Ethan + Helene

In loving memory of
my dad — Aziel Jones
and with prayers for
God's continual working
in our lives and
in the world to bring
those seeking to find
God's living heart to
earth —

Elizabeth
Bernodez

DOUBLE VISION

REACHING A TRIBE FOR GOD
RAISING A FAMILY FOR GOD

AZIEL *AND* MARIAN JONES

DOUBLE VISION

Reaching a Tribe for God

Raising a Family for God

© 2011 Aziel and Marian Jones

First Printing 2011

Cummins Works, Publisher
Ann Arbor, Michigan 48104
USA
Pine Tree logo © 2008 Cummins Works
ISBN 978-0-9640069-5-9

DOUBLE VISION

Reaching a Tribe, Raising a Family

After Costa Rica — 1997 to 2010

Prologue

What? Us! Write a book?

Many friends have asked that we tell our story, but we feel no more qualified to write a book than we did to reach a tribe. In both cases, it was a calling, God's calling. We responded to the call and discovered that God equips those He calls.

We arrived in Costa Rica at the end of 1952, thinking there were fifteen hundred or possibly two thousand Chirripó Indians—or Cabécars, as they are now called. The question then arose, "Is it worth giving our lives to reach so few people?" One thought settled it for me: Would this tribe be worth reaching if I were one of them? As I trekked muddy trails, perspired up exhausting hills, struggled across swift rivers, and slept in isolated huts, I gradually filled my notebooks and files with strange words. I was driven by the story Jesus told about the one lost sheep. Was it worth it? Yes!

Giving the Word of God to the Cabécar Indians was worth the effort, but to write our story? Teachers at college had encouraged me to write. Friends, supporters, and prayer partners asked us to write a book. Their requests became a crescendo. We made a few feeble beginnings. Finally, the words of a missionary friend nailed it down.

"Write your story," Helen urged.

I responded, "But who are we? We're nobody, unknown."

"But we know you," she answered.

So this book is for you who know us: our fifty-year network of loyal friends and faithful supporters. It is also for our children and grandchildren—some of whom will desire to investigate their heritage.

In 2004 at the invitation of our son Philip and his wife, we went to Costa Rica for two months of concentrated effort on the draft of this book. Philip had exhorted us with the words of Revelation 1:19,

"Write what you have seen..." Years have passed since then, years of much activity, while working on the book in between other events.

When Marian and I married, we shared a twofold vision: reaching a tribe for God and raising a family for God. As people asked for our story, we realized that they wanted both stories. Our letters from Costa Rica were always laced with news about the children. Women often told us that they read the last paragraph of our letters first in order to hear news of our children. In recent years as the children became more and more involved in our ministry, news of the work and of the family became more intertwined.

We have read gripping missionary stories without learning much about the family life of the missionaries. In this book we want to share all sides of our lives: the family and the tribe, furlough homes and our home in the jungle, ministry to Indians and to non-Indians, training our children and teaching the Indians, traveling to boarding school and trekking to Indian huts. This may result in a book that is too lengthy, with details of no interest to some. But, for us, all this was the stuff of missions. It is all here.

To write a book with two story lines—the family and the ministry—is not easy. The two lines were intertwined as we established ourselves in the Cabécar area. There, in our home, we created our own vortex, which propelled our twofold vision. As one of our sons said, "Our home was our platform for ministry." As it turned out, our sons unexpectedly were the key to reaching the tribe for God.

Any "soul-gripping drama" may be elusive in the daily details of life in jungle at the end of a jeep road. Over the years we spent time analyzing the language, translating the Word, sowing the seed, responding to needy people—while the tribe more than quadrupled in size. We were also relating to our mission organization and to the national church, as well as tending to the education of our children and spending time in the capital to care for medical needs and legal matters. We took furloughs to visit family, friends, and supporters, to study and to share our vision.

Thirteen years after we arrived in Costa Rica, the Cabécar verb system cracked open in answer to prayer, after thirty-three years the

Cabécar church was born, and finally after forty years the Cabécar New Testament was dedicated. During those years our eight children grew up and finished their education; they married and then scattered all over the world, following their own call from God.

This book may not hold you breathless, but it will reveal to the sensitive reader the spiritual dynamics which enabled us to fulfill our double vision: *"Not by might, nor by power, but by my spirit, saith the LORD of hosts."*

Inside the cover of the first cheap five-year diary that I purchased as a teen were the words "Memory is elusive; capture it." As we wrote the book, Marian and I discovered how elusive memory really is. We were constantly researching our diaries, journals, and prayer letters to capture dates, details, impressions, and feelings. Sometimes neither of us had remembered correctly. The most difficult sections to write were those dealing with tensions, whether in the area where we lived, in the mission, or in the family.

Writing this book has been a team effort with Marian as my co-author. I wrote the original draft in the first person, and she edited it. She has tried to preserve my style, while heavily editing every page—including most of what I say about her. At times she took out things or added details that I had missed. She even rewrote sections, but as from my pen. Nothing is included without both her approval and mine. However, the fourth chapter is her story, untouched by me.

Marian's fingerprints, though hidden, are all over the book as they were when she edited and proofread all of my important letters and other writings, including my M.A. thesis, the Cabécar New Testament, and all our prayer letters for more than fifty years. Since we married, she has edited almost everything I have written. She has done it willingly and lovingly—as unto the Lord. However, at one low point she sighed, "All I ever do is edit your writings." She is weary of it, anxious to organize her family photo albums!

Two friends, both copy editors, have read the manuscript, chapter by chapter, and made corrections and suggestions. A new friend, a professional editor, provided helpful advice on part of the manuscript. The husband of our oldest granddaughter designed the cover and the maps and did the interior layout, while making many helpful suggestions. We are grateful to them—Fran Wise, Joyce Gullman, Linda Ahrens, and Joshua Fleming—but any errors in the final manuscript are due to our own oversight.

I dedicate this book to Marian, my gifted and godly life partner. Yet the glory belongs to our Lord. Without Him, there would have been nothing to write.

Aziel W. Jones

Columbia, South Carolina

October, 2010

Note: The Scripture quoted in this book is from the King James Version because I originally learned these verses in that version as a young man.

−1−
Preacher's Kid from Alabama
1922 to 1940

On a Liberty ship returning in 1944 from the war in Italy, excitement ran high and sleep fled as we—a group of southern soldiers—anticipated arriving in the States the next day. We talked of watermelons, grits, butter beans, fried chicken, and other southern dishes we had missed overseas. I vowed, "When I get out of the service, I'll never leave Alabama again." Yet in the depth of my being I sensed a warning: "Be careful what you say; you don't know what God might have for you to do."

Before going into the army, I had been licensed to preach by the Methodist church, but I was still a self-righteous preacher's kid. I thought God was lucky to have me! I was a *good* boy—at least concerning externals. So were Preacher Jones's other twelve children. We had been taught the fear of God by Daddy.

My father's full name was R K Jones. He insisted that his name be written without periods, for the capital letters stood for nothing. Such a name was common in the old South. I was the third of his thirteen children—five boys and eight girls—but the first to be born in a parsonage. Daddy, son of a godly Methodist farmer, had met and married Leila Mae Tate, daughter of a Methodist preacher, while they were studying at a small Methodist college. After finishing his studies at Birmingham-Southern and working for a couple of years, Daddy became pastor of the Methodist church in Butler, Alabama. In that small town near the Mississippi state line, I was born on February 22, 1922.

Daddy and Mama chose Bible names for all their children. For the older ones they selected lesser known names, perhaps taken from the passage they were reading at the time. My older brother's name was Haniel, and my older sister was named Jedidah. My name occurs

only in I Chronicles 15:20. Aziel—one of the musicians who accompanied King David when he brought the ark to Jerusalem—means "God
is my strength." Since I was born on Washington's Birthday, I was
given the middle name Washington. The brother who came after me
was named Lael, then two sisters, Phoebe and Matred, followed by
two more brothers, Joel and David, and finally "the five little girls,"
Mary, Sarah Mae, Ruth Edna, Lois, and Martha.

The R K Jones family – 1938 (Aziel at back right)

Our world was limited to the southern half of the state of
Alabama, where Daddy moved from one small town to another:
Butler, Silas, Pine Hill, Monroeville, and Florala. At the Annual
Conference of the Methodist churches in that part of Alabama, the
preachers were informed where the bishop had appointed them to
serve during the coming year. Each year we wondered if we would
be moving. If so, we had to move within a week. Daddy often said he
was not given a good appointment, but only moved from one small
church to another. He probably sensed that he lacked the
sophistication to pastor the First Methodist Church in a large city, but
he seemed to think that he was given "bad" appointments—usually
without a raise in salary. I doubt if Daddy ever realized that the

bishop's cabinet saw in him the ability to help a struggling church bring in new members and get on its feet financially.

Daddy loved people and they responded to his leadership. He was a hard-hitting, hellfire-and-brimstone preacher, yet he was jovial and folksy, a great joke teller. He preached against liquor and cigarettes, movies and cards, dancing and mixed bathing. He spoke out against desecrating the Lord's Day, against immodesty and adultery, against lying and cheating. He could make sin look foolish and even silly. He preached that people had to be saved and live godly lives. Many were converted under his preaching, and some entered the ministry. People joined the church and Daddy watched over his flock. He pastored till he died.

Churches prospered when Daddy was pastor. He always preached tithing. If his board members would back him, he put a Tithes and Offerings box at the door rather than pass the offering plate. He successfully led four churches through a building program, one at the height of the Depression. He could lead a church through a building program without a split. Daddy was a diplomat.

Mama also ministered. She played both piano and organ, taught the women's class, and led the monthly meetings of the women's society. Behind the scenes she helped Daddy by keeping track of details. Often she went with Daddy to visit the sick and the grieving. He needed her with him in order to be discreet when he had to visit a woman who lived alone. He always *wanted* her company even though at times she would rather not have gone. If Daddy was out of town, preaching a revival, Mama sometimes led the midweek prayer meeting. They were a ministry team.

We children were an asset to Daddy's ministry. We were proud of Daddy and obeyed him even when embarrassed to follow his custom of kneeling during prayer at church. We attended all the services, although the older children took turns staying home with the babies during the midweek service. During the Sunday evening service the younger ones gathered at the front of the church for the "Children's Hour"—a song and story led by Daddy.

As teenagers we formed the core of the young people's choir that sang on Sunday evenings. At one church we were part of the "Friendly Orchestra" that Daddy organized. I played the violin, teaching myself from a book. Later I learned, after a fashion, to play the clarinet. On Saturdays we cleaned the church, earning a bit of spending money. When churches began to use bulletins, we did the printing. Daddy bought a Multigraph, and later a foot-powered press with movable type, and taught us to print. With thirteen children Daddy had plenty of help. Young people were attracted to the church because he had so many young people of his own.

We validated Daddy's preaching by our obedience and respect. We were not the proverbial "worst kids in town." Daddy established his authority with his razor strap. Mama could wield it, too. Once she broke the strap on me! Another time she left a bruise on my leg, which was embarrassing when I wore short pants. Yet never did I feel over-disciplined or under-loved. If Daddy or Mama overdid any "whipping," we missed a few which would have been in order! I was never rebellious but I did have to learn to obey. Once programmed to obey Daddy and Mama, I found it natural to obey God, as well as lesser authority figures.

My childhood was a happy freedom. We were free to go barefoot, free to fish in the branch behind the parsonage, free to make noise, free to play all summer long. We had few toys but many brothers and sisters to play with. We didn't need money to be happy; we had each other. Outside we played ball and "Hail Over," hopscotch and hide-and-seek, marbles and jacks. Inside we played checkers, dominoes, and Old Maid. We made cars and airplanes; I also enjoyed whittling slingshots. Sometimes we boys played tea party with our sisters or jumped rope or joined them in making paper dolls out of old catalogs. We all read the "funny papers." I read Tom Swift and Tarzan but did not enjoy the Hardy Boys books very much. Except for being preacher's kids, we were typical, small-town children.

School was easy for my older brother and sister but not for me. I studied hard from the time I got home from school until time for bed. Daddy used to say in amazement, "You study, but you don't make good grades." Good grades were important to him. He or Mama would supervise our homework. When I was in the fourth grade, Daddy sometimes whipped me "to help you remember" arithmetic facts. The sixth grade teacher showed one of my English papers to the class as an example of sloppy handwriting. I had gone to school that day confident that I had done a good job; I had rewritten that paper two or three times using Daddy's best fountain pen. In the seventh grade when I failed a science quiz, the teacher, a member of Daddy's church, asked me if I had studied. I answered no, for I was too flustered to remember that I had studied two hours for that test. I did my best always, but could not make good grades.

We were allowed to go to school barefoot. I prided myself on how long it was before cold weather forced me to wear shoes. Mama made most of our clothes. She made our underwear and nightshirts out of old feed sacks, and made the girls' dresses and the blue shirts we boys wore to school. I had two pairs of overalls, one to wear to school for a week, while the other was being washed. We wore hand-me-downs and used worn-out overalls for after school and Saturdays. I was always proud of how Mama could make such neat patches on my overalls. Once I complained about having to wear my old overalls to school. Daddy responded, "If anyone says anything, tell him they're paid for!" Daddy did not buy clothes on credit, but he knew that other parents did.

Money was not plentiful at the parsonage. The house itself was furnished with members' castoffs. Daddy owned nothing but his desk, his glass-front bookcases and, of course, his books, typewriter, and tools. Mama's treasures were her piano and her sewing machine, which we children pedaled for her. Daddy's salary was small, even though he was responsible for country churches as well as the church in town. Yet Daddy managed his money well, watched costs, and put a little each month into a savings account. He lost his savings four times during the Depression when the banks failed, but he usually had a new or late-model car. Daddy tried to leave each parsonage better than he found it, making improvements at his own expense. He knew that churches feared that a large family would be hard on the parsonage, which was perhaps part of the reason he never got well-paying appointments. Daddy always tithed. He once said he was never able to pay off his college debts until he started tithing during his first pastorate. And Daddy always paid his bills. I can remember waiting in the car while he paid various merchants before leaving town for a new pastorate.

Daddy always drove a good car and maintained it well. Cars then were more spacious and trips rarely took more than two or three hours. Each of us children had a place; mine was by the back left window beside my older sister and brother. Some of the younger children stood in the space in front of us. The youngest ones sat up front with Mama. Once at a gas station the attendant, seeing us all in the car, asked incredulously, "Are all these children *yours*?!" Daddy answered with his typical broad smile, "Yes, and I hope they all give the devil a hard time!"

The highlight of each summer was traveling to the Jones Reunion at the "old home place" in Crenshaw County. The old farmhouse in the Camp Ground community where Grandma lived was once known as the "Jones' preachers' house." Daddy grew up there with his four sisters and five brothers, two of whom followed him into the Methodist ministry. Except for the preachers, all the siblings lived near Grandma's house. Grandpa was buried nearby at the Camp Ground Methodist Church. On his tombstone was a quote from Acts 13:36, *"After he had served his own generation by the will of God, he fell asleep."* Grandpa's mother was buried there too, but his father had died, as the family Bible recorded, "on the way home from The War," the Civil War. Among his few possessions when he died was a Methodist hymnal.

Grandpa's parents were both born in Georgia but had migrated to Alabama before he went to war. As Daddy and his siblings gathered each summer on the Thursday after the first Sunday in August, we children never thought about our roots; we just enjoyed the long day of play with our cousins. Without realizing it, we were creating memories that would later help us understand our heritage.

It was different when we went to visit Mama's parents, Grandpa and Grandma Tate in Brundidge. There we had to put on shoes and wear our Sunday clothes. Mama's parents lived in a "superannuate" home, a house donated for a retired minister's residence. The sign over the door read, "Movnomo." Grandpa had that sign painted to express his desire to "move-no-more" from one parsonage to another. At his house there were no cousins to play with, even though Mama came from a family of ten as Daddy did. Three of Mama's five brothers were Methodist preachers, but she was the only girl who married a preacher. When Grandpa Tate died, Mama asked for the "Movnomo" sign to save for the time when her years of moving from one parsonage to another would be over.

Food was simple at our house. Vegetables came from our garden, and all summer long we children shelled peas and butter beans. Mama canned vegetables and made preserves for the winter. When Daddy came home from a week's revival at a country church, the trunk of the car was loaded with more vegetables. Dinner each day consisted of vegetables, followed by rice and gravy, usually meat, and biscuits. For supper we ate cold leftovers, or sometimes pancakes, "batter cakes." We drank milk from our own cow and ate eggs from our own hens. On Saturdays I went with Mama to the chicken yard; she threw chicken feed to attract the chickens so that I could catch a pullet for her to kill and fry for Sunday dinner.

Daddy would order a crate of grapefruit at Christmas, and once a year he ordered a sack of wheat. We would hand-grind it for cereal and for biscuits. Until my teen years, "light bread" from the store was a luxury. We churned our own butter with a Daisey churn, made our own mayonnaise and used it to improve unpalatable vegetables. Mama was not the greatest cook, but occasionally she baked cookies, "tea cakes." Snacks consisted of leftover biscuits sweetened with cane syrup that farmers had given Daddy. Our only desserts were on Sundays; we had little candy except homemade fudge, and no ice cream cones or cokes except as a treat once every summer on our way to the Jones Reunion. Daddy refused to buy snacks for himself when he was on the road, saying, "I eat nothing if the children don't share it."

We were a healthy lot. Rarely did we need a doctor or a dentist. Mama had all her babies at home. Daddy once pulled his own tooth to avoid paying a dentist. Like everyone else we treated cuts by pouring turpentine in the wound and bandaging it with an old rag. And like most of our neighbors, we took our turns bathing each Saturday night in a washtub in the kitchen.

Work was a part of our daily routine; we helped because we were part of the family. We boys brought in wood for the stove and cut kindling, worked in the garden and the yard, and did repair jobs. The girls learned to sew, iron, quilt, and cook. We all took turns doing the dishes.

In the early years we had a wash woman, but when that got too expensive Daddy bought a washer and a mangle iron. As a family we all worked together and got the wash on the line before school on Monday morning. The oldest boy milked the cow every morning and evening, the oldest girl cooked breakfast, the next two children made the beds, and the next two swept the floors—all before breakfast. Mama would tend the baby and help the smaller children get dressed. Daddy washed the dishes on school mornings. He was the manager, harnessing the energy of his thirteen children.

Sunday was special: Sunday School, morning service, and evening service. We wore our Sunday clothes all day long but were allowed to take off our shoes after the morning service. No bicycles or skates were permitted on Sunday afternoon, just quiet play. No unnecessary work was done; clothes had been laid out and shoes polished on Saturday night. We made no purchases; Daddy had the car gassed on Saturday. I felt strange when I had to go to the drugstore one Sunday to get a prescription filled for my little sister Mary who almost died of pneumonia. We were programmed to respect the Lord's Day. Daddy taught us that God has standards. We learned that a godly life could be satisfying, that an orderly home could be pleasant. We didn't need "the world" in order to have fun. Happiness was *home*.

Every morning we read the Bible at the breakfast table before the blessing, but on Sunday the family altar was special. We stood behind our chairs as Daddy led us in a song. Then we said the Apostles' Creed, followed by another song. We recited a Psalm, then usually another song and another Psalm. We often sang "Jesus Loves Me" for the little ones. Each of us recited a verse, usually learned the night before. Then we knelt by our chairs to pray "The Lord's Prayer." Finally we all kissed each other.

Evenings we knelt by Daddy's or Mama's knees to pray "Now I lay me down to sleep..." and "God bless Daddy and Mama and...," then kissed them and ran to bed. As we got older, usually by the age of ten, we began to read through the whole Bible each year, three chapters a day and five on Sundays. If we finished within a year, reading every single day without missing, Daddy gave us a new Bible on Bible Sunday. Daddy and Mama read their chapters aloud to each other, she doing the reading. Then they prayed, he praying one night and she the next. If one of us had not yet read our quota that day, we listened as our parents did their reading and then prayed with them.

As a boy I thought Daddy was the best preacher that existed. He was well-known for his sermon on "Hell and Who's Going There." He preached it at most "revival meetings"—the Southern term for evangelistic meetings. I still have his copy of that sermon, typed "hunt-and-peck" with two fingers as all his sermons were. I heard him preach it dozens of times, and I always trembled because I was not sure of my own salvation.

Each summer at the revival meetings I felt stirrings of the soul. I had joined the church when I was seven because it was the thing to do—and because my sister signaled from the choir for me to go forward. It seemed that in my teen years I went forward in revivals every year but never felt saved. I had heard testimonies like, "I know I'm saved because I was there when it happened," but no one told *me* how to make it happen. Years later when I asked Daddy how *he* knew he was saved, his only response was, "I felt it." I once asked Mama about her assurance of salvation and she only cried. At times I went to the altar in a revival meeting and someone prayed for me, but no one counseled me, not even my parents. Once I got out of bed to talk to Daddy about my salvation, then got cold feet and went back to bed. At seventeen I began to keep a diary to record my feelings so that later, when I did have assurance, I'd have a record of how I had felt. I desperately yearned for salvation—not, *could* I have it, but, *did* I have it?

By this time I was a senior at Murphy High School, then the only high school in Mobile. Mobile was the largest city in the Methodist Conference of Alabama and West Florida, yet Daddy still was not given a good appointment, just *two* full-time churches in working-class neighborhoods. His health almost broke under the load of preaching four times each Sunday. I was doing the printing for the churches, as well as for local businessmen, but when I caught my hand in the press, I had to pass that job on to Lael, the brother who followed me. That injury—the most painful of my life—left me with a bent finger due to a cut tendon. Lael also had to take over the milking, but the city was no place for a cow and Daddy sold it. I found Murphy with its three thousand students quite a contrast to my previous high school. I struggled with chemistry but made a good enough grade on the final exam to graduate in 1940 in the middle of my class of five hundred fifty-five. Even so, I had only C's and D's on my report card that last year.

On one occasion during my senior year, I went forward along with many others in response to one of Daddy's very general invitations. At the end of the prayer time Daddy prayed, "And Lord, if there is anyone here struggling with the call to preach, help him to say yes." My heart leaped. "My need is not salvation," I said to myself, "but God is calling me to preach." I never said anything to Daddy about this, but something clued him in because one day he said to Haniel, my older brother, and to me, "If you're going to get licensed to preach, you'd better get ready for the next District Conference." So we read the required books and met with the committee. This was not to ordain us, but to license us, the first step up the hierarchical ladder of the Methodist church. I was eighteen, had just finished high school, and was a bit uncomfortable with the licensing committee. After a few simple questions one man said, "Brethren, since these are R K Jones' boys, I recommend that we license them." All agreed. Haniel and I were now "local preachers." I was relieved, but in my heart I said, "Men, you didn't do your job. You didn't even ask about our salvation or about our call to preach."

In 1940 I followed my older brother to Millsaps College, a Methodist school in Jackson, Mississippi. Daddy and Haniel had decided on Millsaps because it was cheaper than Birmingham-Southern in Alabama. My faith was shaken at college when liberal professors raised doubts about the Bible, but I reasoned, "My parents don't believe this way. I'll stick with my parents until I have reason not to." Their faith held me for five years until I could stand on my own. However, I had been badly shaken during my short time at Millsaps.

My decision to join the band at Millsaps proved to be a turning point in my life. The only qualification I had was that I had tried to play clarinet—an obsolete "C-system" Albert clarinet—in our little church orchestra, but Daddy urged me to join because we would be paid a dollar for each practice during the school year. Joining the band involved joining the National Guard, since the band was a unit of the Mississippi National Guard. Before the semester was over the National Guard was "federalized"—called into active duty—in the government's attempt to prepare for war. World War II had already started in Europe. We took our final exams before Thanksgiving and then reported for induction into federal service. It was still more than a year before Pearl Harbor suddenly drew the United States into the conflict.

Daddy had few regrets, but he *did* regret urging me to join the Guard. As a ministerial student I would have been exempt from the draft that pulled millions into the war. But God had His plans. My time in the service was revolutionary, transforming. I found the key to what I was seeking. Salvation was only the beginning! Yet Daddy said, "I lost you to the army."

− 2 −
G.I. in World War II
1940 to 1945

The army was a man's world. This naive small town preacher's kid was to learn what men are like when no women are around, and to hear words he had never heard before. And I was also to see more clearly what my own heart was like. I was eighteen and my brother Haniel was twenty-one when our college band was inducted into federal service on November 25, 1940. The band, which was part of the Mississippi National Guard, was to serve for one year. In the army the officers called us "men," but when we were on leave, people often called us "soldier boys." During World War II we became known as "G.I.s," from "Government Issue," the term used to denote all clothing and equipment issued to us.

Three weeks after induction in Mississippi, our unit was transferred from the Millsaps College campus to Camp Blanding, a new installation near Jacksonville, Florida. There were twenty-eight of us in the unit, plus the band director. Along the way our troop train had a two-hour layover in Mobile. Daddy and Mama came to meet us at the railroad station, along with two-year-old Martha, our youngest sister. Then at Easter of 1941 my brother and I got seventy-two hour passes and were able to go home and attend Daddy's Sunrise Service, always the highlight of the year. I had another short leave a couple of months later. This was the last time I would attend Daddy's church until I returned from overseas, a different person.

Camp Blanding

Our band spent over a year at Camp Blanding, playing each morning at 6:00 A.M. as we marched around the perimeter of our regimental area during roll call. We ended each workday by playing "The Star-Spangled Banner" for "Retreat" at 5:00 P.M. We were the regimental band of the 106th Engineers of the 3lst Division, the *Dixie* Division. Our division shared the camp with the *Yankee* Division: a hundred thousand men in all.

The band was attached to the headquarters company of the regiment. Band duties were light, so we were often asked to volunteer for extra jobs. My buddies kidded me because I always volunteered, but I had been conditioned by Daddy to work.

"I've noticed that you frequently volunteer for work details," an old master sergeant, attached to our regiment as an advisor, once told me. "Keep doing it. The guys will make fun of you, but you will go forward in the army because you will have experience. When they need a man with experience, they will say, 'Jones knows how to do that.'"

I never did rise above the rank of corporal since I was ranked according to musical ability, but I did enjoy army life. I liked soldiering, and at one point even considered becoming a career man.

During the summer of 1941 we traveled to Louisiana for the largest peacetime maneuvers ever held up to that time. For us, maneuvers proved more exciting than some of our later service overseas. Over a million men met in mock combat, but the United States was scarcely prepared for war. We used wooden antitank guns, and the trucks had a sign saying "tank." Much of our equipment was World War I vintage, including single-shot Springfield rifles. Not until after Pearl Harbor did the government issue the seven-shot M-1 rifle. The band normally carried .45-caliber pistols. My prized aluminum canteen and mess kit which I used throughout World War II—and still have—were dated 1918!

In August, ten months into our one-year obligation, we heard on the radio that Congress had voted that those in for a year were to stay eighteen months longer. The government saw war coming.

WAR!

The routine days at Camp Blanding came to a sudden end on Sunday, December 7, 1941, when Pearl Harbor was attacked. Our

Christmas leaves were canceled. We kept our ears glued to the radio as Congress declared war the very next day. With the nation at war, we knew we would be in the army "for the duration and six months."

Many of my buddies, and even our band director, foreseeing a long war, had already applied for Officers' Candidate School. As college men we had the potential to become officers, but I personally had no desire to become one. However, I did apply for Aviation Mechanic School, but never received an answer; consequently, I continued throughout the war as a bandsman. My brother Haniel had been discharged by this time because his National Guard enlistment had run out.

Troops were on the move everywhere. Our division moved from Camp Blanding, Florida, to Camp Bowie, Texas. Before we left Blanding, I saw my first Jeep—quite a novelty. For the trip to Texas, our band was assigned to the military police to help guide the long convoy. We were stationed at crossroads, junctions, and bypasses. We were positioned early and picked up late. As the sun arose on a cold, bitter morning in Texas, I sat against a post, huddled in my overcoat trying to keep warm. I dozed, but was suddenly awakened by the crunch of gravel. The general's car was stopping! As he lowered his window, I came to attention and saluted.

"Soldier, do you know the punishment for being asleep at a post in time of war?"

"No, sir," I mumbled.

"You can be shot! What's your name, rank, and serial number?"

The general wrote it all down and drove on, leaving me trembling, but not from the cold! When I got in for a late supper, my sergeant asked me what had happened. I realized that I had been reported! For several days I was overwhelmed by fear. To my relief, however, I never heard any more about the matter.

Changes came as the army mobilized for war. The old square divisions were changed to the smaller, more mobile triangle divisions patterned after Hitler's panzer divisions with their blitzkrieg attacks.

Our regiment was downsized and no longer merited a band. The few men left in the band were now with the 175th General Service Engineers, under direct corps or army command, instead of combat engineers under division command. General Service sounded safer than combat! The engineers were trained to build roads and bridges, to demolish them, and to construct fortifications. In time of battle, bandsmen were subject to duty as stretcher bearers or messengers.

Fort Moultrie

In the summer of 1942, the 175th regiment loaded its trucks on flatcars and the men in Pullman cars and headed for South Carolina. My buddy Hicks and I volunteered to sit in one of the trucks as guards for the three day trip—quite a sacrifice. We unloaded at Camp Jackson (now Ft. Jackson) but soon moved to Ft. Moultrie, a coastal artillery base near Charleston. Moultrie was a lovely permanent army base with all the amenities, but our regiment sweltered in tents on the edge of the base.

By this time I had been in the army almost two years, living a decent life, never succumbing to the temptations I faced in the military. (One exception had been at Camp Bowie when I went to a questionable sideshow near the camp—but left conscience-stricken before it was over.) My buddies even called me "Rev" or "Reverend," though I still had no assurance of salvation.

While we were stationed in Fort Moultrie awaiting overseas orders, a new, young Presbyterian chaplain was assigned to our regiment. Each Sunday Chaplain Mosser preached a simple salvation message. He spoke in a quiet voice and gave no invitation, but ended each message with the phrase, "Claim the promises of God for your salvation."

After five or six Sundays the chaplain's words suddenly clicked in my mind: *"Claim it!"* I knew all about Jesus who died as a sacrifice, but I had never *claimed* salvation. I had been trusting in my *own* righteousness—after all, I was Preacher Jones's kid! Now I began trusting God's promises, trusting what Jesus had done. I found assurance of salvation, but my self-righteousness had yet to be dealt with.

At Moultrie we were also assigned a new band director. As the seven of us who were left in the band marched to the mess hall one day, we noticed a new warrant officer. When he inquired who *we* were, he was told: "That's your band, sir."

Not only was our band just a fourth of proper wartime strength but some of us were poor musicians. What a come-down for young Mr. Anderson who had just graduated from Band Director's School at the top of his class.

Chaplain Mosser

Our new director gradually brought in new musicians, including one who said he could play the bass. When he got into the band, he explained that he played the bass "fiddle," not the bass horn. Mr. Anderson bought a bass fiddle so that the man could at least play in the dance band for the officers' parties, but he couldn't play that either! Eventually the man left the unit, but we had to haul that bass fiddle case—larger than a casket—with us everywhere overseas.

At Fort Moultrie we were issued arctic gear and then told to turn it in. Next we were issued desert gear, then had to turn some of it back in. Were they confusing the enemy or were they changing their plans for us, like a giant chess game? We packed all band equipment in boxes with an APO New York address. Our destination remained a total mystery.

On to the Front

We moved on to Camp Pickett, Virginia, for assault training. There we ran the obstacle course and learned to climb rope nets. In the cold predawn of October 14, we left Camp Pickett on a troop train—my first trip up north. As we traveled through Washington, D.C., and on to New Jersey, I found the trip extremely interesting. Houses were built very close together and factories were everywhere. Everything was fast, especially the electric trains!

We were now at Camp Kilmer, New Jersey, but were ordered not to write our folks of our move but still to use our Camp Pickett address. At Kilmer we not only had time to write letters and read, but twice we were given twelve-hour passes to New York City. I quickly learned the subway system—more impressive to me than the skyscrapers, obscured as they were by other buildings almost as high. I saw Times Square with its night clubs and open sin. My friend Early and I had to drag home a drunken buddy who never forgave us for throwing away his extra bottle of whiskey.

At Camp Kilmer we were issued submachine guns and taught to fire and clean them. The officers held "shakedown" inspections where they rid us of extra items. On October 31, we were told to pack our gear, and then were kept on alert until the next afternoon when we boarded a train for New York. Transferring to a ferry, we arrived at Staten Island after dark, wearing heavy packs and struggling with our cumbersome duffel bags. Walking endlessly through an enormous warehouse, we suddenly turned and entered a small door in the side of a huge ship.

The U.S.S. Monticello was a confiscated Italian luxury liner converted to carry several thousand troops. Our whole regiment was housed in what had been the ballroom. The officers could speak to us all—or the chaplain could preach—without needing a microphone. We slept on narrow canvas bunks installed five high. All we knew was that we were going *somewhere*. Often we quoted the old refrain: "Ours not to question why, ours but to do or die."

Crossing the Atlantic

We woke the next morning to find ourselves already out to sea! Our seven troop ships were surrounded by several oil tankers and freighters, accompanied by a cruiser, aircraft carrier, battleship, and about twenty destroyers darting around the edges of the convoy like little fox terriers. It was an impressive sight stretching from horizon to horizon—awesome!

Several times an hour, the ship's horn would blow to signal a change of direction as we zigzagged through the rough seas to frustrate possible attack from enemy submarines. Inside the ship we lay on our bunks, reading or resting. Card games and crap games went on incessantly. Fourteen hours a day there was total blackout—except for tiny red lights along the narrow corridors. Men gathered near the lights to continue their games. In such close quarters the officers overlooked occasional fights. With so many men on board, we were allowed to crowd on deck, always wearing life jackets, for only two hours a day—some days not at all.

Twice a day we stood in long lines down to the galley to eat as we stood by high tables. One stormy day I missed two meals due to a queasy stomach as the ship pitched and rolled, squeaking at the seams as it crested the giant waves. In preparation for our eventual landing—though we knew not where—we were given cartons of cigarettes and candies to use as barter. Bandoleers of ammunition were issued one day, and another day we received emergency "C" and "K" rations.

As our convoy moved slowly across the North Atlantic, we began to notice after two weeks that the sun was on the "wrong" side of the ship. We had been going in circles! Finally in mid-November we were told, for the first time, that our destination was "still Casablanca." We were also told that North Africa had been invaded on November 8. In a surprise move, the American troops had staged the invasion directly from the United States! The Vichy French government capitulated after a brief fight. Now we learned that the reason for our circling was to wait until the harbor had been cleared of sunken vessels, including a French battleship.

From Morocco to Algeria

On November 16, 1942, we docked at Casablanca and disembarked the next day. We were among the first troops to come off the gangplank, following those who made the initial landing "over the side." Until the kitchen opened on the 28th, just after Thanksgiving, we ate only emergency rations. During our three months in Morocco we slept in pup tents. The weather was so cold that we had to wear overcoats as we practiced marching. In such weather, reed instruments like my clarinet were hard to play, and it was even more difficult when it rained.

For the first week in Morocco several of us suffered from "Montezuma's revenge." Awful! Actually, I was rarely sick in the army, aside from a terrible reaction to a typhoid shot while at Camp Bowie. We were always being inoculated against something—once in both arms at the same time by a medic at each side. At stated intervals there were venereal disease inspections, as well as films about such diseases and morality lectures by the chaplain. A man in our regiment had been treated with penicillin at Bowie for a venereal disease. Penicillin was then a brand-new "miracle drug." Sulfa drugs were still considered the drug of choice for infections.

One day the news reached us that President Roosevelt was coming to Casablanca! My buddies and I hurried to the road. Sure enough, Roosevelt passed by in a limousine on the way to his famous meeting with Churchill. In Casablanca we spent our free time exploring, as well as fixing up our pup tents to make ourselves more comfortable. We did experience an air raid, when a single enemy bomber flew over us. The fireworks were impressive as searchlights ribbed the night sky, and red tracers from our antiaircraft guns tried unsuccessfully to target their prey. At one point I even felt sorry for that pilot—until we heard the whine of a bomb landing in a nearby field. Instinctively, we hit the dirt. My only injury was a scratch as we hit the ground! Later we found jagged, razor-sharp pieces of shrapnel, one of which I kept as a souvenir.

After my twenty-first birthday in February of 1942, we spent six days crossing the beautiful, snowcapped Atlas Mountains into

Algeria. We traveled uncomfortably on the old French railroad in a "40 & 8"—a boxcar with no sanitary facilities, where forty men or eight horses could bed down on the straw-covered floor. One of the stations we passed was Sidi bel Abbas, home of the French Foreign Legion, an international mercenary army under French command. Dismounting finally in Algeria where a U.S. railroad unit was stationed, we heard the nostalgic whistle of an American steam locomotive. A cheer went up, for the sound brought back memories of home! There in Algeria we were attached to the British Eighth Army for rations: never enough sugar.

We bivouacked in a eucalyptus grove. Rains turned the gumbo mud into a nightmare. As always, I shared a pup tent with my old buddy Early, who was also a Methodist preacher's kid. We each carried half the tent in our pack. Next to us our other old buddies, Reagan and Hicks, shared a tent. Later we bivouacked in a pine forest near Tebessa.

On guard duty there one night I memorized Hebrews 11:6: *"But without faith it is impossible to please him . . ."* That was the first verse I ever memorized on my own, not as a Sunday School requirement or to please my parents. For me it was another small step forward.

From Algeria to Tunisia

Before we left Algeria, General Patton took command of our troops. With Patton in command things were different. Orders were *always* obeyed. Specifically, we now wore steel helmets and leggings at all times. Soon we were traveling again, in hopes of intercepting Rommel who was retreating westward after his defeat by the British at El Alamein. We traveled through Kasserine Pass down to the plains in Tunisia where inexperienced American troops had suffered a humiliating defeat. But there Rommel, seeing our equipment, realized that Germany could not win. We ourselves saw no action, but we did see the one hundred tanks that "Blood-and-Guts" Patton had lost to Rommel in a single day. British and American armies continued to battle the Germans and Italians, but my unit remained behind the battle front. We only heard the noise and watched the flares light up the night sky.

We stayed about four months in Tunisia, doing almost nothing—no formal roll calls, only a few band practices. We did play occasional concerts, and I spent hours practicing my clarinet. Mr. Anderson, the director, told me I was improving on my clarinet. I didn't think so but appreciated his encouragement.

My buddies spent most of their time shooting crap or playing penny poker. I had difficulty figuring out the game.

"Put your money in the game, Rev," they said, "and you'll learn."

Instead, I read my Bible and books from the company "library." As we moved east, I even had a chance to visit old catacombs. Entertainment was provided for us, but most of it wasn't worth watching. We preferred playing baseball with British soldiers or watching British Spitfires returning from raids on the front. One "slap happy" pilot even flew under the high tension wires.

We learned that Rommel had already flown back to Germany, but his army evaded capture until they were on the beaches north of Bizerte and Tunis. For days convoys of German prisoners passed us. We watched in silence—no jeering. The Germans, in contrast to their allies, were real fighters.

By the time my unit reached Bizerte, summer had come. We strung our hammocks in a shady olive grove and swam in the lovely Mediterranean. There I finished reading through the whole Bible again. It took four months, at twelve minutes a day. ("No time" is a poor excuse for not reading the Bible!) We did watch a few air raids on the harbor below our camp. The morning following one such raid, I found a 20 mm. shell near my hammock—unexploded!

On to Sicily

Early in August, 1943, we headed north from Africa to Sicily—an overnight trip on an LST (Landing Ship Tank). Disembarking the next evening in Palermo on the north coast, we then moved south to

Licata where we enjoyed a few more months of free time, except for two weeks of taxing guard duty. Camping in an almond orchard near the southern coast, we swam almost daily in the *blue* Mediterranean. On the way to the beach we passed through an arbor, filling our helmets with delicious grapes. As long as the weather was warm, we slept in hammocks outside our pup tents.

That summer I spent many hours studying my Bible, comparing the books of Kings and Chronicles. As I listed the kings, I discovered the difference between the kingdoms of Israel and Judah, something I had never picked up in Sunday School or at home. Studying the Bible on my own was another step in my spiritual pilgrimage.

Aziel in Sicily - September 1943

While in Sicily the chaplain assigned me to preach at outlying companies. I still had plenty of free time for writing letters home, especially to Haniel my brother. My buddies and I enjoyed watching the planes roar in and out of the military airfield below our camp. As the weather grew colder, we built cabins out of plywood salvaged from dunnage used on the ships; stretchers served as beds. Occasionally we practiced, and on Armistice Day we played for a memorial service. Then we flew to the east coast for a concert at Catania, where I was fascinated by the view of Mt Etna, rising to fourteen thousand feet above the sea. Before returning to our camp on the southern coast, we took an express train to Palermo, where the better musicians played at the officers' party. I was just as happy to be sightseeing as I had done in North Africa—Roman ruins, and Arabic art and architecture. My buddies teased me about taking such things so seriously, but a crack into an unknown world had opened to this boy from Alabama.

Meanwhile, across the Strait of Messina from Sicily, the Allies stormed the beaches of Italy at Salerno. Casualties were very high. Planes blackened the skies above us on their way to drop supplies to our men. The French in North Africa had surrendered quickly, as did the Italians in Sicily, but the Germans fought on. Not surprisingly, we heard rumors of a move. Just before leaving I got a Christmas package from home, including a snapshot of my siblings. Stunned, I could no longer recognize the younger ones. I also received a photo of Haniel and Sue, who were to be married Christmas Day. Our ships finally came on December 22. As we headed east and then north, we passed Syracuse. I remembered that the Apostle Paul had stayed there three days on the final stage of his voyage to Rome—exciting to think that he, too, passed through the Strait of Messina!

Up to Italy

Easing past wrecked ships, we anchored in the oil-covered waters of the Bay of Naples. In the background we could see Vesuvius belching black smoke. At its foot, invisible to us, was Pompeii, where U.S. bulldozers kept the streets free of ash for G.I. tourists. We came down the gangplank on Christmas Eve and were billeted in the bomb-damaged, windowless University of Naples. Christmas Day of 1943 brought us our first hot meal in days—a turkey dinner! The next day we headed north in a dreary rain. We bivouacked for the first three months of 1944 at Santa Maria di Capua, twelve miles short of the battlefront. Monte Cassino, covered with snow, stood high in the distance. The Allies made one vain effort after another to dislodge the Germans dug in around Cassino. Day and night the convoys rumbled past our camp, transporting troops, fuel, and ammunition to the front.

As always, we made ourselves comfortable. Here at Capua we set up pyramidal tents, six men to a tent, rather than two-man pup tents. We even made plywood floors to get ourselves off the muddy ground. After two weeks we resumed band practice and played occasional concerts, sometimes in the mess tent at supper or at a nearby military hospital. I spent a lot of time doing guard duty during the bitter cold nights. Often I was corporal of the guard, with the responsibility to see that the others kept at their posts. Usually I would stand with each man for part of his watch—it's lonely out there! Our tents were near the house of a farmer we called Joe. Some of us made friends with Joe's family as we sat in the chimney corner and tried to converse. His daughters did laundry for us; we gave them candy and other goodies. I was attracted to one of them.

During our stay in Italy a typhus epidemic raged. The British troops had many cases but we had none. The U.S. Army strictly enforced sanitation practices. We dug latrines, often before pitching our tents. Before leaving an area, we filled them in and "policed" the area for trash. A medical officer inspected our mess kits and cups as we stood in the "chow" line. In Italy we were issued lice powder for our clothes as a precaution. As the weather got warmer, we were given Atabrine tablets to ward off malaria and were ordered to sleep under mosquito nets. Repeatedly we were told, "A sick soldier is a casualty."

For me, the most significant time in Italy was spent in a little gully at Capua. Though I had come to assurance of salvation a year before at Fort Moultrie, a nagging question came to my mind: "Since I was licensed as a local preacher before I was even sure of my salvation, was I ever really called to preach?" As spring came on, I went each Sunday afternoon to pray in that little gully near our bivouac area. Sitting there by the stream I began reading my pocket Testament straight through, seeking an answer. Not knowing what to expect—just listening to God—I had gotten as far as Luke when my attention was arrested by Luke 9:62: *"No man, having put his hand to the plough, and looking back, is fit for the kingdom of God."* I asked myself, "Is this my answer?"

The next Sunday I found myself going back to Luke 9:62. By faith I finalized it: "Lord, I am taking that verse as your confirmation of my call to preach." This was the first time I claimed a verse as confirmation of a decision. I have never doubted my call since.

The Battle for Cassino

One cloudy night we awoke to the slow throbbing drone of low-flying bombers heading south—enemy planes? Would they drop flares to expose us? Eventually we saw our antiaircraft shells exploding to the south of us. Next morning we again heard the drone of planes—our planes this time—heading north toward Cassino. Through binoculars we saw Flying Fortresses dropping bombs, and we felt the impact on the ground beneath our feet. A second squadron of B-24 heavy bombers followed, then a squadron of medium bombers and a squadron of attack bombers. Our training had enabled us to recognize all planes, whether Allied or enemy. The following day we heard they had dropped hundreds of tons of bombs on one square mile at Cassino.

A week later, a dozen or more German fighters roared over us. One let out a burst of his guns. It sounded like a riveting machine! He then jettisoned a fuel tank—we thought it was a bomb! On his tail came a British Spitfire in hot pursuit. We had been lying around reading or napping but instinctively jumped into the adjacent gully. One bandsman had been practicing when the planes came. The only spot left for him was a pool of water. He jumped in, holding his clarinet in the air. Of course, the planes were gone before we even hit the gully!

Early in April we moved closer to the front, traveling a few miles north to Teano. Every evening after supper we played volleyball on a rise above the Appian Way, which was always full of army traffic. During the six weeks we were stationed at Teano, General Mark Clark came to decorate four men in our regiment who had risked their lives to put out a fire threatening a fuel dump. Our band played for the ceremony. Once at Teano I got a pass to do some sightseeing nearby. At an ancient amphitheater the guide showed us the lion cages where many Christians suffered there under Nero. Another day Chaplain Mosser said, "I'm going to Naples today. Let's go to Pompeii together. I've already cleared it with your band director." What I saw there made me wonder if God had destroyed Pompeii because it had become so base and bold.

The army had now begun a system of rotation based on points accrued for time in service, time overseas, and proximity to a battle zone. With a certain number of points, a man could return to the United States, enjoy a month's furlough, and then be reassigned to a new unit. After we had been at Teano a few weeks, Chaplain Mosser suddenly left on rotation. His departure left the regiment—several hundred men, including our band—without a chaplain. He had once asked me to be his assistant, but I felt I lacked the necessary clerical abilities. Yet now, several of the guys in the regiment asked if I would be willing to hold services, a confirmation of my own feelings. I had nothing available for sermon preparation but my little King James Bible with concordance and cross-references. Feeling my helplessness, I discovered II Corinthians 3:5, *"Not that we are sufficient of ourselves to think anything of ourselves; but our sufficiency is of God."* This was the first time I ever cast myself on a specific verse for a difficult situation. Throughout the week I worked on my message between band practice, volleyball, reading, and mending for my buddies and myself. For the next several Sundays I preached to the usual group of about twenty.

On May 18 Cassino finally fell, leaving only rubble and leafless trees. As I neared there to arrange for preaching the next Sunday, I passed an area curtained off with canvas. The stench of death permeated the air. The Allied dead that had lain frozen all winter were now being buried. Soon our unit moved on to Fondi, keeping up with the fleeing enemy. As usual, the locals watched as we ate our rations, hoping for leftovers. The sergeant made us put the scraps in the garbage can, but even so, we managed to slip food to the civilians at times. There at Fondi we watched the "fireworks" nearby, the last air raid I would ever see.

To Rome—and Home

Sunday, June 4, 1944, was the day Rome fell to the Allies. That day I preached to my buddies at Fondi for the last time. We left the following day on our way to Rome. As we passed the cemetery at Anzio, I tried to count the crosses on the rolling hill. There were ten crosses each way, making a plot of a hundred. More than ten plots each way—the graves of at least ten thousand Allied soldiers. Very sobering.

As we bivouacked just south of Rome, startling news reached us of the invasion of Normandy. It was now June 6, "D-Day." For me personally, that news was eclipsed by even more startling news: I was slated to leave on June 8 for rotation back to the United States! How I hated to miss sightseeing in Rome! I only managed a quick trip to the edge of the city, just to say, "I got to Rome!" The next morning I was on my way south to the Replacement Depot at Naples. There an "on-fire" chaplain held evangelistic meetings every night for the constant turnover of men being reassigned. Even I was asked to preach once at that center, but during my week there I was gripped by fear. I was afraid that, after furlough, I would be reassigned to a combat unit and sent back overseas to the battlefront. I was so fearful that I even asked for permission to return to my old unit, which seemed safe. However, it was too late. Had I given up safety for danger?

Soon we boarded a Liberty ship—an empty freighter—carrying four hundred men and forty officers. The officer in charge asked if I would conduct services. During the four weeks we were at sea, I often stood at the bow of the ship, bracing myself on a life-raft, leading the service as the ship rocked and dipped and rose. With no hymnbooks, I wrote out the words to the songs by hand. As many as sixty or seventy men came to the services. Sometimes card games would go on at my feet as I preached, but there was no disturbance. On weekdays men came seeking counsel, but I was not really spiritually qualified to minister. I did not even encourage them to read the Bible, nor did I pray with them. I had not yet learned that I must first focus on a man's relationship to the Lord and then work from there. I did not even know how to lead someone to the Lord, but God was preparing me to learn.

During the voyage across the Atlantic, the crew asked for volunteers to scrape and paint part of the ship. I not only enjoyed the work but also escaped boredom. We were rewarded with a fresh water shower in the crew's quarters. On stormy days we were not allowed on deck. In our compartment below, I read, or played Chinese checkers, or wrote new sermons.

Excitement ran high as we neared land. Early one morning we rushed to the deck to find that the ship lay in Chesapeake Bay. Unlike the Mediterranean, trees lined the shore, rather than rocks. No jagged mountain rose in the distance, just an old steel water tower. What a beautiful sight! The United States! HOME! We all let out a yell in response to the nostalgic whistle of a steam locomotive in the distance. We disembarked in Newport News, Virginia, on July 10, 1944. After twenty months on foreign soil, I was not the same boy who had left Alabama.

Furlough and Reassignment

Soon I was on my way home for my first furlough in more than two years. Home was no longer Mobile, but Phenix City, where Daddy had been moved while I was in Sicily. I arrived unannounced.

"Aziel's home," shouted all my little sisters.

I hardly recognized my brothers, who had become teenagers. Daddy was about to leave for a week of revival meetings but went to the phone and cancelled the meetings before he even greeted me. I quickly began helping him with a work project, something we Jones boys always enjoyed. However, at church I missed the simplicity of overseas services. Without realizing it, I was in culture shock, before the term "culture shock" existed. But, after thirty days, the dreaded day of leaving came all too soon. Mama felt even worse than I did. That was my hardest goodbye ever.

Reporting back to duty in North Carolina, I was soon sent to Camp Lee, Virginia. To my surprise, we overseas veterans had to take basic training all over again. Our trainers were kind, almost apologetic. Training ended with crawling under barbed wire and machine gun fire, crawling on red clay after a week of rain—then reporting for guard duty forty-five minutes later with a clean rifle and a fresh uniform.

Since I was still classified as a musician, I was then sent to Band Training Camp. There I was submerged in the world of secular musicians, aspiring entertainers.

"Let's face it, Jones, you don't play well," the director told me.

"So will you assign me to Mechanics School, or . . .?"

"No, we'll give you more training."

My playing did not improve, yet in the fall of 1944 I was assigned to a new band made up of about seventy overseas veterans. At that time the band was called the First Combat Infantry Band. Later it became the Army Ground Forces Band, the equivalent of the Marine Band or the Navy Band. I reported to Ft. Meade, Maryland, where I joined the band the day before I began my fifth year of service.

Our first tour was to Boston over the Christmas holidays of 1944-1945. I enjoyed touring historic Boston. During my free time, I met some young people on a street corner handing out invitations to Youth for Christ. They were "turned on" for Jesus—the way I longed to be. I had never before seen such commitment. Going to church with them and visiting in their homes over Christmas, I tasted a new life—another pivotal point in my pilgrimage.

Meanwhile, the war raged on. From Fort Meade, where the band was based, new troops were leaving daily for Europe. As our band "played off" several groups of a thousand new troops on their way overseas, I pitied them, so young and thin, fear lurking in their eyes.

The band practiced regularly and played concerts in nearby Washington. One day at rehearsal the director said, "I've got too many reeds."

"Sentimental reasons aren't enough to keep an inferior man in the band," he continued.

Oh no, he means me.

A week later, searching for the wrong notes he was hearing, Captain Whiting found that we three second clarinets were the problem. From then on we felt like marked men, slated to leave the band and be sent to battle!

Radical Turnaround

In nearby Washington, D.C., I discovered the Navigator Home, run by a middle-aged widow called "Mom." She had left the security of a good civil service job to run the home by faith. As a regular visitor, I became one of "Mom's boys," and she became my spiritual mentor. Soon I began to hear her references to "since I surrendered my life to the Lord..." In my mind I related surrender to the "unconditional surrender" that the Allies were then asking of Germany and Japan. To me it meant signing a blank paper for God to fill in—a radical, mind-boggling concept.

Whenever I was free, I visited the Nav Home. One day "Mom," seeing my blind commitment to my denomination, questioned my becoming a Methodist preacher. A couple of nights later I went to the Home again.

"Why are you so quiet?" asked "Mom."

Actually, I had nothing on my mind.

"Do you want to pray?" she asked.

As we knelt by the sofa, I began with peripheral things, going round and round until I put everything on the altar: my denomination, my family, my basic identity. To me it was a serious matter to surrender fully, because God might then lead me in unexpected paths. Yet I realized that in my life the church had taken the place of Christ.

When I got off my knees an hour later, I had put my "Isaac" on the altar as Abraham did so long ago. I arose shaken, feeling exhausted, yet experiencing joy tinged with fear. My surrender was expressed in the words on a plaque that hung at the entrance of the Navigator Home:

Lord, I make a full surrender,
All I have I give to Thee;
For Thy love, so great, so tender,
Claims this gift from me.
Lord, my life I lay before Thee,
Hear this hour my sacred vow,
What is Thine, I do restore Thee.
Thine forever now.

That night—February 5, 1945—I made a radical turnaround. My surrender proved to be the watershed of my entire Christian life. The longings of my heart since teen years were now fulfilled. The Bible became a living book, not a doctrinal textbook to argue about! I discovered Psalm 107:9, *"For he satisfieth the longing soul, and filleth the hungry soul with goodness."* Jesus became real to me. I was now eager to talk about my Lord. Gone was the reluctance that had bound me for so long.

At band rehearsal soon after my unconditional surrender, my buddy and I were not able to play a difficult piece of music properly.

"We're out for sure," we said to each other. "We'll be sent back overseas."

Suddenly, it didn't matter anymore. My fear was gone! Nothing mattered but God's will—even if it meant the Battle of the Bulge, which was then raging in Europe.

On Tour

The following week, the band left on a two-month tour around the eastern half of the United States. Our convoy traveled behind the command car and two supply trucks, we bandsmen in two buses painted olive drab. On stage we looked good in our special uniforms and we sounded good, in spite of my buddies and me on the back row of the clarinet section. We played concerts at military hospitals and school auditoriums, and furnished music at rallies to raise money for the war effort. Everywhere we went, I had opportunities to witness for Christ, and at Christian Service Men's Centers I found fellowship. "Mom" had given me a list of contacts along our route, for such centers were everywhere. My buddies were amazed that I knew so many people! Always there was time for sightseeing, yet I was glad to return to the Navigator Home in Washington after the tour, and then get back to Alabama for furlough.

We returned to Ft. Meade in time for "V-E Day" on May 8, 1944, marking victory in Europe. How beautiful nearby Washington looked, sparkling once again with lights after years of blackouts! Soon we were off on what proved to be my final tour, this time to the Northeast again. Now I not only played clarinet in the band, but also sang in the Glee Club composed of bandsmen. On the Fourth of July, we played our last concert, one of several bands performing for a huge crowd gathered along the Schuylkill River in Philadelphia. There we watched the most spectacular display of fireworks I had ever seen—a vivid reminder of exploding bombs, whining missiles, and a night sky beribboned with search lights that I had seen overseas.

Discharged—July 31, 1945

We had long since been conditioned to serving "for the duration and six months," so discharge almost took me by surprise. No end was in sight for the battle in the Pacific, yet we were told that those who had eighty-five points would be released soon. I already had ninety-one points accrued for time in service and other factors. Back at Ft. Meade, I began the countdown. With no more band rehearsals my days were free to spend at the Nav Home. Soon I turned in my clarinet and passed final inspection. July 31 was the Big Day! My clarinet buddy, Pulaski, was discharged with me. As always, we stood at attention, saluting as another band played the National Anthem. Then we heard our last command, "Fall out!" Discharge papers in hand, we were free! This American G.I. was now a veteran. I had spent a total of four years, nine months, and five days in the army—including twenty months overseas in North Africa, Sicily, and Italy.

After buying civilian clothes, "civvies," with my discharge pay, I took off for Alabama. I was excited about going home, but fearful for I could not see beyond the next week. All was a blank.

"Will you come back to D.C.?" "Mom" had asked.

"I probably will." For six months she had been a wonderful friend and counselor.

Back home, Daddy asked, "When are you going to school?"

"I...don't...know!!" I answered with a desperate moan.

Daddy's bottom-line concern was that I was wasting precious time, after already losing five years to the war. But I realized that those war years had not been a loss. Furthermore, I was waiting on the Lord for direction. I knew Daddy did not even understand the concept.

A month passed as I did a major landscaping project for Daddy, and preached for him on several occasions. At family reunions, I reconnected with Daddy's family and with Mama's. In my free time, I played Chinese checkers with my siblings and talked with them. "Mom" and I kept in touch through letters.

Startling news came over the radio during that month.

"They dropped a twenty-five-pound bomb that destroyed a whole city in Japan!" exclaimed my younger brother Joel.

"That's impossible!" I argued.

As a soldier, I knew that a two-ton blockbuster could destroy only a city block. The "A-bomb" had been kept secret. We had no idea what an atom bomb was. At the time of my discharge in late July, I assumed that the allies would be island-hopping in the Pacific for at least two more years before Japan gave up. Yet on August 14, 1945, only a week after the first atom bomb was dropped on Hiroshima, then the second on Nagasaki, we were celebrating "V-J Day"—Victory in Japan.

September came and my siblings returned to school. I was restless. Six weeks after I was discharged from military service, I announced to my family, "I'm going back to Washington." Yet as I prepared to leave, I felt a twinge of homesickness. I knew Mama and the rest wanted me to stay. They had waited five long years for me to come home from the war. Now I was leaving *again*, not for college, but for D.C.

My decision to return to Washington was second in importance only to my experience of total surrender to the Lord. Actually, returning to D.C. proved to be the first step toward implementing that surrender, thrusting me into a totally different orbit for the rest of my life.

As I boarded the bus that rainy night in mid-September, I wrote in my diary: "On my way...Wonder what is before me..."

− 3 −
What Next?
1945 to 1951

Returning to Washington on September 15, 1945, made me feel nostalgic. "Mom" met me at the bus station and drove me to the Navigator Home where we resumed our routine. We attended Sunday morning meetings for service men at the Union Gospel Mission and occasionally went to Youth for Christ meetings on Saturday. On weekdays I helped out at the Home and spent evenings studying the Bible with "Mom." When the last of my severance paychecks arrived, I found a job.

"Mom," the hostess at the Home, continued to be a key spiritual mentor. However, I soon realized that I was emotionally attached to her as well. That kept me in Washington for a few months until God revealed my next step.

The first Friday after my return to Washington, "Mom" announced that we would be going to hear Dr. Barnhouse, as though he were someone important. Dr. Donald Grey Barnhouse, pastor of the prestigious Tenth Presbyterian Church in Philadelphia, was conducting a twelve-week series of Bible classes in Washington. From the first, I loved this big, affable, deep-voiced Bible scholar, well-known throughout the nation for his weekly radio program.

"The purpose of the law is to 'slay' you," declared Barnhouse in his booming voice, "not to save you but to convict you, so that you'll cry out for a savior."

During the next week as I was praying, I saw myself in a new light. I had thought I was satisfactorily keeping the law, but now in my mind I saw a picture of myself as the filthy, repulsive entrails I threw out as a boy when Mama killed a chicken. I was reminded that Jesus described the hypocrisy of the Pharisees as being *"like unto whited sepulchres, which indeed appear beautiful outward, but are within full of dead men's bones."* I was convicted that I was as great a sinner as anyone else—an eye opener that would be reinforced a month later.

Perhaps the biggest impact Dr. Barnhouse had was to convince me of the adequacy of the death of Jesus. I learned the truth of II Corinthians 5:21: *"He hath made him to be sin for us, who knew no sin, that we might be made the righteousness of God in him."* I was amazed to realize that God not only placed *my sins* on Jesus but that He also gave *me* the righteousness of Christ. When I was growing up, I had often sung: "Dressed in His righteousness alone, faultless to stand before the throne." Yet I had never heard of "imputed righteousness," nor had I understood that I could be acceptable to God only through what Jesus had done.

From Dr. Barnhouse I also learned about "the flesh," our propensity to sin, that we sin because of sin in us, that our hearts are *"deceitful above all things, and desperately wicked,"* according to Jeremiah 17:9. Barnhouse also talked about practical issues, such as daily devotions and the victorious Christian life. The weeks under his teaching not only raised issues I had never heard before, but built a wider doctrinal foundation than I had learned from preachers as I grew up.

One night as I listened to a preacher at a Youth for Christ meeting, I felt I was standing by the cross, listening to each drop of Christ's blood falling to the ground—for *me*.

"If you were the only person in the world," the preacher said, "nothing less than the blood of Jesus could wash away your sins."

I realized that I personally had caused Jesus' death—not merely that His death was caused by all the sins of the world together! Then it hit me that it took as much of His blood to save me as it did to save a drunk in the gutter.

My self-righteousness was crumbling. The Holy Spirit was convicting me through Dr. Barnhouse and other anointed preachers. I realized that if I could not be good enough to *be* saved, then neither could I be good enough to *keep* saved. Only He could keep me from falling. The enormity of the grace of God impacted my thinking.

A month after returning to Washington, I received a letter from Daddy, telling of his concern that I was losing valuable time by not enrolling in college. Before reading his letter, I had prayed and the Lord spoke to me from Isaiah 26:3: *"Thou wilt keep him in perfect peace, whose mind is stayed on thee."* But though I had peace that it was God's will for me to remain in D.C. and absorb its spiritual offerings, I prayed again after reading the letter.

"Lord," I asked, "do something special to confirm that I am in the right place."

What happened that day was an experience never to be forgotten. I came back from work that afternoon with Titus 3:5 pounding in my head: *"Not by works of righteousness which we have done, but according to his mercy he saved us."* Those words had been swirling in my mind all day long. I headed for my room and fell flat on the floor, overwhelmed by my sins. For the first time in my life I realized that I deserved hell. I felt naked before a holy God. Lying there on the floor, I saw myself standing alone in a "pillbox"—a concrete bunker—as enemy soldiers advanced up the beach. Suddenly, the pillbox disintegrated! There I stood, helpless, totally exposed.

For three days I was overwhelmed by conviction, convicted about my pride, about my attitude toward money, about lack of love for others, about lustful thoughts. I went through great travail of soul as I saw myself as a sinner before a holy God: naked, yet dressed in the righteousness of Jesus.

Ever since that day, the thought of His righteousness credited to my account has motivated me to seek His righteousness imparted to my soul. I developed a total allegiance to Jesus Christ and a passion for holiness of life because of what my sins had cost Jesus—a passion that has only intensified through the years.

A week after the letter from Daddy about schooling, I attended the International Convention of Rescue Missions. Among the many speakers at the convention, the one who moved me most was a crippled man who had been saved in a rescue mission. I felt the Lord tugging and in response, offered myself to serve in rescue missions.

"Thank God, my 'blankness' is gone," I wrote in my diary that night. I had been struggling with a blank feeling ever since being discharged from the army with no clear direction as to my future. Now God had given me a vision for schooling and ministry—plans which would make Daddy happy.

I knew that no ordinary college or seminary could train me for a ministry to broken men. However, I had heard of Moody Bible Institute. One of the speakers at the convention confirmed that Moody would give me good training for work in a rescue mission.

As a veteran of almost five years of active service, I was entitled to forty-eight months of schooling at government expense under the "G. I. Bill" at any institution in the nation. Yet my pride took another blow as I contemplated Moody, for at that time it was not accredited, nor were its credits transferable to other colleges or universities. I was in no hurry to apply to an unaccredited school!

Weeks passed as I hesitated. Finally, in January, 1946, I wrote to Moody Bible Institute for an application form. It was mid-February before I sent it in and applied for the G. I. Bill.

During this delay, a final ingredient was added to my preparation in Washington—I began to "navigate." One Sunday in March, Ed Gray, head of the Navigator Home in Norfolk, visited the Nav Home in Washington. He called us servicemen together and carefully laid out the Navigator memory system. For two hours we listened:

"Learn three verses the first week, reviewing them every day," Ed explained. "Add three verses the second week, reviewing the six every day. Then continue adding verses each week for seven weeks until there are twenty-one verses."

Review was to be word perfect, with the reference before and after each verse—"fore and aft" in the Navy jargon familiar to the sailors for whom the system was originally developed.

"After seven weeks, take the oldest three verses to start a weekly review section, but continue to add three verses a week to the daily section," Ed continued. "When you have seven weekly packs of twenty-one, then with the oldest pack start a monthly review section.

"Eventually, you'll be reviewing the daily pack, plus one pack a day from the weekly section, and one pack a day from the monthly section—a total of sixty-three verses a day indefinitely."

With Ed's encouragement I started the Topical Memory System for which the Navigators were famous. I began memorizing the original 108 verses. Once I learned the Nav verses, I added my own verses. Like every other faithful Navigator, I was impacted by the Word, and felt the joy expressed by the prophet in Jeremiah 15:16, *"Thy words were found, and I did eat them; and thy word was unto me the joy and rejoicing of mine heart..."*

My time in Washington gave me opportunities to learn from many Christian leaders of the day. I heard Clarence Jones, founder of the first missionary radio station, and also Philip Howard, editor of *The Sunday School Times*, a magazine Daddy enjoyed. Dawson Trotman, founder of the Navigators, also spoke in D.C. Without commenting on his baby daughter who had been born with a serious defect, "Daws" moved me as he spoke on Psalm 115:3, *"But our God is in the heavens: he hath done whatsoever he hath pleased."*

One evening several of us from the Nav home went to hear Norman Grubb, son-in-law of the famous missionary C. T. Studd. Before Grubb's message there was a baptism at the church. Suddenly, I felt the desire to be baptized as my own confession of faith. I knew this would hurt my parents, who had me baptized as an infant. Though concerned for my family's feelings, I talked to the pastor, and was baptized a few weeks later. When I wrote to my parents, my mother responded, saying that she hoped I was satisfied. That was the only comment I heard about this major departure from my Methodist upbringing.

Later Norman Grubb taught a series on the "Victorious Christian Life." I had already been introduced to the subject in a tract by Charles Trumbull, but now Grubb plowed new ground. What I remember most vividly was his teaching on "Identification with Christ in His Death and Resurrection." Through him I learned about dying to self, which was at the heart of the message of victory. Grubb's message on "Life in the Spirit" impacted me as well. I was learning and growing, enjoying the Lord to the hilt.

Another speaker who moved me was George Cowan, one of the first Wycliffe Bible Translators.

"I see more of the Lord in you than I have in any other person," I said to him.

"Well, it must be from spending so much of my life in the Word," Cowan responded.

At the time I never imagined I would spend *my* life translating the Word like George Cowan, but the Word was now an essential part of my ongoing walk with the Lord. Listening for God's voice daily in the Word became my lifestyle.

God was working out His purposes in my being in Washington, my staying at the Navigator Home, and even in my ill-advised relationship with "Mom," my mentor. I was not rebelling against my heritage, but rather standing on the shoulders of my parents, hungrily discovering more of God. Washington was my launching pad into a new orbit.

Moody Bible Institute
April 1946 – August 1949

A telegram came on Saturday, April 20, 1946, notifying me of my acceptance at the Moody Bible Institute and telling me to arrive the following Tuesday. For three days I scurried around, preparing to leave. I flew to Chicago on Tuesday evening, arriving at midnight. A sleepy attendant at the reception desk showed me to my room in the 153 Building, the original building built by Dwight L. Moody.

Located a few blocks west of Lake Michigan and a few blocks north of the "Loop," the Institute's neat, orderly buildings blended into the others along LaSalle Street. The winds off the lake constantly whipped up trash along the streets of this "Windy City." The school had no campus—our campus was the city. There we would learn to minister.

Moody Bible Institute was a wider world, spiritually, than Washington. I soon realized that the Middle West was the center of evangelical Christianity and that Chicago was the heart of it all. The Institute had been founded in 1886 to give basic training in Bible and in *practical* Christian work, a need growing out of Moody's Chicago campaign. The school was sometimes referred to as the "West Point of Christian Service." D. L. Moody's original vision was to bridge the gap between the layman and the seminary grad. Everything was geared to the practical. It was my time at Moody Bible Institute—rather than my later studies—that best prepared me for ministry.

"You are our reason for being here!" said Dr. William Culbertson to new students at our first gathering.

"I thank the Lord for sending me here," I wrote in my diary soon after my arrival at the Institute. "It is wonderful to be getting things I've been hungry for for so long, things I used to pray for while I was a soldier in Africa."

I have no idea now what those "things" were! Perhaps I had just been hungry for God and His Word. Also, I wanted to enjoy fellowship with Christians who talked about the Lord Jesus, not just the church—Christians who heard Him speak from the Word. Furthermore, I wanted to learn to share my faith more effectively. But none of this was consciously defined when I first got to Moody.

My first class was Personal Evangelism. The very first day we learned seven simple steps to lead someone to the Lord. Classes in personal evangelism continued for three terms, giving us a mindset and method for talking to everyone we met. With an inner-city campus, opportunities to talk with people were only an arm's length away. Each week during my years at Moody we had to file a report on how many people we talked to, how many professions of faith we had, how many tracts we passed out. No one ever questioned us about the reports, but the requirement created a conscience in us. I no longer feared sharing the gospel.

As this was the Moody Bible Institute, the focus was on knowing and using Scripture. I took courses surveying the Old and New Testaments, and other courses on single books of the Bible. My favorite Bible teacher was Dr. Wilbur Smith—always intent, always serious, always with a pile of books under his arm. Later I had classes on Theology with wise, old Dr. Fitzwater, who had taught at Moody for fifty years. A Presbyterian, he impacted me with his paradox position contrasting free will and God's sovereignty.

"Preach both," he exhorted. "Don't play down either one. Let God harmonize the paradox."

I studied Church History and loved it! I was helped by Historical Theology where I learned how leaders in previous centuries had dealt with complex doctrinal issues. Mr. Springer, our Ethics teacher, gave us each a tract about the victorious Christian life.

We studied Greek under Mr. Wuest, whose popular books contained nuggets from the Greek New Testament. While his focus was not on the grammar and vocabulary I would need for later study, I learned from him that the key to victory lies in realizing that nothing touches us without first passing through the will of God.

In addition to these required courses, I audited a very profitable class on Children's Work taught by Miss Lucy Campbell.

"Mr. Jones," she encouraged me, "you have an uncanny understanding of a child's mind. You ought to go into children's work."

Practical Christian Work was the Institute's hands-on training for ministry. Every student had two assignments each week, one on Sunday and another on Wednesday. My first assignment was to a "Sunday School pickup team." We walked through dirty alleys, up back stairways, into dismal apartments where a drunken mother would say, "Yes, please take my kids"—perhaps glad to be rid of them for a couple of hours. Another time I was assigned to a team that knocked on tenement doors on Sunday mornings at church time.

"May we come in," we would ask the residents, "to read the Bible and pray with you?"

For three terms I was assigned on Sundays to visit the men in the fracture ward at Cook County Hospital, an enormous institution serving all of Chicago. Most of the men were friendless and homeless—picked up on the streets.

Eventually, my Sunday assignment was to direct an afternoon Sunday School at a nearby mission, reaching neglected children as D. L. Moody had once done in the same area. Mr. Moody's "ragged Sunday School" grew into Moody Church, but the kids I worked with all dropped out at the age of thirteen. I was not a Moody!

One of my first Wednesday assignments was with a team holding street meetings: singing, passing out tracts, giving a testimony of salvation, preaching. In cold weather we went by street car, often on bitter, snowy nights, to a "skid-row" mission. There I might kneel with my arm around a sour-smelling human derelict, telling him about the love of Jesus. We knew that Jesus could restore such men, as the song said: "Down in the human heart, crushed by the tempter, Feelings lie buried that grace can restore."

On each team to which I was assigned, I was named the leader for the next term; I never figured out why. Yet I never made the team which ministered at the Cook County Jail, a handpicked group formed of several of my closest friends, mostly WWII veterans and Navigators. They tried me out but felt that I did not fit, except as a substitute.

At Moody I experienced a wide spectrum of Christian work. Chicago was a perfect training ground, but ministry was not just for practice but for real. We knew we were playing for keeps.

Beyond Study and Ministry

Moody Bible Institute provided more than study and practical ministry. Classes began with prayer, and maybe a song or a brief devotional. Each Monday began with a school-wide chapel service where students and staff were inspired by renowned Bible teachers, pastors, missionaries, or presidents of other Bible Schools. Every morning after breakfast a faculty member led a short devotional, and each evening students gathered for a lengthier devotional time, men and women separately. Too much of God? Not for me—I loved it!

Dr. Culbertson, the president, often spoke at the Monday morning chapels. He always moved me. And what speakers he brought! During my first year Dr. Robert Munger spent a week at Moody, teaching us about the fullness of the Holy Spirit. By the fifth day, the service lasted until noon as we prayed, and confessed. The Lord showed me things in my heart that hindered His fullness.

"No matter what experiences we have had, the Christian life is an upstream struggle," commented wise old Dr. Fitzwater as we got back to our regular classes after the week. He was not discounting what we had experienced during the Munger meetings, for these experiences served to provide our "tools" for the struggles of life.

My second year Stephen Olford, a young man from England, came to preach for a week. Though he was only seven years older than I, he rocked the student body. I thought to myself that if he could know God so well, so could I.

Olford touched on a burning question of the students, "How can I know the will of God?" I have never forgotten his telling us to expect three indicators to come together:
"The Word of God,
The Witness of the Spirit, and
Warranted Circumstances."

"Make decisions in line with God's Word," Olford explained. "Listen to what the Holy Spirit says to your heart. Look for circumstances that confirm what you're hearing."

Mr. Olford also gave a message on surrender, particularly on surrendering our love life—a serious concern for us all. Finally, he impacted us with a message on the "Quiet Time." His words reinforced what I was already doing—meeting the Lord daily in His Word. After Olford left, early dawn found many more lights on in dorm rooms as students met the Lord before breakfast. (From Moody, Olford went on to preach at nearby Wheaton, and made a similar impact at the college where, unknown to me, my future wife was then a freshman.)

Each Monday morning after chapel, all students were required to attend the Missions Hour. At my first such hour I heard elderly Dr. Samuel Zwemer, famous missionary to the Muslims. The student-sponsored Missionary Union, met on Saturday night to hear inspiring speakers. Every weekday after breakfast and lunch, students led prayer bands, each group focusing on a different area of the world.

"Someone should go to the Muslims of North Africa!" I spouted off as we discussed missions one evening at dinner. As a soldier, I had seen those Muslims.

"Why don't *you* go?" challenged one of the fellows at the table.

"I'm going into rescue missions," I retorted. Although I did attend Missionary Union meetings, I had no urge to go to the foreign field. Later, that was to change.

Founder's Week, held each February to honor Dwight L. Moody's birthday, was a welcome break during Chicago's bitterly cold winter with its icy sidewalks and piles of dirty snow. During this Bible conference, classes were suspended, and students were expected to attend at least three meetings daily. There were several sessions each day at the Institute Auditorium and then an evening celebration at Moody Church, a fifteen-minute walk north of the Institute. As I hurried there for the evening sessions, the bone-chilling wind off Lake Michigan took my breath away and nipped my ears. Yet the days of Founder's Week were days of glory.

Not only did I learn much Bible and theology during each Founder's Week, but I felt the warm pulse of men who loved the Lord and loved His Word. As we followed along in our Bibles, I began to see how expository preachers handled the Word. They were like an index finger pointing out the meaning with their fine-honed analysis of a passage. For me, Founder's Week was an annual feast! One year I attended all but three of the sessions. I always sat up front, notebook in hand, near my buddies. These weeks impacted me as much as my classes.

I enjoyed social activities at Moody—picnics, clubs, and Senior Sneak. Friends gathered in the lounges or at the "Sweet Shop." Mealtimes in the family-style dining room were occasions to rehash classes, talk about issues, and forge friendships. After supper, or on summer afternoons, we guys enjoyed talking theology while sitting on the railing (dubbed "The Theological Rail") outside the old 153 Building. I counted it a privilege just to go up the stairs of that dorm, where generations of students—and even Mr. Moody himself—had helped wear down the treads.

The greatest impact on my life at Moody came from a few disciplined, mature fellow students. At the core were those Navigators who had been memorizing Scripture and meeting the Lord daily during their years in the Navy, men like Wayne Snell and Charles Zimmerman. Both Wayne and "Zimmie" had a solid walk with the Lord although neither had my Christian roots. I envied their relationship with the Lord and lamented what I felt was lacking in my upbringing. They, in turn, envied my heritage and helped me appreciate it.

"You've got good roots," Wayne told me. "Now that you've gotten some other things straight, you can build on that foundation."

By this time, I had moved into a single room where I was free to pray aloud or even cry out to God. With no roommate, I could read the Word out loud as I knelt beside the bed. Charlie Zimmerman roomed next door. He was always up early to meet the Lord and would come into my room grinning, with his Bible in hand, to share some nugget of truth he had discovered.

Glenn Solum, the Navigators' student leader, mentored me. Each week I recited a set of my memory verses to him, and he recited his to me. He guided my Bible study and taught me the Nav system of recording prayer requests and answers. It was Glen who got me started on a daily quiet time. Later he assigned me another student, Andy Lindvall, to disciple. What I learned from Glen, I taught to Andy.

("Aziel," reminisced Andy recently, "remember how those Nav guys used to ask at the breakfast table, 'What did you get from the Word this morning?'"

"Yes," I replied, "and ever since then I've been asking similar questions!")

During my first year at Moody, I was still emotionally attached to "Mom," my mentor in Washington. We wrote every day and I visited her during vacation. Severing our relationship was agonizing, but Wayne gave me good counsel, and "Zimmie" prayed with me. (I had met him before I went to Moody, for he came occasionally to the Navigator Home in Washington and knew "Mom.") In November, 1947, I wrote her one last letter, which ended the relationship. She had played a key role in my life, but I no longer needed her as a mentor.

Near the end of my time at the Institute, I was asked to teach the college class at Elm-LaSalle Bible Church, at that time a branch of Moody Church. (Later it became independent and was eventually renamed LaSalle Street Church.) This was a personal opportunity, not a Practical Christian Work assignment. I thoroughly enjoyed the challenge and the class grew significantly.

Although my relationship to the Methodist church had been the key issue when I surrendered my life to the Lord in 1945, I had felt no nudge from the Holy Spirit to follow through on this. Perhaps the thought of leaving the church had only been a test, I reasoned, remembering that God had asked Abraham to surrender his son and then had given Isaac back to him.

Occasionally, students would ask me why, being a Methodist, I was not attending a Methodist school. I began to feel my Methodist label was misleading. Moody was an independent institution, but most of my teachers were members of mainline denominations. The school had no objection to my affiliation, but I did not want to be part of a denomination marked by liberalism, nor was I any longer a Methodist in doctrinal conviction. I had been attending Elm-LaSalle for some time and sensed that God was nudging me to join. However, I felt the pull of Daddy's words:

"Every church has a pastor," he often said, speaking about the security of being part of the Methodist denomination. "And every pastor has a church and a guaranteed minimum salary."

Eventually I spoke with the pastor of Elm-LaSalle. He was kind, and had the insight to say that Daddy's counsel arose from love and that he was not being used, even unintentionally, to tempt me to compromise. The pastor's words were helpful in beginning to undo the negative attitude toward Daddy which I had absorbed in Washington from my mentor. This was *my* decision, and I felt *the Lord* was speaking.

Leaving the Methodist church was a big step of faith. It was traumatic for me to leave the security of my denomination and even more traumatic to break the unity of my family. (Both Daddy's family and Mama's had been Methodist as far back as our heritage could be traced.)

Though I wrestled in my soul, I took the step. I pictured myself in an unfamiliar house on a pitch-dark night, ready to step out the back door into the wilderness. I could see nothing—not even one step ahead. I feared stepping into a precipice, but when I stepped in faith, *I stepped up, onto firm footing!*

In March, 1947, I was received into the membership of Moody Church at Elm-LaSalle. I wrote Daddy about my decision, realizing he would be hurt. I knew how much the Methodist church meant to him. He had served the Lord all his life there. I was sad about hurting him, but the Lord encouraged me with Isaiah 50:7: *"For the Lord God will help me...therefore have I set my face like a flint, and I know that I shall not be ashamed."* I have gone back to this verse in many difficult situations, confident that God would vindicate me. *He is enough!*

My conviction to serve in rescue missions — now called inner-city missions—did not wane. At Moody I had plenty of experience in ministering to the "down and out." In my diary I wrote, "Oh, the dirt and filth of the city and the awful places called homes." Those homes mirrored the spiritual condition of those who lived there. Yet God had given me I Corinthians 16:9 at the time of my call: *"For a great door and effectual is opened unto me."*

Then the unexpected happened.

One Sunday morning as I knelt by my bed, I heard myself praying about the possibility of *foreign* missions. I had come to Moody to prepare for rescue missions, but now I perked up my ears whenever foreign missionaries spoke. That week an unusual number of missionaries visited the Institute.

After days of soul searching, and counsel from friends and missionaries, I still sought a "word" from the Word of God to confirm my interest in missions. As I reviewed my verses one night, I realized that the most recent ones I had memorized, Matthew 9:36-38, were classic missionary verses! They were my confirmation to "look on the [foreign] fields!"

The Lord had used my original vision to get me to Moody where He could speak to me about foreign missions, just as He had led the Israelites by a roundabout way, for His purposes. At first my interest was in Mongolia, then Tibet, then northwest China. Eventually I was tugged by an interest in Bible translation, thanks in part to my buddy Wayne, and perhaps as a result of seed sown in D.C. when I first heard about translation work from George Cowan!

By the time I finished "the school that D. L. Moody founded," as the Alma Mater refers to the Institute, my theological underpinnings, my lifelong devotional habits, my concept of one-on-one ministry, and my vision for foreign missions were firmly established.

For my graduation in August, 1949, Daddy and Mama drove all the way from Alabama—quite an effort in the days before interstate highways. I was so happy that they came and that they liked what they saw and heard at the ceremonies. There was no academic procession; only we graduates wore caps and gowns. There were various speakers, but our two class speakers—one for the women, one for the men—were my special friends. Daddy was impressed.

"The students were the focus," Daddy said, "not the faculty."

Despite my earlier hesitancy to attend Moody Bible Institute, I have always been proud of my diploma from "the West Point of Christian service."

However, before graduating, I realized I would still have G.I. Bill funds available for more education. I was attracted to Wheaton College, a sort of Ivy League school among Christian colleges, but what was God's will? Was I just interested in a degree? As I searched my heart, I felt the Lord's approval for more Bible training, so I applied, and to my surprise, was accepted. During graduation weekend at MBI, my friend Bob West helped me and Daddy haul my belongings to Wheaton, thirty-three miles west of Chicago.

In the short interval between graduating from Moody and entering Wheaton, I drove to Alabama with my parents. It was great to be in the South again and great to be home, yet preaching was still in my blood. I preached a week of revival meetings for Daddy and then a week in Montgomery at Cornerstone Bible Church, a new church recently started by Mr. Parker and his friends.

I had met Mr. Parker the year before when he visited Moody. He was from Alabama and had heard about the Institute at a Bible class. My "chance" meeting with Charlie Parker was the beginning of a lifelong friendship with him and others from Montgomery. That summer vacation as I preached in country churches near Montgomery, several people came from that Bible class. I was not a polished preacher but it did not matter to them; they were hungry for the Word.

Now as I preached in their new church, only one person responded to my ministry, a boy named Dick who prayed for salvation during my Children's Hour. Years later, Dick became a personal supporter, and Cornerstone became our first supporting church.

Wheaton College
September 1949 - June 1951

Soon I was back up North to begin my studies at Wheaton. As Moody was not accredited at the time, I had to validate, by exam, any credits transferred from MBI. To my utter surprise, I validated thirty credit hours. But Wheaton would not give me credit for my two years of Greek, as the two schools had different standards. However, if I registered for second year Greek and passed it, I would also be given credit for first year. I took the plunge—by faith. I recorded my feelings in a prayer:

"Lord, I have taken Greek plus the other subjects. My best is not enough but I believe I am in Thy will in taking Greek. At this time I see no way through either Greek or some of the other courses. Lord, I ask for a minimum of equal grade points as semester hours. Lord, lest I forget the fear in my heart—the fear of not making the grade—I record this and give Thee praise for enabling me to pass all and have the points too. May I do this schoolwork in real supernatural power this term."

I signed it, adding: "This paper is to remind me that Thou art to receive *all* praise for what Thou art going to do. I Corinthians 8:2, Philippians 4:13."

During that semester I studied Greek six hours a day for the four-hour-a-week class, plus preparing for four other subjects. That was the year I learned to pray for my studies. In February, 1950, after the semester ended, I wrote in my prayer notebook, "He did it—I made an A, three B's, and a C. *Lord*, all praise to *Thee*!!!"

"I prayed a lot for you, Mr. Jones," said my Greek teacher, a lovely Chinese-American graduate student, as she rejoiced with me over my grade.

The next semester I cast myself once more on the Lord, and wrote: "Lord, Thou didst see fit to do exceeding abundantly above all I asked or thought. I made the grades. But more, I got my rest and am better physically than upon entering. Above all, Thy presence became a reality never before experienced. Thank you, Lord. Now, for this term, in the name of Jesus, I ask for a 2.0 average, a rested body in June, victory in Scripture memory verses (which I neglected before), and attendance at Foreign Missions Fellowship. Father, I trust Thee again as I did before; not on my experience or past success, but as if I had never trusted Thee before. Without Thee, I can do nothing regardless of talents. I now, in Thy presence, yield all my faculties to Thee again to empower and help."

Again I signed the paper before adding these words: "To Thee goes all praise for the victory Thou wilt see fit to give this term! Isaiah 41:10." On June 23, 1950, I added, "I found out my grade point average to be *3.32.* Ephesians 3:20 is my testimony!!!" The Lord had done abundantly above my hopes and prayers.

One of my classes was freshman English. The first week I wrote a short paper which Miss Buck, the teacher, read to the class as an example of good writing. Never had this happened to me! I had written about "faith"—essentially, about resting on Christ, illustrating it with an anecdote about Daddy. He had stopped the car as we approached a crude bridge on a country road. Not until he checked the beams under the bridge did he proceed. He now had "faith" in the bridge.

Later I wrote a description of my first air raid—a beautiful display of lights in Casablanca.

"You have a good feel for words! I want to see you break into print," Miss Buck commented.

Break into print I did. The school magazine printed the air raid story and a later one I called "I Like to Study," a testimony of how prayer and trust bring the supernatural into studying. Learning to "study on my knees" was a pivotal step in my personal walk with the Lord!

Inspired by Miss Buck, I took Dr. Fackler's advanced writing class. Miss Fackler also read one of my papers to the class.

"Mr. Jones has a jerky style, but there's nothing wrong with that," was her comment.

Encouraged by Dr. Fackler, I entered President Edman's essay contest. I won first prize on the assigned subject "The Celtic Irish Church," but it cost me my spring vacation—and more dollars than I won. I considered changing from a Bible major to journalism, but Miss Fackler, though head of the department, discouraged such a step.

"Mr. Jones, you can never develop all your gifts," she said.

That was an earthshaking concept.

Everything that was set in place at Moody was fine-tuned at Wheaton. Daily chapels were often led by President Edman, a man of the same spiritual caliber as Dr. Culbertson at MBI. The spiritual life of the college, thanks to the impact of WWII vets, was at white heat; it was a privilege to experience the Wheaton revival of 1950.

My Bible major filled in any cracks left by Moody, especially in Greek. I also had some great Bible courses, including one on the Minor Prophets and another on the Synoptic Gospels, which I read in third-year Greek. Even reviewing for my Bible major comprehensive exams was a blessing.

At Wheaton I joined no student organizations and attended few sports events, though I did go to a Moody-Wheaton game. It was hard to decide which team to cheer for, but I *felt* for Moody! I never had the same emotional identity with Wheaton as I had at Moody. My interests had narrowed. I was now study-focused, and studies were a bit harder. And I was older—twenty-seven.

Throughout my time at Wheaton, Sundays found me in Chicago, leading the mission Sunday School and teaching the college-age class at Elm-LaSalle Bible Church, where I became a deacon and, for a time, treasurer of the church. In one sense, I never really left Chicago when I went to Wheaton.

My interest in missions and in Bible translation grew, though I struggled to give up my desire to preach. On June 8, 1950, I wrote: "The interest [in translation] continues. Last night at FMF I was thinking of Paul. He preached, but his pen did more for me [than his preaching]. I recall how Miss Fackler said that the Lord has given us more talents than we can ever fully develop. Lord, I can learn other [skills] by Thy power. I am yours that others might have the privilege I had today: The Word in their own tongue."

Two months later, on August 6, after I saw the Wycliffe film, "Oh, for a Thousand Tongues," I wrote: "This is a culmination of a growing and almost settled conviction for several weeks. I have purposed to attend the Translation Prayer Band. I do not see how I could ever do such work...except that Thou hast promised enabling for obedience...Trusting, Lord, that this purpose is wrapped up in Thy purpose, I press toward the mark...that others may have Thy Word."

Marian

While at Moody, I dated only two girls, friends I considered spiritual girls. At Wheaton I dated three different ones, but only one time each. I had been impacted by Stephen Olford who had counseled us not to date to find a wife, but to "sleep in the will of God, till He wakes you up."

In June, 1950, at Wheaton, God woke me up!

My friend Martha Newell came out from Chicago for a visit with her friend Dottie, who was studying at Wheaton. They planned a picnic at a local park with Dot's roommate, Marian Westling.

"Let's invite a guy," Martha suggested to Dottie.

"Ask Aziel Jones," Dottie said, "He's harmless." I was a natural choice since they both knew me.

The Sunday after the picnic, I went to Chicago as usual, dropping in to visit the Newell family between ministry obligations.

"Aziel," said Martha, "I borrowed these socks from Marian for the picnic and need to return them. You can give them to her one at a time if you want to."

Had she thought I was interested in Marian? I had not been aware of any attraction toward Marian, but the next day I gave her the socks—both socks—and later invited her to go with me to the upcoming Moody graduation. My Navigator friend Glen Solum was to be the class speaker for the occasion.

The graduation was to be held at Moody Church in Chicago. Marian and I talked during supper in the dining hall at Wheaton, talked as we walked the dozen blocks to the train station and talked as we rode to the city. After the graduation ceremony I ran into my friends Howard and Corene McMillen, newlyweds who lived near Moody Institute. They asked me for dinner the next Sunday.

"Bring your girlfriend, too," Howard said as they walked away.

Marian and I said nothing about his invitation; just headed back to Wheaton. It had been a great evening—memorable, in fact.

The next Saturday I invited Marian to a special event at the Chicago lakefront. We went, but I sensed the date was a flop (and much later Marian confessed she had decided not to accept another invitation from me). However, when I next saw Marian, I hesitantly reminded her of the McMillen's invitation. Since it was a prior commitment, she accepted. We agreed to go to Chicago early, in time for me to teach the college-age class at Elm-LaSalle Church. Then we would have dinner with the McMillens before going to the Mission where I was to speak to the adults.

A full day in Chicago—on my ministry turf! At the McMillen's apartment we had a delightful time. And before preaching at the Mission that evening, I sang a solo, accompanied by Marian on the piano. That third date did it—a perfect day! Marian and I clicked.

But summer school was ending and Marian was graduating on August 18. I bought her a small corsage of carnations. I wanted to communicate *something* (with flowers) but not *too much* (so keep it small). She responded by inviting me to eat lunch with her family who had just arrived from New Jersey. I enjoyed them: Father, Mother, sister Irene, and brother John. During the ceremonies, Marian was recognized as a member of the Scholastic Honor Society. At my request, Bob Hornish, my roommate, was on hand to take a photo of us before she turned in her cap and gown.

Finding a bench outside the chapel, Marian and I talked an hour while her family waited nearby in their car.

"I'm interested in you," I said, "but I don't know what it means. May I write?"

Marian agreed and soon drove away with her family. Then I moved into high gear. I had to clear my room, store my stuff, and catch a midnight bus in Chicago. Papers and books were in disarray—and so were my emotions. I was running late, too late to catch a train to the city. John Lindskoog, a Moody friend now studying at Wheaton, drove me to Chicago to catch my bus. On the way I lost my supper! John, of course, teased me about being lovesick. We barely made the bus. I was ready for the 24-hour trip to Alabama for vacation—time to rest and think.

After meeting Marian, the rest of my time at Wheaton was anticlimactic. The months went by in a blur: long hours of study, nightly letters to Marian, and occasional times together. I was getting to know and like her, even her neat penmanship. (I had written my first letter on Daddy's church stationery until receiving Marian's letters on special paper; then I bought some nice masculine stationery.)

Although Marian and I had a commitment, I needed to keep her on the altar. This was inherent in my surrender to the Lord in D.C. four years earlier. Early in my correspondence with Marian, I recorded another special decision in my prayer notebook:

"Lord, saints from Abraham to now have been discovering that surrender [to the LORD] involves an altar with 'Isaac' upon it."

Writing down pivotal decisions like this helped to fix them in my mind. As I wrote, I referred to Psalm 9:10, a verse I was memorizing: *"And they that know thy name will put their trust in thee: for thou, LORD, hast not forsaken them that seek thee."* The Lord used that verse to confirm my decision to ask Marian to marry me; it was to become "our" verse.

Early in October, however, we hit a snag in our relationship. Although I was still confident Marian was to be my wife, I was concerned about her church involvement. During her last year at Wheaton, she had attended a Plymouth Brethren assembly and now that she was teaching school in Philadelphia, she attended an assembly with the Macdonald family, at whose home she stayed. I liked the Brethren but wanted to be sure that if we married, Marian would be willing to adopt my church affiliation. Eventually, she joined Moody Church which I had joined a few years earlier. For her, it was not a hard decision, for her mother had once been a member of that church, and Marian herself had attended there occasionally in early years.

Homecoming was approaching. And Marian was coming! I met her train in Chicago. All day we both felt uneasy. I realized that I knew the girl of my letters, not the one here in person. Yet by evening, as we listened to a recording of the *Messiah*, we began to relax in each other's presence, feeling very one but saying very little.

The next afternoon we attended the Homecoming game. It was a bore—I don't remember who played or who won. After supper we borrowed a car and drove to the park where we had met at the picnic just four months earlier. There we talked for hours.

Finally, still unsure of her feelings, I asked Marian if she would marry me. She said yes.

"May we seal it with a kiss?" I asked. Our first kiss—no fire yet, only a formality.

"How many children do you want?" I asked next.

"As many as the Lord gives," she replied.

So much for my desire to have only four, or six at the most! Much later Marian revealed that although she wanted children, she feared she might have trouble having them.

I remember nothing of our emotions that evening, October 21, 1950—a date etched in memory's calendar. Yes, there were emotions, but at the core, our wills were responding to a sense that God was leading us together.

The following afternoon I took Marian to Chicago to catch the train back to Philadelphia. Now that we had agreed to marry, we found it extremely painful to part! The emotional dam had now broken—for both of us. Ever the cautious one, I did not want to make our engagement public immediately.

Marian and I planned to spend the upcoming Thanksgiving with her family. Before I left for New Jersey, I spent most of what was left from my Army savings on a diamond ring. I confided to John Lindskoog that I was taking the ring "just in case."

"If you take it, you won't return with it!" he remarked, knowingly.

I met Marian in Philly, and then traveled with her to her home. I enjoyed the Westlings and felt comfortable with them. At bedtime we joined her parents for their traditional coffee and pastries. We chatted a couple of hours; but when they started upstairs to bed, I finally gathered my courage to bring up the subject on my mind.

"Mr. Westling, how do you feel about me and Marian?" I asked.

"I heartily approve!" he responded warmly.

Before her parents went to bed, we spent a couple of hours telling them our plans for linguistic studies, marriage, and then Bible translation for an unreached tribe. (Obviously, we had expected their approval and were ready to share our plans!)

In the wee hours of that Thanksgiving morning, November 25, 1950, I gave Marian the ring—she loved it! That day was the tenth anniversary of my entering WWII—a very important date to me. At breakfast when I watched Marian show the ring to her mother, I realized it was a precious moment for Marian and a special way to mark Thanksgiving Day.

I returned to the Westlings for Christmas, and experienced some of their Swedish customs. Christmas Eve dinner included *lutfisk*, with rice pudding for dessert. That evening we shared gifts around the tree. Although there were no stockings on the mantel, Christmas Day was more American; yet lingonberry sauce from Sweden substituted for the cranberry sauce at the turkey dinner.

The next day we boarded a bus for the long trip south so that Marian could meet my family. We Joneses were noisy and messy compared to the Westlings' quiet, orderly home. She shared a bedroom with three of my younger sisters, who teased her about her northern "brogue." I enjoyed showing Marian off at church, especially on Sunday night when Daddy asked her to tell the story during the Children's Hour. Privately, Marian pointed out to me positive things about my family that I had been blind to since my time in Washington. She was good for me.

Returning to Wheaton, I finished the semester, then went to the Registrar's office to check out my schedule for the spring semester.

"The long trip south"– December 1950

"With these courses, you'll be finished," the clerk remarked.

"What do you mean, 'finished'?"

"You can graduate in June."

I was a graduating senior and did not even realize it!

During semester break I made a quick trip to Jersey to see Marian, and she came to Wheaton during her Easter break from teaching school. By then our relationship was solid and we finalized plans for the summer and our wedding in September.

Graduation was approaching, which meant that the week-long comprehensive exams loomed ahead — the final hurdle. "Comps" were almost as daunting as the validation exams when I first entered Wheaton; we would be tested on general knowledge and specifically on our majors. That semester I attended a weekly seminar for Bible majors led by Kenneth Kantzer, giving us guidelines as we studied for "comps." We had to be ready to give an outline of any book of the

Bible, to translate any page of the Greek New Testament including parsing the verbs, and to answer questions such as, "What was the relationship between Assyria and Israel during the Kingdom period?" Instead we got this question, "What was the relationship of Syria to the Northern Kingdom?" which I fumbled through as best I could.

To my surprise, I received a "B+" on comps. It was a spiritual victory to graduate; I had prayed my way through.

During my last semester I bought my first car, a ten-year-old DeSoto. Corroded by salt from Chicago's winter streets, it ran well in spite of burning oil. With finals over, I relaxed by washing and waxing it before Marian and her family arrived for my graduation. She liked the DeSoto—I was glad! During graduation weekend, Marian and her mother made final arrangements for our wedding in September. I learned that Westlings plan well, and that I was to have a wonderfully well-organized wife!

As for my graduation on that Monday morning in June of 1951, I remember only that we sat on hot bleachers in the open air and I received my B.A. in Bible. By noon it was over. We ate quickly, said goodbye to Marian's family, loaded my car, and immediately left for an 18-hour drive to Norman, Oklahoma. Classes were to start the next morning at the Summer Institute of Linguistics. We were eager to begin preparations to reach a tribe for God.

—4—

City Girl from the North
Marian Tells Her Story
1929 to 1947

Mine was an American family with a Swedish heritage. My grandfather, Jonas Westling, had carefully laid his plans for emigration to America, traveling to Michigan in 1891 at the age of 25 to scout out the land. When his younger brother Lars died a couple of years later, leaving a brokenhearted sweetheart, Engla Karlsson, Grandpa returned to Sweden to court her. His marriage to Engla was idyllic and their children happy. Their firstborn was my father, Karl Jonas Westling, born in 1897 near Sundsvall, halfway up Sweden's east coast. Karl was followed two years later by Sigrid, then a second daughter, Svea, and finally a second boy, William.

Grandpa earned a good living, doing carpentry and teaching in a technical school. There was money to pay house help, so Engla left her teaching job and spent her time spinning and weaving, knitting and crocheting, and enjoying her children. They loved to hear her tell Bible stories and play the guitar as she sang gospel songs. She lived up to her name, for Engla is translated "Angela."

The peaceful years in the old country did not last. Grandpa yearned for greater opportunity in "Amerika." He also wanted freedom from religious discrimination, for he was a Baptist in a land where every child was registered a Lutheran. Engla did not want to be uprooted from her native soil and cried for days before the move, but in the spring of 1906 Grandpa auctioned off their belongings and left the parish where his family had lived for hundreds of years. He took his sad wife and their four excited children to Goteborg on Sweden's western coast and boarded a ship bound for Chicago—and sorrow.

Grandpa found employment at the Kimball piano factory, working six days a week for $2.50 a day, and at night he attended school to improve his English. The family rented a large upstairs flat—the Chicago term for apartment—and bought nice furniture. The eldest son Karl—now Americanized to "Carl"—was quick to learn English and enrolled in school at his own age level rather than in first grade, like most immigrant children.

Soon the family was asked to leave their pleasant apartment as the kids made too much noise for their downstairs neighbors. Their next home was a basement apartment, roomy but damp and cold. Keeping house with no help, cooking for a family of six, and doing all the washing by hand was not easy for Engla. Homesick for Sweden and overburdened with work, she continued to look after the family. Hanging the clothes out to dry in frigid November weather, she caught a terrible cold. Two weeks of bed rest brought no improvement.

One December morning Grandpa woke to find his precious "angel" had flown away to a better land than America. My father was nine when his mother died. The family's only comfort that bleak winter day was to know that their loved one was with the Lord and they would see her again someday.

What was Grandpa to do with four children while he labored in the piano shop? He soon married Sophie, another immigrant from Sweden. It was a marriage of convenience, he needing help and she wanting a home. Leaving Chicago as Engla had hoped, Grandpa bought a farm in Michigan, near Muskegon where he had lived during his first years in America. The farmhouse was lovely but their home unhappy, for Sophie had a temper and did not like children.

As soon as my father graduated from the country school, he left home—at the age of fourteen. Leaving home meant going to Muskegon to find a place to stay and a job to support himself and help the rest of the family. It also meant leaving the tight-knit Swedish immigrant community, the Swedish Baptist Church, the Swedish language and everything familiar. He aspired to become an artist, but that demanded more training than an immigrant boy could hope for. Eventually he landed a job as a draftsman and then studied at night until he became an engineer.

My mother was also the daughter of Swedish immigrants. Her parents, Nels and Bothilda Erlandson, had met and married while both were indentured servants at a large estate in southern Sweden. Given permission for a holiday in Copenhagen, they boarded a ship there in Denmark and escaped to freedom in the United States. They settled on a farm near Muskegon, Michigan, where my mother, May, was born in 1899, youngest of the four children who lived past infancy. At school she learned English, but the family was active in a Swedish church near their home, the Mission Covenant Church.

May also moved to Muskegon after she graduated from eighth grade. There she got an office job and lived at the YWCA, where she met Sigrid Westling, Dad's sister. The two became fast friends and enjoyed attending revival meetings. Later Mother met Dad's other sister, Svea, and the two girls moved to Chicago in search of better jobs. With other Swedish friends they lived at a boarding house near Moody Church, where May joined the choir and Svea helped in the Sunday School. One day as May and Svea were downtown at a museum they ran into Svea's brother Carl, who had also found work in Chicago. This led to a three-year courtship between Carl and May, climaxing in their wedding in October of 1925.

Chicago Childhood
1929 - 1940

Like most Chicago dwellers, Dad and Mother began housekeeping in a flat but bought a house not long before I came along on July 15, 1929. They named me Marian Ruth. My early memories are fleeting; I do not recall the birth of my sister Irene in 1932, or even the birth of my brother John in 1934. Dad's sister Svea, whom we called "Faye," lived with us at times (his other sister, Sigrid, had moved to Seattle). Since neither sister ever married, and since they had both been very close to Mother before she met Dad, they loved us children as their own. We loved them too!

The Westling family — 1938 or 1939 (Marian at center back)

Growing up during the Depression brought me no hardships. Dad always had work, and we never missed a meal. We lived comfortably in a two-bedroom house on the far south side of Chicago. Streets were safe for us to join the neighbor children playing on long summer evenings.

Our home life was happy—and quiet. On Sundays, however, Swedish friends and relatives came to dinner or we went to visit them. Mother was a very good cook, and Sunday dinner was always an event which included supper. No Swede ever went home until supper was over. We children hated to see the company leave.

Occasionally on Sunday we would go with our Aunt Faye to Moody Church with its cavernous auditorium and magnificent pipe organ. It was an awesome place, yet very friendly. I could understand Dr. Ironside's sermons and loved to listen. As a family, though, we attended a church nearer our home, a church which made no lasting impression on me. What did impact me was the weekly after-school Bible class at the Dutch Reformed Church which I attended with a neighbor girl. At home we did not have family devotions, but in the evenings Mother prayed with us and often read to us from Christian story books.

We children did a minimal amount of work around the house, but gradually I learned small tasks such as setting the table, washing dishes, making beds and helping with Saturday cleaning. Mother was a diligent worker who expected us to do our jobs precisely.

Discipline, not often needed, was usually dispensed by Dad. Mother would scold us and promise a spanking when he came home in the evening. There was no getting out of the promised spanking, nor did we try. (I do not remember what I was punished for, but I always felt I deserved it!)

Our health was good, aside from childhood diseases such as measles, mumps, and whooping cough which were so devastating before vaccines and antibiotics. Dad, however, suffered from asthma, often sitting up all night while struggling to breathe.

Learning at the local public school came easy to me. I loved spelling and reading, and did well in arithmetic. I got high grades and skipped ahead half a year, but developed no attachment to the school or any of my teachers. My only friend was a Dutch girl. (Most of the students were of Dutch, Polish or Italian background.) Recess was unpleasant—no games or play equipment, just a crowd of children milling around the bare gravel schoolyard. My only memento of school is a dog-eared booklet of spelling words required of us from first through eighth grade.

Winters were long and harsh in Chicago. Snow was plentiful—sometimes drifting up to our bedroom windowsill—and beautiful, but soon peppered with soot from thousands of coal furnaces. Snow was fun to play in, but in a few minutes we would be back inside, wet and crying with cold. Heat came from a furnace in the basement. Coal was delivered by a truck and unloaded into a chute leading to our basement window. Dad bought an automatic stoker to feed coal into the furnace, as he was not well enough to stoke the furnace by hand each day.

During the winter, drying clothes was a challenge. They would freeze if hung outside, so Mother hung them in the basement. Dryers were still in the future, and Mother did not have a washing machine in my early years. She boiled the clothes in a copper tub on a gas burner in the basement.

If winters were long and bitter, Chicago summers were short and steamy. Many nights we lay awake sweating until the temperature cooled enough for sleep. But the days were wonderful. We often put on our bathing suits and played under the backyard sprinkler. Most afternoons we sucked popsicles to cool off. In the evenings the children on our block gathered to play tag or hide-and-seek, or we would roller skate on the sidewalk or play hopscotch. When I was nine, I got my first bicycle. A neighbor girl helped me learn to ride it, as there were no training wheels in those days.

In summer, Mother took us to nearby parks or to interesting places around Chicago. We enjoyed the zoo and the museums. Sometimes on a Sunday afternoon Dad drove us to Midway airport (O'Hare airport was not yet built) to stand by the fence and watch the planes land and take off. Normally, Sunday afternoon was reserved for quiet play, or a walk around the neighborhood. We would stay home and play Anagrams or Flinch with Mother, while Dad read the paper and snoozed in his chair.

During warm weather we occasionally traveled away from Chicago on weekends, sometimes for an overnight with Dad's father and stepmother in Michigan. Grandpa Westling had long since given up farming and settled in Muskegon. He was a cheerful soul who loved music and had a piano that played all by itself—quite a wonder to me! "Grandma" always kept lemon drops for us in a sugar bowl in the buffet. Both of them spoke English with a Swedish accent, although my parents had no trace of an accent. There were Swedish books and newspapers on the table beside the sofa. Mother also had relatives that we visited in Muskegon, but we always stayed with the Westlings. Mother's mother had died before I was born, and her father died when I was quite young.

Another weekend destination was Rockford, Illinois, a city northwest of Chicago. Many Swedes had settled there, including some of Mother and Dad's friends from early years in Michigan. Trips to Rockford were very special to us, as there were lots of kids to play with, good Swedish cooking, and Sunday services at the large Swedish Evangelical Free Church where we felt at home both culturally and spiritually.

Dad had only one week of vacation each summer. He would usually spend the time at home on a remodeling project, but twice we did go away for a whole week. The summer I turned seven, Aunt Svea drove with us to Kentucky so we could visit a Moody Church friend of hers who served as a "home missionary" there in Appalachia. A couple of years later our family spent a week at a lake near Muskegon—a whole week to play in the water!

New Life in Christ

More memorable than any family trip was my week at a Christian camp in 1939 when I was ten years old. It was the first time away from my family, and it was there that I came to personal faith in Jesus as my Savior. I went to camp with a friend from school who was also in my Girl Scout Troop and in my Bible class at the Reformed Church, yet I was very homesick. By Thursday of that week I had lost all desire to participate in the day's fun, but the counselor insisted that I attend the evening meeting.

At camp the good news about salvation through Christ was preached every night. I had never heard that I was a sinner who needed to be saved. That I was a sinner I knew, but that there were eternal consequences that only Jesus could save me from was a new idea. That Thursday night I was so miserable that I went to the prayer room after the preacher finished. There a counselor explained John 3:16, and I asked Jesus to save me.

That decision was the beginning of a whole new life for me. The rest of the week I was happy, yet apprehensive because the counselor said that when my parents came, I must tell them about my decision. On Sunday when they arrived, I showed them around camp, then sat on a bench by the lake and told them I had asked Jesus to save me. When I did so, I was relieved, and the subject was never mentioned again—neither by me nor by them. In my heart, I treasured the knowledge that I was secure in Christ, but I had no one to nurture my new faith.

That year was our family's last full year in Chicago. By the next summer, Dad had accepted a new position with an engineering firm in New York City. After our belongings were loaded into the Mayflower moving van, we headed east in the family Ford, leaving behind our life as Swedish Americans. I do not recall being sad to leave nor excited to be moving to a new place.

Teen Years in New Jersey
1940 - 1947

We thought our new home would be in Connecticut, so Dad would have an easy commute by train directly to Grand Central Station. However, my eleventh birthday passed at a hotel in Connecticut during the weeks of fruitless house-hunting. Finally, Dad bought a house in West Orange, New Jersey, on the opposite side of New York City from Connecticut. This involved a difficult commute for him. Mother would take Dad by car to catch a train for Hoboken where he would board a ferry crossing the Hudson to Manhattan, then walk a few blocks to catch the subway to his office. The trip was not only very time-consuming but hard on a man with fragile health.

West Orange was one of a cluster of suburbs called The Oranges—small cities dwarfed by nearby Newark. We lived on a steep street, very different from flat Chicago. Our house was different too, having a garage in the basement, with the main rooms on the first floor, and bedrooms on the second, with a large attic above.

Moving to New Jersey also meant finding a church. Although Dad remained a Baptist at heart, he chose the First Presbyterian Church in nearby Orange because it was more evangelical than other local churches. This church was to impact me far more than the Baptist church back in Chicago.

Soon I was in seventh grade, and continued to do well in my studies. I got my first taste of foreign languages. Latin and math became my favorite subjects, though everything came easy to me—except for physical education classes. As I played on sports teams, I realized I was poorly-coordinated, and that weak vision in one eye kept me from focusing on balls that came at me too quickly.

World War II

One Sunday an event occurred that colored the rest of my school years. I was sick in bed that afternoon when Dad came upstairs to communicate the *shocking* news that our country had been attacked by the Japanese. It was December 7, 1941, and Dad, who always followed the world news closely, had just heard about the bombing at Pearl Harbor. Although I was only twelve years old, I comprehended the seriousness of the situation. The following day Congress declared war, not just on Japan but also on Germany.

Life changed. The school designated a basement hallway as an air raid shelter. In addition to fire drills, we now had air raid drills; sirens would sound throughout the city and citizens would take cover. If the sirens sounded at night, we were required to turn off all lights and wait in total darkness for the "all-clear" to sound. West Orange was within easy reach of the Atlantic Coast where German submarines lurked, and enemy raids were not outside the range of possibility. I never feared an attack and none ever occurred, yet we were always on the alert.

Rationing was a major change that we tolerated for the sake of the "war effort." Gasoline and tires were rationed. This meant more walking and more bus rides, especially on Saturdays when I went to my piano lessons. Certain foods, like meat, were rationed so that there would be plenty for the soldiers. Even butter was rationed, and we began using "oleomargarine" as a substitute, though it was not very agreeable to butter-loving Swedes! But Mother added coloring and salt to the tasteless white substance and we learned to eat it. The war effort even affected the paper on which books were printed; the paper soon turned dark and brittle.

Growing up

Other changes in my life were not due to the war but to growing out of childhood. Jigsaw puzzles still brought me pleasure, but I now began to enjoy crossword puzzles, eventually doing the New York Times puzzles with Dad. We kids discovered Monopoly, playing by the hour on the back porch during hot summer days, sometimes varying with a game of Parcheesi or Chinese checkers.

Reading began to occupy much of my free time. First it was classic children's books like *Heidi*, then the Nancy Drew books that all girls my age were reading. Mother frequently took us to the public library, and I also checked out books from the school library or borrowed them from friends. Both Dad and Mother were readers; they gave each of us a new book every birthday and Christmas.

There was always enough time for reading, despite my now having more domestic chores. Mother taught us girls to sew and bake—which was fun—but we also peeled potatoes, set the table, did dishes, and helped with cleaning and laundry. Mother now had a washing machine with a wringer. I learned to arrange the clothes so as not to jam the wringer—and learned to keep my fingers from being caught between the rollers! We lugged the heavy, wet clothes up from the basement to hang outside in the summertime and also did some of the ironing. There were no permanent press fabrics in those days, so everything had to be ironed. In fact, many items had to be starched and then sprinkled before ironing.

We girls willingly did what we were asked to do, but I do not remember volunteering for extra jobs. To my shame, I confess that I sometimes hid a novel inside a textbook I was supposedly reading, knowing that Mother would not call me to a task if I was studying.

In New Jersey without our Swedish friends and relatives, we rarely had Sunday visitors, so Dad would drive us to nearby points of historical interest, or to the countryside for a picnic. On Saturdays Mother sometimes took us to museums in New York City or to stores like Macy's. We enjoyed those outings, especially riding the ferry and the subway or a double-decker bus.

In the summer Mother occasionally took us to swim at a lake but never to the "shore" where all my school friends went. We were not a beach-loving family. Instead, when Dad had a vacation, we drove to New England or Pennsylvania to visit historical sites—Bunker Hill, Plymouth Rock, Valley Forge, and many more. We always stopped to read every historical marker along the road. Furthermore, Dad had a special interest in old blast furnaces. We would hunt them even if it meant tromping through the woods to find a long-abandoned furnace.

During eighth grade, I was baptized and joined the church along with others my age. I also began going to the church youth group with a boy I knew from school. At youth group I heard again the message I had heard at camp when I was ten. I was hungry for the Lord and began to grow spiritually, but my "boyfriend" wasn't interested and dropped out of the group—and out of my life.

Adults at church mentored me informally. I memorized Scripture and sometimes taught children in the Sunday School. My teacher in the class for senior high girls had been a missionary with Wycliffe Bible Translators. She had a heart for us girls, arranging outings and retreats, and implanting the Word in us.

In high school I met other Christians, including Joyce Thompson who became a lifelong friend. She and her parents took an interest in me and invited me to go with them on Sunday evenings to their church, where the Bible teaching was rich. One summer Joyce and I went to a Bible conference at Lake George in New York State. I had enjoyed Girl Scout Camp during junior high, but the Bible conference was even more memorable. It satisfied my hunger for the Lord, yet whetted my appetite so much that I went again the next summer.

Studies continued to be easy for me. In high school I took three years of Spanish as well as Latin. At that time most students studied French, but Dad insisted that I take Spanish, which he said was the language of the future. (His insistence gave me a foundation in the language I would need—not that I knew it then!) I enjoyed math and took every available class, but avoided science except for required subjects. My grades in all my courses were embarrassingly high.

What high school student wants to be known just for high grades? Actually, I had little interest in studies other than languages and math. I did no more homework than was required, preferring to spend my time reading novels and magazines.

Although I did well in my studies, I fared poorly in gym and was always the last to be chosen for a team. I also wore braces on my teeth for five years, and for a few months I wore a patch over one eye in a vain effort to strengthen it. These appliances did not bother me, for I had supportive parents and faithful friends, and did not aspire to become popular at school.

Classes continued and so did World War II. Each night Dad turned on the radio to hear the world news. (Television was not yet available.) Finally in May of 1945, when I was a sophomore, we got the word one morning in class that the war was over, at least the fighting in Europe. You can be sure that no one did much studying the rest of that day, V-E Day, the celebration of victory in Europe. It took a few more months and two atomic bombs to end the war in the Pacific. Finally in September, V-J Day, celebrating victory over Japan, closed the conflict that had kept the world in mortal struggle as I had grown from childhood into adolescence.

In addition to school and duties at home, I kept up with piano lessons, summer and winter for seven years, studying both organ and piano the last year. My piano teacher was proud of me, but actually, I did not have much talent. Music for me was more of an emotional outlet. My training was in classical music, but more and more I began to play hymns on my own, though I did not find them easy at first. They became an expression of the spiritual life that was budding inside me in spite of a lack of nurture at home.

My parents did not oppose my growing interest in spiritual things, but they wanted me to study other things in order to be well-rounded. I took swimming lessons at the YWCA, and even studied Swedish for a year, but balked at dancing lessons. I had no interest in going to school dances, or to the movies.

In order to earn money I baby-sat, which I found more difficult than teaching Sunday School. However, I gained experience and saved my earnings toward clothes for college. I even earned a bit doing a Spanish translation job for one of Dad's colleagues.

Growing in the Lord

During high school I began attending Hi-BA: "High School Born-Againers." These clubs gave young Christians the support needed to survive and thrive in the secular high schools of the New York City area. We met off-campus each week to receive instruction in the Word and learn how to witness to our classmates. The staff members who led the meetings were campus missionaries who knew how to relate to us and inspire us to share our faith. We carried our Bibles to school on top of our stack of textbooks, but though I wanted to witness, I was too timid to verbalize the gospel.

During my senior year we met at my house, which was near the high school. Meeting with other Christian students—especially those well-grounded in their faith—really strengthened me. We were happy in the Lord and did not crave "worldly" activities. Occasionally there were Hi-BA parties, to which we invited our unsaved friends. These events closed with a staffer giving a gospel message. We were glad when some responded and put their faith in Jesus. One such classmate named Ellis went on to serve the Lord as a missionary. Another, Joan, was one of many Jewish students at school. She was friendly but unresponsive to my feeble attempts to witness. I have maintained contact with Joan, Ellis, and my friend Joyce, plus a girl from Hi-BA, throughout my adult life.

Hi-BA's emphasis on missions began to penetrate my consciousness, as did the staffer's challenge to have regular personal devotions. Responding to this challenge, I asked my parents for permission to move out of the bedroom I had always shared with my sister, and into the unfinished attic. There, alone with the Lord, I relished my time in the Word and in prayer.

My final year in high school, I went with girls from my Sunday School class to a rally at Madison Square Garden in New York City. Preceding the message by well-known evangelist Jack Wyrtzen, seven young women who were soon to leave for the mission field gave their testimonies. As I listened, I had the uncomfortable feeling that the Lord might also want *me* to become a missionary. Before that night I had assumed that after college I would simply settle down and raise a family. However, I now felt that the Lord was speaking to me about serving Him. Latin America—particularly Colombia— attracted me. When I was required to write a paper in Spanish about my future plans, I told about my desire to take the message of salvation to some place in the Spanish-speaking world.

High school graduation neared, which meant choosing a college. My parents were the ones who made the decision, but I was in on the process. I was grateful that the only colleges they seriously considered were Christian schools. I applied to Wheaton College in Illinois and was accepted for the fall semester of 1947. The thought of college studies was not daunting, for my high school had prepared me well. The transition from home to college was eased by knowing that my friend Joyce would be my roommate. For both of us, attending college near Chicago meant a reconnection to our families' roots.

In June of 1947 I graduated first in my class from West Orange High and received a small scholarship from the school. My parents gave me a typewriter as a graduation present, and I spent the summer teaching myself to type in preparation for college. Leaving home was exciting, yet sobering. I sat at the piano and played away my nervousness until time to go.

Wheaton College
1947 - 1950

At Wheaton College a whole new world opened to me. The campus atmosphere was totally different from what I had been used to. Here, everyone was a Christian, classes opened with prayer, and chapel services were held daily. My spiritual hunger was being satisfied—yet it only whetted my appetite for more.

I felt privileged to attend chapel every morning, not just church on Sundays and Hi-BA once a week. Now I was with more than a thousand fellow students in chapel, all singing praise to our Lord—a stirring experience, especially when we joined in our favorite hymn, "Wonderful Grace of Jesus." I listened attentively as speakers brought powerful messages from the Word.

Besides the regular chapels, there were special services at the beginning of each semester, providing me even more blessing and challenge. Classes were shortened and chapels lengthened, with an even longer service in the evening. During my first semester Stephen Olford impacted us for a week. That was when I surrendered my whole life to the Lord—what else could I do when the Lord had given His life for me? Then, during my second semester Robert Munger challenged us to open each area of our life to the Lord as he preached on "My Heart, Christ's Home." My heart responded.

Each Wednesday night a few hundred students gathered for the Foreign Missions Fellowship. My interest in serving the Lord in some foreign field escalated as I gleaned inspiration and information from the missionaries who spoke at those meetings. I also attended— sporadically my first couple years, then regularly my last year—a daily prayer meeting for missions. I felt like a baby among the more mature students as they poured out their hearts to the Lord for the world. (Many of them were World War II veterans who brought to the campus a vision of the world's needs.) Besides the daily prayer time, I eventually participated in a round-the-clock prayer chain for missions, treasuring my 15-minute slot in the college prayer room.

Wheaton was not a Bible School but a liberal arts college. My parents had sent me there to study and I did. No more reading novels! I made good grades and enjoyed my classes, at least most of them. Bible courses were required, and I drank in all the teaching—Old Testament Survey my freshman year, then New Testament Survey, next Bible Doctrine, and finally Archaeology and Apologetics.

Choosing a major was difficult. I knew it would not be math or science, but I had no clear direction. My freshman advisor, Dr. Kenneth Kantzer—who later became well known as the editor of *Christianity Today*—helped me think it through. I chose to major in elementary education. I had never considered teaching, but realized it would be useful both on the mission field and in raising a family.

Some of my elementary education courses were not particularly stimulating, but I did enjoy courses in history of education, psychology, and an elective in the teaching of reading. That latter course opened an interest the Lord would use in the future. One elderly education professor was avoided by most students, but I liked him. Another professor whom I did *not* like once chided me for cutting most of his classes. My grade point average was high enough that I was allowed unlimited cuts, which I took advantage of in his course. Did my conscience bother me? No, but perhaps it should have.

The climax of my training was "practice teaching" during my senior year. Interested in the growing Christian school movement, I appreciated being assigned to the Wheaton Christian Day School. I found I *loved* teaching, and very much enjoyed being with the children. Had I inherited the genes of the Swedish grandmother I never knew, who had once been a teacher?

Although I majored in education, and the required Bible courses amounted to a minor, I took almost enough courses in Spanish to equal another minor. After the basic Spanish courses, I found myself in classes with missionaries on furlough, missionary kids, and nationals from Spanish-speaking countries; including a girl whose brothers I would later come to know in Costa Rica. It was challenging to keep up with such classmates, but I wanted to learn as much Spanish as possible.

My other courses were mostly those required for graduation, including history, which I enjoyed. (In fact, my interest has increased over the years.) There was no math requirement for my major, but everyone was required to take a science course. In high school I had avoided biology and chemistry, taking physics instead. Now I chose geology. The professor, Dr. Paul Wright, was a favorite at Wheaton. All the students loved him and learned not only about the earth and its history, but also about the Lord. We had a lot of fun on field trips, especially a three-day trip to Wisconsin to see in the field what we had been learning about in the classroom.

Term papers were a recurring assignment that kept me busy as deadlines approached, because I tended to procrastinate. I put to good use the typewriter my parents had given me—personal computers were still in the future! During my senior year I was elected to the Scholastic Honor Society, but academics was not my main interest. Rather, I continued to draw closer to the Lord and to others who were serious about following Him.

College was not only about studying and attending chapel services. We did have fun! I got to know many special people and made some lifelong friendships. Parties, outings, concerts, and football games provided occasional breaks from studies. Sometimes on a weekend I went to Chicago to visit my Aunt Faye and attended Moody Church with her. Occasionally Joyce and I went to Chicago or Rockford to visit Swedish relatives and friends.

Besides the fun activities, I went a few times with fellow students to witness to Mexican migrant workers. One year I volunteered to go regularly to Chicago with a team from Wheaton, although sharing my faith remained as difficult as it had been in high school.

My years at Wheaton flew by, as I did four years' work in three by taking classes each summer. I was able to graduate before my sister started college, easing the financial burden on my parents. Although summer courses were more intensive, the atmosphere was relaxed. Sometimes I was invited for a weekend at a friend's home near a lake. Only in late August and at Christmas did I make the long trip home to New Jersey by train, bus or with classmates by car. Back then, airplanes were only for emergencies.

Whatever the season, Wheaton was a beautiful place. The tree-lined streets of the town and campus were shady in the summer, gorgeous in the fall with the leaves turning gold and red, awesome in winter when ice etched the branches and snow covered the ground, then lovely again in the fresh green of spring. I was happy at Wheaton, responding to the stimulus of peers who were more mature in the Lord, as well as to the constant stream of speakers at chapel and at Foreign Missions Fellowship.

The Wheaton Revival of 1950

My third year at Wheaton was my last. I was now twenty years old and ready to make lifelong decisions. During the second semester Spiritual Emphasis Week, the Lord visited our campus with His cleansing presence. For months, many on campus had been praying for revival including our daily missions prayer group. Yet the Lord's answer still amazed and awed us.

No one predicted or even suspected that the Spirit would do such a powerful, pervasive, permanent work in those few days in February. Hardly a student was untouched. The faculty was also affected. Even the townsfolk of Wheaton became aware that something unusual was going on at the college. The news spread to Chicago, thirty miles away. The story appeared on the front pages of national newspapers. Teams of students traveled to other Christian colleges to spread the fire.

What happened that week was beyond human explanation. The speaker, a pastor with a quiet message about being channels for the Lord to flow through, spoke on Monday and Tuesday, but on Wednesday, a student asked to be allowed to say a few words before the message. Actually, it was a confession. Then another wanted to confess, and another and another. A classmate, Bill Kornfield, had gone to President Edman that morning asking if he would extend the meeting if the Spirit was moving. Dr. Edman, a Spirit-filled man, allowed the testimonies to go on.

The speaker never spoke that night, nor the rest of the week, as student after student stood to make things right with the Lord and with others. The meeting continued all Wednesday night, all day Thursday, all that night, and on into Friday. Classes were suspended. Dr. Edman never left the platform as students and even faculty confessed. Some students confessed cheating or breaking the school pledge not to engage in worldly practices. Others confessed bad attitudes toward professors or fellow students. Some told how the

Lord had been calling them to His service but they had chosen a different path. Even a Greek professor confessed he had avoided the Lord's call to the mission field.

Few students were left unaffected. I, too, was convicted and knew I must speak up. My own public confession concerned pride and self-centeredness. Privately I confessed to some fellow students that I had harbored wrong attitudes toward them. The hallways were crowded with students seeking to make things right with others.

The impact of the revival was lasting. There was a new spirit on campus. Some students changed their majors, and that Greek professor ended up working with the Bible Society in the Philippines. We seniors were deeply affected. The "senior sneak" was not just a fun getaway, but a final chance to fellowship before we dispersed to serve the Lord around the world.

The Foreign Missions Fellowship—we called it FMF—took on fresh meaning for me. That year Bible translation was the emphasis, particularly the need for Scriptures for the tribes of Latin America. Wycliffe Bible Translators was expanding from Mexico to Peru. The more I learned about the need, the more interested I became. Yet I hardly dared hope that I could be involved other than perhaps teaching in a school for missionaries' children. To me that seemed a suitable ministry for a single woman.

My last semester I led one of the weekly prayer groups focusing on specific areas of the world. I also continued attending the daily prayer times. Our first gathering after the revival was unforgettable; we were in awe of what God had done. Jim Elliot, later martyred in Ecuador, led us in prayer that day. He had been part of the group before graduating the year before and had returned to rejoice with us.

Increasingly, my friends were those in FMF. Eventually we would scatter to the four corners of the globe, but we kept in touch, exchanging news of what God was doing in our part of the vineyard. One of these friends was Dot, my roommate during my senior year. We went together to the daily FMF prayer group, and on Friday nights the two of us sang hymns together as we did our laundry by hand. Dot's boyfriend, Bob Weeber, who had been Jim Elliot's roommate, was head of FMF that year. I would cross paths with Dot and Bob all my life, as I did with my friend Joyce.

Churches abounded in the city of Wheaton—my aunt called the place "Saints' Roost." My first two years at school, I usually attended the Gospel Tabernacle, pastored by Dr. Merrill Tenney, respected head of Wheaton's grad school. The "Tab" became my church home, for I had left the Presbyterian Church I joined in junior high school. Now, as a senior, I joined Dot and Bob in attending Bethany Chapel, a Brethren assembly where worship was spontaneous, meditative, centered around the Lord's table. At Bethany I thrived and drew closer to the Lord.

Meeting Aziel

Between the spring semester and summer school I took a short course on Galatians taught by Dr. Tenney. More than a hundred of us were seated alphabetically, as usual, which put me—Westling—near the back of the room. My mind was on studying: four stimulating class hours each morning, with eight hours of homework each evening. I was not thinking about my classmates and never noticed a fellow sitting midway to the front, an older student whose last name began with "J."

For a short break from the pressure of the course on Galatians, I went with Dot for a picnic at the Lagoon—a park on the edge of town. Her friend Martha supplied the transportation and suggested asking a guy to go along. Dot suggested Aziel Jones, saying, "He's harmless!" Dot knew Aziel because both majored in Bible, while Martha had met him during his years at Moody Bible Institute. On the way to the Lagoon that evening Aziel sat in front conversing with Martha, while I sat in the back with Dot. Aziel turned out to be a fellow student in the class on Galatians.

Eight weeks of summer school remained. I spent them studying a grad level course in Greek. Now that my courses on education were over and I had taken "comps" (three days of comprehensive examinations required for graduation), I was free to take an elective.

Wanting to study New Testament Greek, I enrolled in an intensive course that gave me a rudimentary knowledge of grammar and then a chance to read through the epistles of John in the original.

Halfway through the summer, who should ask me for a date but Aziel Jones! He invited me to go with him to Chicago to attend the graduation of a friend at Moody Bible Institute. I had only had a few dates while I was at Wheaton, yet I was praying for a husband—praying very earnestly, in fact. However, the reason I accepted Aziel's invitation was not that I was attracted to him, but because I had no reason to refuse.

A date to Chicago would involve spending several hours with Aziel, this fellow I had met only briefly. There was a quick meal at the college dining hall, followed by a hurried walk to the station, then a train ride to Chicago, another walk to the "L"—the elevated train—then another walk to Moody Church for the graduation. To my surprise, I greatly enjoyed his company, and we never ran out of subjects to talk about. After the graduation, as Aziel was introducing me to his friends, one couple, the McMillens, invited him to Sunday dinner a couple of weeks later, adding, "And bring your girl along!"

A week later, Aziel asked me to Chicago to see an exhibit and drama about railroad history. It was a rather tiring and boring day. As we talked on the return trip to Wheaton, he emphasized the need to memorize Scripture. I had memorized a good bit of the Word as a teenager, and at Wheaton had memorized the whole first epistle of Peter, but I was annoyed by Aziel's insistence on the Navigator system. My reaction to the day was that I would not have accepted another date with him, except that I was already committed to go to dinner with his friends in Chicago.

That third date was an all-day affair. We left Wheaton early Sunday morning in time for Aziel to teach the college class at his church in Chicago. Dinner at his friends' tiny apartment was memorable; I felt totally comfortable with Aziel. It was that August day in 1950 that launched our relationship. I had just turned twenty-one; he was twenty-eight. We both were ready to settle down.

Commencement—*a New Beginning*
1950 - 1951

Summer graduation was five days later. My family arrived from New Jersey for the occasion. As I came down the stairs of the classroom building from my final exam in Greek, Aziel was coming up the stairs to meet me. In his hand was a graduation gift, a corsage. Surprised at his gesture, I responded by inviting him to join the family for lunch before the ceremony that afternoon.

The graduation ceremony was short and simple, with none of the elaborate proceedings of spring semester graduation. I graduated with honors and was elected to the Scholastic Honor Society. Afterward, on the lawn, I greeted my family and was about to turn in my cap and gown when up walked Aziel, wanting to talk. He asked his roommate to snap a photo of the two of us—our first picture together. My parents retreated to the car to wait while Aziel and I sat on a bench and talked about continuing our new relationship.

An hour later I joined my patient family to begin the long drive home, stopping for the weekend with Swedish friends in Rockford, then driving north through Wisconsin into Canada and east to Niagara Falls, then down through New York to New Jersey—a week's drive. All the way my mind was on Aziel. Several days after arriving home, I received his first letter. He had mailed it from his home in Alabama soon after graduation, but mail between the South and the North was slow in those days.

As I moved on from home to my first—and only—teaching position, my days began with a quiet time of prayer and Bible reading and ended with a letter from Aziel. He filled my life and my thoughts. I had a job at Northeast Christian Day School in Philadelphia, an hour and a half from my parents' home. To say it was a school was a misnomer; I had actually been hired to restart a defunct school. I began my teaching career with one little girl in first grade. She and I sat together day by day while I taught her to read and write, to add and subtract.

Teaching was enjoyable, but with only one pupil I found myself getting sleepy as I taught. Yet in time other children enrolled until I had my hands full with nine children in five different grades, including a big fifth-grade boy who kept hitting my little first-grade girl. One day at recess his behavior was so provoking that I slapped him. To my surprise I never had another problem with him.

During the week I stayed in the home of Jim and Eunice Macdonald, dear folks who had been involved in the original school. Since the school was unable to pay me the full salary, small though it was, the Macdonalds gave me room and board. I had no car, nor driver's license, so my mother drove each Friday from West Orange to take me home for the weekend and then brought me back each Monday.

As the school year progressed, I became increasingly interested in teaching reading. For fun, I analyzed Scripture passages for Christmas and then Easter, writing lessons to prepare the little ones to read from the King James Bible, the version everyone used at the time. I was delighted at how easily they could read the unfamiliar words. Preparing those reading lessons foreshadowed my work years later in Costa Rica.

My days were full with teaching, but my heart was with Aziel in Wheaton where he was completing his senior year. I looked forward to spending Homecoming weekend there in October. Yet when Aziel met me at Union Station in Chicago, he seemed like a total stranger although we had been exchanging letters daily. By evening I again felt comfortable with him and conversation flowed easily. He borrowed a car and we found a quiet place to talk.

That night, October 21, 1950, Aziel asked me to marry him. (We still celebrate each year on that date!) For both of us

"The Ring!" – November 25, 1950

it was a momentous decision, involving not only serving the Lord together but raising a family for Him. We prayed and talked long into the night, sealing our commitment with our first kiss. We decided not to share our joy with others just yet, but when I got back to Philadelphia, the MacDonalds guessed my secret.

"I saw the stars in your eyes," said Mr. Mac.

Thanksgiving weekend brought us together again. Aziel came to West Orange to ask Dad's permission for us to marry. Dad was expecting the question, of course, and readily gave his consent. It was November 25, 1950, the tenth anniversary of Aziel's induction into the Army. He marked the date by giving me a diamond, the most beautiful engagement ring I had ever seen! How thrilled I was to wear it—a constant reminder of his love during long days of separation.

Soon it was Christmas, and the best gift was being together. It was so nice to have Aziel with me in New Jersey at our simple family celebration. The next day we boarded a bus for the overnight trip to Alabama so I could meet his family. His home was a different world from mine—a busy, noisy parsonage with several of his younger siblings still at home, and married siblings coming to visit. I slept in a room with three of his sisters, who enjoyed trying to mimic my "Yankee" accent. I became increasingly conscious of the distinctions between Southerners and Yankees that shaped the thinking of Aziel's family. Although I was raised in the North, I did not consider myself a Yankee, for my family's thinking was shaped more by the Swedish immigrant culture than by the general American culture. These differences were no stumbling block; Aziel's parents and siblings treated me kindly.

Our holiday was short. After another wrenching goodbye, Aziel returned to Wheaton and I went back to teaching. Yet he got a ride to New Jersey at semester break when we had a few days together to begin plans for the summer and our wedding. During Easter vacation I spent a week in Wheaton, enjoying the loveliness of spring, enhanced by young love. As Aziel and I parted, I was comforted, knowing that the next time I saw him our months of separation would be over.

At the end of the school year, the mothers of my pupils surprised me with a bridal shower. My little first-grade girl and a second-grade boy dressed up as bride and groom and carried in a bushel basket full of gifts for "Miss Westling" — a happy occasion to mark the end of my teaching career. Soon Mother and I were on the road to Wheaton to attend Aziel's graduation and make arrangements for the wedding. After graduation, Aziel and I would drive to Oklahoma to spend the summer studying linguistics and then return to Wheaton for our wedding. No longer would we be separated. Our lives were becoming one.

— 5 —

Joining Our Lives
June 1951 to January 1952

Striking south from Wheaton after my graduation, Marian and I and two friends headed for a summer of linguistic studies. Crossing the Mississippi at St. Louis, we drove on through the night. By dawn we had reached Oklahoma. As the only driver, I began to feel sleepy, but we pressed on to Norman, an eighteen-hour drive from Wheaton. Arriving at the Summer Institute of Linguistics shortly after 8 a.m., we were greeted with "Hurry to the lecture hall! The first class just started." Finding seats near the back of the big room, Marian and I listened to a linguistic lecture that made no sense to me.

We were immersed in a new world—complex concepts, the names of famous linguists, and an array of new vocabulary: phonemes, minimal pairs, morphemes. I didn't even know what was meant by the syntax of a sentence, much less the morphology of a verb! Yet it was great to be with Marian, courting in person, no longer by mail. We were now building a reservoir of shared experiences, making new friendships as a couple, and learning to know God together. In class and outside class, we were being equipped for reaching a tribe with the Word of God.

The Summer Institute of Linguistics, usually known as SIL, is the academic arm of Wycliffe Bible Translators. Without a campus of its own, it was housed on the campus of the University of Oklahoma in buildings that had been built hastily during World War II for Navy trainees. The accommodations were at best "spartan." Staff families, married students, and singles shared the dorms. All of us—adults, children, toddlers—ate in a common dining hall.

There was no air conditioning to temper the Oklahoma summer. There were only fans to stir the hot, dry air and a few window units where water dripped through straw to bring some relief. One Sunday after church the drugstore thermometer stood at 110. During that week the temperature inside Marian's dorm didn't drop below 100 even at night. She pulled her mattress off the top bunk and slept on the floor. I was no cooler in the small WWII prefab that I shared with Jim Wroughton and Don Van Wynan. Don, a friend from Moody, had asked for me as a roommate, but rarely saw me. Why? I was "romancing."

Marian and I spent our afternoons studying outside under a shade tree, as other engaged couples did. There were also several newlywed couples at SIL who had graduated in June, married the next day, and then spent their honeymoon sharing bunk beds in the dorm. Marian had hoped for a June wedding, but I didn't want to spoil my honeymoon studying!

Although the university provided the academic credit, the staff of the Summer Institute of Linguistics was made up of Wycliffe members, most of whom served tribes in rural Mexico. Each summer they drove to Norman, took everything out of storage, and then, when the summer was over, returned things to storage before heading back to their fields, only to repeat the process the next summer. These were the casual, happy, dedicated individuals who taught us and shared our dorms and our meals. Overall, I felt that SIL, both students and staff, was the largest conglomerate of individualistic individuals anywhere! Yet there was a pervasive oneness, a communal spirit, a shared academic seriousness. And beneath the casual lifestyle was an underlying vision of giving the Word of God to the unreached. That spirit impacted me!

Dr. Kenneth Pike, the chief linguist, always wore his Mexican sandals and a brightly-colored shirt—even when he introduced a noted visiting linguist dressed in a business suit. Dr. Eugene Nida, who taught morphology and anthropology, always dressed in a plain white sport shirt and rode to class on a bicycle. As Marian and I walked from class to class, she often took off her sandals to walk on the grass—cooler than the sidewalk. We dressed as comfortably as possible, preferably in seersucker because it was cool and did not need the starching and ironing of our generation before the advent of permanent-press fabrics. Only on Sundays did we dress up—she with the customary hat and hose and I in a suit—for at least the church was air-conditioned.

After supper in the relative cool of the day Dr. Pike led the volleyball game with the same intensity he showed while teaching linguistics. Staff and students joined in the game or relaxed on the sidelines. Others sought the old Navy pool a mile away for a cooling swim. But as darkness fell, it was back to the library or dorm to study.

"How-to" Approach

Although there were serious lectures on linguistic theory, the main focus was on practical linguistics: how to reduce a language to writing, how to determine an alphabet, how to describe tone and stress, how to organize thousands of 3x5 slips covered with language data. This was before the days of computers or even tape recorders! Our professors had advanced degrees in their areas of expertise, but they were always encouraging, never intimidating. Dr. Pike would frequently say, "You're not linguists, but we'll make linguists out of you!" In addition to the lectures we had daily practice "labs" with experienced missionaries.

We learned what happened—with the mouth, lips, tongue, teeth, nose, throat, and lungs—to produce the hundreds of sounds known to human speech. We were responsible for diagramming and symbolizing each of these sounds when pronounced by the instructor. Conversely, we had to correctly pronounce the sounds indicated by the diagrams or symbols. Finally, we were required to "learn" a language with the aid of a Native American helper. For the exam we had to carry on a short, one-on-one conversation with the helper while our instructor observed! Furthermore, we were taught how to determine which of the sounds in our new language needed to be symbolized in our alphabet. Fortunately, they also told us that no single language uses an inordinate number of difficult sounds.

All this was just the beginning! We learned about different types of verb systems, about ways of referring to objects and their characteristics, or referring to persons. We were taught about relating objects and actions in phrases, clauses, sentences and even paragraphs. We studied how to determine the inherent patterns that govern intelligent communication. And we learned how different cultures think about themselves and the world around them, as well as about the unseen world.

One characteristic of exams at SIL was the use of humor. Sometimes we had to "transcribe" a joke written in phonetic symbols. As the test proceeded, chuckles would be heard around the classroom as one student after another came to the punch line. It was a "learning-made-fun" approach. But behind the casual approach of our instructors—many of whom were almost as young as their students—was a serious intensity. They were preparing us to reach a tribe for God.

Inspiration Personified

Rubbing shoulders daily with translators fresh from the field, experienced missionaries from various areas of the world, and missions-minded graduates from many Christian colleges, offered an undercurrent of inspiration at Norman. Even though they were practical, fun-loving, friendly people, all were serious about analyzing a language, penetrating a culture, and changing the values and worldview of an unreached tribe. We were blessed to be taught by Dr. Bob Longacre. Despite being a stutterer, Dr. Longacre had "cracked" the first known five-tone language, a process like cracking a code. We were blessed to see Dr. Pike's translation of the New Testament into Mixtec come fresh from the printer. It was Wycliffe's first Testament—the product of fifteen years of work squeezed in between getting his doctorate, teaching at the University of Michigan, and writing textbooks on linguistic theory.

Dr. Pike led Wycliffe's monthly half-day of prayer. This, I believe, was our first experience in a group day of prayer. Dr. Pike usually led Sunday afternoon vespers as well. A great devotional speaker, he also loved to lead the singing, applying speech rhythms to music according to his mood. One of his favorites was "Oh, the Deep, Deep

Love of Jesus," from the IVCF *Hymns* so popular with students at that time. Kenneth Pike is indelibly related in my memory to that song.

Church and Ministry in Norman

Finding a church home for the summer was difficult. Marian and I didn't quite fit the typical Southern denominational churches of Norman with their cultural Christianity. It took us until the end of the summer to find the delightful Gospel Chapel, a Plymouth Brethren assembly in Oklahoma City twenty miles north of Norman.

To our surprise we found opportunities for service that summer. A few times I spoke at a mission church in the morning service. Several Sunday evenings we drove to a small rural congregation, meeting in a country schoolhouse. It was fun to minister together with Marian. One Sunday we took Bob and Betty Morse to that little schoolhouse to show their slides. They were from the North Burma Christian Mission, part of a second-generation family team. My brother Haniel, who was then a Methodist missionary, had gotten to know the Morses in Burma and wanted me to meet them. Bob showed slides of their work among the Lisu, a group similar to the one Marian and I would later reach. The Morses became part of our lifelong network of friends around the world.

"Romancing"

Until we went to Norman, Marian and I had related primarily by correspondence, but at SIL we were together most daylight hours and evenings. We were getting to know each other—relating in person. Since most of our courtship had been by mail, we needed this. It was, of course, delightful—I thought she was so pretty at the welcome party. We were also storing up shared experiences: the heat, the studies, the new friends.

Each day we found convenient places to be together. Once we went to a state park for a holiday picnic together. On another occasion we drove to Kansas for the wedding of one of Marian's FMF friends from Wheaton. Each night on campus we had a semiprivate place to read the Word and pray before saying goodnight. But we did have to establish guidelines for our behavior. A year before, when my Wheaton roommate Bob Hornish got engaged, he asked for guidelines as to expressions of affection. My answer? "You can kiss, hold hands and hug, but keep hands above the waist and only on her back." Those guidelines worked for us. We didn't want to spoil our own future, and we wanted to be able to say to our children, "Do as we did." Above all, we wanted to please the Lord.

"Romancing" at SIL

That summer at SIL we were wrestling with the reality of the "Faith Principle." Wycliffe Bible Translators is a "faith mission" and we were moving in faith mission circles. On July 31, 1951, I wrote in my prayer notebook: *"Lord, after last night as we read Thy Word, and Thou didst give us Matthew 6:33, I trust it is the basis for faith missions—the faith principle of support—which we have been seeking. But there are two ramifications which Thou must keep us doing. One is the condition of the verse: seeking first Thy kingdom (extension of Thy spiritual kingdom) and to be holy. The other is of trust for support. Before Thee, we cannot and will not be beggars of money, whether directly or indirectly in deputation work and prayer letters. Lord, we trust Thee to take the initiative in support, whether directly or through deputation meetings. Lord, furthermore, we purpose not to say more to Elm-LaSalle [Church] by way of hint or otherwise, about their promised partial support. Lord, Thou must take the initiative. Prove Thy promises for Thy name's sake."*

Our talks about the Faith Principle may not sound like "romancing" but this matter was part of our nightly time of prayer and reading the Word, of our being one in the Lord—that's what oneness is all about. And the bottom line? Loving Him more than each other is the glue that holds couples together.

Applying to WBT/SIL

We had gone to Norman expecting to apply to Wycliffe Bible Translators—WBT. Once we got there, we liked what we saw. We really enjoyed the orientation meetings. We heard Cameron Townsend himself tell how he got the vision for providing translations for tribal people, then how he stumbled onto the idea of gaining entrance into countries not as a missionary organization but as a linguistic organization, the Summer Institute of Linguistics. We thrilled to hear how "Uncle Cam," as he was called, had moved in faith to take his first team to Mexico. They all had the money he had requested, but he kept delaying their departure. The problem? He didn't yet have his own funds!

As our orientation proceeded, we came to agreement on the Faith Principle of financial support, but we struggled with the idea of joining two separate organizations with identical membership: WBT, the organization relating to churches, and SIL, the organization relating to academic institutions and government entities. We were also troubled by the practice at that time of requiring translators to leave their work periodically to take turns staffing field headquarters—doing administration or accounting or purchasing.

Finally, a couple of weeks before the end of summer school those who had applied to WBT/SIL were interviewed by board members. When Dr. Nida summed up their evaluation, he told us, "Well, I see no reason why you shouldn't be accepted." They would have a letter, hopefully of acceptance, awaiting us in New Jersey. Then we would get married in Wheaton and honeymoon by driving leisurely to Mexico City where we would study Spanish. Our financial needs would be covered by the G. I. Bill. Afterward we would go to southern Mexico for SIL's Jungle Camp.

Never once did it occur to us that driving to Mexico with our last hundred dollars might not be realistic. Nor that studying Spanish as newlyweds might be as difficult as studying linguistics as newlyweds would have been. Nor did it occur to us that we might not be accepted by WBT. Nor that LaSalle and Moody Church would not automatically start giving to us when we became members of Wycliffe. We were moving in faith! Or was it presumption? Or just plain naivety? Our plans were about to disintegrate. Our vision was to be severely tested!

On to the Wedding

With eleven weeks of linguistic study behind us, we left Norman, Oklahoma, heading out under a blazing sun. At last we were on the way to our wedding. All day we drove—no power steering, no air conditioning. The two-lane roads were straight, hot and endless. Marian lay across the back seat, not feeling well. By night we arrived at my brother Lael's parsonage in Louisiana. Next day we ate the midday meal with my sister Jedidah in Mississippi, then continued on to Alabama for a quick visit with my friends from Cornerstone Church in Montgomery. We were greatly encouraged when one couple promised to support us—our very first supporters!

Late that night we reached the parsonage in Phenix City where Daddy and Mama lived—too much driving on two-lane roads for one day! We had been adding oil to my old DeSoto more often than water, so we stayed long enough at Daddy's for his friend to put new rings on our car and for me to preach on Sunday. Marian had wanted one of my sisters to be in our wedding, so Lois joined us on the two-day trip from Alabama to New Jersey.

At Marian's home in West Orange we found our letter from SIL waiting for us. Expectantly we tore it open. To our dismay, we were *not* accepted! The letter stated that they did not know us well enough, but that we could go ahead to the orientation program for new candidates, after which they would make a final decision. We were not only dismayed, but perplexed. To go to orientation in October, our plans to study Spanish in Mexico after our wedding would have to be canceled and the rest of my G.I. Bill funds would be lost. On the other hand, if we decided *not* to go to orientation, then what *would* we do? We were in a daze. Wycliffe's doubts about us brought our latent doubts about Wycliffe to the forefront again. Once more we cast ourselves on God for guidance.

With our wedding only days away we *had* to make a decision. Marian's parents offered to let us house-sit their home in New Jersey until it sold. They were moving to Pittsburgh where Mr. Westling had already begun a new job. Staying in their house would give us time to decide whether or not to proceed to orientation in October. It was now early September. That Sunday rather than go to church with the Westlings we chose to attend Bethany Evangelical Free Church, beginning a relationship with Bethany that continues to this day.

On Labor Day we headed for Pittsburgh in caravan—Marian, my sister Lois, and I in our car; Marian's parents, her sister Irene, and brother John in their car. It was fun to drive the Pennsylvania Turnpike, the first modern toll road, precursor of the interstate system. We were all in a holiday mood, anticipating the wedding on Saturday. In Pittsburgh we camped out in the empty house the Westlings had bought, then traveled on to Wheaton the next day, leaving us three days for final wedding preparations.

It was so good to be back in Wheaton where Marian and I had met. We enjoyed the lush green beauty of the place, now so full of memories. We were back at the college where I had begun studying two years before with so many uncertainties. Every step had been bathed in prayer. And now, marrying in Wheaton was a crowning blessing!

On Friday afternoon my folks arrived: my mother, my brother Joel, and my sister Matred with J.C., her husband. To me it was special that they had made the long trip from Alabama. That evening after the rehearsal, Dad Westling treated us all to a meal at a Swedish *smorgasbord*. Perfect! My folks, however, had no concept that a *smorgasbord* was a symbol of the Westling's Swedish origin, for the South had never been impacted by any major ethnic immigration.

Marian and I had memorized our vows—traditional vows, biblical vows. I awoke the morning of my wedding day repeating my vows aloud. I had let myself sleep late, so I had only a brief time with the Lord that day. John and Carrie Lindskoog, my Moody friends at whose home I was staying, had even set up a place for my quiet time. I still regret not having a special time with the Lord that morning—my wedding day!

I would not see Marian that day until I saw her walk down the aisle. That morning she went to a studio in Chicago to have her wedding portrait made. The photo was glamorous, but we much preferred the photo taken on the spiral staircase at the chapel as Marian descended after dressing for the ceremony. She had once seen a bridal picture made there and always thought she would like to marry at that chapel.

"I, Aziel, take thee, Marian"

We were married on September 8, 1951, at Bethany Chapel in Wheaton, Illinois, a place special to Marian during her last year at the college. The chapel was full of college friends, as well as people from the town of Wheaton and from Chicago. Marian's father's sisters came: Svea from Chicago and Sigrid from Seattle. Both were special to Marian, for Svea had lived with her family for a time and Sigrid had prayed faithfully for Marian since she was born.

The chapel was decorated very simply. Marian carried white flowers on a white Bible, for our marriage was based on the Word. Her dress was simple and modest, and so were the dresses of her maid of honor, Irene, and bridesmaid, Lois. My brother Joel and my friend John Lindskoog were the groomsmen. Marian's father, who brought her down the aisle, was suffering from an attack of asthma that dampened his happiness.

Pastor Gibbs of Elm-LaSalle Bible Church performed the ceremony. Marian chose him, for she appreciated what I had told her about his counsel when I left the Methodist church. His message from the Psalms was appropriate. A Wheaton friend sang "I Take Thy Promise." The first line expressed our feelings: "I take Thy promise, Lord, for all my days." The other song, "Together with Jesus," was one I especially wanted. I had heard it at a wedding I sang in and had decided then that I wanted it sung at my wedding. Marian ceded her choice to me, but over the years we sang hers many times, and never sang mine again. In fact, we sang hers, "May the grace of Christ our Savior..." as a prayer at our 50th wedding anniversary. But "Together with Jesus, life's pathway we tread" verbalized our commitment first to the Lord and then to each other.

"Hapily Married"

The rings we exchanged were each engraved with Psalm 9:10, the verse the Lord had used a year before to confirm my decision to marry Marian. When I kissed her to finalize our vows, I unwittingly knocked her veil off! Irene picked it up and replaced it—maybe a bride does need a maid of honor!

My mother's only comment on our wedding was that she missed the traditional songs, "I Love You Truly" and "Because." Pastor Gibbs comment to me was, "I'll never forget your look as you watched Marian come down the aisle." Nor will I ever forget how Marian looked; her simple, pure beauty—the beauty of the Lord. She didn't even have on make-up that would hide her natural beauty, the beauty of a "meek and quiet spirit." I was marrying a woman of God. I always felt that our simple, Christ-centered wedding set the tone of our married life.

The reception was as simple as the wedding had been. In the reception line a friend made a very significant comment. As we told Millie about our dilemma with Wycliffe, she suggested, "Why don't you try The Central American Mission? They're looking for a translator for a tribe in Panama." We had been impressed with that mission because of a film shown on a prayer day at SIL. We liked William Walker, the general secretary of the mission. We also knew that Cameron Townsend, who founded Wycliffe, had been a missionary of The Central American Mission when he did his New Testament. Furthermore, Ed Sywulka, our first and favorite teacher at SIL, was a member of the Mission. Millie's suggestion to try The Central American Mission would be God's key to our next step—though not without doubts on my part.

After the reception guests left, Joel brought my car from where I had hidden it, and my folks left for the long drive back to Alabama. Marian and I settled down to open all the gifts. We had prayed that the Lord would meet all our basic household needs through our wedding gifts, and that we would not receive a lot of showy items that would be impractical to take to the mission field. The Lord abundantly answered that prayer! Then as we were about to drive away, Dad Westling—I'd have to learn to call him "Dad"—handed us a check for one hundred dollars. We felt so blessed!

Mr. and Mrs. Aziel W. Jones

Down the road a few miles as we neared Chicago, Marian suddenly said, "I'm hungry!" We had hardly eaten all day. We spotted a White Castle, the only fast food place that existed in those days, and went in for a hamburger—the first meal of our married life! Unwittingly we set a tradition. Each anniversary since then we've gone out for a hamburger, or Marian has fixed hamburgers for supper in the jungle. Many years later the children made hamburgers for our anniversary, serving them in White Castle hamburger holders they had brought from the States to surprise us!

For a honeymoon suite I had been able to arrange the one normally reserved for special donors at Moody Bible Institute. For the first time I signed in as *"Mr. and Mrs. Aziel W. Jones."* We were shown to the suite, which was just opposite the window of the dorm room I had occupied for three years as a student. It was a perfect honeymoon suite—Marian loved it. I didn't know until later how much a special room meant to a girl for her honeymoon—and at other times too. As we sat on the sofa, we pulled out our Bibles and went through the Scriptures reviewing all the passages we could recall relating to marriage. Then we knelt and prayed. The wedding ceremony had declared publicly the "tone" of our marriage. Now we reaf-

"Newlyweds!" – September 8, 1951

firmed it privately, laying the foundation for a lifetime together. We desperately wanted God's blessing on our marriage, so we tried to start right. Each anniversary we have reviewed those passages again. The Word of God and prayer are still the basis for our life together, f or our home and our work. Nothing less could build a lasting foundation for marriage—and we were in this for keeps!

We were united in Christ, happy in Him. We loved Him before we loved each other. We delighted in each other, in our new married love, unspoiled, untried. Next morning we ignored the breakfast bell and even missed Sunday School, but we did go to the main service at Elm-LaSalle, where I had taught the college class and where I was still a deacon. How I enjoyed showing off my wife to friends there!

The next day we began our leisurely trip back to New Jersey, stopping early each evening and leaving late each morning. Checking in that afternoon at Winona Lake, we ate supper at the hotel dining room. The Grace Seminary student who served us put on a record, "I Love You Truly." How did *he* know we were newlyweds, we wondered? Newly married couples don't realize how obvious it is! From Winona Lake we continued east to Pittsburgh to spend some time at the Westlings' new home and do some sightseeing. Choosing scenic roads rather than the Turnpike, we finished the last lap of our trip to New Jersey on Saturday and settled in at the Westlings' old house in West Orange.

On Hold in New Jersey

We had only one day, Sunday, before reality set in. That Sunday we decided to go back down the hill to Bethany Church where we had attended the day before leaving for the wedding. Marian had known about the church during her high school days. The Norwegians at the church not only accepted Marian, a Swede, but me, a Southerner. Bethany became a church home to us.

On Monday morning we faced the reality that I needed a job. We had less than a hundred dollars left. Marian phoned Mr. Ramsland, a contractor from Bethany's mother church. His daughter-in-law had been a high school friend of Marian's. "Come on over," he said, so I started to work that same morning at a dollar an hour. After a week he raised my pay, saying, "It costs a lot to live." I enjoyed working with Mr. Ramsland and learning more about carpentry. It was the Lord's provision for us naive newlyweds.

Marian and I settled down to married life. This unplanned interlude in New Jersey was far better than our elaborate plans for study in Mexico. The Lord knew we needed this time to bond without the pressures of travel and study in another country. I soon observed that Marian set a pretty table and was a careful cook, although still a learner. She was organized, and as the years went on I saw this as a major distinctive.

We loved our church home, a family church composed mostly of descendants of Norwegian immigrants. Occasionally, there would be a *fest* on a Sunday afternoon with typical music from the string band—one old man even playing a musical saw. I loved the "feel" of their singing. Then after the preaching and an offering for missions, there would be Norwegian goodies at the fellowship hall in the basement—things like goat cheese and cold meats and rye bread, cookies and pastries, and of course coffee, always coffee. But Marian hadn't yet learned to like it, in spite of being raised in a Swedish home.

The church building was small, but always full on Sundays. Not so many came to prayer meeting, but we always attended, sitting beside Mrs. Egli, an elderly Swiss lady who loved the Lord and loved us—old people appreciate the friendship of the young. Years later she sent us a large gift that enabled us to attend a linguistic conference in Guatemala. We made other friendships in the congregation when folks invited us to dinner. I learned that an invitation to Sunday dinner in a Scandinavian home meant staying for a light supper before the evening service. The food was wonderful and the families were so loving to us newcomers.

Pastor Louis Hess and I developed a close relationship. He was a great student of the Word, a good preacher and a good shepherd. Once he had me preach. Sometimes I would sing a solo. We had many a good chat around his kitchen table. Interestingly, he was German, not Scandinavian, yet he fit the church. Pastor Hess was a mentor to young men in the church looking toward ministry, fellows like Ted Martin, Don Condit, and Ron Manus, none of whom were Norwegians. They had been high school classmates of Marian's sister, but now they became *our* lifelong friends—Ted, later pastor of a supporting church; Don, a Christian worker who visited us in Tsipirí before his tragic death; Ron, fellow translator in Peru.

Sometimes Marian and I would visit other churches where she had friends. Once we went to a Word of Life rally to hear Jack Wyrtzen, the evangelist I had learned of in Boston during the war. It was at one of his rallies in New York City that Marian as a teen had committed her life to missions. Occasionally Marian and I invited friends, usually Ted and Ron, for a simple meal. Once John and Carrie Lindskoog spent a night with us, and we went with them a couple hours' drive to Philadelphia to see Independence Hall and the Betsy Ross House.

Just up the steep hill from the Westling's house on Eagle Rock Avenue was a forest preserve with an overlook where we could see the skyscrapers of New York City. Even from our attic window we could see New York on a clear day. Down the hill, not far from Bethany Church, was the Edison Museum. As a boy I had been fascinated by Thomas Edison. When we visited the museum, what interested me most was Edison's enormous roll-top desk on which he would catnap while working around the clock on an invention. Even the power company that served West Orange was named for Edison.

Though we were happy in New Jersey, our future was still up in the air. Should we go ahead to orientation? Friends urged us to go. John Lindskoog even phoned long distance, not common then, to encourage us. Other couples, who had gotten the same letter we received, did proceed to orientation and were accepted. But we had no liberty. The Lord had not spoken.

Fall passed—so lovely. Then winter came—so dreary. The Westlings arrived from Pittsburgh, for their house had sold. They needed to settle their affairs, and we needed to find a place to live. Apartment hunting was another "first experience" for us. Right away I learned a lot of things very close to Marian's heart—what she wanted in a house. It had to be clean, neat and hopefully, pretty—not just something that "would do." As a child, she had learned to draw house plans and had opinions about what she wanted. She could walk through an apartment, sizing it up quietly and quickly, seeing every detail, seeing things I never noticed. We settled on a small basement apartment in East Orange—the only tolerable place we could afford.

One day, working all alone on the ridge pole of a roof, I began thinking about our future, and said to myself, "I'm no linguist! I'm cut out to be a preacher!" About this time Herman Kroeze, an active layman at Bethany Church who had been one of Marian's teachers in junior high, invited me to fill in for him as pulpit supply at Riverdale Bible Church, half an hour north. I jumped at the chance and preached there most Sundays during the winter. We loved this new storefront church. The folks liked us and invited us to their homes for dinner. We kept active at Bethany during the week.

On to South Carolina

The weeks rolled on—not really many, for we were in Jersey less than five months. I began to feel restless, a desire to attend the Graduate School of Missions at Columbia Bible College. I had no definable reason, except that I wanted to see what the place was like. So I applied and was accepted for the second semester.

Then in January 1952 Riverdale Church dropped a bombshell! "Would you be our interim pastor until Pastor Smith arrives in June?" What a test! I might have been sidelined in the pastorate for life. We would gladly have agreed had I not already been accepted at CBC. I don't know why we felt we should go on to South Carolina. We had no clear leading from the Lord. Yet we went, motivated only by my desire to go back to school.

Late in January we loaded everything we owned in the old DeSoto, filling the trunk and the back seat. Happily we headed south, where some of our Wheaton friends were already studying. Unknown to us, there in Columbia the Lord would soon reveal the next step toward our life's work.

– 6 –
Off Square One
1952

"Four Chirripó Indians recently went to the capital of Costa Rica and asked for a missionary," announced the leader of the prayer group.

To him it was just another item in a list of prayer requests. To us those words were to become a call, as clear as when the Apostle Paul heard the man from Macedonia say, "Come over and help us." I had just enrolled in the Graduate School of Missions at Columbia Bible College in order to make good use of my time while waiting for God's leading to a place of service. The first Saturday night there in South Carolina we sought out the missions prayer group. There we heard the prayer request about the Chirripó Indians that God used to get us "off square one."

Marian and I had been married just four months when we drove to South Carolina in January of 1952. Before leaving New Jersey, we had sent a letter of inquiry to The Central American Mission after a friend mentioned that the Mission was looking for a translator for a tribe in Panama. Yet when spring came to Columbia, the application to the Mission, later known as CAM International, lay untouched. Marian was enjoying being a housewife in our little apartment—just a kitchen and a bedroom. She was so pretty to come home to after classes at grad school and my Fuller Brush sales route. It was exciting to walk with the Lord together, but again I felt stirred to move on.

"I've had enough school—first Moody, then Wheaton, and now grad school at Columbia Bible College. I'm thirty years old. It's time to get into ministry," I said to Marian as we lingered over breakfast on March 17.

Marian felt the same. Two hours later Dr. Robert McQuilkin spoke at chapel on Psalm 31:3, *"...for thy name's sake lead me, and guide me."* My heart latched onto that verse. After chapel I went to the college post office and found a letter from The Central American Mission. That letter was the final key to God's call.

A "Macedonian Call"

I opened the letter and read: "We noticed on your letter of inquiry that you have had linguistic training as well as Bible training. Would you be willing to consider an assignment to work among the Chirripó Indians? Four of these Indians recently went to The Central American Mission in San José, Costa Rica, and asked for a missionary." Marian and I were amazed that the Mission was offering us an assignment when we hadn't even submitted our application yet. In our hearts we knew that this was *it*, the call we had been waiting for.

"Let's send off the application right away," urged Marian.

Always the cautious one, I hesitated. "Let's wait a week. If the Lord is in it, it will still be 'hot' then."

That night it was Marian who hesitated, "But who are we? We're just *us*."

"I know," I countered, "but 'the Spirit and the gifts are ours.'" In my diary I wrote, "Things will get rugged; but I don't care, now that a door has opened."

Our perfect "Macedonian call" was really just simple guidance, in line with three principles I had learned from Stephen Olford: *Warranted circumstances*—the letter from CAM; the *Witness of the Spirit*—our feeling that it was time to get into ministry; and the *Word of God*—the verse that Dr. McQuilkin had preached on that morning.

A week later the call was still "hot." We completed the application and mailed it to Dallas. It was all so romantic. "Even 'Chirripó' sounds pretty," Marian said, "like 'cheery-oh.'"

In the weeks to follow, Psalm 2:8 summed up our leading, *"Ask of me, and I will give thee the heathen* [a tribe] *for thine inheritance."* Yet we said, "With such perfect guidance, we'll surely be tested."

That week I added Psalm 2:8 to my pack of verses to memorize—following the Navigator system—and then wrote on the back of the card: "3/23/52. This ties in to verses like Numbers 36:2, *'...give the land for an inheritance,'* and verses in Deuteronomy 1 and 2 about possessing our inheritance. This is the basis for responding in the affirmative about the Chirripó Indians. This verse summarizes the trend of Scriptures this week."

At the same time I added another verse, Romans 15:14, "And I myself am persuaded of you, my brethren, that ye also are full of goodness, filled with all knowledge, able also to admonish one another." This verse was the key Scripture that professor Art Glasser used in the class I was taking on "Indigenous Church Principles." It molded my thinking that among the believers in a church are the necessary gifts and resources to develop the church. In the ensuing decades as I desperately tried to plant a viable church among the Indians, this verse kept me from depending on outside money or ministry.

Our doubts sometimes returned. Could we do the linguistic job? While at Moody and Wheaton I had doubted my ability to translate, but the day after receiving the letter from the Mission I wrote in my diary, "I feel it's God's voice to tackle the job. Marian isn't sure." Yet she already had been encouraged by Isaiah 41:13, *"For I the Lord thy God will hold thy right hand, saying unto thee, Fear not; I will help thee."* Then, as now, we expected confirmation from the Word when making major decisions.

The following day other realities hit us—finances, including the next month's rent. That evening was our weekly time for fasting and extra prayer, but I was tired and in no mood for it. Yet before the evening was over, we had real joy in the Lord and in each other.

Time was as tight as money. It was almost April. There were medicals to complete and references to be checked before we could be invited to the June session of Candidate School in Dallas. At the last meeting of the missions prayer group for that semester, the leader shared an answer to prayer from The Central American Mission—a couple had volunteered to work among the Chirripó Indians. The group was astounded when I announced that *we* were the couple! Until we received our invitation to Candidate School, we had not felt free to reveal that we had applied to the Mission.

Candidate School

In June we packed our belongings in fifteen boxes to ship to Marian's parents in Pittsburgh. As usual, we had no money. A new Christian came to supper and gave us five dollars. A fellow student gave us ten. That money not only paid for shipping the fifteen boxes but set the stage for seeing God intervene regularly in *all* areas of life. We were more excited about those fifteen dollars than about a more miraculous two thousand dollars to buy a Land Rover two decades later.

We still had to get out of Columbia—and get to Dallas for candidate school. An unexpected tax refund helped. On the way, at my parents' home in Alabama, I sold some scrap iron—more gas money.

From Columbia to Dallas was more than a thousand miles on two-lane roads. No interstate, no cruise control, no air-conditioning. Driving was hot and tiring; I was more tense than I realized. Somewhere along the way Marian made a suggestion about my driving, and I slapped her. I had never done it before, nor have I done it since. Neither of us said a word. She didn't even cry. But it scared me—that I was capable of slapping my perfect bride of ten months!

We were welcomed at the guest home of The Central American Mission in Dallas by Bill and Erma Walker. During the years that Bill was General Secretary, the Walkers came to personify the Mission to us. The large, well-kept home in a nice neighborhood fit the Mission, and it fit us. Two other couples and three single girls also arrived for Candidate School. We began to forge friendships—the bond of a common call.

Mrs. Walker showed us our room. On the back of the door we noticed the daily rates. We were to learn that this is common practice in mission guest homes. But we had arrived in Dallas with about forty dollars and still had to drive to Pittsburgh after the two weeks of orientation. The other couples were in the same dilemma. Marian and I cried out to God for help. What relief we felt the next morning when Mr. Walker began the orientation session by saying, "You will be our guests during your stay. We'll also pay your trip home."

We had been invited to Candidate School with a view to working among the Chirripó Indians, but this was contingent upon our being approved by the Board. One purpose of the time in Dallas was for the Mission to look us over. Would we candidates come through in person as we had on paper? We ate family-style, did the cleanup and a bit of other work around the Mission property. We went out to an Hispanic neighborhood and sold Scripture portions in Spanish. Marian commented, "If this is missionary work, I like it!" We visited churches to speak about our future ministry, but there was the edge of uncertainty. Would we be accepted?

In the orientation sessions we learned about the policies and procedures of The Central American Mission. We also learned that it was founded in 1890 by Dr. C. I. Scofield, who later became well-known for the study notes of the "Scofield Bible." Scofield had become interested in Central America through a travel lecture, then had investigated and discovered that most of the area was without a gospel witness. He and three men from the church he pastored founded the Mission "on our knees" in his dining room.

For Marian and me, it was even more fascinating to hear about Lewis Jamison who in 1895 had gone to work among the same Indians we were hoping to reach. Jamison was soon forced out, accused of raising a British flag. The flag he supposedly displayed was actually a chart which he used in teaching the Bible. The immediate cause of his being expelled was evidently that the archbishop had made an unprecedented trek through the area at that time.

We felt it was a special privilege to take up Lewis Jamison's work after an interruption of more than fifty-five years. Later we learned that the son of a man who received Jamison was an uncle of one of the four Indians who had asked for a missionary. Eventually I even met a few people who still remembered "Mr. Jamis," as they called him. One even recalled a song about the blood of Jesus. However, none had any personal faith even though thirty-two had been baptized when young Jamison preached through an interpreter. Mr.

Woman who remembered Mr. Jamison

Jamison was still alive when we joined the Mission. We wrote him and received a reply before his death soon afterwards.

On the last day of Candidate School each of us candidates appeared, somewhat nervously, before the Board of The Central American Mission—a dozen or so older men. All of us were accepted! Then we were commissioned, a meaningful service at Scofield Memorial Church. For Marian and me, the icing on the cake was that Bea Cooper, a secretary at the Mission office, committed herself to being our first prayer partner. In the years to come we had more and more prayer backing—a major factor in what the Lord did for the Indians and for us.

At last we were "off square one." As we drove away from Dallas, we felt proud of CAM's history, happy with its policies, and excited about how we fit into its original vision to reach the Chirripó Indians. We were on our own, cast on the Lord for our financial needs. The Mission guaranteed no salary, had neither medical insurance nor a retirement plan. We needed to raise two hundred dollars a month for our support, as daunting for us then as two thousand—or more—is for today's new missionaries. But at least we were "off square one."

Stuck in Pittsburgh

Two excited missionary candidates, we arrived at Marian's parents' home in the suburbs of Pittsburgh, Pennsylvania, early in July of 1952. We were ready and eager to reach the Chirripó Indians of Costa Rica—ready to reduce their language to writing, learn the grammar, and translate the New Testament.

We had no friends in the "Steel City," not even a church contact. However, we had been assured of full financial support from Moody Church in Chicago, where we were members. "Just let us know," one of the pastors had said. And we did let him know when we passed through Chicago on our way from Candidate School in Dallas to Marian's home in Pittsburgh. We assumed we would be in Costa Rica with full support for the September session at language school.

"Now to go!" With these words we enthusiastically began our first prayer letter on July 12, 1952. We only lacked support, setup funds, plane fares, passports, and visas. Only that? That was everything! The next day I was doubting the Lord's leading, but was encouraged as I recalled the miracle gift of fifteen dollars the day before we left South Carolina. Furthermore, since that gift we had already received five more gifts, totaling over a hundred dollars. Yet a week later my doubts returned. In my diary I wrote, "The Lord must provide, or we are paralyzed."

We did finally find a church home in Pittsburgh at Sandusky Street Baptist, an old downtown church then pastored by the brother-in-law of a college friend. The building was a massive monument to a glorious past. The small remaining congregation met in the basement. Though the group was small, the fellowship was intimate. We attended Sunday School, morning and evening services, and prayer meeting—a pattern we established wherever we lived, for we believed in identifying with a local church.

"I know you need support, but we can't do anything right now," Pastor Boyko said to us. However, he gave us the names of sixteen pastor friends in the area.

Some responded and let us show the Mission film and share our vision for reaching the Indians. One contact was in a "Gospel Barn." Another group met in a firehouse where Pastor Oyer said, "If we can get the group to take you on at even five dollars a month, maybe they will increase it."

We contacted our circle of acquaintances throughout the eastern United States, and the Mission gave us a few contacts. Some sent invitations to share our vision. Whether speaking in churches or writing letters, our appeal was for prayer. We agreed with our Mission's policy of "information without solicitation." Our first prayer letter went to one hundred eighty people. That number has increased, but we keep it down to five hundred, about all we can handle. I wrote the letter in the first person, rewrote it twice, then Marian typed and edited it while trying to preserve my style. Then together we fine-tuned it. The process would usually take two or three days, or even a week. We have followed this pattern ever since.

Marian and I worked together on the focus, content, and format of our letters. We also prayed over each letter as we wrote it. When it was done, we prayed that the Lord would touch, empower, and anoint it—that it would raise up a new wave of prayer for us and for the Chirripó Indians. Often we wrote personal notes on the form letters or even enclosed a lengthy personal epistle. This practice was very time-consuming, but we were building relationships. We were also answering questions and discussing various issues. We found correspondence with some people to be very stimulating. We considered all correspondence as a ministry.

Praying Desperately

Prayer took on new meaning for me during those early weeks in Pittsburgh. Often on Sunday afternoons I would go to our room and pray out loud—"praying desperately," as we had said in our first prayer letter—that we would get to Costa Rica. Marian, embarrassed that her family might hear me, would go downstairs and play the piano, hoping to cover up my loud praying!

Years later a young Mission candidate repeatedly asked me, "Mr. Jones, tell me, how do I raise support?" My answer was always, "Get on your knees!"

Although we feared we might be stuck indefinitely in Pittsburgh waiting for the Lord to meet our financial needs, a couple from Cornerstone Bible Church in Alabama had already promised to send a small amount each month toward our support. Soon we made a quick trip to share our vision at Cornerstone Church in Montgomery. While we were in Alabama, a woman from a country church where I had once preached also made a financial commitment.

Even so, support came with agonizing slowness—or so it seemed! Yet in August two churches in New Jersey invited us to show the Mission film, and share our vision and testimony. Bethany Free Church had been our church for four months as newlyweds. Now they promised a portion of our support. Riverdale Bible Church, where I had preached several times, promised support as well. In addition, two couples from Riverdale also committed to support us. One gave monthly for twenty years or so, then stopped when he retired, only to begin again with a larger amount! The widow of the other couple continued giving—as regularly as clockwork—until she entered a nursing home. We discovered that support grows out of relationships, friendships, and ministry.

Twice after our New Jersey trip in August, a college student drove the eight hours from New Jersey to Pittsburgh to get counsel about possible mission service and training. To our joy, he and the girl he married have spent their lives translating the New Testament for a tribe in Peru.

A Providential Delay

Occasionally we received gifts in the mail or at meetings locally, but we did not have enough monthly support promised to get to Costa Rica in time for the September session of language school. To earn money toward plane tickets, I began working for a contractor. One day as I helped an electrician named Ralph Groetzinger put in a conduit, I talked with him about our vision. Ralph, though an elder in a local church, didn't quite understand the gospel, nor did he truly know the Lord. Marian and I invited him and his wife to a Billy Graham Campaign, then to Sandusky Street Church. When they invited us home for a snack after church, we explained the gospel more personally. At midnight Ralph asked the Lord to save him. Two hours later Mae did the same. Soon they began supporting us—and continued until they went to be with the Lord, after which their daughter began to support us.

Our delay in getting to Costa Rica was providential for the Groetzinger family, but for us the weeks were ticking away. It was now fall. We sent out our second prayer letter in October, and then made a trip to Philadelphia to speak to the children at the Christian school where Marian taught before we married. The school promised to give monthly toward support in lieu of the back pay they still owed Marian. Even with these promises, we still needed almost half of the two hundred dollars per month required by CAM.

Still no word from our church in Chicago! Unknown to us, Marian's aunt—also a member of Moody Church—talked with another of the pastors about our support. Finally we got a letter from the missions committee, inviting us to meet with them in Chicago early in December!

In faith, we hastily started packing to leave the United States. I had already coated all our books with shellac to protect them from tropical insects and then mailed them. In November we packed twelve footlockers—including two wooden containers I made for odd-size items—and shipped all our personal possessions to Costa Rica. Yet we wondered as we boarded the train for a restful trip to Chicago, "What if we don't get the rest of our support?" Yet the Lord honored our faith. Moody Church did take on the needed remainder!

Ready to Go!

Suddenly we were ready to go! Our support was fully pledged, our belongings were on the way to Costa Rica, our passports and visas were in hand, and our tickets were purchased. Several times we had shown the CAM film, scores of times we had shared how the Lord had been working in our lives. We had recounted the story of the four Chirripó Indians who had recently asked for a missionary, and how Mr. Jamison had gone to the Indians in 1895. We had spent five months praying, visiting churches, writing letters, and talking to people about our plans. Then everything fell into place so quickly that we were hardly ready psychologically to leave!

We left Pittsburgh on December 16, 1952. That morning before leaving on a business trip, Dad Westling told Marian goodbye. As she cried, he held her firmly in his arms until she was quiet. I appreciated his understanding. There would be nothing but letters, a cable, and a few photos for the next four years. God calls missionaries, not their parents, but parents also pay a price. Will He not in some way recognize and reward them also?

Heading south in our old DeSoto, we reached Alabama the next night in time to surprise our friends gathered for prayer meeting at Cornerstone Church in Montgomery. Then we continued on to Fort Walton Beach, Florida, where my father was then pastor at the Methodist church. Most of my twelve siblings came to visit. For Christmas, Daddy gave each of his five sons a pair of vise grips. I treasured those vise grips, but was so concerned about shipping weight that I didn't even take them to Costa Rica—until twenty years later. Eventually I would learn that airlines were not always stringent about baggage allowances!

Before leaving Florida, I located some motorcycle fenders in a junkyard to ship to a missionary in Costa Rica. I was becoming part of the "pony express" system that provides missionaries with items not available overseas. The "pony express" would serve us well in the future!

After we sold our DeSoto, my brother Joel drove us to Miami to catch Flight 621 on LACSA, the Costa Rican airline. We were excited—glad to be on our way, but totally unaware that it would be thirteen years before we would discover the key to the Chirripó verbs, twenty-five years before the first baptism, over thirty years before there would be a Chirripó church, and more than forty years before the New Testament was available in the Chirripó language.

—7—
The Language of the Angels
1953

Boarding the DC-3 in Miami early in the morning of December 31, 1952, we waved goodbye to my brother Joel, still visible in the glass-front waiting room. There had been no security check, and the terminal was easy to navigate. Most of the twenty-five passengers were new missionaries like us, on the way to study Spanish—the "language of the angels"—in the best missionary language school in Latin America. When we touched down in Cuba to refuel, I took a picture of Marian on the steps of the plane—her first flight. After Havana it was nonstop to the grass landing strip at the edge of the capital of Costa Rica. From the plane we thrilled at our first view of San José, nestled in a bowl-shaped valley.

"Welcome to Costa Rica!" shouted a crowd of missionaries from the balcony of the terminal six hours after we left Miami. After a quick customs check Dean and Colista Lewis, our senior missionaries, drove us off in their Jeep.

"Aziel, you drive the rest of the way to the Mission Home—I have to go to a meeting," said Dean as he stopped at the CAM church. There wasn't enough traffic to bother anyone, no stop lights, no one-way streets, and no parking restriction in those days. It was easy for me to figure out that the red hexagonal signs saying *Alto* meant "Stop."

That night Dean drove me over narrow, winding roads to a small CAM church in a coffee plantation. There he would be preaching at the "watch night" service. Colista took the bus to the watch night service at CAM's main downtown church in San José. Marian, who was five months pregnant, stayed at the rundown Mission Home to rest. Alone there on New Year's Eve, she cried herself to sleep on an old army cot. The romance of missions was fading fast! The real

romance would return four decades later at the dedication of our
New Testament in a large gathering of Indian believers—I would cry
and she would laugh with joy.

Role Models

Dean and Colista were role models for us. They had already been
on the field ten years, having come very young during WWII, yet
Dean was a month younger than I was. Their command of Spanish
and their rapport with the brethren were without equal. They
possessed little, lived a simple life-style, and were model
missionaries, totally committed to the Lord's work and to the
Mission. For us also, the Lord's work was our life. I found social
needs met in evangelization and in Christian fellowship. I found
physical needs met when working on the house or yard (or later the
road to our Tsipirí jungle home). And I had long since found spiritual
refreshing in my daily devotions and in meeting with believers. This
seems in line with Jesus and the apostles, even though now this level
of commitment is seen as lopsided.

Dean Lewis (front left), Dick, and Jim in Chirripó - 1950

Reaching the Chirripó Indians, or the Cabécar as they are now called, was originally the vision of Dean Lewis. Both he and his wife had studied linguistics. Dean had met the four Indians seeking a missionary and had visited Chirripó. He cried when he shared his vision with his fellow missionaries. They backed Dean and Colista's desire to give half their time to the Indians and for colleague Dick Richey also to give half time. But "the Mission"—as headquarters in Dallas was called—had said, "You're too involved in Spanish work; let's look for a new couple."

Before we arrived, Dean had made one more trip to Chirripó, this time with Ed Sywulka, veteran Bible translator with The Central American Mission in Guatemala. Ed's linguistic expertise confirmed the need of a translator for the Cabécars, but Dean kept asking for the Lord's confirmation. On that trip a beautiful rainbow appeared after an afternoon rain and spanned the whole Chirripó Valley. Dean felt the Lord say, "I love these people. Someday there will be a church among them." That was Dean's confirmation. It was after this that Marian and I heard about the need of the Chirripó Indians at a prayer meeting in South Carolina and applied to the Mission.

Dean was a "fix-it" man. He had asked me to bring him a pair of fenders for a motorcycle he was rebuilding for a pastor. Besides being a practical servant, Dean was the liaison to the national churches and to the government. A few days after we got to Costa Rica, he took us to the Department of Immigration to sign for our residence permits, which he had arranged before we arrived. Colista, in addition to caring for their children and ministering to women, ran the Mission Home, providing meals, beds, and a welcoming smile for CAM missionaries. Dean and Colista provided us a wonderful introduction to life in Costa Rica, not only in practical matters but in attitudes.

Living at the Mission Home

The "Mission Home" was a vital institution in foreign missions in those days when most missionaries worked in outlying areas. It was a symbol of identity and security in a foreign land. It was the answer to families with recurring needs for a secure place to stay when in need of medical attention, or for renewing residence permits, and making travel arrangements. It also was the place for committee meetings and the annual conference of the missionaries. Mission Home guests were paying guests, yet the Mission Home was truly a home away from home. The Mission becomes a surrogate family as shown by the custom of having the missionaries' children call the adults "Aunt" and "Uncle."

Marian and I settled down in an apartment in the Mission Home during our year of language study. We had a very small kitchen, rather sparsely equipped, and a living room which served as a hallway to the upstairs guest bedrooms, one of which was for us. We lived out of suitcases until our twelve footlockers arrived by boat.

Downtown there were stores stocked with local and imported commodities, but near the Mission Home were small shops for daily needs: the vegetable stand, the meat market where they wrapped the fresh meat in pieces of banana leaves, and the *pulpería*, a tiny general store. There were no super markets in those first years so when we shopped, we had to use what Spanish we knew, or else go hungry.

Living in the Mission Home gave us opportunities for meeting other missionaries like the Houk family—real church planters arriving after a dusty, twelve-hour jeep ride from western Costa Rica. Or like hearing Dean, Jim, and Andy strategize: "Man, if we only had a little bulldozer to make roads to the country churches." Or seeing Dorothy come in from the "Line"—the railroad line to the Caribbean where she coordinated her children's classes and women's meetings between the schedules of three daily trains. Or sympathizing with Catharine who came in crying—she'd cashed her remittance check, taken the train to San José, and had her month's money robbed at the station. We were too new to digest all we heard, but it was invaluable to hear leaders discuss church issues and missionary/national relationships. Bill Taylor, the diplomat, would often quote a Spanish proverb: *Mejor un mal arreglo que un buen pleito.* ("Better a bad settlement than a good fight.")

Spanish Studies

Language study is neither dramatic nor glamorous, but all our previous training and our knowledge of the Lord were locked securely within us until we mastered Spanish, the medium for later learning the Cabécar language. We also needed the language to establish credibility in our adopted land since the Indian population was only a fraction of one percent of the total population of the country. We needed Spanish just to get around!

Each morning we'd catch a bus—an experience in itself—to a point where we could walk the last mile to school. We still recall the pleasure of walking in the crisp air of early morning under skies of unmatched blue with mountains forming an ever-present backdrop to the city.

School was hard, at least for me, like studying at Wheaton all over again. I struggled with Spanish even though it is relatively easy to learn. My mainstay was Philippians 4:13, *"I can do all things through Christ which strengtheneth me."* I prayed desperately, yet the nagging question would come, "If Spanish is so hard for me, how will I ever learn Cabécar, still unwritten, or translate the New Testament?" I continued on by faith!

Day after day we studied grammar and pronunciation and memorized vocabulary. One class was devoted to conversation practice and still another to ministry practice. We memorized verses and learned how to read Scripture aloud with proper emphasis. The women practiced giving Bible lessons, and the men practiced preaching.

Six weeks into language school I was called on to pray at the Saturday night men's meeting at church. I wasn't sure I'd heard right, but the silence confirmed my guess. I prayed in English.

"From now on I'm going to pray in Spanish at all meals," I said to Marian when I got home. One can prepare for a message, but not for impromptu prayer! Within a couple of months I was able to pray in public, albeit very simply, but I continued the practice before meals until our first furlough!

As part of our orientation Dean Lewis took me and some other language school students to a rural area called Cabeza de Buey, "Ox Head"—a three-hour jeep ride followed by a five-hour trek, which included crossing a river in a homemade cable car.

Aziel crossing the Pacuare in an "andarivel"

Dean was to perform the wedding of a couple who had lived together many years and whose children were grown. Now they were legalizing their relationship—the woman had divorced a man she had lived with only a short time, so as to be free to marry her lifelong companion.

On the trail I watched Dean, observing how he related, counseled, encouraged, and put up with us newcomers! Inwardly, I criticized him for drinking from the creek and for accepting lemonade made with water from a ditch, yet how good that lemonade tasted after hours on the trail. By then germs didn't matter! I came back from the trip refreshed and ready for Spanish classes each morning from 7:30-11:50 with a midmorning coffee break—that's where Marian learned to drink coffee! I was even ready for five hours of homework every night.

CAM missionaries in language school were expected to go to church three times a week as orientation to the Mission churches. Marian and I attended services downtown at the CAM church in San José—the first Spanish-speaking evangelical church established in Costa Rica. We enjoyed getting to know the believers and made some lasting friendships. Attending services also provided good language practice.

"What does *pecado* mean?" I asked Dean after I kept hearing the word during an evangelistic sermon—*pecado* wasn't in the vocabulary list at school.

"Sin." he answered. "Going to church is helping you learn new words!"

Traveling around Costa Rica

During our first year we got to know much of Costa Rica. My first outing was to the nearby volcano Irazú, looming large on the eastern rim of the central plateau. Our bus had to leave by sunrise to get to the top of the volcano before the clouds moved in. On a clear day one can see both the Caribbean Sea and the Pacific Ocean from the peak. The volcano was quiet in those days, but ten years later began erupting violently the day of President Kennedy's assasination. Volcanic ash fell on the city of San José like black snow, except that the ash didn't melt and had to be swept away. That day someone wrote in the black ash on the trunk of a car, "Even nature is in mourning"—a fitting expression of Latin America's feeling for its favorite U.S. President.

Another outing was to a nearby area to visit old Mrs. Ross, daughter-in-law of an English-speaking family who had immigrated to Costa Rica in the late 1800s to establish a coffee plantation. Our colleague, Jeanne Chew, wanted us to meet this woman whose mother-in-law had prayed for years that the Lord would send missionaries to reach the people of her adopted country. For Marian and me it was a special privilege to connect to this link in the history of the gospel in Costa Rica. It was also a nice drive with Jeanne in her old Jeep, seeing another part of *our* new land.

One sunny Saturday I borrowed a van from a colleague, and Marian and I drove an hour or so west toward the Pacific Coast over narrow, winding roads. It was good to be driving again; good to be out as a couple, but this was not just a *paseo*, an outing. We were headed for a furniture factory to buy some local wooden chairs. Before coming to Costa Rica we had lived in rented apartments. Now we were settling down for a lifetime of service. Buying furniture was part of the process.

A few weeks after arriving in San José we got to experience another facet of life in Costa Rica. We felt a strange jolting sensation—an earth tremor. Even though we'd never felt one before, we realized immediately what it was. We were to experience many more tremors over the years, and several earthquakes.

First Contact with Indians

During our first trimester Chamorro arrived at the CAM church downtown. He was the police agent in the Chirripó area, one of the four Indians who had asked for a missionary. Chamorro had come with his wife and two children to seek medicines. They were barefoot, but dressed much like the Latins, and were able to speak about as much Spanish as I could at the time. When we asked the name of their three-month old baby, Chamorro responded, "Oh, she doesn't have a name, she's just a baby." Eventually we learned that in those days the Indians didn't name their babies until they were sure they would live.

Years later I asked Chamorro why they had wanted a missionary. He confessed, "To learn Spanish." I wasn't surprised, for I had learned in my studies that mixed motives are often involved when people respond to the gospel. We later observed that if an Indian did not want the gospel in his own language, but only in Spanish, he was interested in "upward mobility," not the message.

My First Trek to Chirripó

At Easter break I saw Chamorro again. Dean drove me in his Jeep to Moravia, a cattle ranch near the Chirripó area where most of the Cabécars live. We walked five hours through the mud to the first house while Dean kept commenting on how dry the trail was! He walked erect and never paused, while I slipped in the mud and tripped on the roots which are characteristic of jungle trails.

In those days the Indians lived in thatched-roof huts scattered widely through the hills. We visited Chamorro's father's old cone-shaped house, and met Chamorro's teenage siblings who are great-grandparents today—we would grow old together! From there we went up to Chamorro's own house which was also conical, with beds made of river cane around the edges of the hut. The place was clean, and they kept shooing out the chickens, dogs, and pigs.

In the middle of the hut was a cooking fire. I learned that their staple diet was green boiled bananas. For them it was like rice or potatoes or pasta in other cultures. Dean gave them a package of soup mix. Chamorro's wife made it up and added eggs to the soup before serving us. They killed a chicken for us one day, and the next day served us steaming hot beans.

The last day Chamorro took us on a day's walk, up and down exhausting hills, making a circle touching four or five huts. The people served us coffee and ripe bananas, roasted in the ashes. In one house they served us corn *chicha* in large gourds. *Chicha,* whether made from corn or bananas, was their real staff of life—drunk fresh or fermented, depending on its age. Everywhere we went I made linguistic notes, beginning language study. Dean already knew the greetings. The visitor comes in silently, sits down, and is greeted by the host, *Jishtä ma shkina?* ("How did you wake up?") The visitor responds with *Bäi.* ("Fine, good.") Upon leaving, he stands up and tells each one, one by one, *'smajiapa* ("I'm going") and then leaves.

Dean pointed out to me how happy and carefree the young men were. At the Chirripó River we helped the guys build a temporary fishing dam. Each night, at their request, we sang Spanish hymns as we sat around a low round table, hewn from a log. Our seats were smaller versions of the same.

As we trekked back through mud and around twisted roots to the Jeep we stopped at Tsipirí, the cold, clear creek where eleven years later Marian and I would establish our base. Dean drank from the fresh mountain stream while I tolerated the miserable boiled water in my canteen.

"Can this creek really be contaminated?" responded Dean when I questioned him about the safety of the water. He never argued or discussed.

Afterwards when I took new people on the trail I knew what they were thinking. Some voiced the same questions I had asked Dean! In years to come, each of our children would stop at a stream, look at me before drinking and ask—verbally or with their eyes—"May I?" I learned so much from watching Dean.

Our First Child

Soon after the Easter trip to Chirripó, our first child was born on April 22, 1953, at the *Clínica Bíblica*, a hospital founded by Marie Cameron in the 1920s. Dr. Cameron asked me to give a hand as she delivered the baby. Then, turning the baby over to a nurse, she went up and talked to Marian as a mother would—a lovely side of this precise Canadian doctor!

I had wanted a son named "Peter," a rock for God. We gave him Karl as a middle name, after Marian's father Carl, and also to echo my father's name, R K.

As soon as Marian and I were alone together, we looked over our beautiful baby and then dedicated him to the Lord—a special moment with our first child.

With our first child— January 1, 1954

After spending the night on a cot in Marian's room, I hurried off the next morning to catch the bus for language school. Suddenly I stopped at a street crossing, thinking, "I'm a father now. I have to be more careful!" Before boarding the bus, I sent a cable to Marian's parents—international phone calls were unheard of, not even to announce the birth of a first grandchild. It was fun breaking the news about Peter at school and later showing him off at church. In a couple of weeks we dedicated Peter to the Lord publicly. We took Peter with us to church each Sunday, even at night. Churches in Costa Rica didn't have nurseries in those days. A young girl named Thais, who lived upstairs at the church, would take him out if he cried during a meeting—the beginning of a fifty-year friendship!

Marian didn't want to leave Peter with a sitter. She was glad to have part-time help with the extra work caused by lack of stateside conveniences, but she wanted to care for the children herself. She was able to skip the second trimester of school and stay home with the baby, since she was doing so well in Spanish. When speaking on the telephone she was sometimes mistaken for a local. Once when a pastor phoned the Mission Home, he said to Marian, "I need to talk to one of the missionaries." He mistook her for a *Tica*, as Costa Rican girls are called.

Marian's First Trip to the Indians

In August during the break between trimesters Marian and I made our own trip to the Indians, but not to Chirripó. We took the bus to Turrialba and left baby Peter with missionary friends, who converted a dresser drawer into a temporary baby bed. From there we took the train, since there was no highway beyond Turrialba. Down near the Caribbean coast we got off close to the banana town of Zent. We were hoping to visit Alfredo, a brother of one of the four Indians who had requested a missionary. Alfredo, who knew a good bit of Spanish, had heard the gospel at a CAM church in the area.

At Zent we spent the night in the home of a believer, a foreman at the banana company. Next morning we rode for over an hour sitting on a flatcar as a mule pulled us along abandoned tracks. Then for the last two hours of the trip we crisscrossed the Zent River thirteen times in water that was still hip-deep even though we had waited for a flash flood to subside. The trails were ankle deep in mud, but at least there were no hills.

We did not find Alfredo, but his brother Aristides and brother-in-law Demas were there in the thatched-roof hut. Demas fed us wild meat, bananas, beans, and coffee. Both Marian and I recorded language data in our notebooks. Aristides even gave us their traditional flood story. Then all of us sang together in Spanish and prayed before bedtime. Bedraggled, we slept in our wet clothes on one of the sleeping platforms that lined the edge of the hut!

"Bedraggled" — 1953

On our way back we stopped again at the foreman's house to clean up before a Spanish service with the believers who worked for the banana company. The key believer, Ramón, had been saved from drinking, tobacco, and womanizing. He kept a supply of Bibles to sell, but when someone asked for the book on credit, Ramón would say, "When I was unsaved and wanted liquor or tobacco, I managed to find the money. If you really want a Bible, you can find the money." Amid the loose living prevalent in the banana towns, men like Ramón were the "salt of the earth!"

To Chirripó on My Own

Right after Marian and I went to Zent, I made another trip to the Indians before the final trimester of school. Since I had only been to Chirripó once with Dean, I wasn't sure of the trail. I asked Dick Richey to go with me, for he had gone there with Dean before I got to Costa Rica. Another CAM missionary in language school accompanied us.

On this trip I carried a fourteen-pound phonograph and four records made by Gospel Recordings the year before, using Alfredo from Zent as the speaker. When we finished playing the records, our bored host said, "I already know that language. Don't you have any Spanish records?" The Indian's intense desire to learn Spanish was a barrier I would have to overcome. But as I tried to learn the Cabécar language, some of the Indians began to realize that their own language had value.

My friend Chamorro was not at home. We spent all our time with his father, old *don* Joaquín. Joaquín's youngest daughter, Flor María, still unmarried, was the one who fed us. (She was later to become the mother of Isaac, one of the first Cabécars to be baptized.) Joaquín had built an unusual two-story storage building out of hand-hewn lumber. It even had a permanent roof of corrugated metal, the first one in Chirripó. Joaquín let us sleep in that building, though seeing scorpions in the rafters wasn't very conducive to a restful night. Eventually Joaquín's place became my jumping-off point in Chirripó. For months I went first to his house before branching out from there.

Finishing Spanish Study

As we started our third trimester of language school—when the smart students begin to feel comfortable with Spanish—I was in a store downtown trying to buy something. The clerk didn't understand me and asked, "Will you please speak in English?" That was humbling, but not as embarrassing as when I was asked to sing at a wedding. I had practiced with Marian at the piano and could handle the song although it was new. Yet when I stood up to sing at the church, another woman was playing, and on a pump organ. I couldn't catch the tune and had to give up.

Once at coffee break that trimester surprise visitors appeared at the language school. No one knew Jim and Elisabeth Elliot in those days, but his martyrdom less than three years later made his name familiar to believers everywhere. Jim and Betty had just been married in Ecuador and had taken a side trip to Costa Rica on their honeymoon to see Betty's brother, David Howard, who was studying at the language school. Dave had been my wrestling coach at Wheaton, and Marian had known Jim through the Foreign Missions Fellowship there. To us Jim and Betty were just acquaintances from college days that we enjoyed seeing again.

During the third trimester Marian returned to school part-time. She did an elective in orthography, and we both took the required course in advanced grammar. The men were required to preach in Spanish to their fellow students, which I did with fear and trembling. My message was about personal devotions, so basic to spiritual sustenance for missionaries who must challenge the kingdom of darkness. Marian's turn came when she was chosen to speak for the women of the class at our graduation ceremony in December.

Changing Focus

We ended our year of study by celebrating a unique Christmas. It was our first in Costa Rica, first with Peter, and first of our very own—we were not with either of our families. As we went downtown one evening to buy some toys for Peter and trimmings for a tree, we found the streets closed to traffic and thronged with noisy shoppers throwing confetti. On Christmas Eve we enjoyed fellowship with the believers at the downtown church. As each one left the building, he was handed a gift of candy and an apple, a lovely tradition at a time when apples were a once-a-year luxury—even for missionaries.

On New Year's Eve we were back at church for a long evening of singing and rejoicing at the Lord's goodness during the year. The preaching of the Word was more understandable than at the watch night service I had attended a year before on my first night in Costa Rica. We ended our first year in Costa Rica on our knees in prayer with the brethren, rising to sing *"Santo, Santo, Santo"* — "Holy, Holy, Holy" — as firecrackers outside signaled the New Year.

From now on, our focus would be on reaching the Cabécar Indians. We were confident that the new administrator of Moravia, near Chirripó, would soon let us set up a base on the ranch. After all, he was a fellow American. We were optimistic, not knowing that our search for a good location was to last ten years!

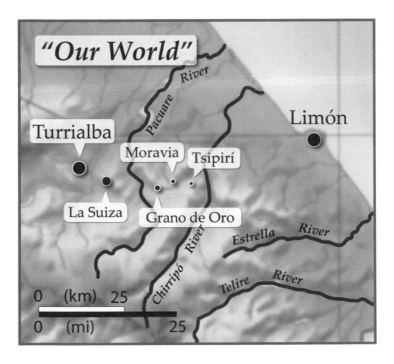

– 8 –
Jump-start from Turrialba
1954 to 1957

With language school behind us, we had no reason to continue living in San José. No one was pressuring us, but we began to feel increasingly uneasy about living in the capital, just waiting for a place to open up near Chirripó. I marked time by repainting and wallpapering the decrepit living room of our apartment in the Mission Home.

We were still hoping for a place in Moravia, but a trip in January of 1954 convinced me that the new administrator had no intention of selling or even renting us a place. Mr. Harvey told me in no uncertain terms, "I want everything on the farm to be under my control." At that point fellow missionaries Dick and Jean Richey were leaving the town of Turrialba and suggested we take over the duplex they had been renting. We jumped at the chance, for at least we would be a couple hours closer to the Indians. Moving early in March, we settled down to raise our family and figure out how to reach the Indians.

Turrialba, although not so close to the tribal area as we had hoped, proved to be a good place from which to jump-start our ministry. It was strategically located about two hours east of the capital. Buses ran several times a day to San José and once a day to outlying areas like Moravia, the jumping-off point for reaching the Indians in Chirripó.

In the '50s Turrialba was a sleepy town, with

Boarding the old bus to Moravia

one paved street and one telephone: a place where farmers came on Saturday and tied their horses to hitching posts; a place where Indians came when they had money from the sale of their bean crop; a place to buy supplies and to seek medical aid or government help. But it was also a progressive town, stimulated by the presence of a research station and school of agriculture sponsored by the Organization of American States.

Still Getting Oriented

We had finished formal language study, but I was still getting accustomed to speaking Spanish. Not long after we moved to Turrialba I was invited to preach at a country church in Cabeza de Buey. I had visited this same rural area a year before, during my first trimester of language school, but now I was on my own—still needing to read my painfully prepared message. As I began to speak, a downpour hit the tin roof of the little chapel made of hand-hewn lumber. I had to shout to be heard. There I lost my *pena*, "embarrassment," at speaking Spanish. One never speaks freely until he gets over being embarrassed about making mistakes. I buried my *pena* there in Cabeza de Buey!

Another matter of orientation was to finish studying the required books on Costa Rican history and geography. At that time new missionaries of our Mission were not allowed to vote in business meetings until we read these books—in Spanish— and passed a test, also in Spanish. In addition we had to memorize and sing the national anthem of our new country. Later recruits were not required to pass these tests, but we appreciated being obligated to learn more about Costa Rica—we might not have done so otherwise!

"The Lord Let Me Down Easy"

We very much needed our years in Turrialba. Marian always says, "The Lord let me down easy!" First, we had a year in San José getting oriented to Costa Rica. Then we spent several years in Turrialba learning to live near the area we would be working in for the rest of our lives. Finally, a decade after we first got to Costa Rica

we moved to the isolation of Tsipirí, three hours by jeep from
Turrialba. Why did the Lord delay our move to Tsipirí in spite of so
much prayer for a location close to the Indians? *He* knew we needed
those years of preparation.

Turrialba became a "hometown" to us. In fact, I ended up living
there longer than I'd lived in any other place up to that point. We still
went to San José to see doctors, to take care of government
paperwork, and to attend business meetings, but Turrialba was the
center of our universe. We enjoyed watching the town grow. Old
wooden buildings were rebuilt with cement. The dirt streets were
eventually paved and the hitching posts disappeared. Buses with
wooden bodies were replaced by modern ones, and the train quit
running after the highway to the Caribbean coast was opened.

Home Church in Turrialba

We loved the CAM church in Turrialba, one of the most active
evangelical churches in Costa Rica at the time. There was also a small
Baptist church in town and a large Catholic church that served the

whole area. Later, other churches would be established, but the church started in the 1930s by missionaries of The Central American Mission was the main evangelical church, located diagonally across the central park from the Catholic church.

The congregation was characterized by hearty singing, fervent praying, righteous living, and love of the brethren. The believers had already outgrown their need for missionary leadership. Although they did not need our input, the brethren loved missionaries and were glad for our participation. Marian taught a class of *señoritas*, helped oversee several child evangelism classes, and also helped with the weekly women's meetings. However, I refused to accept an office on the church board because I needed to keep my main focus on the Indians. Yet I did attend all services when I was not trekking.

Although there was no nursery in the church, we took Peter to all the services. If he got noisy, Marian would join the other young mothers on the sidewalk in front of the church. On rainy evenings she would take him home if he misbehaved during the meeting, for there was no shelter outside the church. Even when I was away Marian would take Peter along, carrying him three blocks until he was old enough to walk by himself.

We did not have to convince the brethren of the Indians' need for the gospel, for they fully shared our vision. They were accustomed to seeing Indians on the streets of Turrialba and were concerned for their souls. The church provided a place for Indians to sleep when in town overnight—others slept on the porch of the priests' house. Over the years the brethren prayed faithfully for our outreach to Chirripó—and still pray!

Trekking Alone

Even more than a hometown, Turrialba was a base for beginning to reach the Indians. I soon began a pattern of monthly trips. I would usually be on the trails among the Indians a week or ten days out of every month. From Turrialba I could reach Chirripó where the largest concentration of Cabécars was found, as well as the Pacuare area which had a fairly large number. I could also catch a train to Zent, Estrella, and other Indian areas.

Chatting on the trail

As I alternated trips to the various areas I kept pushing back the limits of my ignorance. Before we got to Costa Rica, we had only heard about the Indians of the Chirripó River Valley. Now I was discovering Indians in other areas who all spoke the same language. It was not until many years later that the term Cabécar became a unifying name for all these scattered groups, a name chosen because the people claimed to have migrated westward from an area near the border of Panama called San José Cabécar. In Chirripó the people would tell me, "God left us in San José Cabécar, and then we came here."

At first I felt reluctant to trek alone, so I began where Dean Lewis had taken me, the only area I knew. I took the bus from Turrialba to Moravia, found a family who would give me a meal and a place to sleep, and the next morning started off to Chirripó. On that very first trip alone the people in Moravia realized that I was a missionary. A few sought me out to inquire and talk of spiritual things. Though my goal was to reach Indians, I needed to "do the work of an evangelist" among these people as well.

A typical hut in the old days

How would I break into an unreached tribe with an unknown language? There is no formula, no "right" way. I observed, related, and acted in faith, always keeping tuned to the voice of the Holy Spirit. On early trips I would go to Chirripó or to other Cabécar areas and stay a few nights, gradually lengthening my stay to a week as I branched out, looking for more trails, making new friends, feeling my way. I always carried a pocket notebook to write the names of people and places, as well as to record words to be filed later. If there was a visitor in the home where I stayed, I would ask to go home with him so I could get to know a new family, a new area. Also, the young men were often glad to take me to new areas, even three days upstream—they were wife hunting!

Awesome Silence

I loved the long silent hours on the trail, passing giant trees choked with underbrush and vines. You can be sure of one thing: no

Tarzan could swing through those trees on vines—so thick was the vegetation! I sloshed through deep mud, over roots and rocks, saw wildflowers and strange birds—and occasional snakes. I trekked the chilly highland rain forest, panting up exhausting hills. I struggled through white-water rivers or walked through torrential rains. In the hot, humid lowlands I sweated profusely.

In those early days I took a snakebite kit for protection against the dreaded fer-de-lance, the most common poisonous snake in the area. And I carried my old canteen from army days, along with halazone tablets to purify the water. I carried a machete in a sheath strapped to my waist just as the Indians did. I needed it to cut vines and over-hanging branches or to chop a trail around a fallen tree. However, the Indians taught me not to use a machete to kill a snake but to cut a pole so I could be at a safe distance. And I also learned never, never to cut my own shortcut through the jungle—and to avoid trekking at night.

Alone, I could set my own pace. I learned to avoid falling headlong in the mud. One time my face barely missed the knife-edged stub of a plant. Another time I stumbled and fell, lying on my back at a 45-degree angle with my head in the bushes and my feet on the trail. I felt embarrassed, even though no one was there to laugh at me! Later as I jumped to the next "step" downhill, my foot wedged under a root—some trails were so steep the roots of trees formed "steps." I shuddered to think that with the momentum my ankle could have snapped, hours from nowhere, alone. But the Lord kept me safe.

Cutting a walking stick

I learned to cross rivers going diagonally upstream against the current, bracing myself with my pole upstream to keep my balance. I also learned when *not* to try to cross, and when a river was too deep. Muddy, raging rivers are not safe. I waited for the water to clear even if I had to wait a day or more. I learned to find a proper crossing place, usually a wide spot where I would find a trail to the edge of the river and cast-off poles of others who had crossed. If no pole was handy, I would cut one in the canebrake by the riverside.

Friends asked, "And what if you get hurt?" I used my best judgment, prayed for the Lord's covering, and moved in faith. Never did I get hurt. As I became accustomed to the jungle, I lost my uneasiness about its dangers. In fact, I developed my own proverb: "We feel secure among our accustomed dangers."

Undivided Attention

Traveling alone, I got better food, my own bed, and undivided attention. Also my host got undivided attention from me. Alone I could hear the Lord better, and I was not self-conscious about what a traveling companion might think. Trekking alone forced me to think for myself, to evaluate, to make decisions. I never knew if the Indians considered me a novelty or a nuisance. Nevertheless, they did give me something to eat and a place to sleep.

Giving hospitality to strangers was their "law." Nicanor, an old man down in the lowlands, once told me, "We have a legend that someday a white man will come speaking our language. God knows all languages, but Cabécar is the language God speaks. Someone who comes speaking Cabécar must be from God." This belief lay behind his hospitality.

The Indians would share their food—rather unappetizing to me. Their staple food was green bananas or plantains, boiled in a pot of beans or of meat if they had any. I never learned to like boiled bananas, but I needed the carbohydrates. Green boiled bananas are neither soft nor sweet. They have little flavor of their own. Occasionally I would be served a fried egg with a boiled banana which made the banana more palatable. As a drink, the Indians would give me their weak black coffee—homegrown and home-toasted. In the lowlands I would drink their homegrown cocoa, a greasy drink with no milk or sugar. Later I began carrying a small bottle of liquid sweetener.

Eventually I began to travel lighter. I no longer carried an air mattress—it weighed five pounds. With only a blanket, I would be given one of their crude beds, but with an air mattress I would be given the damp, dirt floor. I even left the snakebite kit at home, for I discovered there was little danger of snakebite if I kept to a trail. But I still carried an old army blanket, one change of clothes, a New Testament, a notebook to record observations, towel and soap, toothbrush and paste, as well as a razor. Shaving regularly helped me feel clean. Brushing my teeth satisfied my hunger for a familiar taste—the taste of toothpaste. I did not take any food, but kept a bit of hard candy in my pocket to assuage the longing for something more palatable than half-cooked beans and boiled green bananas. If I had my own food, my host gave me none. I wanted to be dependent on the Indians. Why? Their response was a good barometer of their feelings toward me.

Health Concerns

Health-wise, I had more concerns about food and dishes than I did about water. I would be concerned when my hostess handed me a gourd full of banana drink—water mixed with ripe banana. It was a great thirst quencher and very nutritious, but I wondered about germs when she would still be mashing the banana with her hand as she served me. Once a young mother picked up her baby in her left arm, then filled her mouth with water, held out a dirty plate in the other hand and rinsed it with the water she spewed out of her mouth. Fortunately, what she served me on that plate was food that I had to peel before eating.

My friends would serve me the best they had, but when I traveled in unknown areas it was not always that way. One time a woman served me a plate of rice that had maggots in it.

"Did you eat it?" asked Marian when I told her about it later.

"Yes, of course," I said. "It was cooked, wasn't it?"

Shocked, she retorted, "Yes, but *when?*"

Marian later had her own experience when she was handed a dirty fork to use. She asked for my dirty, sweaty bandanna to remove the old food. I guess she preferred fresh germs.

Indian mother bathing her baby with water from a seep hole

Water from a sparkling mountain stream was usually clean, especially if no one lived upstream. I learned that Indians do not drink from big rivers, or downstream from their bathing areas. I found out that even without outhouses in those days they did have fixed areas to relieve themselves. Once an Indian cautioned me not to drink from an apparently clean stream but said I could safely drink from the next small stream. Yet I did drink a lot of murky water from seep holes. When there is nothing else to drink, murky water is better than dehydration.

Perhaps the fear of germs and worry about amoebas is as dangerous as sickness and parasites. I did suffer from parasites and I did get diarrhea those first years, but I did not worry myself into a nervous breakdown. I just took my medicine and continued trekking. God has not died, and I did not die either.

Gathering Information

During our first year in Turrialba I spent a hundred nights in different Indian homes. I was always probing, making notes, drawing pictures, making observations on the culture, the clans, the customs, the religion. Once I asked Chamorro for a word and he replied, "Look in your notebook. You already wrote that word." As I traveled about, I used every word I knew, which delighted the Indians. When they realized I really wanted to learn their language, they would teach me new words. And since I alternated trips to various areas, they noticed the progress I had made since my last visit. As far as I was concerned, however, my progress was painfully slow.

I felt sorry for any Indian helper who answered my questions. I felt I had turned his brain inside out. I knew that what I needed to find out was in every Indian's head—language, culture, beliefs. But I *had* to get it out. At times I felt I was invading the secrets of his heart. But I *had* to find out. I never got all the information from any one person, just bits and pieces from many different people.

The language intrigued me. I learned that c*a* meant "place," but it also meant "time" or "weather" depending on what went with it—"pretty" c*a* meant "nice weather," but "good" c*a* meant "good land." Furthermore, to have a "good liver" meant to have good will, but to have a "hot liver" meant to be thirsty. The language also frustrated me—especially figuring out the verb system. I finally learned how to say "to be able." I had to say, "To me it is doable." I also discovered seven ways to express desire: "to wish for," "to hope for," "to pine for," "to need," and others—all very similar forms.

As far as the culture, one of the complexities that I soon learned was the matrilineal system, meaning that the clan name was passed through the mother. An Indian's mother and her sisters were all called "mother." And his sisters and the daughters of his mother's sisters were all called "sister." Never marry a "sister," for that would be incest. However, the daughters of your father's sisters are not sisters. They belong to a different clan. You may marry into your father's clan. In fact, to do so is preferable to marrying into an entirely different clan.

I also investigated their belief system. They believed that the seat of the emotions was the liver—not the heart—and that the mind was the seat of morality. However, they did not think of God as holy or moral, which would be "straight minded." They spoke of God as "clean," but to them that signified a sort of ritual cleanness, not moral purity.

In addition to all the information I gathered while on trek, we tried hiring an Indian to come to Turrialba for a month at a time so I could sit across the desk from him by the hour, pumping him for language data. The fellow who helped us in those early years was Alfredo, a bachelor with no family obligations. If he had been born in a different culture, he might have been a scholar. For him it was no chore to sit for hours discussing words. When I needed a break, Marian would work with him for a while, taking down data for later study.

Endlessly Filing 3x5s

When not on trek I worked at home in Turrialba, even if I did not have Alfredo's help. I would study the data I had gathered while on trek or had gotten from Alfredo. I spent hours analyzing all kinds of data—words and sentences I had recorded in my notebook, stories about where the Indians came from, legends, and beliefs about the spirit world.

Each word had to be recorded on a separate slip of paper with the date and the name of the person who gave me the data, as we had learned to do at the Summer Institute of Linguistics. I filled up thousands of 3x5 slips of paper. I would file them alphabetically in metal files, keeping separate files for nouns, verbs, and other parts of speech. Marian also helped file when she could fit it into her schedule.

Filing was only the beginning of the process. Everything had to be analyzed. Which sounds were significant enough to symbolize in an alphabet? What about tone and stress? How did nouns and adjectives go together? What about tenses of verbs? And on and on—a project to last a lifetime.

Not only did words have to be analyzed, but the culture had to be studied—the family structure and marriage customs, customs relating to birth and death. I also investigated beliefs about the afterlife and the spirit world. All this research into beliefs and customs, as well as the language, went on for years as I made more trips and gathered more information.

As I struggled to understand the language and the culture, I got bogged down. In my prayer notebook I recorded another stanza to my personal version of "My Faith Looks Up to Thee"—"My faith looks up to Thee, Oh Thou Ability, Enlightening God, Oh Thou to us Wisdom made, Who to us the promise gave, Take Thou my simple mind, And make it wise." Then I added this prayer affirming my faith: "Lord, by Thy grace I'll learn, not only to speak Chirripó but to make my analysis linguistically accurate."

Housekeeping in Turrialba

In between trips we were happy in our little duplex—just a bedroom, a living area, a small kitchen, and a little room barely big enough for Peter's crib. There was a tiny bathroom off the kitchen, with the lavatory actually in the kitchen. The kitchen sink was a small cement tub accessed through the "window," a wooden shutter.

We always worked together, arranging things so Marian could work as easily as possible in the circumstances we had to cope with. I built shelves for storage, as there were no cabinets. Our propane gas stove was a blessing, for the electricity in Turrialba at that time was hardly adequate for lighting, let alone cooking. While still in San José we had ordered a kerosene refrigerator from a missionary supply outlet in anticipation of living where there was no electricity at all. Every Saturday for more than forty years I filled it with three gallons of kerosene.

Outside the kitchen door of the duplex was a cemented area covered by a roof. There Marian could hang clothes without fear of the daily rains. In that area was the *pila*—a large cement laundry tub which was a feature of every Costa Rican home. Marian used the *pila* as a bathtub for baby Peter and also for scrubbing and rinsing clothes. Beyond the laundry area was a nice grassy *patio* surrounded by high wooden walls. Tropical plants and flowers grew along the wall—a private spot for our enjoyment and a safe place for Peter to play.

Painful Lessons

Peter was ten months old when we moved to Turrialba—such a joy to us as we watched him grow and learn. But one night not long after our move we had an unforgettable incident. We had put him to bed as usual, singing a song, praying for him, kissing him goodnight, then turning out the light and shutting the door. He had always been good about going to sleep, but that night we heard a sound and opened the door to find a triumphant-looking Peter who had discovered how to climb out of his crib—even though he had not yet learned to walk. Marian put him back in the crib and shut the door. Soon we heard him climb out a second time.

"Do you want him to stay in the crib?" I asked Marian.

"Yes."

"Are you willing for us we teach him?"

"Yes."

So I spanked Peter and put him in bed again and shut the door. Soon he was up a third time, so I repeated the spanking. And so it went, again and again. Peter was no longer smiling when he got up. Marian was drained emotionally. So was I. Finally, he stayed in bed and slept. The next night he got up several times, and we disciplined him. The third night he only got up three times. Never again did he get up without permission.

The process was so painful we have never forgotten it. It was agonizing to keep on punishing him, but we needed to learn to be consistent and Peter needed to learn to obey. Spanking was a teaching tool, teaching obedience by making it painful to disobey. Spanking was more than a punishment, it was a training method.

Once Peter learned to submit his will, we never again had such a battle. Of course, he tested the limits again, but the crucial battle had been won. To train a child, his will must be brought into submission. Usually there is a crisis that must be followed by consistent expectations and occasional spankings.

Irene's Visit

Family visits to the mission field were not very common back in the 1950s, so we were thrilled when Marian's sister, Irene Westling, spent a few weeks with us after she graduated from college. Her visit gave us the impetus to do some traveling around Costa Rica. We drove to the top of the Irazú Volcano, and then climbed on foot to a point where we could look down into the fearsome crater—not a placid crater lake but a murky greenish cauldron that was to erupt only a few years later. Alfredo, who was with us at the time, was exceedingly fearful—not of any visible danger but because of his perception of the spiritual forces connected with such mountains according to the Cabécar worldview.

We visited colleagues from the east coast to the west—for the country is less than two hundred miles wide. Near the end of Irene's visit we were in the Mission Home in the capital when a young man came to the door, looking for her. He had met Irene a few weeks earlier at a wedding in the States and wanted to connect with her again as he traveled on a missions trip. Both Irene and Marian were standing in the hallway when Dick appeared, but he could hardly tell which one was Irene. Marian and I made sure they had opportunities to get better acquainted before Irene returned to the States. Their brief acquaintance was happily to develop into marriage and a lifetime of ministry together.

One of the highlights of Irene's visit was an overnight to Chirripó, Marian's first trip to the main Cabécar area. With them along it took eight hours instead of my usual five. We had started at around 3,800 feet in Moravia, climbed a few hundred feet on a logging road, then went down a steep foot trail to the Tsipirí—a small stream. Then it was up again a few hundred feet, and finally down almost 2,000 feet—downhill was always harder, though uphill was more exhausting. Marian said the trek was even worse than I had led her to expect. Irene was amazed at the quantity of mud but disappointed not to see any snakes!

Chamorro's well-built house

Along the way we stopped at Chamorro's place. Marian was impressed with his friendliness and with the orderliness of his well-built hut. When she inquired about the ages of his children, he pulled out his notebook and figured out their ages from the records he had made of their date of birth. In those days the Indians did not celebrate birthdays and did not know how old they were. From Chamorro's we went around to his father's place. Old *don* Joaquín welcomed us kindly, even going two hundred yards to a spring to get water for Marian and Irene to wash their feet, for the seep hole near his house was dry.

The next morning we retraced our steps up the hill, stopping to rest in a pasture. The whole Chirripó River Valley was spread out below us. We saw no villages or roads, but noticed a few clearings and several patches of banana plants which indicated a hut must be close by. Looking to our right, we saw the mountains rising toward the central range where the river was born. We could see *Cerro de la Muerte*, "Death Peak," but could not quite make out the massive *Cerro Chirripó*, the highest peak in Costa Rica, over 13,000 feet high. Across the river from us was the Matama Range, beyond which lay the even more isolated Telire Valley where a few Cabécars lived. To our left smaller mountains obscured the Estrella Valley—home to other Cabécars—and the Caribbean Sea less than thirty miles away. Beyond the mountains far to our right was the Pacuare River along which more Cabécars lived.

Chirripó Valley – "Nothing promising about it"

The panorama that sunny morning was impressive. No white man lived anywhere in this area.

"Marian, this is our promised land!" I exclaimed. "This is the land the Lord spoke about when He gave us the promise of Psalm 2:8: *'Ask of me, and I will give you the nations as your inheritance.'*"

"There's nothing promising about it to me," groaned Marian, already exhausted from the trek.

I recognized she was not made for trekking, but she had other more important gifts, without which we would never succeed. She was the helpmeet I needed. Together we would fulfill our then embryonic vision!

Climbing up from the pasture, we turned off the main trail to pay a visit to Antolín. At least that gave us an hour's rest before finishing the trek back to Moravia where we could clean up and change clothes before catching a bus to Turrialba the following morning, and then another bus to San José where we had left Peter with fellow missionaries. When we got to Mr. Harvey's place in Moravia— George Harvey was the new administrator of the ranch—he had news for us.

"Did you know that the bus that brought you here is not running anymore?"

Now what? The next morning I decided I would walk the six miles to where some men were logging. Perhaps I could find a truck to town. As I was leaving, Mr. Harvey called me back.

"Look," he said, "I realize I need to go to Turrialba. Let me get ready. I'll take you and Marian and her sister." For him, that was a big kindness. For once, Mr. Harvey was an angel!

Disappointed Hopes

As the months wore on, informant work was most discouraging—Alfredo was not available. Parasites and minor ailments sapped our strength. A trip I planned to make in order to scout out the Talamanca area did not materialize. I did, however, make a couple of trips to an area where a group of Cabécars lived along the Pacuare, a river running roughly parallel to the Chirripó. At home we worked on language analysis and enjoyed little Peter—active, alert, inquisitive, and mischievous.

On a routine trip to Chirripó I had a chance meeting with a man who owned land close to Moravia, the ranch which was the jump-off point to the main trail to Chirripó. This fellow was an Austrian duke now residing in Costa Rica, who—like Mr. Harvey—had acquired the land by extending credit to the original developer of the whole Moravia area. The developer defaulted, leaving the duke with unwanted property. He promised to give me a piece!

We still kept hoping for permission for a hut in Chirripó territory as well. But we realized that even if we lived there, we would have difficulty contacting any Indians beyond our immediate neighbors. With no villages, nor any market where people congregated, it was a hut-to-hut ministry—with huts separated usually by an hour of more of steep, muddy trails.

To live in the Moravia area would provide access to Chirripó, as well as bring us into contact with Indians who came there to sell corn and beans and buy soap, sugar, and other supplies. Furthermore, we would be connected by road to Turrialba and the outside world. True, it was just a one-lane unpaved road snaking through the mountains, but it was usually passable in spite of occasional landslides and cave-ins.

The duke's lawyer was to meet me in Moravia to arrange the deal. I made more than one trip, but he repeatedly failed to keep his appointments. Then suddenly, only a few months after I met the duke, he died leaving no will. Now we were back where we started, living in Turrialba with no prospect of any place closer to the Indians. Even though Turrialba was a convenient and strategic location, to us it was always temporary. We were sorely disappointed not to get property closer to Chirripó. But we kept on praying, and many prayed with us.

Scouting out Talamanca

As I alternated trips to Chirripó, to Pacuare, and to Zent where Alfredo lived, I kept hearing references to Talamanca and to the

Bribris. I found myself puzzled as to what was in the Talamanca area near the Panama border. Were the people there the same as those in Chirripó and other areas I was becoming familiar with? I was already aware that the Indians in these areas all spoke the same language. They considered themselves to be *ditsä si*, the "true people." I needed to survey Talamanca to better define the limits of my field of ministry. If the Indians in Talamanca were different, I wanted to survey the need for a couple to work among them.

The trip I hoped to make to Talamanca with a colleague did not materialize, so early in 1955 I struck out on my own. The Lord provided an unexpected companion, a believer I encountered on the train. Mario was going to Talamanca and agreed to take me—one of the few times I ever paid a guide. He knew the area and proved to be an excellent guide. At the end of the railroad line we crossed the Estrella in a dugout, and then took a *burro carril*, a mule cart running on old narrow-gauge tracks abandoned by the United Fruit Company. I was fascinated to ride through groves of cocoa trees, interspersed with the homes of Jamaicans whose forebears had come to Costa Rica to build the railroad. These folks still spoke English, although I sometimes had a hard time understanding them.

After spending the night in a crude hut poorly protected from the rain, Mario and I crossed the Sixaola River by dugout to visit his brother in Panama—there was free access between the countries in that isolated area. Once back in Costa Rica we walked for hours over abandoned tracks, finally reaching Suretka where a Jamaican gave us supper. In Talamanca three races—Jamaicans, Latins, and Indians—lived together and intermingled, sometimes intermarrying and learning each other's languages.

The next day we reached Amubre—the center of Talamanca. Simón Mayorga, an Indian leader, hosted us very graciously like my friend Chamorro in Chirripó. Simón was trilingual—speaking not only his own language but Spanish and Jamaican English. He served us chocolate, a greasy sugarless drink, even less palatable than the black coffee in Chirripó. Simón took us all over the area. We saw the rundown Catholic church, where at that time a German priest came once a year to say mass, baptize, and marry, as another German did in Chirripó. Simón also took us to see the "princess," the descendant of an American anthropologist who had married a Bribri in the late 1800s. She spoke no English and looked like an Indian.

Simón's house, like all the others in Talamanca, was built on posts and had a split palm floor—easy to keep clean because trash fell through the cracks in the floor. Quite a contrast to the dirt floors of the Cabécar Indians. The hammocks which served for seating were neatly woven, unlike the crude bark hammocks of the Cabécars. Furthermore, these Indians carried loads in baskets on their backs, rather than nets as in Chirripó. Another contrast was the proximity of the homes, only fifteen minutes apart along flat trails rather than an hour apart by steep trails. And the rivers were navigable in contrast to the white-water rivers in Chirripó and Pacuare. I almost found myself wishing I had been called to Talamanca!

From Amubre I hiked another four hours with Mario up to San José Cabécar. I wanted to see the place, for in Chirripó the people had told me, "Sibu [the name of their god] left us in San José Cabécar. Then we came here." There really wasn't anything to see, just a few huts, but at least I could tell the people back in Chirripó that I had been to their motherland. It would be several more years before I learned the true significance of San José Cabécar as residence of the *sakichawí* who guarded the sacred stones which the people believed controlled the destiny not only of the Indians but of the whole world.

Return from Talamanca

On our way back the next afternoon we lost our way. Darkness fell, but we continued on by moonlight, finally reaching a hut on the bank of the Urén. Unwelcome there, we walked downstream to where Mario cajoled a boatman into poling us in a dugout to the petroleum company camp. Next morning we traveled back through land the United Fruit Company had abandoned a generation before when a disease ravaged the bananas, and floods devastated the plantations and bridges. Reaching the Caribbean, we took an old WWII Landing Ship to Limón, the port city where I caught a train for Turrialba.

The last few days trekking through Talamanca, my right leg kept itching. When I got home someone identified the cause of the itching—five *tórsalos*! Larva of the botfly had penetrated my skin through insect bites and were burrowing and growing. The local remedy worked well: cover each spot with a piece of adhesive tape for twenty-four hours until the worm dies and can be squeezed out. That simple remedy stood us in good stead many times over the years of living in the tropics.

During my time in Talamanca I recorded language data to compare with my Cabécar data at home. Many of the words I wrote down were very similar to Cabécar. Others were quite distinct. One of the interesting things I noted was that the Indians in Talamanca could count to at least one hundred in their own language. In Chirripó folks could count only to five, then had to resort to Spanish numbers—which they had learned as they sold their crops and bought supplies. The two languages turned out to be closely related, but different enough to warrant a separate translation of the New Testament. They were two separate languages, not dialects of the same language. However, both groups shared the same religion and social system.

Even before this trip Marian and I had begun praying for the Lord to raise up a testimony in Talamanca. Now my data confirmed our desire for new workers to cover this territory, workers who would be prepared to translate the Scriptures for this tribe—now known as the Bribri Indians. When I reached home I wrote to CAM headquarters, communicating the need for workers for Talamanca. I hoped someday to see Bribri churches relating to Cabécar churches.

Our First Daughter

After the trip to Talamanca I made another to Chirripó, and then Alfredo came to work with us for a month. Soon it was time for us to go to San José to wait for the birth of our second child. We settled in at the Mission Home, where Peter, now two years old, had fun playing with other missionary kids. Since meals were served at the home in those days, Marian could get more rest and would be close to the hospital of the Latin America Mission.

Priscilla May arrived on June 7, 1955. For each of our children we asked the Lord to guide us about a name, but we had a hard time settling on a girl's name. We wanted a Bible name, but had no special reason for choosing the name Priscilla; yet it turned out to be prophetic, as did the names of all our children. We hoped their lives would reflect the characteristics of the one for whom they were named. Priscilla's middle name, May, was for Marian's mother, May Westling, as well as for mine, Leila Mae Jones.

We rejoiced in the Lord's blessing us with another child, for *"children are an heritage of the Lord"* according to Psalm 127:3. The day we brought Priscilla back from the hospital, Peter came running up for his first glimpse of his baby sister. He loved her from the start and never showed any signs of jealousy. He proved to be a wonderful big brother to her and the siblings born later.

Our Costa Rican friends rejoiced that the Lord had given us a daughter. Everyone exclaimed, *"Ya tiene la pareja."* (Now you have a pair—a boy and a girl.) To Costa Ricans this was important. We too were happy to have both a son *and* a daughter.

Larger House for a Larger Family

Within two weeks we were back at home in Turrialba. In preparation for Priscilla's birth we had found a larger house. The little duplex, though inexpensive to rent, was now too small. We took the plunge of faith, paying fifty dollars a month instead of just six, out of a total of slightly more than two hundred. We had also increased our giving beyond a tithe, another act of faith. As we increased our giving, the Lord increased our support, but first we gave.

Our new house was old and termite-ridden, but large and airy. Across the hall from the bedrooms was a dark room that we used for a study, large enough for a desk for each of us. The kitchen was filthy and still had the sink outside the shuttered window, but at least it was big enough to work comfortably. Best of all was a very large, fenced-in yard full of fruit trees.

Peter and Priscilla—early in 1956

Peter had plenty of space to play, both in the house and outside. Thais, the young girl who had volunteered to tend Peter in church in San José when he was an infant, was now back in Turrialba with her family. She came often on Saturdays to entertain Peter, pulling him around the yard in his big red wagon. Soon Priscilla was a passenger as well. Peter himself delighted in entertaining his baby sister and finding ways to make her laugh. Sometimes Thais would take both Peter and Priscilla to the park. Her sweet spirit continued to bless us year after year.

Life with a Maid

Behind our house was a small room and bath for a live-in maid. Yes, we had a maid. Friends in Turrialba had recommended a girl from the country church in Cabeza de Buey. She lived with our friends while we were in the duplex and worked for us by the day. Once we had a larger place, she moved in with us. Celina became almost like a member of the family.

Household help was not expensive in those days, but having a girl around the house was a potential source of problems, even with a good girl like Celina. Marian and I had snagged on this with occasional part-time help while we were still in language school. At first, having a maid seemed like a blessing, then it just seemed like a necessity, or even a necessary evil. Occasionally it seemed like an evil. Celina was truly a blessing, but even so, Marian and I did not always agree about how to manage her work. It was I who had to learn over the years that *Marian* was the one to give orders to the maid and to pay her. One day as I was seeking victory over this issue, I wrote still another verse to the hymn that had inspired my faith before. This new verse read, "My faith looks up to Thee, Oh Thou omnipotent untiring God, Thou who exhaustless art, Gird up my fainting heart, Infuse in me Thy power, Almighty God."

In those days there was more work than Marian could manage by herself. Every day the unvarnished wooden floors had to be swept, mopped, and polished with a long-handled brush until they shone like a mirror. Once a week they had to be waxed. This was standard routine in every Costa Rican home. In the kitchen all food had to be prepared from scratch. Marian did most of the cooking, but appreciated Celina's help. Convenience foods were not available, and the few canned goods were beyond our price range. Besides, with fresh vegetables and fruits available year-round, who would want to eat canned food? Supermarkets were nonexistent in those early years, so every day the "girl" would take a *bolsa*, a colorfully woven bag, and make the rounds—meat market, vegetable market, bakery, and grocery. Peter would beg to go with her, but when he tired he gave Celina a hard time, refusing to walk.

When our family increased, Marian's aunt gave us money for a washing machine. It was just a wringer washer, but it was a blessing not to have to do diapers by hand any longer, to say nothing of the muddy clothes I brought home from trips. I would wear the same clothes every day as I trekked, saving my one set of clean clothes to sleep in each night and then to wear on the trip home. Washing was a joint project: Marian would wash and rinse the clothes and Celina would hang them out to dry, rushing outside to rescue them if the daily afternoon rains started early.

Of course, the clothes had to be starched and ironed as well in those days before permanent press clothing. Marian even had to cook the starch on the stove. Celina, like all Costa Rican girls, did a superb job of ironing, and would have ironed even underwear and socks if Marian had allowed her to do so. Ironing was a cultural value, like shining the floors and keeping cars waxed.

Welcome to Newcomers

Just a few weeks after Priscilla was born, Marian's sister Irene returned to Costa Rica, now as the wife of Dick Foulkes whom she had met the year before. This time it was not just a visit. They came to settle down and begin teaching at the seminary of the Latin America Mission in San José. Few missionaries have such a privilege—family members living in the same country!

Around that same time we also welcomed Bob and Dot Weeber and their two children to Costa Rica. They had joined The Central American Mission and were slated to work in Talamanca after finishing language school. We were thrilled at this answer to our prayers for someone to work among the Indians of Talamanca. What made us especially happy was that we had known the Weebers for several years—Dot had been Marian's roommate at Wheaton. The Weebers were prepared for translation work, having majored in Greek and then studied at the Summer Institute of Linguistics the summer before Marian and I had our linguistic training there.

A few months after the Weebers' arrival as I was on the train in January of 1956 returning from a visit to the Indians in Zent, a pastor handed me a newspaper account about five missionaries killed in Ecuador at the hands of the Auca Indians. One was Jim Elliot who had been Bob Weeber's roommate, and two of the others had also been students at Wheaton during our time there. The story of these martyrs became well-known among the believers in Costa Rica. Marian and I hosted Phil Saint, a brother of the pilot who had been killed, when Phil presented the story of the martyrdom at the CAM church in Turrialba.

Help from a Language Expert

By this time we had been working on the Cabécar language for a year and a half, and felt the need of advice about the alphabet, as well as confirmation of our phonetic analysis. One of our professors at SIL was Dr. Eugene Nida of the American Bible Society. As head of the Translation Department, Dr. Nida spent some time in Costa Rica in 1955 working on a revision of the Reina Valera, the standard version of the Bible in Spanish. He was gracious enough to give us some help with our analysis.

Alfredo traveled with us to the capital for an afternoon with Dr. Nida. We needed a native speaker to pronounce words so that Dr. Nida could check our analysis. We had already written up our tentative conclusions and had even recorded illustrative words on tape, although tape recorders were not yet in common use.

Dr. Nida confirmed our analysis as to what sounds were significant and needed to be symbolized in an alphabet. Up to this point we had written data with a modified phonetic alphabet. Now we had to switch to characters available on a typewriter. Deciding on the alphabet for an unwritten language was quite a responsibility! We wanted the language to be as easy to read as possible. We hoped to use letters available on a Spanish keyboard. A few Cabécars had already learned to read Spanish, although their understanding was minimal. Since Spanish is written phonetically, it was easy to learn to read—even if you could not understand what you were reading!

The Cabécar language has certain consonants common in English but not in Spanish, such as "sh," "w," and the "j" sound as in "Jones." Our biggest problem was the "j" because the Spanish alphabet uses "j" for the sound we symbolize in English with "h." Marian and I struggled with that decision even after Dr. Nida left. Our decisions lasted for a generation, until English became so widely known in Costa Rica that other symbols could be used.

How would we write the vowels? Cabécar has "a, e, i, o, u" with the same sounds as those vowels in Spanish, which made it easy. But Cabécar also has nasalized vowels, which we symbolized by underlining: "a, e, i, o, u." Nasalization makes the difference between the meaning of certain words: *ca* means "no, not" whereas *ca̠* means "time, place." The most common vowel in Cabécar turned out to be one pronounced somewhat like the "u" in the English word "but." Since Spanish does not have this vowel, we had to decide how to write it. At first we chose to use an upside down "v" and even had our typewriter modified for it. Obviously, this was not a good long-term solution! Dr. Nida advised us to use an "a" with two dots over it: *ä*.

Analyzing the sound system is the first, and easiest, stage of preparation for translation. Later we would have to analyze the morphology—the way words are constructed—and the grammar also. We were grateful for Dr. Nida's help in getting over this first hurdle.

Back to Mundane Routine

After the excitement of welcoming a new baby and the arrival of Marian's sister and husband, as well as the arrival of colleagues for the work in Talamanca, plus the session with Dr. Nida, life settled back into a routine. I resumed my treks to the Indians and the tedious language study when home in Turrialba. We all took turns being sick—nothing serious, just parasites, or colds, but still debilitating. Leishmaniasis, an unhealing tropical sore caused by an insect bite, led me to seek medical attention in the form of thirteen large daily injections with a drug also used for venereal disease.

On my trips I was not battling direct opposition but rather what I called *the numb indifference of satisfied paganism*. The Cabécars were steeped in animism covered with a very thin veneer of Catholicism. The old German priest who lived in Turrialba made an annual trip to Chirripó to marry those who had started living together since his last visit, and to baptize babies born during the year. Of course, only those who lived near one of the two chapels he had built years before were in any way affected by his visits. As far as I could tell from talking with the Indians, Padre Enrique had done no teaching. The people still continued the practices handed down from their forebears.

Unwelcome

As I trekked one day, impeded by the ever-present mud, rocks, and roots, I was exhausted from climbing. I was also hungry, for I had eaten nothing all day but an egg and a few bananas. Now rain was beginning to fall and night was coming on. My pack pained my shoulders though it was loaded with only the minimum gear. I was alone on an unknown trail, for my guide had only taken me part of the way.

Through the banana patch I spied the hut that I had been looking for. As I approached, several men greeted me, but no one invited me to enter. Glancing in the opening that served as a doorway, I made out a crude curtain surrounding a bed. Finally, the man of the house spoke.

"Do you want to spend the night?" he asked.

"Yes, if it's all right with you," I answered, for there was no other hut within an hour.

"You sleep here," he said, taking me to a smaller hut behind the main house. "We'll give you a guide tomorrow."

I sensed that I was most unwelcome.

Later another man invited me to the main house for a drink of their home-brewed beer. I made it clear that I did not drink, but he still insisted I would be welcome. The place was full of people when I entered. They seemed to resent my repeated refusals to drink.

"Didn't I tell you not to come into this hut?" barked the man of the house, stepping from behind the curtain.

At that instant I realized that he was a shaman, trying to cure a sick person behind the curtain. Apologizing, I retreated hastily to the little hut, feeling somewhat fearful—the only time I ever thought I might possibly be in danger from the Indians.

The next morning I needed a guide to find the trail across the ridge between Pacuare and Chirripó, but no one wanted to leave the healing ceremony, not even for money. Finally, a man guided me an hour to a fork in the trail.

"Follow this one," he said. That afternoon I got to the Chirripó River—and familiar territory.

Still Trekking, Still Learning, Still Praying

As I continued to trek the lonely trails, I ran into a round of all-day *chicha* parties. It was years before I learned that the corn harvest was the reason behind these "festivities." For this celebration the women made the *chicha* by chewing the corn and spitting into a trough and then leaving it to ferment. It was their strongest brew, a real corn beer, made not from the corn they grew to sell to outsiders, but from Indian corn which they raised only for themselves. The five types—white, yellow, red, black, and mixed—were sacred. During the celebration they placed some corn on the trail so that "the mother of the earth" would notice their respect and grant them a good harvest the following year. When I told Marian about this, she began to pray that someday these celebrations would be replaced by a Thanksgiving celebration to the true God.

Isolated Cabécar compound

When I ran into *chicha* parties, it was useless for me to do more than move on. The parties went on for days. Everyone was drunk, even the children. Fights broke out, babies were neglected, illicit relationships occurred. When the *chicha* finally ran out, the family was left in a stupor and the hut was littered with filth.

Each trek added to my knowledge of their customs and language, as well as giving me orientation to the Indians' worldview. In time, we would see how their worldview made sense—at least to them. Once I understood their point of view, I could relate the gospel to their life. Trekking also gave me a picture of the total area inhabited by the Cabécars, who were scattered throughout the mountains of the Caribbean watershed along four major rivers: the Pacuare, the Chirripó, the Estrella, and the Telire. Their territory extended from the Turrialba area all the way southeast to Talamanca—and a few even lived on the Pacific side of the central mountain range.

The constant clash with immorality, decadence, and filth, in addition to the linguistic and geographical barriers, constituted a challenge that demanded all that I was spiritually, mentally, and physically. Yet I knew that someday God would raise up believers from the huts scattered through the mountains. Marian and I continued to pray for the people. Many others were praying as well.

Translation Conference

We kept feeling the need for advice and stimulus in our preparation for translation, so we were glad when a special gift made it possible for us to fly to Guatemala in April of 1956 for a conference sponsored by the Bible Society. We would be gone several days, which made it hard to leave the children, but Marian's sister was willing to keep them.

For us it was the first of many trips to Guatemala, almost a thousand miles north of Costa Rica, and a much larger country. Indians in tribal dress were everywhere, in contrast to the few isolated Indian areas in Costa Rica. At the conference we did not get much help as the sessions were focused on the various Mam languages of Guatemala, but we did get the stimulus we were looking for. Even though the Guatemalan highlands were chilly, very chilly for Marian who always was sensitive to cold weather, we were delighted to mingle with other translators and hear of their problems, and to interact with Dr. Nida again, as well as Dr. Wonderly of the Bible Society's work in Mexico.

Among the attendees were Ed and Pauline Sywulka. We had contacted them by mail before joining CAM and Ed had been our first teacher at SIL. He had also done the linguistic survey that led CAM to seek a missionary couple to work among the Chirripó Indians. After the conference the Sywulkas invited us to go with them for a couple of days to see the work in their field in northern Guatemala, fairly close to the border of Mexico. The time spent with them was delightful and strengthened our link to this special couple who were our role models, not only as translators but as parents of a large and godly family.

Back to Turrialba

Returning from Guatemala, we were glad to be home with our own little family. The children were a deep, satisfying joy. Priscilla's first birthday was a happy day for us. Marian had a special time of prayer for her future, as she did for each child on his birthday. We took Priscilla to a store and bought her some pretty shoes to match the dress that a college friend of Marian's had made, and then went for a walk in the park—Priscilla had just learned to walk. In those days we had to pay a heavy duty on gifts like that little dress, but we learned to accept the cost rather than disappoint the giver. Priscilla looked so cute in that outfit that we took her to a local photographer to capture the moment. That picture still hangs above our bed, with the one-year photos of our other children.

Peter was now three years old, but still didn't talk much. Our pediatrician told us it was common for children growing up in a bilingual environment to be slower to learn to talk. He certainly wasn't slow in any other area! Except in potty-training—we were still learning how to raise kids.

Talamanca Again

During the time Bob and Dot Weeber were in language school, I traveled again to Talamanca to introduce Bob to the territory where he hoped to work. I still needed a guide, so that made three of us trekking together, plus a friend who came along with Bob. Four people together on the trail naturally break into two groups, which meant Bob could not fully benefit from the trip. Furthermore, I felt awkward appearing at the door of a hut to ask for hospitality for so many strangers. I was doing a serious piece of diplomacy, hoping to establish an entrance for the gospel. As I felt my way in the evenings with my host, he was distracted by my companions.

Not fully convinced that Talamanca was the place the Lord wanted him to serve after he finished language school, Bob later surveyed a tribe across the border in Panama. While he was on that trip, his baby daughter came down with polio during the last epidemic to hit Costa Rica before the development of polio vaccine. Such a large number of children were afflicted that there were not enough physical therapists in the country to tend them all, so the Weebers had to return to the States. They have continued to support us and to pray faithfully for the Indians of Talamanca and Chirripó.

Aziel, Mario, and Bob pray during the survey of Talamanca

More Help from the Experts

A year after Dr. Nida's visit to Costa Rica, Dr. William Wonderly came from Mexico to continue the revision of the Spanish Bible, but gave us a few hours of his time. Again we took Alfredo to San José for the occasion. With Dr. Wonderly's help we made a few changes in the practical alphabet we had worked out with Dr. Nida. More importantly, he checked out with Alfredo our suspicion that Cabécar might be a tonal language, something which translators fear.

Yes, Cabécar *was* tonal, meaning that the difference between a high or a low tone on a word could change its meaning. We had already observed that the word for "father," was -*ká*, but the word for "tooth" was -*ka*. There were other pairs of words differentiated only by tone. Fortunately for us, this did not turn out to be a major feature of the language.

Dr. Wonderly urged us to move closer to Chirripó. He realized that living in Turrialba was a hindrance to our learning progress. We were quite aware of our need to move, but where? We had followed all the leads we had. Each had led to a dead end. What could we do but stay in Turrialba, praying until the Lord opened a door?

Shortly after Dr. Wonderly's visit, we tried out our revised alphabet. Within minutes Indians who could read some Spanish were easily reading a simple account of the creation story. Only twenty-three lines, but it was a beginning! After that we worked out with our helpers a short version of the Ten Commandments and a story about the birth of Christ. Though it was just a tiny beginning, to us it was a big stimulus—especially since the alphabet seemed workable and the Indians showed much interest in this first attempt to write their language.

1957—First Furlough

By the fall of 1956 we began wrapping up our work. We would complete our four-year term on December 31. Furlough was due in January, and our thoughts were on showing off the children to their grandparents. Just before we left for the States we celebrated New

Year's Eve once more with the brethren in the Turrialba church, as we remembered His faithfulness to us fledgling missionaries.

We were to fly to Miami where my family—three carloads— would meet us. But Peter was sick, very ill with pneumonia. The pediatrician insisted we postpone the trip until the next flight three days later. Yet my parents had already left Alabama. How could we notify them? The airline assured us they would page the family at the Miami airport. Imagine our chagrin when we arrived on January 17 to find the family frantic after a three-day wait.

"You should have seen your mother's face when you didn't show up on Monday!" said Von, my sister-in-law, for they had *not* been notified and one car had already returned. The others were preparing to leave Miami without us.

With hardly a moment to greet each other, they hurried us into the cars for the eighteen-hour drive to Phenix City, Alabama—an inauspicious beginning to our year of furlough! David, my youngest brother, had bought a car for us to use on furlough, but I had driven only occasionally during our four years in Costa Rica. I asked Daddy to drive the first few hours until I could readjust to the States.

Endless Furlough Travels

Soon we were on the road again, this time to Pennsylvania, a hard two-day trip from Alabama. Priscilla, now nineteen months old, refused to eat anything but cornflakes when we stopped for meals. Yet as we drove she amused herself by the hour, folding and refolding a handkerchief! During our stay with Marian's parents in Pittsburgh, Peter and Priscilla had their first experience with snow. We bundled them up in the warm clothes the Westlings had bought them and went out the back door with the camera. Peter and I had fun making a snowman, but Priscilla stood in the snow and cried with fear as she touched the cold stuff.

We really ran our little green Chevrolet that year, driving twenty-eight thousand miles, touching twenty-three states, D.C., and Canada, and speaking almost a hundred times. We have never topped that! But we were free to move—twelve dollars a day covered gas and meals. At night we usually stayed with friends, relatives, or supporters. We had come home from Costa Rica feeling not up to par physically, and travels were wearying, but the Lord's people were very kind, and our hearts were refreshed as we fellowshipped with them.

"We pray for you every morning at 5:30," an older couple told us in Alabama.

"We know you better than you know us," said a Sunday School superintendent in New Jersey, indicating that our letters helped them pray intelligently.

Some asked, "How is Alfredo? Is he helping you?" This showed us that they were praying for our language helper, as well as for us.

"This is the first time I ever really understood what you are doing!" remarked a business man, after we'd shown our slides and demonstrated the technique of reducing a language to writing.

As we reported to churches on Sundays or at prayer meetings, our focus was that people might understand and pray more effectively. Though we needed more financial support, we determined not to hint at our needs. When folks occasionally asked about our support, we told them our situation. But we knew the Lord could provide whether people knew our needs or not. God had already proved that to us!

SIL — More Linguistic Study

Furlough travels included a prolonged stay in Oklahoma. From mid-June to mid-August we studied at the Summer Institute of Linguistics for a second time. I took the intermediate course and Marian took second year. Before we left Costa Rica we had gathered materials to work on at SIL, but our main goal was to get help with analyzing the Cabécar verb system. While Marian's classes were more theoretical, mine were very practical, giving me a thorough review of first year as well as extra help with analyzing sound systems and tone. I was able to solve a nagging problem with the way "d" alternated with "r." But no one found the key to the verbs, although the professors, with field experience in Mexican languages, gave us personal help.

"You have a problem!" said one linguist. Discouraging!

Each day at SIL Marian wrote a postcard to Peter and Priscilla, who stayed that summer with her parents in Pittsburgh. We had been advised not to bring the children if we could find someone to keep them. Marian had more free time for study, but it was hard for her to be away from them for so long.

In the SIL dorm and dining hall we made friends with other budding translators—more names on our mailing list! At church on Sundays we enjoyed fellowship centered on the Lord—and developed more friendships. Exchanging letters over the years with these new friends and others scattered around the world enriched our lives, as well as informed us about what God was doing worldwide.

Final Months of Furlough

From SIL we headed straight back to the children. Marian was anxious to see them and to settle down for the last few weeks before our third child was born. I continued to travel, but missed one missions conference because the baby was late. Before our return to Costa Rica I responded to a last minute, urgent invitation to speak at a conference in Maryland. At three of the meetings only a dozen people were present. Never were there more than thirty-five at any meeting, but the Lord was present. Amazingly, one couple began to support us financially, and another couple became missionaries themselves! One never knows what God has in a non-promising contact. So we kept our eyes on Him: What were His purposes? What was He doing?

Our Third Child

Susanna Faith was born October 16, 1957, in Pittsburgh. We named her Susanna after the Susanna who was one of the followers of Jesus, according to the gospel of Luke. In line with my Methodist heritage we also named her for Susanna Wesley, the mother of John

Wesley. An exemplary mother, she prayed with each of her many children and instructed them in the fear of the Lord. The name "Faith" was an echo of our own faith for our family. In announcing her birth we included the phrase from Psalm 127:3, *"Lo, children are an heritage of the Lord."* We were raising a family for Him. In our prayer letter that month we wrote:

> *We know that you will pray for Peter, Priscilla, and Susanna's physical well-being, but to us their spiritual well-being is far more important. Already we are systematically planting the Word of God in their minds in order that "from a child" they might know "the scriptures which are able to make...wise unto salvation." Pray that the Lord will very definitely be dealing with them, bending their wills and inclining their hearts to Himself. This He must do if our efforts to instill scriptural truths are to produce God-fearing children. We are keenly conscious that "Except the Lord build the house, they labor in vain that build it."*

Furlough Trials

Before baby Susanna was a month old the whole family was heading south for more meetings and visits. Sickness plagued Marian and the children as we traveled to Alabama and South Carolina. Marian ended up in the hospital for several days with tonsils so swollen she could hardly breathe, let alone swallow. And I ended up with three little ones to look after. But the Lord was good. Our missionary friends from Guatemala, the Sywulkas, were on furlough in Columbia at the time and put up with us very graciously, though their house was small and their family was large.

On our way back to Pittsburgh in December the roads through the mountains were snowy and icy and the temperature near zero. By the time we reached Marian's parents' home, Priscilla was almost frozen—unknown to us the heat in the back seat was not functioning. Grandma Westling sat by the fireplace cuddling Priscilla until she warmed up.

Back to Costa Rica

Soon it was Christmas and time to say good-bye to Marian's parents. From Pittsburgh we drove to Alabama for a last visit with my family and finally to Miami for the return flight to Costa Rica on January 16, 1958. In our prayer letter we wrote:

> *"The hearts of the saints have been refreshed through you." As furlough ends, these words of Paul express the blessing that many of you have been to us. Your hospitality, sacrificial gifts, and serious prayer interest in the Chirripó Indians have enriched us and deepened our appreciation of your vital part in our ministry. We need you in reaching the Chirripos, for we are all "laborers together with God."*

– 9 –

From Turrialba to La Suiza
1958 to 1963

House hunting after our return from furlough in January of 1958 led us to a large second-floor apartment in the center of Turrialba. Our new home was right by the Moravia bus stop, very convenient for language practice with Indians who came by for coffee while in town.

For the family, however, the apartment was confining, with no yard for the children to play in. We did have a nice tiled patio upstairs, but the people downstairs resented the noise when the kids bumped the corrugated iron wall. Peter turned five not long after we moved in, Priscilla was not quite three, but Susanna was just a few months old, so they couldn't have made too much noise. Yet one day the neighbor yelled up to us.

"What have you got up there," he complained, "a herd of cattle?"

In Turrialba I settled back into my routine: meeting the Lord each morning, then hours at the desk working on Cabécar language data. Marian spent time at the desk in between other duties. Celina returned to work for Marian, and Alfredo came from time to time to spend a month helping us. I also resumed my monthly treks to various Cabécar areas and even back to Talamanca. Each day we spent time with the children, reading Bible stories and praying, memorizing Scripture verses and singing.

For Marian, having three children meant a lot more involvement than with two. Previously I could take one and she the other. Now that we had three, life was different.

"I knew I had to settle down to raising a family," she said.

We had married with a desire to raise a family for the Lord. Now that our family was growing, she realized what was involved. Even with a maid to help with the housework, Marian still spent most of her time either cooking or caring for the children. Was it worth it? As we faced the implications of a growing family, we took time to rethink our convictions about not limiting the size of our family. After talking

With our first three in 1958
Peter, Priscilla, and Susanna

it over, praying, and reflecting on Scripture, we decided to continue in faith that the Lord would enable us to fulfill our twofold vision.

Living in the center of Turrialba gave us a good chance to develop friendships and try to evangelize the Indians who visited us. Within six months of renting the apartment we had counted almost ninety such visitors. These contacts only increased our desire to live nearer the tribe. Sometimes the Indians spent the night in our living area. With no yard outside, they used our extra bathroom, but some had never seen a toilet. I tried to teach them to use it, and also cleaned up their messes. Occasionally our visitors arrived drunk or smelly—our apartment looked out on four bars and a dance hall. Peter used to stand on the front balcony and watch the police load drunks into the paddy wagon. On Saturdays the noise lasted late into the night. Only on Sunday afternoons was it relatively quiet.

Church and Mission Duties

We were back at our beloved "home church." Every Sunday we put Susanna in the stroller, and walked with Peter and Priscilla the four blocks up to the CAM church by the central park. Marian taught the Sunday School class for *señoritas*—young ladies. She also was secretary of the church council for a time and served as pianist when needed. On the other hand, I kept avoiding local involvement. I loved the brethren but needed to be free to trek regularly.

As missionaries we had an obligation to attend the conferences and retreats of the national church association, but I rarely accepted preaching invitations except during Holy Week when every Costa Rican went to church. Each time I was invited to preach I had to sense whether this was God's will for me. I knew there was time to do the will of God but constantly needed to discern His leading.

Marian and I found it a blessing to fellowship with the brethren at conference and even to be challenged occasionally by the preaching. A side benefit was seeing different parts of the country, as conferences alternated between churches from the Pacific to the Caribbean. Facilities were minimal—many slept on the church benches, but the brethren tried to arrange better accommodations for missionary families. We made lasting friendships with some who opened their homes to us.

At the annual conference of the church association I made it clear that I did not want a position on the governing committee, but one year I narrowly avoided being named president by unanimous acclamation. I could not accept such a heavy responsibility, nor did I want to deprive my Costa Rican brethren of opportunities for leadership. Besides, I was quite aware that their acceptance of me would not necessarily even last until the next election—no one remains popular indefinitely!

For several years I served as legal representative of the Mission, which meant that I needed to get clear titles for church properties and to secure residence papers for new missionaries. It was my job to investigate how to incorporate the churches so that ownership could be transferred from the Mission to local authority. My search for a capable lawyer was frustrating.

The process of establishing a legally recognized church association seemed interminable. I was never able to complete the job, although I worked at it diligently and prayed faithfully for a solution to the complex legal situation.

The group of CAM missionaries in Costa Rica was not large, never more than twenty-five or thirty, but we were required to meet yearly for spiritual refreshment and Mission business. After we finished our language study and passed our orientation exams, Marian and I became voting members. During our first term I was elected president because few others were available for the job. After that I was named secretary and was reelected for most of the years we served with the Mission. I discovered that I enjoyed organizational matters. In fact, I enjoyed it almost too much! I had lots of ideas—not always appreciated! Marian also had a group responsibility for a few years, leading the orientation of new missionaries.

Traveling to missionary conferences and church conferences with the children was always a feat during the Turrialba years when we had no car. I would go to the bus station and hire a few of the street boys looking for work. They would follow me home to carry the suitcases back to the bus, while Marian and I took the children. Quite a parade for people to gawk at! We had more baggage than the rest of the passengers combined, but Marian learned to put up with the embarrassment. Fortunately none of us were prone to motion sickness as the bus lurched around the curves through the mountains that covered most of the country—beautiful scenery but treacherous driving.

Who Was Doris Stone?

During our first year in Costa Rica we kept hearing about the anthropological studies of Doris Stone, an American who had spent most of her life in Costa Rica. Mrs. Stone had made a lifelong study of the Cabécar and Bribri Indians. Early in 1954 I had visited her school for Indians in southern Costa Rica in a vain hope that she might help us find a place to live near the Indians. Now in 1958 Doris Stone came to Turrialba to solicit our help with Cabécar kinship terminology in preparation for her book—which was eventually published by the Peabody Museum at Harvard under the title, *The Talamancan Tribes of Costa Rica*. Later I was asked to review her book for a journal on missions; I called my article, "Without God and Without Hope," portraying these Indians as I saw them.

Doris Stone also asked us to present a paper at an upcoming gathering of anthropologists, archaeologists, and linguists interested in the native peoples of the Americas. This Congress, which was held every two years in a different country, was to be in Costa Rica for the first time. Mrs. Stone wanted to make a good showing, so for a week Marian and I mixed with scores of leading authorities. In one sparsely attended session Marian presented our study of the sound system of Chirripó. This study was published in the proceedings of the Congress, and years later I also published two studies in Spanish on the Cabécar verb system. On one occasion the wife of the president of the country invited me to participate in a seminar on the Indians of Costa Rica. But our heart was not in the academic study of Indians nor in linguistics. To us linguistics—though interesting and necessary—was merely a tool to help us get the Word of God into the language of people that God loves. Our goal was to share the Good News about Jesus.

A Banquet in the Wilderness

Besides trekking to Chirripó and other areas accessible to Turrialba, I sometimes took the train down to the Caribbean coast and from there made my way to more distant areas. Eventually I headed for Telire, the most remote area. I would be on the trail eleven days, walking about a hundred miles over steep muddy trails, crossing swift rivers and eating native food. I had traveled two days from the last store and had finished the last sandwich Marian had made for me. The next day I took the trail up around the sacred mountain of the Cabécars, and then stopped for the night at a hut near the Telire River. Leaving my pack at the hut, I headed toward the river to bathe and change to my dry clothes.

Suddenly a Latin carrying a heavy pack came up from the river, then another, and another, until there were perhaps a dozen or more, each carrying a pack weighing eighty to a hundred pounds! They were taking supplies from the coast up to an American geologist searching for petroleum two hours further upstream. Tired, they decided to make camp.

"Do you want supper?" they asked.

Breaking out their supplies, they served me ham, potatoes, canned vegetables, and canned fruit. For breakfast they gave me bacon and eggs from Chicago. A feast in the wilderness!

On a trip to Talamanca near the Panama border, I was served five consecutive meals of green plantains and greasy chocolate—called "the drink of the gods" by the Bribri Indians. Five meals in five houses. After the last I vomited.

Two hours later in Amubre, the priest's caretaker, an old black man of Jamaican origin, greeted me in English.

"Are you an evangelist?" he asked.

"Yes," I replied.

"Are you hungry?" was his next question.

"Yes," I admitted.

The old fellow told me to take a nap on the porch while he fixed me some food. I awoke to a full British-style meal!

Wake for the Dead

Pausing on the trail one day, I listened to the drums beating in the clearing below. Another funeral was in progress with pagan rites and plenty of *chicha* to drink. In 1958 death was striking hard in Chirripó. Whooping cough was killing the little ones. Flu, fever, and old age devastated my friends, who were still "without hope and without God."

Once as I crossed the ridge between upper Pacuare and upper Chirripó, my guide invited me to a wake for the dead. He, it turned out, was to preside over the ceremony. The hut we entered was filled with men and women sitting separately, on long benches pointing east and west. The seating arrangement was crucial to the ritual. The women of the family served gourd after gourd of meat with green boiled bananas, and then gourds full of chicha. The dead man's animals had to be eaten. The souls of those animals would strengthen the deceased to get past the place where boa constrictors—demons— tried to hinder the soul from reaching the nether world.

The trail to God's place had been lost, I'd been told, so the soul must travel below to the place of Sulá. Otherwise it would remain on earth as a ghost. During the wake, the man who presided conducted a ceremony in which he lit a fire by twirling a green stick on a board until it sparked. This was the signal that the soul of the deceased had returned and was happy to be remembered and would now proceed down the trail.

Wakes for the dead were among the few times I ever saw a large group of Indians gathered. This time I counted forty-five. To them it was more than a social obligation. It was for their own future peace of mind, not to be harassed by departed spirits. There was more than one wake for each person who died. There were initial wakes, final wakes, and in-between wakes. Death stalked the lives of these seemingly carefree people. In the language there were terms not only for those who cursed or cured, and for those who divined the future, but for those who officiated at wakes and those who handled the body.

When I would suggest to the Indians that Jesus was the way to God's place, they would respond with dull eyes.

"Why would we want to go to God's place? All our people go to Sulá's place," they insisted. "We want to be where our people are."

Many years were to pass before their eyes were opened, and some would express a desire to go to God's place.

Language Analysis Continues

Back at home I continued studying the notes I took during treks. I studied six to eight hours a day, analyzing, filing, memorizing. When Alfredo came to help us, Marian and I took turns transcribing stories he dictated. Once when he visited us we spent three tedious hours doing a rough translation of the Lord's Prayer, which takes up only three short verses in the Bible. As someone has said, "Translation requires the patience of Job and the wisdom of Solomon."

Alfredo was not a typical Indian. He was more interested in words and their meanings than in practical matters. A confirmed bachelor, he was rather picky about many things, including food. In fact, he refused to eat salad, saying, "I'm not a rabbit, so why should I eat weeds?" Yet Alfredo was the Lord's provision for our early years of language learning. No one else would have been content to spend hours responding to my probing questions about words, especially when I asked paradigms such as, "I saw, you saw, he saw; we saw, you saw, they saw," or "I run, you run, he runs; we run, you run, they run."

Of course, I knew ahead of time that the Cabécar language would not function grammatically like English or Spanish, but I kept on asking questions. I was desperate to figure out how the language actually *did* function. It would take several more years and much more prayer before we finally got a handle on the verb system. In fact, time after time we asked our friends to pray that we would find the key to the Cabécar verbs.

Family Life

The children kept growing. Susanna learned to walk, Priscilla had eye surgery, and Peter started school. We sent him to first grade at the bilingual elementary school for children of the staff at the agricultural institute near town. A special family event was the visit of Marian's parents. With both their daughters and all their grandchildren in Costa Rica, they came to spend the Christmas holidays.

As the children began to mature in understanding, we increased our teaching. Eventually we wore out more than one copy of *The Bible in Pictures for Little Eyes*, one of the first Bible story books for young children to include questions with each story. Every night we read a story or two and asked questions to help the children stay alert and focus on the content. Marian and I were both involved; both of us taught, questioned, and prayed with the children. Each of the children prayed as soon as they were able, even if only repeating after us. It was a *family* time, a time for us to meet the Lord together. When I was away, Marian took over.

We continued to train the children in obedience as well. The lessons we learned in training Peter helped us with the other children even though the particular issues were different. While we were living in the apartment, colleagues visited us who had a little girl about Susanna's age. We were distracted, talking with our friends, until we began hearing noise in the children's bedroom. Marian discovered Susanna and her little playmate, happily crawling in and out of a portable crib, tearing the fabric. Marian spanked Susanna, which put an end to the fun. But it was a learning experience for Marian—she had given Susanna too many licks for her tender age, and for an offense that was not deliberate disobedience.

Children at Church

One difficult area of training was to teach the children to behave at church. My Daddy used to say, "Never let a child play on the floor at church." We began with Peter, then the girls, teaching them to sit quietly—not an easy task. We did not normally bring toys or books to entertain them during the service. Toys can be noisy and books encourage talking. We knew that children sat quietly in a Catholic church. Could we teach ours to do the same?

Of course, there were times when we had to take a child outside—there was no foyer in the church. Once Peter, who was then perhaps three years old, caused a bit of a stir as we sat on the back row during the evening service. When the preacher eventually finished, Peter sighed loudly.

"*Ya!*" he exclaimed, meaning "Finally!" Those sitting nearby all turned and smiled.

Marian sometimes got discouraged with having to take the children outside and even questioned the value of going to church. But she did enjoy most of the service before they got wiggly, and she also enjoyed chatting with the other young mothers out on the sidewalk with their little ones. Our children did learn to behave and eventually to be attentive. They needed to learn to participate with other believers beyond the family setting.

Blessed with our Fourth Child

Our second son was born on July 6, 1959, a few days before Marian's thirtieth birthday. We named the baby Steven Paul, for Stephen, the man of faith and wisdom who eventually gave his life for the Lord, and for Paul, the great apostle. Steven's birth was a matter of special praise to the Lord who brought him safely into the world despite complications three months before his birth and during delivery. Marian had to spend those last months at the Mission Home in the capital to be near good medical help.

While we were in San José those three months I began to be troubled with asthmatic bronchitis, and then barely three months after Steven's birth he came down with pneumonia. I was away on Mission business at the time. Steven was barely breathing when I got home. At the local hospital there was no pediatric ward so Steven lay—pitifully small—under an oxygen tent in a full-size bed, fighting for his life as we prayed by his side. The whole church prayed with us. The Lord was pleased to spare Steven, as well as to heal me.

"What does the Lord have for this child?" Marian and I asked each other. "What is God's purpose in sparing Steven these three times—before his birth, during delivery, and again now?"

English Church in Turrialba?

By the time of Steven's birth in 1959 we were getting desperate for a place to live near Chirripó—away from the pull of Spanish work, as well as communication with the capital and its distractions. Yet God still had a job for us to do in Turrialba.

One Sunday morning a new family appeared in church, a British-American couple and their five little girls. The Cuanys had just arrived in Turrialba the day before. Dr. Cuany was to work in the nuclear research program at the Inter-American Institute of Agricultural Sciences nearby; his wife had been a missionary before their marriage. Although they did not know any Spanish, they inquired whether there was a Protestant church in town. Their love for the Lord and desire to be with His people drew them to the CAM church.

Our contact with Robin and Carol Cuany led to meeting other English-speaking professors at the Institute. Soon we began services early on Sunday mornings at the Cuany's request. I led the singing and Marian played the piano; then she had a class for the children while I led a Bible study for the adults. To avoid time-consuming preparation I limited my study to reading the chapter every day in a different version and then on Saturday night making a few notes and checking out any potential difficulties in the passage. The inductive Bible study approach proved very effective, as each person took part in the discussion. Most who attended were Ph.D.'s in some field of agriculture. They were highly intelligent people—but, except for the Cuanys, with no knowledge of the Scriptures.

Friendships developed. At Christmas over thirty people gathered in our apartment for a lively tamale supper and carol sing, with Marian playing our new piano. In January—vacation month in Costa Rica—Marian held a Vacation Bible School for the children, with help from her sister Irene. By Thanksgiving of 1960 we had enough contact with internationals to sponsor a potluck meal at the Institute—another opportunity for witness. We enjoyed this ministry with those at the opposite end of the social and educational spectrum from the Indians. The brethren at the Turrialba church were happy about our outreach too, for several of them held responsible positions on the Institute staff.

Meetings went on for the last year and a half of our time in Turrialba. Near the end of that time one of the couples, Joe and Eileen, invited us to dinner at their lovely home, filled with furnishings gathered from the various countries where they had worked. During the meal I was trying to clarify their relationship to the Lord.

"Aziel, this is your last chance to save us before you go on furlough, isn't it?" blurted Eileen.

We all laughed, and I pressed no more!

The final Sunday we received a special gift when Millie, one of the professors at the Institute, asked to say a word during the service. We had spent extra time with her explaining the gospel, so we were thrilled with what she said.

"As a going-away present to Mr. and Mrs. Jones," she testified, "I want to say that through these services I have accepted Jesus Christ as my own personal Savior."

When we left Turrialba, colleagues traveled weekly from San José to continue the services, but the group soon broke up. Yet for over forty years these families have kept in touch with us, some sending occasional gifts.

Continuing Cabécar Ministry

Although we were occupied with the English services on Sundays, I continued my trekking a few days a month. At home I kept working on the linguistic analysis necessary to beginning translation. With no Cabécar church yet on the horizon, we envisioned "the New Testament not as a commodity to satisfy a demand, but as a seed to create a demand," as another translator expressed it.

Careful attention to language details was sometimes rewarded with fascinating discoveries. In studying the verb "to come," I found several different forms all translated "he comes." There was *idaju*, "he comes," *idamiju*, "he comes" (arriving), *idawaju* "he comes" (down), *idakaju* "he comes" (up), and *idaksaju* "he comes" (out of). I spent many hours filing and cross-checking such data. Marian helped when she could, but served mainly as my consultant.

Besides filing and analyzing data, I made initial attempts at producing literature in the language, preparing a booklet to explain God's holiness, man's sin and its consequences, Christ's death in payment for our sin, and our salvation through active trust in His death as our substitute. When I took the booklet to Chirripó, it caused quite a stir. Obviously the basic message was beginning to get across.

However, whole areas of their thinking needed to be transformed: their concept of God, of sin, of heaven and hell.

The Deity of the Cabécar Indians

In April of 1959 we wrote to those who backed us financially and in prayer:

> *How would you explain a man-made satellite in orbit (and the related movements of the solar and planetary systems) to an illiterate Indian? That is no harder than communicating a Biblical concept of God to the same Indian. He will modify his idea of the universe far more quickly than his theology — and he does have very definite convictions about God even though we see them as an inextricable mixture of paganism and perverted Christianity.*
>
> **Sibu** *is the Chirripó god of whom we are learning through conversation and stories. Though creator of all, he has an impersonal relation to creation with his agent or "foreman,"* **Sulá**, *doing the actual work. Pictured in crude charcoal figures as a grotesque feathered creature with an equally unattractive father,* **Sibu** *also has a sister, an older and younger brother and is said to be the size of a child. Though he is considered supreme, in the Chirripó dualism of good and evil, the latter usually wins. While not thought of as bad we have found nothing about his moral virtues in their legends... This god's love for man is "not like we love our children, but as we love animals which we are fattening for the slaughter" and "he has us for that purpose until he orders his brothers to kill us."*
>
> *The Bible message once translated, in addition to overcoming the natural barriers to the gospel, must also penetrate and transform this defective concept of God. We would say that the obstacles are insurmountable except that the gospel "is the power of God unto salvation." Furthermore, we remember that God broke through all our misconceptions and reached* **US!**

At the time we wrote this, we were still learning the language and the culture, and still discovering what the people believed. I was still trekking, getting to know how and where the Indians lived, and getting acquainted with people in various areas. It would be several years before our command of the language was sufficient for us to begin serious translation work. We assumed that the Scripture, once translated into their language, would show the Indians what God was really like.

In the booklet I had recently produced, I had used the native name for god. It never occurred to me to look for a different term. In our study of Bible translation theory both the lectures and books suggested using the native term unless the natives conceived of their god as an essentially evil being. The people of Chirripó did not think of their god as evil but rather as being indifferent to them. Hence, I continued to use their term in my efforts at evangelism.

Still Praying for Land

Often in our letters we asked our friends to keep praying for a place to live near the Indians. In our minds we were thinking of a couple of acres where we could build a house for our family, plus a building for translation and for hospitality for traveling Indians, and perhaps a clinic. Then in 1960 the association of churches began investigating property for a camp. I went with two of the brethren to an area near Moravia to look at acreage suitable not only for a camp but also for our ministry. The church committee decided that the area was not central enough for a camp, and we personally could not finance the purchase. In our disappointment we intensified our prayers, and rejoiced in the offer from a carpenter in the Turrialba church to build a house for us once we obtained land.

Meanwhile we continued in the apartment on the main road through Turrialba. Celina, the girl who had become like a daughter to us, got married and moved away. Without her help Marian could hardly handle the housework, let alone help me with language work. We tried a succession of girls. One stole from us, another quit after three hours, another could not get my muddy clothes clean after a trek. She quit, but at least her mother came to do the washing. No one could replace Celina, yet Marian was grateful for whatever help she could get and for the knowledge of local customs and cooking that she had gleaned from various helpers.

At this point Marian had major surgery that left her even less able to cope, then a siege of amoebas and a case of hepatitis, all within two months. On top of all that, we moved. We found an old house with a large yard, located on a peaceful street. Life did eventually settle down to "normal" again.

Normal life for me still included trekking. A college student was with us as a summer missionary. Doug was interested in translation so I took him along on my trips. Peter, then seven years old, accompanied us to visit my helper Alfredo. Peter took the abundance of mud like a real trouper. He was thrilled that we saw and killed a snake,

Peter, Priscilla, Susanna, and Steven in 1960

apparently poisonous, the first such I had ever seen on a trail. Doug found his interest in translation waning as he realized all that was involved in reaching a tribe.

Encouraged!

As I trudged up the last hill from Chirripó in October of 1960, I paused to survey the little farm plots dotting the rugged ridges behind me. I felt that Chirripó was such a friendly place! On these primitive farms lived our friends, whose casual lives centered around their homes with animals and children underfoot and women cooking over the fire while men lounged in their hammocks after work. Mists rising from the narrow valleys far below enhanced the jungle beauty.

Just a few years earlier I had trudged up that same hill feeling like a discouraged Elijah with my faith and vision dulled by the numb indifference of satisfied paganism. The Indians' only interest then was in learning Spanish in order to better themselves materially. This time, however, I was encouraged. Without exception I had been asked to sing in their language rather than in Spanish as before. One young man copied our translation of John 8:12 in his notebook.

"Bring me a primer in my language; it's easier than Spanish," said another, previously uninterested in his own tongue.

In hut after hut I witnessed the first real interest in God's Word in the language of the "true people," as they called themselves.

The "true people" hungered, albeit unconsciously, for the sure Word of the true God. Their carefree happiness masked their lack of hope in the face of frequent sorrow and death. At one home on that trek I had arrived at the end of a wake for a young father who had just died of the all too frequent snakebite. The death of another youth, who had recently disappeared in the swollen Chirripó River, was blamed on Dínama, the "Water Tiger," a spirit which causes drowning.

With another furlough coming up soon, I made a farewell trip in January of 1961 to see Alfredo and his relatives in the lowlands near Zent. Marian was with me, her first trip to that

Carrying Peter across the Zent River

area since language school days in 1953. Although there were no hills as in Chirripó, there were the usual rivers and muddy trails through jungles and cocoa plantations. For me it was special to have not only Marian but also Peter to share with me the Indian's hospitality and food, including on this trip, wild goat, wild chicken, monkey, and toucan. Marian had learned enough of the language to enjoy simple conversations with the women. Peter hoped to see another snake and to his delight he saw two!

Short Furlough in 1961

Times were changing and the Mission accommodated to the increased ease of travel. Our first term had been four years: one year of language study and three years on the field. Now, however, the Mission allowed the option of a six-month furlough after three years. As we laid plans for furlough, we needed to consider our children's education. Peter had completed two years of bilingual schooling on the Costa Rican schedule, which did not coordinate with the U.S. schedule. We ended up putting him in Spanish school for the six weeks of the new term before furlough and then skipping school until we returned, for he would still be up to grade level. Priscilla went to the public kindergarten, looking so cute in her red and white uniform. We still remember the songs she learned there!

Incredibly, Peter got sick on the eve of our departure for the States, causing us to postpone our flight as we had done in 1957 for the same reason! My brother David met us in Miami, drove us to Alabama, and then lent us his station wagon for our furlough. In the Lord's goodness, we enjoyed a furlough free of sickness and accidents.

Studying at SIL Again

The centerpiece of our furlough was another three months of study at the Summer Institute of Linguistics. We did visit family and friends both before and after the course, but the main reason for this furlough was to study advanced techniques that would help us in further analysis of the Cabécar language. Again we hoped to discover the key to the complex verb structure. Again we were disappointed, though many were praying with us specifically about this.

All four of the children were with us that summer at SIL, eating in the dining hall and living in the dorm with other families. Quite an interesting experience! Peter and Priscilla enjoyed their time in a day camp run by the SIL staff, but Susanna and Steven did not fare so well in the preschool program. In fact, Steven got a reputation for biting other kids as they spent the hot afternoons milling around in a fenced enclosure—the "wailing wall" we called it, as the crying kids lined up along the fence.

Studying with us at SIL that summer were Ellis and Katherine Deibler. Ellis had graduated from high school with Marian. In our long search for a couple to work near us in Talamanca, the Deiblers had become interested, but were disappointed in their hopes to join CAM. That summer they joined Wycliffe and went on to serve in New Guinea, while Marian and I continued to pray for workers for the Bribri tribe.

Preparing to Return to Costa Rica

Once SIL was over we headed to Alabama for a Labor Day reunion of my family—parents, brothers and sisters, and their families—sixty-one of us. My father had recently retired after more than forty years of faithful service to our Lord in the Methodist ministry. From Alabama we headed north to visit supporters and Marian's family. During our furlough we spoke more than sixty times to groups, besides numerous delightful personal visits over coffee cups. To us it was enriching to fellowship with God's choice saints.

Difficult decisions pressed in on us as we faced our return to the field in November. Would a place in the Moravia area open to us? If we did not live in Turrialba, what of Peter and Priscilla's schooling? If we lived closer to the Indians, how would we manage without a vehicle? Around this time my brother David called with a question.

"Would you like to have a car to drive back to Costa Rica?" he asked.

We took him up on his offer of an old DeSoto—not suitable for our use in Costa Rica but certainly an economical way to transport the family back to the field. Just before we left, we visited my parents one last time. My mother, who had just been released from the hospital after a heart attack, got out of bed to say good-bye. We took a photo to remember the occasion. I treasure that picture now, for I never saw her alive again.

Our First Drive through Central America

On November 10, 1961, we crossed the border into Mexico and arrived in Costa Rica 2800 miles and ten driving days later. Traveling as a family over breathtaking mountains and desolate wastes, seeing modern capitals and old Indian villages, was an unforgettable experience. Along the way we visited missionaries and national believers in the six countries we passed through.

The first flat in Guatemala

We still talk about the Lord's kindness one dark night in Mexico when our lights went out. We drove a tense fifteen miles by the light of the car ahead of us, as the driver kindly guided us until we came to a repair shop. The delay made us so late that we arrived at our colleagues' home at midnight, only to learn that they had not received our letter and were not expecting us!

A few days later we were stranded on a rocky road in the mountains of Guatemala after a second flat tire. Again we experienced the Lord's care. The man who stopped to help us gave me and eight-year-old Peter a ride to the nearest town to get the tire repaired. In the town I found a missionary at a nearby Bible Institute who kindly took us to lunch and then drove us back up the long winding hill. Not a single vehicle had passed during the three hours Marian was alone on that desolate hillside with the younger children.

By the time we arrived at the border of Costa Rica I had become accustomed to filling out the necessary paperwork and laying out the baggage for inspection. As for duty on the DeSoto, the authorities charged us ten times what the car was worth but gave us the option to proceed to our destination. Within thirty days we were required either to pay the duty or take the vehicle out of the country. For the time being, we were just glad to be "back home." As we drove the last stretch to the capital we joyfully sang the national anthem of our adopted country.

Finding Housing

The first two months back in Costa Rica proved to be an unsettled time for our family. Weeks rolled by as we tried to find a place to live. The administrative structure of the Mission was becoming more directive. The head of the local committee told us we could not return to Turrialba even temporarily, for another missionary family had moved there in our absence. We felt pressured to find housing elsewhere. But where could we find a house outside of Turrialba for a family of six with another child on the way?

Meanwhile, I had plenty to do, taking care of legal business for the Mission and working on a paper I was soon to present at a conference in Guatemala. Furthermore, we had to get our freight shipment out of customs, renew our residence papers, and obtain visas for our next trip. Marian was busy getting clothes ready for Peter and Priscilla, who would be going to boarding school. During this time all six of us stayed in one room at the Mission Home except for a couple of weeks when acquaintances asked us to housesit. At least we were able to have a family Christmas at that house and to spend time with Marian's sister and her family who lived nearby.

In January we left Susanna and Steven with colleagues and drove with Peter and Priscilla to Guatemala in the old DeSoto—a three-day trip. There we gathered with one hundred forty CAM missionaries to strategize for the next ten years. My paper on the relation of the missionary to the national churches was one of many presented at the conference. At the end of the meetings Peter and Priscilla left for Las Américas, the Mission's boarding school in Honduras. They went happily, but it was hard for Marian to see them go. The Mission did not require us to send the children, but in view of our hope to live closer to Chirripó we came to peace about sending them. We had visited one of the Mission schools a few years earlier and were impressed at how happy the children were and how lovingly the teachers cared for them.

We stayed another week in Guatemala while I attended business sessions of the Field Council, which guided the Mission's activities throughout Central America. Mission business really cut into my time for Indian work—though I would not admit it. I enjoyed the annual sessions of the Council, as well as the business meetings of CAM missionaries in Costa Rica.

On our return trip to Costa Rica we stopped in Nicaragua long enough to sell the DeSoto and buy an old Willys from Dean Lewis—the same Jeep in which he had welcomed us eight years earlier, when we first arrived in Costa Rica. Even after many miles on the back roads of Central America, it was still serviceable and best of all, affordable. I had always said I wouldn't buy a car until I needed one, for I tried to maintain a simple lifestyle. Now, as we faced living beyond public transportation, we definitely *needed* our own vehicle.

A House in La Suiza

Late in January of 1962 we finally moved into a tiny house in La Suiza, a small town eight miles from Turrialba on the road to Chirripó. If the two older children had not been away at school, we could not have fit into the house, for it was only sixteen feet by twenty-two. Four little rooms and a tiny porch were squeezed into that small space. We took what little furniture we could, leaving the living room and dining room furniture with our colleagues in Turrialba. The piano and a desk filled the living area, and the refrigerator had to go in the children's bedroom.

Living in La Suiza allowed us time to transition. For Marian it was another gentle step down. Again her testimony was, "The Lord let me down gently." Life was quieter, for there were only a few stores, a school, a Catholic church, and a telegraph office. With no electricity we learned to make do with candles and kerosene lamps. Our kerosene refrigerator and propane stove served us well. A friend who worked in a machine shop in Turrialba rigged our wringer washer to a gasoline engine.

With fewer interruptions we poured a lot into the children. The absence of the older ones led to an unanticipated pleasure—the "discovery" of Susanna and Steven. Yet we needed to prepare for the return of Peter and Priscilla. They wrote each week, Peter telling of hikes and swimming and fishing, Priscilla of books and studies. Anticipating their arrival, we added a back porch and an extra room.

Indian visitors were few. All were hurrying to Turrialba to do their errands. I spent more time in prayer and the Word and began to read Christian classics during my quiet time, a few pages a day. This strengthened my devotional habits, which proved more vital once we lived near the Indians, isolated from any other spiritual input. I wasn't conscious of a need; I was just satisfying a desire to know the Lord better.

New Ministry Opportunities

How we enjoyed La Suiza—the brisk morning chill, daybreak over the hills, pungent coffee blossoms, barefoot farmers passing by, children hurrying to buy bread for morning coffee. Early icy stares at us, the "false prophets," turned into friendlier greetings and conversations. Our quiet, unpublicized Sunday afternoon Bible studies attracted a few neighbors. Others were afraid to come. Our landlord was reproved by the priest for renting to us. Occasionally passersby pelted the house with stones at night. Once they aimed at the front window, scattering pulverized glass all over the piano and even in my hair. Another time they threw stones while we were in the midst of a Bible study. The results of our ministry were not encouraging, but it did eventually lead to the establishment of a stable church after we moved away.

Each week we drove from La Suiza to the agricultural institute in Turrialba for a weeknight home Bible study in Spanish, the only language we all had in common. The key couple was from Brazil. One man was from Peru. Another was a German fellow married to an American girl. As I pondered how to avoid certain possible objections and irrelevant questions, I set some ground rules: We would study the book of John, not questioning whether the book was true, or whether they believed it, but trying to honestly see what John meant to say.

Each week we read a chapter in a modern Spanish version, everyone taking a turn at reading a paragraph. Then I would ask, "What impresses you? What strikes you?" They were responsive—we bonded together. It was beautiful to see the Word come alive even to those who had never read it before, as they studied the Scripture thoughtfully with an open mind. When we reached chapter twelve, we came to verse twenty-five: *"He that loveth his life shall lose it; and he that hateth his life in this world shall keep it unto life eternal."*

"And what does *that* mean?" asked the German.

"I think it means what you fear it might mean," I responded, for I suspected the concept was too strong for him.

"If that verse means what it says," he said after a long pause, "there are blankety-blank few people who will be saved!"

When the class gave us a good-bye gift several months later, the Brazilian thanked us for our "open Bible approach." Years later the German's wife wrote from Canada, "You need to come help us convert folks here." Obviously they had felt the power of the Word of God.

New Baby Adds Joy

Peter and Priscilla's return from boarding school reunited our family for a few months. They flew alone from Honduras, with nine-year-old Peter allowed to sit on the pilot's lap and lower the landing wheels as they touched down in Costa Rica. Marian and I hugged each other emotionally as we watched them wave to us from the tarmac.

We did not immediately proceed to La Suiza but stayed in the capital for the birth of our fifth child, Elizabeth Joy, who was born August 28, 1962. We named her for Elizabeth, the "devout and blameless" mother of John the Baptist. She was our joy girl from the start! Guiding the total development of five children was for us a privilege that was laden with sobering responsibility.

Back in La Suiza we all managed to fit into our little rented house. There was not much privacy for any of us, but at least we were together! New baby Elizabeth was in a bassinet in our room, Priscilla was in the other little room with Susanna, and Steven was out with Peter in the room we had added. It was a large room that we also used for a Sunday afternoon meeting place and for a study as I kept analyzing the Cabécar language.

Hard Times

Our tiny house had an adequate yard for the children on sunny days, but rainy season kept them cooped up for weeks. A couple of flash floods surrounded us with water, but fortunately the water did not rise high enough to seep through the wood floor. Then Priscilla had surgery and Marian was sick for weeks, first with pneumonia and then with depression. Spiritual warfare brought deliverance. Soon it was time to pack for the children's return to boarding school.

In January of 1963 I drove the Jeep seven hundred miles to Honduras to leave Peter and Priscilla at Las Américas. We had already been impressed with the good impact the school had made on our kids, but the visit left me even more impressed by the love and happiness and order there. It was harder to part from the children than it had been to send them the first time, but I felt comfortable leaving them in the hands of such a dedicated and qualified staff. Peter cried when I left, but dear "Aunt" Kay, one of the teachers, was right there to comfort him.

Last Days in La Suiza

Back in La Suiza once more, I busied myself reproducing some little hymn booklets for the Indians. By now I had my own mimeograph machine and could avoid trips to the capital to get things printed. What a thrill it was to sell the first hymnbook! The growing interest encouraged me to reproduce the illustrated alphabet book we had been working on. Even in trial form it was already popular.

In between working on booklets, we continued analyzing our data on the Cabécar language, and I made regular trips to the various Indian areas. A Mennonite couple, Ray and Susie Schlabach, had arrived to begin working in the neighboring tribe. I took Ray to Talamanca to survey the area—my last exploratory trip. He and Susie were to become close friends of ours, united by a shared vision and a common love for our Lord. The Schlabachs were the Lord's answer to our long-standing prayer for workers to give the Word to the Bribris. And the years of prayer for a place to live at the edge of Cabécar territory would be answered shortly!

—10—
Building a Base in Tsipirí
1963

From day one, we knew we needed to live among the Indians—or at least as close as possible. A major prayer request that we shared in our letters during the first ten years in Costa Rica was for property near the Indians. We had been told of a law restricting outsiders from living on Indian lands. Again and again we asked for prayer. We ourselves constantly brought this request before the Lord.

To live in the tribe would be daunting, for there were no roads or villages, only tiny farms scattered over the steep hills. At best we would have only one neighbor, so we were willing instead to live along the main trail entering the area. Hopefully, we would have contacts with passersby. Certainly living along the main trail would be easier for the family.

Those first years as I trekked through all the Indian areas, I kept a sharp eye out for a possible place. I made an early attempt to get land on the Pacuare River where that first missionary, Lewis Jamison, had lived for a few months back in 1895. Another possible location was down in the lowlands where a number of Indians lived along the Estrella River not far from the Caribbean coast. I really liked the thought of settling there, but we could not afford the available land. I even had a house promised for rent in the lowlands near the Zent River where a few Indians lived, but nothing ever materialized.

Yet all along we had focused our prayers on the area near Moravia, an enormous *hacienda*, a cattle ranch and coffee plantation at the end of a one-lane gravel road from Turrialba. Indian land, considered reservation, bordered the edges of the *hacienda*. From Moravia, trails led to the largest concentration of the Cabécar Indians, the "true people." Several hundred lived in scattered huts in the mountains bordering an eighteen-mile stretch along the Chirripó River.

When the original developer of the Moravia Valley went bankrupt, an American named George Harvey had ended up managing the largest section for his uncle who was one of the creditors. Time and again I asked Mr. Harvey for a lot to build on, but he was adamant. Could I buy? Or rent? Or even build something he could take back at any time? He said a firm "no" to *all* offers. An Austrian duke who had been another creditor promised me a free lot in the Grano de Oro section of the original ranch. Three days before we were to close the deal he died without leaving a will.

What I really wanted was a piece at the back edge of Mr. Harvey's land, between the two branches of a sparkling, icy creek called Tsipirí by the Indians. Living in Tsipirí would give us access at least to passing Indians, for this land was on the *Camino Real*, the main trail to Chirripó, about a four-mile, hour-long trek from the center of Moravia. We needed a place where the Indians were still in the jungle and in their native mindset. During the years we searched for a place, an elderly woman in Alabama wrote us, "I'm praying every morning at 5:30 that you'll get a place in Moravia." Prayer would open closed doors.

Chance Contact Leads to Land

Early in 1963 we had a visitor in La Suiza, where we lived at the time. The pastor of Bethany Evangelical Free Church in West Orange, New Jersey, came for a whirlwind visit. As he and I were on the trail to Chirripó, we caught up with a local Latin woman named Modesta who was on the way to check on her bean crop. Her plot was just across the Tsipirí from Mr. Harvey's land on what I had heard was reservation land. On our return from the Indians later that day I paused, looking toward Modesta's little hut half-hidden in the jungle.

"Wouldn't that make a wonderful base for reaching the Indians?" I remarked to the pastor.

"Yes—for the person who has the vision for it!" he said, though he was in culture shock and already stretched to the limit.

The next time I returned to Moravia, I found that Modesta was willing to make a deal. Marian and I decided to take legal steps to try this option and see how far we could go. Would we be stymied by a reservation law? We could only try. And pray!

Now the complications began. Modesta would sell only if I would also buy a large piece of adjacent land from another Latin named Nino and give her a piece of his land in exchange. Furthermore, I realized that her steep little piece was not really suitable for a house. I actually needed part of Nino's property. But between these two pieces and the trail to Chirripó was a corner of land claimed by a third Latin named Lupe. I would need that piece in order to provide an entrance from the trail.

On later trips I discovered new angles. Nino and Lupe were willing, but they wanted ten times what they had paid Indians for that land. I decided to accept their price without haggling, for I had to have all three pieces—or none. To further complicate matters, none of the people from whom I was buying actually lived in Tsipirí. So I was negotiating between them in San José the capital, Cartago the provincial capital, and Moravia.

At the time there was only one lawyer in Turrialba, *don* Ricardo. After a lifetime of dealing with farmers—and squatters—he knew everybody. It was quite an event to go to his one-room office, where all clients listened while one was being attended! *Don* Ricardo handed me a legal document listing more than twenty requirements for getting a title to previously untitled land. The first requirement was to bring a bill of sale from the owners—provided they could prove ten years of possession. Modesta and Nino and Lupe agreed on a date to accompany me to the lawyer, but Modesta failed to show up. Marian and I kept praying, and eventually she signed. We paid a total of $500 for the three pieces of land, a large sum for us in those days.

Yet I was still a long way from obtaining a title, including time for each legal step to go through the bureaucracy. There was one big hitch. One of the men who owned property bordering my purchase refused to sign the necessary paper stating that I was not infringing on his land. Why would he not sign? Modesta had never paid him for the piece she was selling me! So it was *his* land I was buying.

"Go ahead and build,"said the lawyer as he leaned back in his chair, smiling confidently. "You'll get your land. The worst that can happen is a delayed title."

"Put up a barbed wire fence," he counseled on another occasion. "Squatters respect a fence more than a title."

The land itself was no prize. It was a steep, narrow peninsula hemmed in by the Tsipirí and the Dukurdí, squeezed between Indian land and Mr. Harvey's land. Furthermore, it was covered with second-growth jungle and worn-out patches of coffee trees. It was located three miles beyond the end of the road. For the squatters, however, it was a piece to sell at a big profit. For us it was a prize, a long delayed answer to prayer!

This land would not only put us close to the Indians, but it would put us in the Indian mode. It's hard to "think Indian" in a Spanish-speaking village like Moravia. For the Indians, Tsipirí was a place to bathe and change their muddy clothes before proceeding to the village. They would be glad to stop at my house for a cup of coffee. And I would need Indians not only to help me translate but also to chop the grass, plant bananas, and haul heavy loads, as well as to sell us fruit and eggs and beans.

Although building a house and raising a family in such a location had its problems, Tsipirí would prove to be a great place for kids to grow up, a place not only to reach a tribe for God but also to raise a family for God. At the moment, though, we were looking only at the problems involved in building there!

"We will build..."

On subsequent trips to Chirripó I usually stopped at Tsipirí to chop weeds and study the broken terrain, trying to decide where I would put my house and the road—someday. What would we do for a water supply? How would we get building materials to the site? A bulldozer had once come to within a few hundred yards of the property. An oxcart could come as far as the bulldozer had entered. Though slow and awkward, it was feasible. There were horses available, and even men willing to carry heavy loads.

Our old Jeep was a real workhorse, but it could not get much more than a mile past the center of Moravia. We had to figure out how to negotiate the last three miles. We would need to hire an oxcart from Mr. Harvey. Oxcarts are famous in Costa Rican history, crucial to the early development of the coffee trade. The brightly colored, intricate designs painted on the oxcarts are a symbol of the country, but Mr. Harvey's carts were crude and unpainted. In addition to renting an oxcart from him we would need to hire his *boyero*, the man who drove the oxen.

When I brought Marian out to see the property, she seemed satisfied, even though she saw the problems. We knew that living three hours from Turrialba—actually only thirty-one miles—would be difficult in terms of supplying food for the family and meeting medical emergencies. But we were encouraged that the Lord had at last provided land. We had a vision for what He would do there.

Marian drew up a very simple floor plan, with measurements not in feet and inches but in *varas* or rods, the way lumber was measured at the time. Then we started cutting the measurements back to meet our tight budget, ending up with a house roughly twenty-seven feet by thirty-seven feet. We had received a few gifts toward construction and had been able to save a bit of money toward it. We also borrowed some money from a revolving fund of the Mission. Still our budget was extremely limited. Our immediate plan was for a house with four walls, roof, and floors—a shell. Inside walls, sanitary facilities, and water tanks could wait if necessary.

Don Emilio, a contractor friend from the Turrialba church, visited the site with me to get the lay of the land. He volunteered his services, but I would need to pay his helpers. To save us money, he bought logs and had them sawed at the local mill. By February of 1963 the flooring and siding were sawed and set out to dry in the sun. Three Latin friends from a country church which *don* Emilio pastored went to Tsipirí with me and spent a day clearing the building site on the least sloping part of the land. It hurt them to cut down coffee trees, for they themselves grew coffee. But they loved the Lord and shared our vision to reach the Indians!

We were disappointed in our hopes to start building before the end of the short "dry season." Moravia averaged one hundred inches of rain per year, so the area was never really dry. On May 24, four days after the rains began in earnest, Marian was struck by the words of Neh. 2:20: *"We will begin and we will build, for the God of heaven, whose servants we are, will enable us to accomplish our aim."* Rain or not, this gave us hope and boosted our faith!

Troubles

The next morning, unannounced—there were no phones in La Suiza—*don* Emilio and two helpers appeared in the rain on their way to Moravia. A lumber truck carried not only the siding and the hardwood flooring, but also the galvanized iron roofing. Emilio's old Dodge Power Wagon carried four dozen meter-long, cement foundation posts, the lumber for framing, the nails and tools, plus basic food supplies. Ready or not, I gathered a change of clothes, plus some cooking and eating utensils I had bought to use during the construction, and followed them in my Jeep. We expected to unload the lumber in Moravia so that the truck could return immediately to Turrialba, but to travel the nineteen miles from La Suiza to Moravia took us the whole day—a long, discouraging, exhausting day.

After twelve miles through the hills, we crossed the Pacuare River at 1,800 feet altitude, and started up the five-mile, serpentine climb which would crest at just over 4,000 feet overlooking the Moravia Valley. Less than half a mile up, the lumber truck stuck in the mud. After vain efforts to free it, *don* Emilio went ahead in the Power Wagon to leave his load in Moravia and return to shuttle the lumber. Twice he had trouble with a universal joint, and twice the motor failed. Eventually he too got stuck. I shuttled between him and the lumber truck, helping each of them and towing other vehicles which were having trouble passing ours.

Finally at twilight we unloaded the lumber by the wayside so the trucker could go back to town. Abandoning the Power Wagon, Emilio and I went on in the dark in my little Jeep to Moravia to spend the night. We were loaned a room with cots to sleep on. With nothing to eat since leaving La Suiza, we broke out some dry bread and cheese for supper and drank suspect water from the tap.

"*Don* Aziel, if we ever get your house built, it will be a *victoria*," commented Emilio before we fell asleep.

For me, it was the lowest moment of the saga. *Don* Emilio called it "*el día de la tragedia*"—the day of the "tragedy." Only the Lord could turn this mess into a victory.

The next morning we drove back to the Power Wagon and finally got it started by towing it. Then with the Jeep pulling, the Power Wagon made it up the hill through the mud and on to Moravia without its front-wheel drive. There we arranged for an oxcart to haul the foundation posts as far as possible. We hired a passing Indian to take the heavy nail boxes on his horse and then packed food, tools, clothing, and bedding on our backs before heading to Tsipirí on foot.

"*Don* Aziel, we now have possession!" said *don* Emilio triumphantly, when we got everything stowed in Modesta's old thatched hut—with her belongings still there.

I still had no title, but I had taken possession of my property.

After a word of thanks to God, Emilio and his two helpers started building and I left for La Suiza. Along the way, I arranged for a boy to guard the lumber we had left by the wayside near the Pacuare River. Then without help I loaded each of the hundred sheets of galvanized roofing that had been left on the road. When they slid out of the Jeep, I loaded them all again. I stored them under the house of a man I had met down at the edge of the river. If left on the road, such valuable items would have "walked away." Under this man's house they would be safe. I had learned the local unwritten code.

I spent a couple of days in Turrialba buying provisions for the carpenters and locating a new universal joint for the old Power Wagon, as well as getting my old Jeep repaired. Heavy rain continued to fall. On my way back to Tsipirí, I stopped by the lumber we had piled beside the road, opened my windshield, and loaded two 4x4 beams through the front. They were so long that they extended out the back window.

During the construction my job was to keep materials moving to the building site. The oxcart left everything two miles short of Tsipirí, so I paid locals by the load to carry the lumber and roofing on their backs as they slopped through rain and deep mud. We began with 4x4 and 2x8 hardwood beams, then the hardwood for framing and rafters, and finally the siding, as needed on the site. Frequently I returned to Turrialba to bring more supplies. I lost twenty pounds in the five-week saga of the construction.

The rains continued. Mud was often up to the axle of the oxcart. The *boyero* carried an ax to cut roots in the deep ruts. On one occasion the cart fell off the edge of the "road." The oxen would have broken their necks if he had not quickly cut the thongs binding them to the long, heavy yoke.

We had contracted with Nino, the man from whom I had bought part of the land, to transport the heaviest items—the concrete posts, which were the first items needed—from the oxcart to the site. He owned a horse, so I thought he would have no problems, but after hauling about half the posts he gave up. Then a fellow named Tomás volunteered to carry the rest of the posts on his back! With superhuman strength he made four trips a day for five days, each time carrying one post—weighing almost one hundred pounds—more than a mile down the hill until his back was rubbed raw.

Every piece of lumber and roofing arrived muddy to the site. But in spite of squabbles among the men, the human chain of carriers worked successfully. However, this cost me more money than I had paid to the trucker!

Don Emilio's first task had been to clear all trees large enough to fall on the house from the hill above the site. He knew that after weeks of torrential rains the steep land might slide, carrying even large trees with it. Tomás, the strong man, was a godsend to Emilio in felling trees. Using some of the roofing, Emilio built a small metal shed to keep tools and other valuables safe. He had no power tools, but even hand tools were valuable in the jungle. He slept in the shed while the helpers slept and cooked in Modesta's tiny hut.

The project formed a lifelong bond between Emilio and me. We became "mud brothers." I let him take responsibility for all decisions when I was not around. He was building the house as a service to the Lord—though not without payment. We settled later, though he asked for less than he deserved. The construction, including materials, transportation, and labor, cost us $1500—far more than we were prepared to pay.

"*Don* Aziel," said Emilio one day, "no other contractor would have done this for you."

He wasn't bragging, he was telling the truth. Why did he do it? He shared our vision to reach the Indians.

Interrupted by Sad News

On June 21 I went to town for more supplies. Late that afternoon as I was leaving for Tsipirí, a telegram arrived, written in pencil in English. My older brother Haniel had sent a cable that morning. The central office in San José had retransmitted it to La Suiza. It came without an error, though our friend who ran the local office knew no English. As best I remember, it read: "Mother died. Funeral tomorrow. Call collect."

Changing to "city clothes" and substituting shoes for my rubber boots, I drove two hours to the telecommunication office in the capital, at that time the only place in the country to make an international phone call.

"No collect calls, internationally," stated the operator flatly.

In my pocket I had the equivalent of ten dollars, the price of a three-minute call to the United States. Daddy told me that Mama, already under treatment for congestive heart failure, had gotten up in the night and fallen over dead. She was sixty-six; I was forty-one. I was sorry my three minutes didn't allow for all the details Daddy wanted to tell. He wanted to talk!

There was no way I could go to the funeral! It was impossible in those days to obtain immediate permission to exit the country. Nor was it possible to leave the construction, so I drove home to La Suiza, glad to be alone with my thoughts. The next day I headed back toward Tsipirí. At the hour of Mama's funeral, I was slopping through mud up to my boot tops. As I followed the oxcart loaded with lumber, my eyes filled with tears and I choked up.

I asked my twelve siblings to write me their own accounts. Some did, so I have a composite picture of the funeral—the sun streaming through stained-glass windows and Mama with her pink necklace and earrings "she'd wanted all her life." I could visualize my twelve siblings, united in memories and sorrow. Although I couldn't be there, I did not feel sorry for myself, for God is sovereign. I was in His will, in His timing.

The Victory—Moving Day

We *did* begin, and we *did* build, as the prophetic word had said. And it *was* a victory. Moving day was June 27, 1963, five weeks after "the day of the tragedy." We left La Suiza on a sunny morning taking the gas stove and propane tank and whatever else we could fit into the old, but priceless, army trailer. The children's red wagon perched on top of the Jeep.

In Moravia we loaded the oxcart. Marian sat on top of the stuff with baby

Goodbye, La Suiza

Elizabeth in her lap. Susanna and Steven also climbed in the cart. The skillful *boyero* led—bump, bump, bump, bump, bump, bump—as the springless cart creaked over the uneven ground.

"Never again!" said Marian as she dismounted two hours later. "I'd rather slop through the mud on my own two feet."

The ride was miserable, but Marian did learn to appreciate the skill and patience of Nino Flores, the wiry little *boyero,* as he led the reluctant oxen. He walked in front of them, facing them, occasionally glancing behind himself at the road ahead of them. With goad in hand, he would poke them to indicate which direction or to spur them to continue. He had trained them to walk toward him, *toward the pain.* They lumbered along, ever so slowly, balking when they got angry as they pulled the cart through mud up to the axles. He was good to his animals, and so kind and patient with Marian and the children. Afterwards, however, baby Elizabeth would scream whenever she saw him!

"Here comes the architect!" said *don* Emilio, waiting nervously as we approached. "Will she like the house?"

Marian "the architect" with Emilio the builder

We all posed in the sunshine for a triumphant picture—Emilio holding Elizabeth. Then we toured the place before beginning to settle into the house that would be our home for the next thirty-three years.

We had said we would be willing to camp out, and that is what we did! We came to a house with no windows, no ceilings, no furniture, no refrigerator, no sink, nor even a kitchen counter. The house was small, only a thousand square feet—just living room, dining room, kitchen on one side; the study, our bedroom, the bathroom, and a second bedroom on the other side. No closets, but we did have interior partitions which we had not expected. Hastily thrown up with leftover siding, the partitions were only head high at first, nor were there any interior doors.

In the kitchen *don* Emilio's helpers were cooking on a little kerosene burner which didn't work properly. Marian shed a few tears trying to cook on that burner. A bucket held water from the creek. We were always running out of water. Everything was rustic, *too rustic*. Why didn't we wait a week longer to move?

The first few nights we all slept on the floor. Old quilts covered the gaping window openings in a vain attempt to ward off the penetrating chill at 3,700 feet. With no ceilings, the wind—and sometimes rain—blew down on us through the opening which ran the full length of the roof in the local style of that day.

The next day we installed the gas stove and a temporary counter. We cut a hole in the counter for a galvanized iron "sink" which drained into a bucket. Eventually we cut a hole in the floor for a drain pipe, a major improvement! Soon we also had barrels under the eaves to catch the rainwater running off the roof. Life was becoming easier for Marian.

At first we used a makeshift latrine at the edge of the hill, with green banana leaves for a "wall" and dry leaves for paper. Within a couple of days we had a flush toilet in the bathroom—even though we had to flush it with buckets of water. We put the paper in a waste basket and burned it every day. In a single day Tomás, the "superman" who had hauled the foundation posts, dug a six-foot hole in the clay under the house for a septic tank. We topped it with heavy planks, covered it with dirt, and used it for over thirty years, occasionally uncovering it to siphon out the contents and drain it off the edge of the hill beside the bathroom.

First wash day - 1963

Furniture continued to arrive by oxcart and then was transferred to the backs of men as they walked through the woods, down across the Tsipirí and back up the hill to the house. One worker appeared at the door with our large translation table perched on his back.

"Where do I put this?" he questioned.

All the furniture was muddy. Even the unpainted walls of the house were decorated with muddy footprints.

The heaviest item we managed to bring to the house was a large cement *pila*, a typical Costa Rican laundry tub. It took four men two days to get it from the oxcart to the house. With the slope of the land, there was space under the back of the house for a partial "basement," where we could hang clothes in rainy weather. We set up the *pila* there, and eventually the old wringer washer, but at first Modesta, the woman from whom we had bought part of the land, did the washing by hand at the creek.

We continued to park the Jeep about two miles away at the *descanso*, the "resting place," a flat spot at the top of the ridge between Tsipirí and Moravia. I would buy supplies in Turrialba and bring the meat and vegetables home from the Jeep in my backpack. Next day I would send a local boy back for the rest: flour and sugar, rice and powdered milk, soap, hardware, and kerosene.

The kerosene refrigerator was too heavy to be carried in, so we left it in town with colleagues. The chilly weather kept vegetables from spoiling quickly, so our only real problem was preserving meat. Salting it or smoking it proved unsatisfactory. Instead, Marian would cook all the meat as soon as I returned from Turrialba. She would bring it to the boiling point the next day and again the following day if any remained. After that we depended on eggs, cheese, and hot dogs, all of which would keep indefinitely. Canned tuna and sardines were further sources of protein.

The Indians would sell us whatever was in season—oranges, corn, beans. Chirripó was a major bean-producing area of the country. We were already accustomed to eating beans and rice every day, for this was the staple diet of all Costa Ricans. The combination provided another source of complete protein. The people would also sell us eggs. Once when our supply ran low, we prayed during our family devotions that night, asking the Lord to send us more eggs. The very next morning a man came to sell us thirty-four. Another time someone brought ninety eggs, a suspiciously large number. Sure enough, half of them were rotten. Marian soon learned to crack open and inspect each egg before using it.

Every evening I lit two Aladdin lamps, two other kerosene lamps, and several candles. As we ate supper under the hanging lamp, moths of all sizes and descriptions would be attracted by the light. They would flutter down through the opening in the roof and land on the table. Beetles were more seasonal, but we had plenty of those too. If moths or beetles landed in the food, we'd fish them out and go on eating. They were much preferable to the cockroaches that came out of the cracks once we blew out the lights.

Early Days in Tsipirí

We were fairly well settled by Steven's fourth birthday a week or so after we moved to Tsipirí. That day a friend came to visit who was an excellent photographer. We treasure the photos he took, including one of Steven holding his birthday gift, a little tin truck. A few days later a hubcap came off that cheap truck. Elizabeth, then ten months old and crawling, picked it up and swallowed it. She choked and started to turn blue until Modesta put her finger down Elizabeth's throat and pulled out the hubcap. God was watching out for our baby!

Peter and Pricilla's first trip to their new home

Another month passed, and it was time to meet Peter and Priscilla at the airport. Marian was glad to see civilization again after six weeks in Tsipirí. As we stood on the balcony of the terminal, Marian and I grabbed each other in an emotional embrace as we watched the plane descend, bringing our ten-year-old son and eight-year-old daughter home after their second year at boarding school in Honduras. We snapped a picture as they walked across the tarmac to the terminal.

How exciting it was to take Peter and Priscilla to the house for the first time! Though Marian had said, "Never again," she rode in the oxcart with the youngest children while the older ones slopped through the mud with me. Susanna's boot stuck so firmly in a mudhole that she needed help to pull it out. Finally we reached the house that was to become "home" to us all.

Sunday in Tsipirí — 1963
Marian with Elizabeth, Steven, Susanna, Priscilla, and Peter

For the children there was no end of running and playing outside—and plenty of the same inside. How good to have room after being so cramped in La Suiza. One of their favorite pastimes was running their little Matchbox cars on "roads" they carved in the side of the hill in the front yard. They loved the icy swimming hole and kept it dammed, repairing it after floods. All of us usually bathed there—except Marian, who did not like the cold water. One of Peter's chores was chopping weeds with a machete, "helped" by young Steven wielding a smaller machete. The boys also helped haul water from the creek in buckets when we ran out of rainwater.

Our living room became the focal point of our family devotional life. Every night we gathered to read a Bible story for the younger children and a chapter from the New Testament. Then all of us would pray, starting with the youngest. We also continued the practice we had started our last year in Turrialba of reading Proverbs at breakfast, Old Testament at the midday meal, and Psalms at supper.

The God of heaven had indeed enabled us to accomplish our aim, as we had read in Nehemiah. We, His servants, had built in Tsipirí not only a base for reaching the Indians but also a place for raising our children. We would continue there for over thirty years until all the children were married and the New Testament was published.

– 11 –

The Jeep, the Neighbors, and the Horse that Died

1963 to 1967

Living in Tsipirí provided us with many stories about the Jeep, the road, and the neighbors. The three-mile "road" up from the edge of the wide Moravia Valley—the last edge of the Spanish world— dropped sharply down into the narrow Tsipirí Valley, the beginning of the Indian world. Most of our difficulties with the Jeep and the neighbors could have been avoided by settling closer to civilization, yet living in Tsipirí put us in a perfect location for reaching the Indians in the vast Chirripó Valley and beyond.

In Costa Rica the term "jeep" is a generic term for any four-wheel-drive passenger vehicle, not just for the original military vehicle produced by Willys during World War II. In our thirty-three years living in Tsipirí we went through a Willys, a Land Rover, two Toyotas, and a Trooper. All of these vehicles except the last had a winch mounted on the front, which we used frequently on the final three miles of the road to our property.

In spite of a few occasional problems, our vehicles had almost miraculous capabilities. They were strong, tough, work horses. One local said that my jeeps never broke down! Once moving, I usually made it to town and back, alone or with the family, at all hours, through pouring rains, sticky mud, and swollen creeks, with practically no exceptions and only a few delays. God also protected us from accidents and brake failures. We never fell over the precipice of the cliff-hanging roads that snaked around the steep mountains. At times the road would be closed for days or even weeks when bridges were out, or when landslides or washouts made it impassable. The Lord was good not to let such things happen when we needed to get to town.

Except in very dry weather I could not climb the steep hill up from Tsipirí without engaging the four-wheel drive. Usually I had to put chains on all four wheels as well. On every trip to town—three hours away counting time to take off the chains—I used all forward gears. Twice we had to climb that hill with a broken axle. I made it with the help of the winch, but it was a two-hour, muddy ordeal to climb the first few hundred feet.

One fine morning we loaded up the Willys for a trip to San José and prayed that it would start. There was no mechanic within three hours, and I had been having trouble starting the Jeep.

"Pray, Daddy!" said young Steven when it wouldn't crank.

I felt a bit peeved, for I had already prayed. But I prayed again, and to my amazement the engine started.

Many a time we prayed ourselves up the first hill out of Tsipirí. Our property was in a narrow valley, with hills rising on every side. That first hill was very steep and had only been bulldozed once, never graveled. If the weather was dry, I could sometimes make it up without chains unless we were pulling the trailer. Actually, we used the trailer—an old WWII army trailer—more often than not. The Willys was not large enough to hold the family plus our baggage and supplies.

On a cloudy morning during the first year after the road was opened all the way to our house, I kept hurrying Marian to get ready to leave for town. I was hoping to reach the top of the hill without having to deal with chains, but the rain began before we had gotten even a hundred feet up the hill. The clay got slick and we got stuck. I tried revving up, but nothing happened except that mud was splattering all over the Jeep. The engine roared, frightening Elizabeth who was about two years old—old enough to realize we were in trouble. She started screaming at the top of her little lungs. Five-year-old Steven joined in. Had we remembered to pray? I don't know.

There was nothing I could do but get out in the rain and put on the chains—much more difficult to do in the sticky mud than if I had done it at home. Then we inched our way up, engine roaring, kids screaming, mud flying. The children finally screamed themselves to sleep. It took us half an hour to reach the top where the "road" leveled off somewhat.

At such times Marian would always shut her eyes. The road was the bane of her life. I never could figure out why it bothered her so much, but then, I'm not a woman. The frontier is a man's world. Such events—and they were frequent—were just part of life in our frontier world.

Keeping clean on trips to town was difficult for Marian. Just getting from the house to the Jeep was sometimes a challenge because of the mud. If I had to put on chains along the road, I would wipe the mud off my arms as best I could with a rag. Inevitably, some of the mud rubbed off on her when I got back in the Jeep. The floor of the Jeep would be caked with mud from our boots. When we got to town we stopped first at a friend's house to clean up before proceeding to do our errands.

Marian was not the only woman who didn't appreciate the road! A neighbor lady who begged me for a ride was so terrified that she screamed for me to let her out. Unfortunately I could not hear her above the roar of the engine. When revved up, the old Willys made a piercing noise like a siren.

Once I left Tsipirí before daybreak to take two visitors to catch the once-a-day bus in Moravia. I was hoping to avoid taking them all the way to Turrialba after their weekend visit. We made it up the hill all right but then got stuck in a mud hole. The ladies stood at the edge of the road while I struggled to get the Jeep out of the hole.

"I'd have cried," confessed one of them later, "if I hadn't been embarrassed to cry in front of Aziel."

Years later as we were plowing through the mud on our way to Tsipirí with friends, another woman made a comment about the road.

"If the Lord gives Brownie points," remarked Joani to Marian, "you certainly deserve some for putting up with this road!"

Winching around the Curve

Traveling home from town one dark night with the whole family—six children by then—in the Willys, we reached the first sharp curve after cresting the ridge separating Moravia from Tsipirí and promptly get stuck. At every bend in the hill there was a sharp inside curve where water flowed down when it rained. The rainwater collected on level sections of the road, producing some of the worst mud holes. This particular mud hole was one of the most problematical, but all mud holes were long stretches with sticky, gumbo mud filling the deep ruts.

With only the headlights of the Jeep for light, Peter walked ahead to feel his way in the weeds beside the road as he searched for a stump to which he could hitch the winch cable—a hundred feet long.

Peter helps with the winch

We worried that he might step on a snake. After he found a stump and hooked the steel cable around it, I cranked the engine of the Jeep and started winding up the cable, a process similar to winding thread on the bobbin of a sewing machine. Since we were pulling at an angle around a sharp curve, the Jeep would only move a few feet before the cable began to jam up at one end of the drum. Then we had to unwind the whole cable so that Peter could hitch it to a stump a bit further ahead before I started the winch again.

For two and a half hours, we kept repeating the process until the Jeep finally pulled itself onto solid ground. We had driven straight from San José, five hours away. We had not had any supper, yet none of the children complained, nor did the baby cry. We have never forgotten that night. As we look back on it now, it seems like a miracle. Who was praying for us that night?

On another night at the same spot, again with the family in the Jeep, I unwittingly hitched the winch cable to a dead tree. I got quite a scare when the whole tree fell—with the top landing just a yard from the hood of the Jeep! But that winch was a blessing from the Lord. Over the years it got us out of many a tight spot.

Bridges and Fords

The Moravia Valley is an extensive, relatively flat, swampy area crossed by a river and several small streams. Perhaps the valley had once been a lake before some earthquake opened an outlet and drained it. The road through the valley skirted the edge of the swampy area, crossing the creeks on simple wooden bridges. As the water weakened the wooden supports of these bridges, they would be damaged by floods. Sometimes we would have to detour through the swamps for weeks or even months before new bridges were built.

When the bridge over the largest stream at the eastern edge of the valley washed away a second time, it was never rebuilt, leaving us to ford the stream permanently. Fortunately, when this creek rises, it goes down quickly. We never had to wait for it to recede, although it was a bit tricky to negotiate the rocky bed. The two branches of the Tsipirí at the edge of our property were easy to ford, but at flood stage they could not be forded, nor did they recede quickly. Sometimes we would be cut off from the outside world for days, giving us the feeling of being "snowed in" or "rained in!"

Doing Favors along the Road

One day as I was driving up the Pacuare hill in the Willys, I came upon a log truck spinning on a slick place in a relatively level spot. Loaded with a dozen eleven-foot logs, he was not able to move, but with my little Jeep I managed to pull him off the slick spot.

Another time on that same steep hill I came upon the "bus"—an old converted Willys station wagon like the jeepneys used in the

Philippines. Overloaded with about twenty passengers, it was stuck in the ditch beside the road, facing uphill. The driver asked if I would pull him out. I doubted that I could, but I turned my Willys around to face the bus and hitched my winch cable to it. The winch refused to work! I felt helpless. The bus driver got out and studied the problem.

"Do you have a three-inch nail?" he asked.

I happened to have just bought a fresh supply in Turrialba. Putting the nail in a slot where a pin was missing, the driver got back in the bus.

"Try it," he commanded.

It worked! I pulled the bus out of the ditch.

"That nail won't last long," he warned me. "Get a proper pin the next time you go to town."

One night after dark on my way home from town in my old Willys I approached the rickety narrow suspension bridge over the Pacuare River. A light rain was falling and the bridge planks were slick. As usual, some of the boards were loose and floppy. A loaded log truck was stalled in the middle of the one-lane bridge, facing me. His starter was not working.

"Will you pull me off?" asked the driver.

Since I wanted to get home, I was willing to take a chance.

"With this little Jeep I don't know if I can," I said, "but we'll see."

I already had the four-wheel drive engaged, so I put it in low-low and drove toward the truck. The logger hitched up his chain. I prayed, then put the Jeep in reverse, let out the clutch, and revved the engine up all the way. The truck moved enough to crank! Within seconds he was out of my way. Yes, my clutch was smelling.

Once as I was on my way to San José for a committee meeting, a man hailed me.

"Will you go get my brother in Paso Marcos and take him to the hospital in Turrialba?"

The daily bus had already passed by, so his only hope was to hitch a ride with some passing vehicle—infrequent in those days. I thought of the parable Jesus told about the priest and the Levite who passed up an injured man—were they on the way to a committee meeting? The brother got in my Jeep and we drove a few miles on a side road, then stopped at the edge of the Pacuare, a major river. Relatives brought the sick man across the river on a hand-pulled cable car and settled him in the Jeep. I dropped him off at the hospital and continued to the capital.

Another time we were about halfway from Turrialba to our home in Tsipirí, when a man hailed me.

"Will you take this fellow to the bus? He's been bitten by a *bicho* ['bug,' local slang for 'snake']."

The bus had already passed by on its way to Turrialba, so I unloaded the baggage and Marian stood by the wayside with the kids while I turned the little Jeep around and took the fellow back a mile to catch up with the bus on its way to Turrialba.

These favors—and many others over the years—impressed some of the locals. People knew I would help in cases of genuine need. But did these favors bring people to the Lord? Not that I know of. Yet I continued to do these favors as unto the Lord.

Emergencies

Over the years that we lived in Tsipirí I made many emergency trips to the hospital in Turrialba. A familiar scene would repeat itself. I would be working at my translation desk with a helper. At midmorning a young couple would bring a small, listless child—hot with fever, eyes pitiful, breathing hard. They had walked since daybreak. I would dismiss my helper, ask Marian if there was anything she wanted me to add to the shopping list I always kept in my wallet, and then crank up the Jeep. Once in Moravia, I would take off my shirt so I wouldn't get it muddy when I took off the chains, then wash the chains in the creek and wash the mud off my arms.

After leaving the child at the hospital in Turrialba three hours away, I would do a few errands and get home by night.

On one occasion Tomás, the incredibly strong man who had hauled the cement posts for our house, asked me to take his baby to the hospital. The sick child died in her father's arms a few miles short of medical help. I drove back to Tsipirí alone and walked twenty minutes up the hill to tell his wife the sad news.

Coping with other people's emergencies became a lifestyle for us, whether it was an illness or a machete cut or a snake bite. But in thirty-three years of living in Tsipirí, we never had to make an emergency trip to town for one of our own children, though on a couple of occasions I took one of them out to the doctor just in case they needed attention. Each day I committed all of us to the Lord for His covering: physically, mentally, and spiritually. In Tsipirí I felt that my margin of safety was narrowed by half. Yet over the years there, God seemed to double in size!

"The Mother Can't Deliver"

By the local grapevine we had heard that a landslide had covered about fifty feet of the road on the steep Pacuare hill, about ten miles away. We were at home in Tsipirí, waiting for some missionary friends to arrive for a weekend. I would need to drive out to the landslide to meet them there. Around eight that morning a young Indian came running up to my door, exhausted. Celín had left his home near the Chirripó River at daylight.

"My mother's been in labor twenty-four hours and can't deliver. Will you take her to the hospital?" he asked, stating that they would bring her in a hammock with four men carrying her up a hill that even without a load was a three-hour climb.

"How long will it take you to get her here?" I asked.

"We'll be here at four p.m.," he answered.

Mentally I calculated that I could pick up our friend Bert and his family at the landslide and bring them to Tsipirí, then take the woman to the landslide and transfer her to Bert's car for the trip to the hospital. The risk? That our friends would hear of the landslide and turn back.

"Go bring your mother," I said to Celín in faith.

Guessing when Bert would reach the Pacuare hill, I drove to the landslide, parked my car, and crossed the slide, slopping through the slush and mud filled with rocks, roots, and branches. An hour later I heard a car. It was Bert and his family! I told them the plan. With some difficulty we got the family and their baggage across the landslide and back to Tsipirí. At four p.m. we were chatting and drinking coffee on our porch. I had left the Jeep parked at my gate, ready for a quick getaway when Celín arrived.

When Celín appeared, Bert and I went to the Jeep. Removing the passenger seat, we laid the woman on the floor. Bert, Celín, and the husband sat on the sides as we drove to the landslide. It proved very difficult for us four men to carry the lady over the fifty feet of deep, slushy mud and rocks, but we made it to Bert's car. At the Turrialba hospital they saved the mother, but lost the baby. The woman remained in the hospital, but Celín and the father returned with Bert and me.

Arriving at my door at midnight, Bert was in a daze. Without saying a word, he went straight to bed while I fixed up a pallet on the floor for the Indians. The sad sequel to this story is that when I was on furlough a year later, the same woman was again unable to deliver. With no one available to take her to the hospital, she died.

Since I had the only vehicle in the area, there were many requests for my services. I did favors such as purchasing sheets of galvanized iron roofing for the Indians as they began to replace thatch with more permanent material. If I did not buy it for them in Turrialba and take it to Tsipirí in the trailer or on the rack of my vehicle, they had to walk as much as a day to reach Moravia, then take the bus the next day to Turrialba to purchase the "zinc" and return to Moravia, and finally carry the roofing four miles from the end of the bus line to Tsipirí. They would spend the night at our house, then carry the roofing for several more hours from Tsipirí to their homes. A few owned horses, but many had to carry the heavy rolls of roofing on their backs.

What I did *not* offer the Indians was taxi service for personal trips to town. But usually when I made supply trips to Turrialba, some Indians would show up, asking to go along. The grapevine evidently informed them that I would be going to town. In such cases I took occasional passengers, charging them nothing. When I made special trips to the hospital for emergencies I charged only the actual cost of the fuel. Emergency trips were exceptions to my policy of not offering taxi service. I was not running a bus line, nor a trucking service. My job was to translate the Word and to plant the church.

Maintaining the Road

When Beto, a local logger, finished bulldozing the road from the edge of the Moravia Valley to Tsipirí, it was still only an access road—a logging road. There were no ditches along the edge, nor was the road "crowned" so that rainwater would run off. It was merely an opening adequate for loggers—and for a jeep.

"*Don* Aziel," counseled Beto, "if you want to save the road, you'd better ditch it."

At first I did not take his words seriously. I waited, hoping for help from local settlers. They did eventually give me some help. It was to their advantage to join the work crew, for the government would give them a receipt toward the small property tax that settlers had to pay to substantiate their claims. Those receipts would help them prove possession, if they eventually tried to title their land.

With their help I put in culverts at four crucial points—on inside curves. We also ditched some of the worst spots. But the ongoing work fell to me. I was the only one who really cared about keeping the road passable for vehicles. On Saturdays I often took my boys and my *peones* to work with me on the road—a pattern for thirty years.

We dug ditches and shoveled landslides—new roads cut through steep hills produce frequent slides. But the big work was hauling rocks from the creek. We loaded river rock into wooden boxes and then dumped the rocks into my trailer. Twenty-five boxes would fill—actually, overload—the half-ton army trailer. We kept putting rocks in the worst ruts, the ones where we could only pull out with the winch if we got stuck. With three miles of road to maintain, the need for rocks was endless!

A New 4x4

In the summer of 1965 a couple from California came to visit us. On a hot, dry afternoon I was driving Colgate Clark, a high school shop teacher, and his family to Tsipirí. As we neared the top of the five-mile climb up from the Pacuare River, climbing over two thousand feet in that stretch, the engine stopped. Although Colgate was something of a mechanic, he couldn't get it started. Then the bus—at that time a worn-out school bus from the States—came along on its daily run from Turrialba to Moravia.

Quírico, the bus driver, left his engine running—his starter was not working—and got out to help us. In that isolated area every truck driver or bus driver was, of necessity, a self-made mechanic. The bus was full, the passengers were tired, a baby was crying. Unperturbed, Quírico studied our problem, found a leak in the gas line, managed to seal it temporarily, and we drove away. The Clarks were amazed. No one on the bus complained. Quírico accepted no money for his services. Such was life on the frontier.

The last three miles through the woods to Tsipirí were impressive—and uncomfortable—as the old Jeep bumped and jolted over the hard ruts. Only in rainy season did we have a relatively smooth ride, for mud is at least soft! The Jeep was worn out from the previous owner's travels all over Central America, Mexico, and the States. But it ran—and it had a winch!

That little two-door, five-passenger Willys could hold a lot of people. Once we had twelve crowded in it. Marian always sat in the tiny, homemade seat between the driver's seat and the passenger seat, trying to keep out of the way of the gear shift. The back seat occupied space that was needed for baggage, so we took it out. The children sat on pads covering the panels over the back wheels. The floor and the wheel panels were rusted out in spots.

"Daddy," one of the children would often cry out as we splashed through a mud hole, "my bottom is getting wet!"

Seat belts were unknown in those days. I had the steering wheel to hang on to, but my passengers just hung on as best they could. Sometimes they bumped their heads against a window or even the roof when we hit an especially bad hole in the road. But we were grateful to have a vehicle. It was an answer to prayer.

After Colgate—the kids called him "Uncle Toothpaste"— returned to the States, he sent us a gift of $50 "for baling wire to hold the Jeep together until you can get a better vehicle!" That gift was a real boost to our faith.

During Colgate's visit, he and I had discussed our need for a better four-wheel drive. We continued our discussion by mail, but Marian and I were indecisive as to what we wanted. We did check out all the alternatives in San José and even saved up a little money. Finally we settled on a Land Rover Safari, a twelve-passenger, four-door vehicle that also had a back door accessing two side benches. There was plenty of room for the kids and even some space for baggage inside, as well as on the roof rack. We would only need to use the trailer occasionally. Once we settled on the Safari, I wrote Colgate for the first time in months.

Colgate answered me quickly: "I just sent $2000 to your mission toward a Land Rover for you." Then he told this story: "You couldn't make up your mind about a vehicle. So I told the Lord, 'If I get a summer job at the photo shop, and if Aziel Jones tells me what vehicle he wants without my asking him again, then I'll give him everything I earn this summer for a vehicle.'" Then he added, "I got the job, made over $900 and sold my stamp collection to round it off to $1000. I was so happy about it that I told Mrs. Winters at church. Right away she said, 'I'll match it!' So I just sent $2000 to your mission for a better vehicle."

The Land Rover

Soon we learned of a recent model Safari being repainted and refurbished at the Land Rover dealership. The dealer gave us a few hundred dollars credit on the old Willys and the winch—the most valuable part of the Jeep. With that credit and Colgate's gift plus our small savings we were able to purchase the Land Rover for cash.

What a thrill it was to drive away in that "new" 4x4. We were humbled to receive such a sacrificial gift from the Lord's servants. As we showed the Land Rover to colleagues, Anne made a comment to Marian.

"I bet you feel like a queen in that Land Rover!" said Anne.

"I feel like the Queen of England on safari in Africa!" Marian replied.

Our first photo of the Land Rover was with Steven. He had prayed fervently and ceaselessly. We felt that the Safari was an answer to *his* prayers.

Eventually I drove that Safari all the way to the States for furlough, with six children, and Marian expecting our seventh. Our luggage all fit in the roof rack. On our return from furlough we stopped in Houston for the manufacturer to install a winch made just for Land Rovers.

That vehicle was the most comfortable of all our four-wheel drives, but it didn't hold up as well as the others we had. It gave us a smooth ride, but with only four cylinders it was underpowered for the loads we carried and the "roads" we traveled. Yet

Land Rover stuck in the mud

what an improvement it was over the old Willys, and what an answer to prayer!

Frontier Neighbors

Our move to Tsipirí impacted the local scene. Locals who had already claimed small parcels of land near Tsipirí began to settle there too. Previously, they came only occasionally from their houses in Moravia to check their crops. Others perhaps imagined I would open up a whole new area, as the legendary Fernando Alvarado Chacón had opened Moravia in the 1940s. Some of the men I hired to haul lumber during the construction seemed to assume I would be an ongoing source of employment. At one time or another every neighbor became a *peón*, working for me by the hour, some long-term. I would need them for years, until the area became a reservation and the land was given back to the Indians.

While these neighbors might have hoped for personal gain from my presence in Tsipirí, they perhaps also feared I might see too much, know too much, or talk too much. By settling near Tsipirí they were beyond observation by the police agent in Moravia, but what about me? Would I report illegal bootlegging or exploitation of the Indians? Unwittingly I became a sort of conscience awakener. After all, they knew I was an "evangelical pastor." Evangelicals had a reputation for uprightness.

Everyone living across the Tsipirí was a *precarista*, a landholder with no legal title. All in some way had obtained land from the Indians, paying less than the going price of land *afuera*, "outside," closer to civilization. The Indians did not sell their land: "The land is God's," they said. In their minds they were only selling the right to use it; therefore, they sold it cheaply. The Latinos had a completely different concept of land tenure. And a few of them were not above getting an Indian drunk in order to buy his land even more cheaply.

Five such settlers were now our neighbors—shouting distance away. They were handy when I needed help hauling things or cutting trees that had fallen across the road. I paid them the going hourly rate and they were happy to get some cash. Cash was hard to come by except at harvest time.

Just after our first Christmas in Tsipirí an enormous oak fell across the road, blocking the way for the oxcart to get to our house. It was time for us to take Peter, Priscilla, and now Susanna as well, to the airport for the flight back to boarding school in Honduras. The cart was to take all the baggage to the Jeep, for the final stretch of "road" to Tsipirí had not yet been opened. The Tsipirí—a creek normally less than knee-deep—was a roaring, waist-deep torrent following a week of heavy rain. The oxcart driver came to our rescue, along with Nino, the neighbor from whom we had bought part of our land. Dressed in clean, starched, and pressed khaki for New Year's, Nino helped me get Marian and the children through the water. One misstep and we might have drowned. Then Nino and the *boyero*—the ox driver—helped carry the baby, the duffle bags, the suitcases and boxes up the hill to the oxcart.

The Still

Forty-five minutes up the hill from Tsipirí toward Chirripó lived another settler named Albino, the most influential man in the whole area. For many months he sold us milk, which his son brought us daily. Albino was the head of the local "road board." I helped him out, taking him and some of the other neighbors to Turrialba to ask the municipal authorities to send a bulldozer to finish the road as far as Tsipirí.

Once the road was opened, it gave government vehicles access to the area. One day men from the rural police force in Turrialba appeared at my door, asking where Albino lived. Two hours later they were back with the evidence that he was bootlegging. They had found his still, with his son stoking the fire. To get out of jail and pay his fine, Albino sold his cattle—the beginning of his downfall.

Later I had an occasion to do a favor for Albino, driving his ailing wife—who had not left the area for seventeen years—to live with a grown daughter near Turrialba. Still later I was called upon to taxi family members to a funeral. That was a twenty-four hour ordeal, for I had to spend the night in the Jeep.

Albino had a daughter who eventually worked for Marian; but his son, the milk boy, left the area and became a drunkard. When I ran across him in the port city of Limón years later, he gave a glowing testimony of how he had come to the Lord and married a Pentecostal woman. Although we had nothing to do with his conversion, we had been praying for Albino's family to be saved.

Whatever the results of our favors to neighbors, we did what we had to do, as the Lord led us. They needed help and I gave it, but I did it for the Lord. In Tsipirí there was no one else to help those in distress.

The Mummy

On a later occasion some rural police came to our house, asking to park their jeep in the front yard—safer than parking at the spot where the public road ended by the creek. Carrying shovels, they headed for an Indian hut hours away across the Chirripó River. Questions had been raised about the death of a young woman. Her parents had gone to Turrialba to make a formal accusation against the son-in-law, claiming he had beaten their daughter to death with the butt of his rifle. (The young husband was a friend of mine; I had once taken a risk crossing the swollen Chirripó River to give him a Spanish Bible he had requested.)

The next day the police returned carrying the body, wrapped in plastic, strung from poles.

"When we disinterred the body," they reported, "we found it wrapped in a blanket inside a deep chamber topped with poles covered by rocks and dirt. The body was in perfect condition—dried up like a mummy."

The bones, including the skull, were taken to San José for the proper authorities to make a judgment. The husband was vindicated when no fracture was found.

The Horse that Died

Modesta's horse became the source of a story that we have told over and over again. Modesta was the woman from whom we had bought part of our land. Soon after we built our house, she settled on land behind us. She was a source of information—and local gossip. She also became our maid, providing invaluable help in those early days. Modesta was tough. She washed clothes for us on the rocks at the creek when rainwater in our barrels ran out. She helped wax the hardwood floors after I had washed, planed, and sanded them by hand. At that time in Costa Rica no one varnished wood floors, but merely waxed the bare wood.

Nino, from whom I had bought another piece of land, also moved from Moravia with his wife and family to a spot down the Tsipirí from us. He had come, it seemed, thinking I would build an empire—not just a house—and would need his services. He also came to be near Modesta, who was his cousin and lover. Nino worked for me from time to time—until I caught him cheating. But Modesta's teenage son continued to cut weeds for me occasionally.

When we made trips to the capital, we employed Modesta to guard the house. Twice, however, we returned home to find the house had been robbed! Marian even saw a piece of her own clothing on Modesta's clothesline one day when we went to visit. Later when Marian mentioned it to Modesta, she quit on the spot.

I had already started making a fence between our land and hers. But soon I really needed to finish it, for Modesta bought a horse and started using my driveway and front yard as a trail to her house. Her son could look directly into our bedroom window as he rode within a foot of the house. Previously they had used another trail.

A few days after I finished my fence, Albino came to bring milk—and news.

"*Don* Aziel," he confided, "you should know that a petition is being circulated, signed by all your neighbors, saying, 'Arziel Jones, an evangelical pastor, has closed a public road.'"

I appreciated that Albino was friendly enough to tell me, but then a nagging question arose. Had he also signed the petition? The misspelling of my name gave me a clue as to who might have been behind it all, for only one person ever called me "Arziel"—a man who had laid claim to a big area downstream from us.

If all my neighbors had signed, I had no defense. I was facing the local mentality: Stake a claim, and if no one challenges it within ten years, you will have the right of possession—albeit *posesión en precaria*, "precarious possession," not a title. I knew that continuing to allow passersby to cross my land could result in my trail becoming legally public.

Marian and I went to the study that morning and knelt by the cot. From the window we could see Modesta's horse contentedly grazing.

"Show Your hand!" we cried out to God. "Show us Your glory!"

That afternoon a friend of Modesta's came with a request.

"Modesta wants to borrow your pick and shovel," he said.

We were glad for a chance to do a favor for an angry neighbor. Peter was curious and ran over to see what was happening. As a child, he could get away with it, but he returned quickly.

"They're burying the horse!!" he exclaimed.

God truly had intervened!

Easing Tension

Modesta still was not on speaking terms with us, so I was hoping for a chance to do her a favor. I had the impression that Modesta's mother, who was ill, needed to get out to a doctor. So I went over to ask Modesta if her mother needed medical help, but she brushed off my inquiry. When she finally realized that I was serious, she asked me to take her mother to Moravia to catch the bus to town. Then I offered to take her all the way to Turrialba, if that was what the family wanted. In order for them to get the mother to my Jeep I unstapled the barbed wire fence I had made. She and other family members got a free trip to town. That broke the tension over my closing the trail to Modesta's house. Later she returned to work for Marian.

Eventually we discovered who had robbed our house. On a trek to an Indian house I found some of our missing silverware. I showed it to the police agent in Moravia as evidence, then bought some silverware in Turrialba to compensate the Indians. They had innocently purchased it from Nino's grown son who bought and sold items to the Indians.

"You're an evangelical pastor. You should have pardoned my son," said Nino, furious that I had shown the evidence to the police. But we learned that the fellow was already suspected of other robberies in the area; we were merely the first to report him.

Another Fence

Sometime later I put a gate across my driveway to prevent horses and cars from entering without my consent. Tourists from San José wanted to use my yard as a parking lot. Alongside the gate I made a *pasagente*, a small opening through which only people could pass. Eventually, I encircled my acreage with barbed wire—except for one inaccessible area at the bottom of my land. One day I discovered that someone had made a trail through that area across a narrow strip of land at a bend in the Tsipirí. I put up a short stretch of fence which ended the problem, or so I thought. As for who had made that trail, I found out that Modesta's son had done it, paid by a man who had properties both below and above mine.

The *Camino Real*, the main trail to Chirripó, still bisected my land—which was no problem. However, no other trail across my property had existed before I bought the land. In Turrialba I went to the authorities to investigate my rights.

"If you've got a title saying there's no right-of-way through your property," they told me, "then you don't have to worry."

Fortunately, by this time I did have a legal title. When I consulted my lawyer, he leaned back in his chair and smiled reassuringly. He knew that the term "no right-of-way" was in my title, for he had included that phrase when he drew up the document.

When Nino, Albino, and a third man—the one who had actually drawn up the petition against me—appeared at my door, I was prepared.

"Would you please be so kind as to allow us a trail across the bottom of your land, just the very edge?" they asked politely.

Addressing Nino, I said, "You could have kept that piece of land, which I didn't even want when you sold it, or sold it with the condition that you could put a trail there. But you didn't."

To the third man I said, "When I was away, you paid a man to open that trail."

Directing my words to all three, I said, "My answer is no." Then I showed them my title.

"Let's go. We don't have a case," said Albino as he stood up and spoke to the others.

Years later someone told me that the locals said, "Don't mess with *don* Aziel. He knows the laws."

Another Robbery

During our first year in Tsipirí we had to park the Jeep at the top of the ridge two miles from the house. Only once was my locked car bothered. Someone let the air out of the spare tire and also emptied the glove compartment, reaching through an air vent near the floor by the passenger seat. A few weeks later when our family paid a visit to a woman who lived in the area, I happened to notice the small English Bible which I had always kept in the car. Her son, she said, "had found it."

Chepe

Chepe, a nephew of Modesta's, was not a close neighbor, for he lived three miles away in Moravia. A few years before we moved to

Tsipirí I had given him a Gospel of John. Now he came to see us, repented of his sins, and prayed to receive Jesus. To follow up, I supplied him with a simple Bible correspondence course.

One day a runner appeared just after I got home from a supply trip to Turrialba, having carried a forty-pound pack two miles from the Jeep to the house. The runner delivered a message from the administrator of Moravia where Chepe worked as a *peón*: "Manuel struck Chepe in the head with a machete, and we can't stop the bleeding. Please come take him to the hospital. There's no other vehicle available." Quickly I retraced my steps to the Jeep and drove back to Moravia where I found Chepe, deathly pale, lying in a pool of blood. Kneeling by him, I prayed for him, for Manuel, and for all in Moravia. Then in record time I drove him to the hospital in Turrialba. I found out later that the administrator's Willys station wagon had actually been available at the time of the incident, but he had refused to take Chepe to the hospital. Nor would he pay for my gas, for he said the incident was not a farm accident, but rather the result of an old feud between the two *peones*.

Once recovered, Chepe began to work for me on Saturdays—as my *peón*. It was with his help that I rolled giant logs out of the way and cleared tangled growth from the steep acreage in order to fence my property. From him I learned to dig post holes with a shovel and *macana*, a narrow digging tool. I also learned how to treat a *peón*—some of the "do's and don'ts." I learned, too, how a good *peón* treats his *patrón*: he never asks the boss to go get him a tool, and he never talks back. Chepe was a very good *peón*, but sadly he fell away from the Lord and eventually left the area. After he left, I employed only Indian helpers.

Other Neighbors

Manuel, the man who had attacked Chepe, was an old contact from my first trips to Moravia while I was still in language school. I would stop at his house and talk to him about the Lord. Eventually I loaned him a hand-cranked Gospel Recordings phonograph with records in Spanish. A seed was planted in the heart of his son, a boy named Javier who loved to crank that phonograph. Later Manuel asked me for a Bible, but afterward returned it, asking instead for a Catholic Bible. When I supplied it, he wanted me to sit and explain to him the Catholic notes—but not the Scriptures. I quit visiting him.

After we moved to Tsipirí, a new bus driver came to live in Moravia. Claiming to be an evangelical, he asked me to start services at Manuel's house. Once a week I drove out in my old Jeep, but the meetings didn't continue long. Neither did the bus driver. He absconded with the money raised during a *turno*, "a fair" to finance a local project.

There was, however, one local settler who gave us much joy. In those days we held meetings at our house in Spanish for the neighbors in the Tsipirí area. Eduardo, who owned a bootleg still an hour downstream from our house, was one who attended frequently. He had been the best *peón* among those who hauled lumber when we built our house. Eduardo always chose the heavy pieces that the other men avoided, particularly the 2x8 floor joists, which were heavy because the wood was still green. He would work overtime, hauling lumber on his back for a mile and a half down the hill over a difficult trail crisscrossed with roots. He never complained nor quarreled about pay.

Eduardo had already professed faith before I met him. Now he came to our meetings. He was the only local Latin I ever baptized in the creek at Tsipirí. On the day of his baptism, a teen from Moravia came to gawk and make fun of us. Within six months that young man was dead—he had ridden his horse too hard on the only straight stretch of road in Moravia and the horse threw him.

Eventually Eduardo moved away from the area and attended a CAM church, but he never became a stable Christian. Marian and I continued to pray for our neighbors. For a while we visited one neighbor each Sunday—each family that lived within a two hours' walk of our house. All the children went with us. We would chat a while, then read a Scripture, and pray. But there was no response, no interest. Real fruit among Spanish-speakers would come much later.

Our problems with the neighbors and with the road were part of the greater context of learning the Cabécar language, translating, and trekking to plant God's Word in a new culture. We were always looking to the Lord, always praying about current concerns, yet paradoxically, as we sought the Lord we were drawn to a new spiritual level. We grew exponentially, though not consciously at the time. Actually, it seemed that God grew! In those early years in Tsipirí God doubled in size!

− 12 −
Translation at Last
1963 to 1966

As we drove from the United States back to Costa Rica after our short furlough in 1961, we had stopped in Mexico for a quick visit to the SIL translation center at Ixmiquilpan. There we happened to meet John Beekman. We had heard a lot about this Wycliffe missionary who had finished his own translation and was now training new translators. He was a pioneer in developing the science of translating idiomatically. During the three summers we studied at SIL in Oklahoma we had learned much about linguistics, but nothing about the how-to of translation.

Beekman had conceived the idea of bringing translators and their helpers to a center where they could stay a while, away from the distractions of the tribe, and translate under supervision. He strongly encouraged us to attend such a workshop and then gave us two booklets, full of questions applicable to any language. Before attending a workshop, we would need to write out our answers to those questions. I felt a desire to participate in a workshop someday, but was fearful. I knew I would be embarrassed for an experienced translator to see my ignorance after almost a decade on the field. Putting aside the thought of a workshop, we continued our trip back to Costa Rica.

The Alphabet Book

When I organized my study after moving to Tsipirí in 1963, I set aside the booklets that John Beekman had given me, planning to work on them "someday." Instead I went back to work on current projects. My study schedule increased as we became more settled. Indians dropped in frequently, giving us plenty of language practice. I was anxious to complete the alphabet book I had been working on since we lived in La Suiza. I did the drawings and Marian the lettering.

On a trip to the capital, we took the finished manuscript to a mimeograph agency—no photocopying in those days. We had a mimeograph at home, but needed help to cut the stencils for any material that was not typed. The dealer not only made electronic stencils of our originals and ran them off, but also collated, stapled, and trimmed the books, charging only cost!

Soon we used the book to introduce a middle-aged Indian to the idea that those marks on the paper stood for sounds. To him those characters were no more intelligible than Chinese characters are to me. He was convinced that he could not learn. But over the years many Indians taught themselves to read with only that little booklet to help them. That alphabet book went through many printings and became our most widely distributed piece of literature. Everybody wanted a copy!

Another project was to translate, with the aid of a helper, several simple Bible stories. We did the creation story, the fall of man, the flood, and a few others, writing them all on 3x5 slips of paper until Marian found time to type them. How pitiful those initial attempts look now! But we had to start somewhere. I also kept adding to my "hymnbook"—a tiny collection of songs, handwritten at first on 3x5 slips, later typed on quarter sheets of paper.

Finding the Key that Unlocked the Verbs

People cannot communicate without verbs. They can point to objects and name them, but without verbs they can't get a message across. Verbs are the key to any language.

We had already learned a lot about Cabécar verbs. But every time we thought we had figured out the whole system, we'd snag on some pesky particle. We could not fully conjugate any verb without an Indian helper. That meant we were not really qualified to start translating. We desperately needed to know what was going on!

It was now May 19, 1965. For years friends had been asking if there were any converts, but we were still learning to talk! Twelve years had passed since I wrote down my first Cabécar word. During those years we had returned twice to the States for further studies in linguistics. But not even the experts could solve our verb problems. One successful linguist told us, "You've got a problem!" It would be a while before linguists would categorize this type of verb system.

On that memorable day in May, I had spent the morning in my office poring over data. When Marian called me to dinner, I left the puzzling data spread out on the desk and sat down at the head of the table. Marian was at the foot, with the children in between. After our customary Bible reading and prayer, I discussed our verb conundrum with Marian. (Our linguistic table talk eventually led daughter Susanna to quip to a friend, "We eat more linguistics with our meals than any other family in the world!" Ironically, Susanna went on to study linguistics herself and to marry an expert.)

As Marian and I talked that day, she came up with a hunch. "Maybe each Cabécar verb has two roots." Our discussion almost turned into an argument as we considered the preposterous idea. Finally, toward the end of the meal I threw out a problem word: *xäk* (to say). The root was "*x-.*" Could "*dzi-,*" which didn't even look related, possibly be the other stem, with *dzinak* as the second infinitive? Marian got up from the table and wrote the two forms on the children's blackboard, which hung on the dining room wall. We ran through a full paradigm of the verb. To my amazement, it conjugated perfectly. So did the next verb we tried, and the next, and the next.

The children disappeared while I continued calling out one verb after another. Marian kept writing conjugations on the blackboard. That mysterious suffix "*-r*" fell into place. The negative forms all made sense. Then, like a complex jigsaw puzzle, other chunks of material fit into the bigger picture. We kept at it all afternoon until finally at five o'clock it was too dark to continue. We stopped to light the kerosene lamps and to close the jalousies against the damp evening chill of the highland rain forest. As I went outside to close the chicken house against jungle predators such as skunks or possums, I knew we had found an important piece of the puzzle.

The pattern we discovered that afternoon proved to be the key to understanding how to talk Cabécar. Every verb had two stems, or roots. One stem carried the simple active tense markers: present, and past, as well as markers for positive and negative commands. The other stem carried the more complex aspects: perfect tenses, past negative, impersonals, and passives. The pesky particle "-te" that had puzzled us for twelve years turned out to be the marker that indicated the subject of a transitive sentence containing the first root of a verb. Another pesky particle, "-wa," turned out to indicate the subject of a transitive sentence using the other verb stem. Then there was another particle, "-cu," to mark the subject of transitive commands. Eventually we arbitrarily labeled one stem "A" and the other "B."

Each pair of verb stems would form a double entry in our dictionary file, but we found no way to predict one stem on the basis of the other. However, if we knew one stem and asked two or three questions, we could always derive the other and conjugate the whole verb. The conjugations looked like this, in the alphabet we were using at the time:

A - Stem		B - Stem	
xäk	"to say" *(infinitive)*	dzinak	"to be said" *(passive infinitive)*
ite ixe	"he says it"	idzina	"it is said"
ite ixa	"he said it"	iwa idzile	"he has said it"
bacu ixo	"say it"	ca iwa idzine	"he didn't say it"
ke ixa	"don't say it"	iwa idzinak	"it is to be said by him"
		iwa idzir	"it is said by him"
		idzinopa	"may it be said"

Did we realize at the time that this was a breakthrough? Marian did. In her diary she wrote **"BREAKTHROUGH?!"** in capital letters, followed by a question mark and an exclamation point. Ever the cautious one, I wrote in my diary, "We believe we hit upon a simple description of verb patterns." But a few weeks later in our prayer letter of July 10, 1965, I wrote confidently: "God who confounded the tongues at Babel has granted us new insight into the complex Chirripó verb system. We have discovered a way by which we can predict how almost any Chirripó verb will behave." For years we had asked our friends to pray that we would find the key to the Cabécar verbs. Now they rejoiced with us at God's answer.

Preparing for the Translation Workshop

About this time we were invited to a workshop to be held at the SIL center in Guatemala early in 1966. John Beekman himself was to be there to lecture on translation principles, and we could concentrate on translation for three months. Experienced translators would check our work daily.

Now it became imperative to answer the questions in those booklets I had set aside—seventy-two pages of questions! As we organized our data in order to answer the questions, we discovered things we had not realized before. For one thing, we learned that a number always came after the verb, for example: "I dog saw two," rather than "I saw two dogs." Also, in order to answer a question about how our language used words borrowed from the trade language, we had to go through page after page of Cabécar stories, looking for borrowed terms and analyzing them.

Marian did not have as much time as I did to spend on study, but she was a full partner with me. Both of us had received the same training in linguistics. But whereas my "linguistic antenna" was always up, she turned hers off when not actually studying.

One fear still bugged me: I had been told at SIL, "You're ready to translate when you're able to discuss linguistic problems with your helper without resorting to the trade language"—in our case, Spanish. I could not do this. Although my conversational ability had increased rapidly once we lived in Tsipirí, I was still limited to everyday talk. Would I be disqualified at the workshop if I resorted to Spanish?

Urgent—Helper Needed

Writing up the answers to the questions in those booklets was not the only requirement for attending the workshop. We also needed an Indian helper willing to leave the jungle and go to Guatemala with us for three months. I was on the alert for prospective helpers. In Tsipirí I would try out any Indian willing to sit across the desk from me and answer questions. Some Indians only worked a day or two. *Don* Emilio, the friend who had built our house, brought me a young Indian named Benjamín from a country church. Emilio thought he had potential. He had befriended Benjamín and bailed him out of jail for chopping a man with a machete. Benjamín had responded by going to services at the country church where don Emilio was lay pastor. Eventually he made a profession of faith.

Benjamín helped me for months. He chopped weeds, guarded the house in our absence, and helped translate simple Bible stories. At that point he was not good at exact translation but was useful in correcting Bible stories and supplying native stories. I needed the native stories to provide vocabulary, grammatical insights, and insights into Indian thinking. Once Benjamín got angry and quit because I corrected him about some small matter. I apologized but he ignored my pleas. How this humbled me before the Lord. Eventually Benjamín came back—and returned again and again to become my most loyal helper over the years. Yet at this point he was not the man I wanted to take to Guatemala.

The other Indian who helped me at times for extended periods was Alfredo. He used to come to Turrialba in the early years, then later to La Suiza. He lived in the lowlands near the Zent River, but since his family was from the Chirripó area, it was not out of the question to invite him to Tsipirí. Yet to do so I would have to go to Turrialba, catch a train to Zent—no road to the lowlands in those days—then walk four hours to make arrangements for him to come.

Alfredo came that July but promptly got sick with one of his recurring ailments. When he finally recovered, he did work for two weeks, finishing several Bible stories and the fourth chapter of Mark.

Our main project, though, was grammatical analysis in view of the upcoming workshop.

When I had no helper, I sometimes worked on literacy materials, but my main focus was on writing up answers to the questionnaire for the workshop. The workshop was postponed three months, giving us time to finish the write-up and to arrange for Alfredo to travel with us to Guatemala.

Alfredo to Guatemala?

We were ready for the workshop, but would Alfredo arrive in time? We had watched his pattern: undependable, always complaining, full of self-pity. Many a time he had stopped me on the trail, pointed to an airplane overhead, and commented, "You [Americans] are smart; you make things like that. We Indians don't know anything." Yet he knew quite well how to make the most of his being an Indian to get favors from whites. When in a good mood, he could be very likable. Although he had never been to school, he could read and had learned Spanish well. His prized possession was a Spanish dictionary which he pored over by the hour.

Alfredo professed to be an evangelical and had studied a Bible correspondence course in Spanish. He refused to consult the witch doctor, even though his brothers pressured him. On the other hand, when I asked how to say "believer" in his language, his answer was not "one who believes in Jesus," but "one who knows God." To him that meant, "one who can handle the Spanish Bible."

In spite of my fears, Alfredo did appear in time for the trip to Guatemala. It took us a week to get all the paperwork done for the trip. We needed exit and reentry visas, permits to take the car and the kids out of the country, and transit visas for Nicaragua, Honduras, and El Salvador, plus a visa for Guatemala. We also had to get passports and visas for Alfredo and for Loida, a girl who was working for Marian. She was a minor, an extra complication.

We crowded into the little Jeep —Marian and I and the two younger children, plus Alfredo and Loida—and loaded our baggage in the old trailer for the trip of almost a thousand miles. (Our older children were at boarding school.) We spent the first night at our Mission's guest home in Managua and the second at the one in San Salvador. In Guatemala City we had arranged for a small apartment in the sprawling building of our Mission's main Bible Institute.

Alfredo stayed at the translation center in quarters provided for translation helpers. He did not like the quarters, or the food—tortillas, black beans, and rice—the staple diet of Indians in Guatemala. Nor did he want to take his turn chopping firewood. He missed the jungle, wild meat, his dogs, and his family. He was homesick! Furthermore, Alfredo did not like the fellows with whom he shared accommodations. They were Mayans, in contrast to the Cabécars who are the northernmost extension of the Chibchan culture of Colombia and Panama. To him they were "sophisticated, city Indians." To them Alfredo was quite a joke—going around bragging about being "a legitimate Indian from Costa Rica." In Costa Rica, Indians are a curiosity, forming less than a half percent of the population. In Guatemala it was quite the opposite, with around two-thirds of the population being Mayan, although many no longer used their tribal languages and were ashamed of being Indians.

For Marian and me, life in the biggest city in Central America was interesting. On Saturdays we explored the markets and shops. On Sundays we attended one of our Mission's many churches or else went to the Union Church for English services. We socialized with the Wycliffe missionaries, forming lasting friendships. We attended their Sunday evening vesper services, a Wycliffe tradition we had learned to appreciate during our linguistic studies in Oklahoma. Sometimes on weekends we visited missionary friends in other cities. For Marian it was like a vacation, even though she worked with me at the translation center part of each day and spent hours at the apartment studying or typing the manuscript of Mark.

Translation "Know-how"

During the weeks that John Beekman was at the workshop, he held lectures and discussions on how to translate meaning, not just words. In the mornings I would drive to the translation center from the apartment where we stayed at the Central American Bible Institute and work with Alfredo for a while. Marian would come by bus in time for the lecture.

We both were fascinated. We were learning to translate idiomatically. We wanted our translation to sound as natural to the Indian reader as it did to the original reader in the early church. For example, when we translated "Jesus opened his mouth and taught them, saying...," we would say, "Jesus began to teach. He said..."

Beekman counseled us to say "river Jordan," "region of Judea," and "city of Jerusalem," in order to make Biblical place names intelligible to the Indians. Later we could eliminate the extra words when the Indians began to understand the Bible. I did have trouble convincing Alfredo that Galilee was a freshwater lake. After all, he knew that the Spanish Bible said "Sea of Galilee." A "sea" is salty, isn't it?

A major piece of advice was to change certain nouns in the original text to verb phrases when necessary in the "target language." So Mark 1:4 that I had struggled with became: "John appeared in a deserted place; there he baptized us [people]. He began to teach us; he said we ought to be baptized in order that it might be apparent that we despised our badness, in order for God to leave our debt quiet [forgive our guilt]." The nouns "baptism," "repentance," and "remission" all became verbs.

Another principle we learned was: "Be honest with the text. Your linguistic sins will find you out. Don't slant your translation to favor a certain interpretation or doctrine."

We studied how to translate Biblical figures of speech into languages that did not use those figures. We had never found a metaphor in any Cabécar story, so when we later translated the Gospel of John, Jesus' metaphor, "I am the good shepherd," became a simile, "I am like a good sheep caretaker."

There were lessons on how to translate Biblical terminology. How were we to translate "lamb" for Indians who had never seen one? We could not substitute another animal, for lambs were crucial to the sacrificial system. Until the Cabécar Indians learned about sheep, we had to call a lamb "the young of a tame animal called a sheep," borrowing the term "sheep" from Spanish. And what word could we use for "cross," "synagogue," "temple" and over a hundred other terms?

The lectures also dealt with New Testament references to the Old, and quotes from the Old Testament, plus matters of Biblical chronology. How often my translation helpers over the years would say something like, "Wait, let me get this straight. Was Abraham before or after David?"

We felt so encouraged by John Beekman's teaching and the experiences of fellow translators. We now felt free to make our translation sound like the New Testament might have been written by a Cabécar—or at least that God knew his language. We had heard the story of how Cameron Townsend's vision for translation had sprung from a question asked him by an Indian. As he traveled around Guatemala selling Spanish Bibles door-to-door in outlying areas, Townsend was asked, "Don't you have any Bibles in my language? Doesn't God know my language?" This question eventually led him to found the Wycliffe Bible Translators.

Marian and I wanted the Cabécar Indians to know that God is omniscient, that He does know their language. Those months in Guatemala of daily lectures and rubbing shoulders with a score of other translators, while we struggled with the translation of Mark, were profitable, encouraging, and just plain fun!

Fear Overcome

Aside from translation theory sessions, Alfredo and I would spend most of the day translating. Marian would take over for a couple of hours after the lectures so I could study special problems—or get ready for the next session. I would try to think through the next passage, writing up a tentative draft if I could.

Of course, I was forcing myself to talk to Alfredo in his language and trying to get him to respond in kind. We had been accustomed to communicating in Spanish—his Spanish was better than my Cabécar. The night before our first session with the consultant, I was apprehensive. Yet the session went fairly well and my fears faded. I did wonder, though, if the consultant could cross-question my informant in Spanish, why couldn't I?

All the other translators were working on Mayan languages. The consultants had all done New Testaments in those languages. Consultant questions were often based on problem areas in Mayan groups. Mayan culture was highly developed in social and political structure, but the Cabécar language had no terms for "government," "kingdom," or "king." Yet it was a stimulating situation for us.

Most of the consultants were easy to work with, trying to adjust to Cabécar problems. I particularly enjoyed working with Ken. We would sometimes get off the subject and talk about mission policy. He was interested in the way The Central American Mission operated. I was curious about Wycliffe's policies! Marian and I felt fully accepted by the Wycliffe missionaries and were treated as equals.

Gospel of Mark Completed

Struggles with Alfredo were our most difficult problem. His homesickness continued. Everyone tried to make concessions because of his complaints. We struggled every inch of the way. He even convinced one consultant that we had used the wrong term for "the devil." He wanted to use the name of a specific Cabécar demon rather than a generic term. He also tried to use words we had never found in any text—apparently terms from the so-called "secret language of the witch doctors." Several times he would not even answer my questions! When I asked him why he didn't respond, he said, "If I tell you, you'll put it in the translation."

In working with Alfredo on the translation we learned a lesson: A good language teacher may not make a good translation helper. That is an axiom among translators! Alfredo had been a good teacher, but in Bible matters I was the authority. He was not flexible enough to make the change, but in spite of our struggles, we finished the Gospel of Mark.

Dealing with Alfredo was not our only problem. Loida was homesick and unhappy at the Institute with us. Marian and I disagreed on how to handle her, so we also were unhappy. Furthermore, Marian had a miscarriage while we were in Guatemala and was hospitalized. Both Marian and I suffered from a series of very painful boils. Three-year-old Elizabeth came down with asthmatic bronchitis.

Amazingly, we not only translated all of Mark, but had it checked verse by verse with a consultant. Marian typed it on our manual typewriter. The manuscript was approved for publication by the American Bible Society pending further checking. The consultant said, "You've got the point. You can handle things now on your own. Take your manuscript back to Costa Rica, check it with two or three more Indians, and then send it back for printing."

Helper Needed—Again

We left Guatemala early in August with the completed manuscript of the Gospel of Mark. Once back in San José, I paid Alfredo and put him on the train for Zent. I knew we were through with him. He'd had it with us, and we'd had it with him. Yet we remained friends. There was an unspoken bond—we had needed each other. After sending Loida home, we ourselves finally got back to Tsipirí, walking the last two miles after both the winch and the four-wheel drive quit. It was good to be alone as we settled back in to begin checking Mark with fresh helpers.

Who could I get to help with further checking? I concluded that I must find helpers near Tsipirí. I had to trust the Lord that there would be some who had the gifts we needed in a helper. At that point Célimo was "chopping" my yard—cutting the grass with a machete. I looked out the window at him, and then looked back to the manuscript lying on my desk. "Try Célimo," I thought.

Although Célimo was not as linguistically sensitive as Alfredo, he was responsive and communicative—a delight to work with. Yet he was perhaps the least qualified of any man I ever worked with long-term. But he was available because he lived nearby. Célimo went through Mark with me verse by verse. Was everything clear? Did he understand it? When we checked out the term for "king," I tried to find a better term than the one Alfredo had suggested. Célimo said, "Why don't you try *sa tsakui*, "our head"? We've used it ever since!

The translator has a lot to do with what he gets from his helper—gifted or not. The information is in the helper's head, but sometimes it takes much questioning to draw it out. I felt sorry for my helper when I had to keep on probing. Sometimes I discovered ways that I myself could improve the translation—and Célimo could evaluate. I used him for many years. But his younger brother, a very sharp guy who knew the name of every leaf in the jungle, quit after only one day at the desk. "This is the hardest work I've ever done," he complained. Nor was he a good farmer. He was only happy while hunting!

At the translation table

We finished the first check in a few weeks. Greater than the satisfaction of finishing was my joy at seeing Célimo understand the message of Mark. It was exciting to see him learn for the first time about the resurrection of the body! In Cabécar thinking, only the soul lives on. The resurrection of the Lord Jesus became a key point in their acceptance or rejection of the gospel.

Final Checking of Mark

Now I needed to find someone to do the second check—someone who could evaluate, criticize, and suggest. I tried more than one man, finally finishing the second check during a three-day stay in an Indian home—the hard way to do it. I trekked to and from the hut with books, papers, and blankets, sleeping on gunny sacks, eating Indian food. My host, whom I paid by the hour, was most cooperative, but he had his own designs on my stay. He wanted me to write down native stories which he dictated and which he read slowly and repeatedly until he was sure of himself. They contained the usual concept of the beginning of the world—bat dung forming the first soil on the eternal rock. And there was the usual fusing of deity with objects and animals so typical of animism.

We were checking Mark for comprehension and clarity. I would read it aloud with no explanation, then ask questions in order to discover possible misconceptions lurking behind the most innocent word or phrase—not to mention the words I knew would be difficult, such as "kingdom," "synagogue," "Son of Man," "sin," "parable," "sign," "love," "believe," "repent," and many others. We worked on the premise that the New Testament made sense—at least on the surface—to the average first-century reader. But for an Indian oriented to a religious system that was not mentally stimulating, we hoped to produce a translation that made sense without taxing the mind.

It took us months to finish the second check, but then our old friend Benjamín, who had left angry two years before, returned and finished the third check within weeks. Marian had at times helped check with a helper, but her main contribution was to go over the notes I made while checking. She evaluated my suggested alternatives, wrote penetrating questions in the margins, and sometimes suggested other alternatives. Her notes, penned in red, led to further checking at my next session with a helper. The helpers were learning. Marian and I were learning. We were also learning to work as a team, each with our different gifts and responsibilities.

After the third check, one major task remained—a freshly-typed manuscript, free of any corrections or errors. It was our turn to check and recheck for accuracy and consistency. Finally, in May of 1967, a year after the workshop, Marian shouted to me from the study, "I finished!" It was after bedtime but I was in the kitchen washing dishes to free her for typing. In fact, I had done most of the housework for two weeks while she tediously typed, frequently consulting me to decipher the hundred pages of notes I had made during the three revisions. Now the eighty-six pages of the final copy of the Gospel of Mark were stacked neatly on the desk.

Discussing the translation

Almost fifteen years had passed since we came to Costa Rica, not knowing Spanish, or even a word of Cabécar. Based on the estimated population and literacy rate of the Chirripó area, the Bible Society agreed to finance one hundred fifty copies of Mark. There was no demand for the Scriptures in Chirripó. We were not producing a commodity to meet a demand, but to create a demand! In faith we looked ahead to the day when Cabécars would be hungry for the Word.

– 13 –

Family Life at Tsipirí
1963 to 1966

In the days following our move to Tsipirí in 1963 I began to pray differently. Our "margin of safety" had been reduced by one-half. Our Jeep was an old rattletrap, and I was the only driver. We were thirty-one miles—three hours by jeep—to the nearest telephone, doctor, hospital, mechanic, and gas station. In case of an emergency there was another Jeep in Moravia four miles closer to outside help. The next closest vehicle in those early years was thirteen miles away at the Pacuare River, almost halfway to Turrialba.

Our isolation moved me to begin a lifetime routine of covering the family in general prayer daily—physically, mentally, and spiritually. We needed God's protection and provision. We needed His power to walk in victory over the world, the flesh, and the devil. We wanted the joy of the Lord. As the head of my household, I felt an obligation to "cover" my family daily.

Housekeeping in Tsipirí

Just "living" took all of Marian's time those first few years in Tsipirí. Even with the help of the children—especially Priscilla when she was home—there was much that only Marian could do. She did have help from Modesta off and on for quite a while. Modesta was strong and able to cope with heavy tasks like washing clothes down at the creek, then hauling the wet load up the hill to hang on the lines behind the house. Modesta also did other heavy tasks like mopping and waxing the floors, then brushing and polishing them Costa Rican style. She was cheerful but moody. Often she would come late or resist Marian's directions. Actually, once we managed to get the washing machine to the house, I ran the machine myself. The gasoline engine was so cantankerous that Marian could not keep it running. Instead, she hung the clothes when Modesta was not available.

Cooking occupied much of Marian's time. Everything had to be made from scratch. There were tedious jobs like picking over mounds of beans in order to cull out bits of trash, clods of dirt, pebbles, weevils and worms. Sometimes rice was so trashy that it had to be picked over as well. It took a lot of rice and beans to feed not only the family but also *peónes* and language helpers. There were lots of dishes to wash, but that was a job for kids or maids. When the older children were away at school, I washed the day's dishes in the evening and Marian dried them.

Although living was time-consuming, Marian had adjusted to it gradually. "The Lord let me down easy," she always said: First, a year in San José getting used to life in a foreign country; next the Turrialba years, adjusting to life in a small city with no public phone at the time; then a year and a half in La Suiza, a little town which then had no electricity; and finally the move to Tsipirí, hours from any medical help or source of any but the most basic supplies. In spite of adjusting gradually, Marian sometimes found life in Tsipirí difficult with its isolation and inconvenience.

More Creature Comforts

In January of 1964 Fabio, who had helped *don* Emilio during the construction, returned to put up the ceiling boards. What a difference the ceiling made! Though the house was still chilly and damp at night, at least it was less drafty. Marian no longer needed to drape Elizabeth's crib with a blanket to keep out the wind. Enough lumber was left over from the ceiling to finish walling up the bedrooms so that we could warm them with our kerosene heater on the coldest mornings and evenings. The average early morning temperature inside the house that January was fifty-five, but a few times we saw it drop into the upper forties. The penetrating chill was almost as trying to Marian as the road was. She often said, "I'm glad the Lord didn't call me to Alaska!"

In spite of the hard work and the chilly weather, Marian was content to be in Tsipirí where we could begin to develop our work among the Indians and where the children thrived without the negative influences of city life. They played happily with each other and worked together at their chores. The five months of vacation from boarding school was a bonding time for the whole family.

The Road Arrives!

A year after our move to Tsipirí a bulldozer appeared in our front yard. A very welcome sight! The municipal authorities had sent the dozer to open the road as far as the Tsipirí, the creek which bordered our property. Then we paid the operator to cut a driveway out of the side of the hill between the creek and our house, a distance of about a hundred yards. I had already arranged for our piano to be crated for the rough trip from Turrialba. In fact, I was at the creek with the piano in my trailer when the bulldozer left. It took six men to get the piano off the trailer and into the living room a few steps away, for it weighed about six hundred pounds. Not wanting to risk the chance that rain would make the new road impassable, I went back to Turrialba two days later to pick up our kerosene refrigerator, also crated for the trip.

Now we were really living! We had a piano to enhance our family devotional times, as well as for the children to enjoy. They were not to bang the piano with anything but their fingers, and they had to wash their sticky hands first, but they were free to make as much noise as they pleased! We also had a kerosene refrigerator, a little eight-cubic-foot model with a small freezer section. The freezer was too small to hold enough meat for a family our size, for I only made a supply trip every two weeks. At least we could have meat three times a week, and we could cool the powdered milk so it would taste more palatable. We even had ice on Sundays for tea and on weekdays for *fresco*, a drink concocted with any available fruit. Usually Marian made *fresco* from oranges we bought from the Indians or from the acid fruit of the tangerine trees that grew in our yard. Every day she fixed a gallon of milk and at least two gallons of *fresco*.

Three months later we were rejoicing in fresh blessings. With the addition of a front porch we had a place to chat with passing Indians. The porch also served to keep from tracking so much mud into the living room. At the back of the house we added another porch and closed in part of it as a bedroom for the boys. Now Peter and Steven no longer needed to sleep in the dining room. We had eliminated these porches from the original plan until funds were available.

A year after we built the porches, we had saved up enough money to paint the outside of the house, as well as the ceilings. We made improvements gradually, as funds and workers became available. Any major improvements involved providing accommodations and meals for workmen—an extra load for Marian—but we were gratified to see the house becoming more practical and pretty.

Las Américas Academy

Early in January of 1964 we sent Peter, Priscilla, and now Susanna as well, off to school in Honduras. It was harder to see them go than previously, but they went happily, proud to fly alone on their own tickets. The airline, however, was not happy about children traveling alone.

"Sorry," said the ticket agent as we checked in, "we don't accept unaccompanied children."

Now what could we do? No one had warned us. We left the ticket counter to think through our options. Missionaries in Honduras were soon to meet the children at the airport there. Marian was thinking fast, surveying the other passengers.

"That young woman over there may be a missionary daughter returning to college in the States," she said to me.

Approaching the girl, Marian asked if her guess had been correct. Yes, she was the daughter of a family serving with another mission.

"Would you be willing to accept responsibility for our children so they will be allowed to fly?" Marian asked.

"Sure," responded the girl. Problem solved. The Lord always had his "angels" when we needed them!

The children almost always began their letters home: "We love you. We are having fun." Las Américas was a wonderful school, so homelike. With less than fifty children it was like one big family. The teachers and house parents were called "Uncle" and "Aunt." Long after our children were grown, they kept up with "Aunt" Kay, "Aunt" Beulah, and others. Marian and I did too, for the staff became our friends as well. They saw the school as an extension of the missionaries' homes. Parents were always welcome to come and visit.

Four months after the children left for school, Marian and I, along with Steven and Elizabeth, drove the three days to Las Américas— 767 miles from Tsipirí—an uncomfortable trip in that era with miles and miles of unpaved "washboard" roads. A hard trip, but it was worth it for the happy time we had with Peter, Priscilla, and Susanna.

For four days we ate with the children in the dining hall, enjoying the homemade bread and honey butter they had raved about. We also had fun socializing with the staff at mealtimes. We went to the daily chapel services, and in the evening I sat in on devotions in the boys' dorm with Peter while Marian attended devotions with Priscilla and Susanna in their dorm. Marian, a former teacher, even attended classes with the children. On Saturday we went along with all the kids and "Uncle" Ralph to the river and watched them have fun in the water. For Marian our trip to Las Américas Academy was a wonderful vacation from household duties.

An M.K. School for Costa Rica?

Returning from Las Américas, we were doubly burdened for the Lord to help us start a school in Costa Rica. The Mission's two existing schools were anticipating capacity enrollment, and the children of our colleagues in Costa Rica were now school age. We parents were praying and planning for a new CAM school. We envisioned a school that would serve not only CAM but other missions as well, and even children of students in the Spanish Language School.

Together with our colleagues, we had already formed a school board. Marian, with her degree in education, was a resource person. She became the secretary, not only doing correspondence and minutes, but helping me prepare a handbook for parents. Our school would offer five-day boarding for children who lived close enough to go home on weekends. There would be three long weekends during the school year so that those who lived further away could also go home and the staff could have a break. The school would free parents from the grueling overland trip to Honduras, or from the expense of air travel.

What would we name the school? We decided to call it McConnell Academy in honor of the first missionary to Costa Rica. The descendants of William McConnell sent a donation to help start the school. The Mission gave its approval, although somewhat reluctantly, for around the world schools for missionaries' children were beginning to phase out in a move to relocate personnel to the cities.

Part of our personal urge to start a school was that with five children and a sixth on the way, we faced a long future of constant separation and time-consuming travel—not only the week-long round trips to Honduras with two border crossings each way, but days spent obtaining car permits, exit and reentry visas, and permission to take the children out of the country. Yes, I had to have a permit from the Child Protection Agency to take the children outside Costa Rica if I traveled without Marian. After all, I might be taking the children without her consent, in effect, kidnapping them— not an uncommon occurrence.

Our Sixth Child

On December 17, 1964, Timothy Mark was born. We named him after Timothy whom the Apostle Paul called "my own son in the faith," as well as for Mark, the helper of the Apostle Peter. Marian and I were challenged by the potential wrapped up in his life, as well as the lives of our other five children. We remembered God's words to Abraham, "For I know him, that he will command his children and

his household after him, and they shall keep the way of the Lord."
We were raising a family for God, and our confidence was in Him.

As Marian left the Clínica Bíblica in San José with the new baby,
our older children crowded around to get their first look at little
Timothy. Two-year-old Elizabeth tried valiantly to get a glimpse as
her taller siblings blocked her view. Later we took a photo of the six
of them, sitting on the step of the Mission Home in the capital. We
lined them up from oldest to youngest, with Peter holding the new
baby.

With Elizabeth we had broken the "baby barrier" of the Mission.
Now with Timothy's birth it was obvious that we planned to raise a
family, as well as reach a tribe. The Mission had no rule against large
families, but if our support was low, they would not grant temporary
subsidy for more than four children. However, the Lord was faithful
to provide enough so that we never needed a subsidy, though we
had many lean years.

Baby Timothy with (clockwise) Peter, Susanna, Priscilla,
Steven, and Elizabeth

Although there was no rule about the size of families, we began
to feel increasing social pressure: "Missionaries with large families

don't get their work done." However, the largest family in the Mission—seven children—actually worked harder than most. Furthermore, the oldest son of that family eventually became head of the largest evangelical seminary in Latin America, and another son became head of the largest Christian radio station in Central America.

A week after Timothy's birth, while we were still in the capital, we loaded all the children in the Jeep and drove downtown to do a bit of Christmas shopping. While we walked to the store from the parking lot, Peter watched over the baby, asleep in a cardboard box on the floor of the Jeep. There were no infant seats in those days, nor would there have been space in the tiny Willys.

Our major purchase that day was a new short-wave radio. We had lost our radio during a robbery a few months before. In the isolation of Tsipirí we really needed a radio—not only for news but to reset our watches to the correct time. That radio served for over thirty years to keep us in touch with the outside world.

We stayed on at the Mission Home over Christmas, not only for Marian to recuperate, but also because the new school year was about to begin. Marian needed to get the older children's clothes ready. She had come to the capital more than two weeks before Timothy's birth to shop and sew—her little portable sewing machine was of no use in Tsipirí without electricity. Complete outfits for three children, plus sheets and towels, pillows and blankets, all had to be tagged. Down to the last sock and hankie—no Kleenex at school—each piece needed a name tag. Marian ordered the tags from the States, or else wrote the names on iron-on tape with permanent ink. A formidable job each school year!

McConnell Academy

When we took the children to school in January of 1965, it was not to the school in Honduras, but to the Mission's new school for missionaries' children. McConnell Academy was located half an hour's drive west of San José, a central location for parents working in various areas of Costa Rica. Parents could drop in for a quick visit if they happened to be in the capital.

By the end of February the children were already home for their first long weekend. Even though it was not so exciting as coming home from Honduras, it was just as hard to see them return to school after a rich weekend. Rains didn't dampen Peter's enthusiasm for cutting weeds, while Priscilla helped with the baby and the cooking. Susanna, our most voracious reader, buried her nose in a favorite book.

As usual, once the "big kids" left, we would see the "little kids" with fresh eyes. There was time to give them more personal attention, whereas if the older ones were home, it was they who doted on the younger ones. Steven now had his turn to be the big boy. We also had a new maid: Loida, a teenager from a country church. It was hard for her to be away from home and friends and hard for us to have a stranger in our home at all times. But she stayed—not without problems—until the children came home in August for their five-month vacation. Then we wanted to be alone and re-bond as a family. Besides, the children's help compensated for the extra cooking and washing they caused. Each child had a job listed on a chart on the kitchen wall. Marian switched the jobs every week.

Medical Matters

The Lord mercifully spared us from having to make any emergency trips to town with seriously sick children. He did hear my prayer to "cover" us physically! Yet we had our concerns. Elizabeth, the baby when we moved to Tsipirí, got sick in the drafty days before we had a ceiling. Was it just a cold, or possibly pneumonia? We rubbed her with Vicks and wrapped her with extra sweaters and watched over her through the night. When she didn't get better in a few days and was running a fever, we started her on antibiotics.

Before we moved to Tsipirí, Marian had asked our pediatrician in San José what to do for various situations. Dr. Ortiz knew there would be times when it would be impossible for us to get out of the jungle to seek medical help, due to the weather in our area and the state of the roads. He prescribed certain medicines and gave directions as to when Marian should use them. Then he added, "If there's no improvement within seventy-two hours, you need to come to the capital."

Over forty-eight hours passed without improvement in Elizabeth's condition. We increased our prayerful vigil, but began to think about closing the house, arranging for a guard, and heading to San José. Finally, just before the seventy-two hours ended, she took a definite turn for the better. It was quite a while before she recovered fully, but the Lord spared us an emergency trip.

We did have an emergency with Elizabeth a few months later, but it happened while we were in the city for a conference of churches. She suddenly became deathly ill with vomiting and diarrhea, the dreaded *gastro* that killed so many children in those days.

"This child is severely dehydrated," said Dr. Ortiz when we took her to his office. "Give her a spoonful of rehydration liquid every three minutes. If she's not better by tomorrow morning, I'll have to put her in the hospital for intravenous rehydration."

Elizabeth was too sick to swallow a spoonful of liquid. What could we do? We forced the liquid down her with a medicine dropper, taking turns all night. By morning our precious little one was beginning to rally. The Lord is good.

There were ongoing concerns with the children. Peter needed his teeth braced. Both Priscilla and Susanna had eye muscle problems. Elizabeth's growth did not satisfy Dr. Ortiz. We attributed it to the short stature of my parents and most of my siblings, but he wanted to be sure that heredity was the real cause. He prescribed a growth stimulant, but Elizabeth continued to be shorter than normal for her age.

Marian suffered periodically from colds and bronchitis, as well as from amoebas. She became run down and occasionally depressed, but she kept going by taking a daily *siesta* while the children napped. Steven and I were the healthiest ones.

The neighbors and the Indians also had medical needs. They came to us to be treated for serious cuts or to seek medicine for some ailment. Neither Marian nor I had any medical training, but we did what we could. We knew that folks wouldn't go to Turrialba unless they were desperate. Why would they borrow money and walk hours to catch a bus, if it was not serious? We kept simple remedies on hand to sell—or give—to people. Marian was the one who pre-scribed, while I was the one who took care of cuts. I would warm a pan of water to wash the first layer of dirt away, and then douse the cut with hydrogen peroxide, finishing up with Merthiolate and a bandage.

Our main problem with medicines was that everyone asked for penicillin. No matter what the condition, they always wanted an injection of penicillin. Pills would not satisfy them. For a while we kept a small supply of penicillin for serious respiratory illnesses.

One day we sold an ampule of pediatric penicillin to a teen-aged Indian who came with a sad story, replete with convincing details, about his baby brother. When another brother came by a few days later, we asked if the baby was better.

"The baby hasn't been sick," he said, surprised.

"Then why did your brother ask us for penicillin?" I questioned.

"Oh, that was for his horse," the brother replied.

The fellow had obviously surmised—correctly—that we would never have sold him penicillin for a horse. Marian and I had a good laugh over the thought of trying to treat a horse with one tiny ampule of pediatric penicillin. We discontinued keeping penicillin on hand. If they wanted it, they could buy it without prescription in the village two hours away.

1966—an Eventful Year

When McConnell Academy opened for its second year in January of 1966, Steven joined the older three. He seemed anxious to begin first grade, yet as the time drew near he grew very quiet. When we took him to have his picture taken, as we had done for the first three children when they started school, the photo revealed his distress and gloominess. Although we didn't realize it at the time, it was a foretaste of years of homesickness. Peter had experienced times of homesickness in Honduras, but it was never to the same degree as Steven. Peter settled down quickly at boarding school and became a "happy camper" like Priscilla and Susanna. To Marian it was rather distressing to leave Steven at McConnell unhappy, but he did perk up somewhat after the first few days.

Marian and I returned to Tsipirí to enjoy three-year-old Elizabeth and baby Timothy, who at one year was almost as large as Elizabeth. We wrote our weekly letters to the kids at school and they wrote to us, but in Tsipirí we could only send and receive mail every couple of weeks. There was always a communication blackout—for them as well as for us—their first few weeks away until the letters started arriving. We coped because we knew we were in the Lord's will in sending them—and also because we knew that if anything serious happened, our colleagues would find a way to let us know.

A month after we left the older children at McConnell Academy we had a special visitor. Marian's mother flew from the States to see her daughters and her grandchildren. The day we drove Mom Westling to Tsipirí was the first time in months that we made the trip without getting stuck! After we took Mom back to San José, we had a little family reunion with Marian's sister's family. The administrator of McConnell very reluctantly gave permission for us to take our four older children for dinner with Grandma at Aunt Irene and Uncle Dick's house. All nine of the grandchildren were there for the historic occasion.

We returned to Tsipirí just before a record-breaking rainfall closed the road for many days—in the middle of dry season. If Mom Westling had still been there, she would have missed her return flight! Rain fell in torrents—twenty-five inches in twenty-four hours—causing landslides I needed to clear. The road which we rejoiced in when the bulldozer arrived in 1964 did not hold up well after the first year, for it was never graveled. We went back to chains and winch, but at least we usually could make it all the way to the house. Our battered but cherished Jeep was symbolic of struggles— and lessons from the Lord.

Soon after we reopened the road we had another special visitor. My brother David, pastor of a church that supported us, came for ten days. A born driver and mechanic, he was itching to get behind the wheel of my Jeep. When I met him at the airport he said, "All I could think of on the plane was the fun I'd have driving the roads I was seeing from the window." To accompany me to the Indians, however, he had to trek up the mountain through the mud. Worse yet, he was offered unpalatable food and a slat bed. He ate nothing, nor did he sleep that night. Back home, though, we had fun working together on the road and around the house. Elizabeth was charmed by her uncle, and Timothy learned to walk while David was visiting.

A month after David's visit we were off to Guatemala for three months to attend our first translation workshop, returning early in August with the completed manuscript of the Gospel of Mark. We arrived home on foot, walking the last two miles after both the winch and the four-wheel drive quit. Our deteriorating Jeep now had around one hundred twenty thousand miles on it. The faithful old workhorse needed to be replaced.

Changes at McConnell Academy

While we were in Guatemala we received a letter announcing a change in the school year at McConnell. The school year at the M.K. schools provided and staffed by The Central American Mission ran from January to August with no break. Children heading for furlough could enter the next grade in September in the States, while those returning from furlough had a vacation from June to January. The system also coordinated somewhat with public schools in Central America which usually began sometime in February and ended late in October or November. Missionaries' children would be on vacation during the end-of-year vacation for local children.

Now, however, the Mission's schools switched to the American system with a three-month vacation in the summer and a month at Christmas when local schools were out. We personally were not happy with the change, for we would lose the sense of family pro-vided by the five-month break. Furthermore, during the changeover our children would get out in August and return in October. We wrote a letter expressing our concerns. Perhaps our letter was too strong. At any rate, it was not well received.

More fundamentally, although we did not realize it at the time, the Mission itself was in transition, with a new general secretary. There was a move toward relocating missionaries from rural areas to concentrate on strategic cities where there would be other educational opportunities for children. This meant a decreased need for boarding schools. Questions were also raised about the validity of sponsoring schools exclusively for M.K.'s. In addition, the new homeschool movement was beginning to provide an option.

At the same time there were problems at the school itself. The teachers were not happy with the administration. They felt over-loaded with duties outside school hours, and one of them broke down in tears at a school board meeting. We parents of boarding students were also unhappy, for the administrator had trouble cop-ing with homesick students and with parents' visits.

Home Again

With all this on our minds, we brought the children home after their second year at McConnell and settled in for their short vacation. I hired an Indian to help check the translation of Mark, but found studying less attractive than digging ditches or cutting weeds with Peter and Steven. Elizabeth and Timothy were overawed by the big kids who, in turn, smothered the little ones with loving attention.

Peter was now thirteen and taller than Marian. Priscilla at eleven was showing many womanly traits. Susanna, almost nine, was the musician. Steven, seven, was a beautiful specimen of body and mind. Elizabeth, who turned four that month, was a show-off—and a bit vain? Timothy at twenty months was a perfect delight.

We were quite encouraged with their development spiritually, mentally, and physically, but we were serious about their training. We aimed to lay a foundation of good discipline and build well on that foundation. We had only one chance—and precious little

time—to do it right. During the children's vacation from boarding
school we continued our mealtime Bible reading and prayer, as well
as our family devotions each evening. On Sunday mornings—with
no church anywhere near—we gathered in the living room for a
simple Bible study with the children and any neighbors who showed
up. Sunday nights were a time for singing. Marian and I wanted the
Word to be in our own hearts and to teach the Word diligently to our
children, taking advantage of every opportunity.

Tarzan or Peter?

All the children were constantly reading, writing, or drawing. At
times they would turn scientist and catch beautiful butterflies and
enormous beetles. They even hitched a Matchbox car to a horned
beetle with a thread, and gleefully watched it pull the tiny car across
the waxed floor. They loved to run in the front door and see how far
they could slide in stocking feet across the floor. Sometimes they
would put one of the little children on the woolen mop we used to

polish the floor and give him a fast ride while providing extra pressure for shining the floor. They had a large wooden train they pushed from the front door to the back door, until we could stand the noise no longer. And always there was the swimming hole for Saturday baths and water fun. Marian and I had fun watching the kids have fun.

A Saturday at the swimming hole during the 1970s

Outside they played with cars, carving roads for them on the hillside beside the house. If it rained they played in the dirt under the house. Susanna and Steven had a little "nest" up under the house where there was headroom only for little kids. One day, hiding out together, Susanna talked to Steven quite seriously and he prayed to receive Jesus.

Third and Final Year at McConnell

All too soon we left for San José to prepare for school again: medical checkups and shopping for new shoes and clothes—all of which needed to be tagged. After taking the older four to school, we stayed on at the Mission Home for the annual business meetings. Most business was routine, but this year we had to deal with the issue of McConnell Academy. After a painful day with all factions together—the Mission representative, the school administrator, and the parents—the matter came to a vote. Even Marian and I voted to discontinue the school when the current school year ended in June of 1967. Why did we vote against the school which meant so much to us personally? We had read the handwriting on the wall. We knew the Mission was not in favor of the school. Furthermore, there was no point in continuing to operate a school with so many internal problems.

For us this was a "before and after" experience, when colleagues with a common calling, and a common vision to reach the world, could not agree on the education of their children. I did not get immediate victory over my resentments. In fact, I suffered for months. Though I knew—in principle—the secret of the victorious Christian life, I was now in the crucible of reality. Yet I still loved the Mission. My tensions with the organization would come later.

– 14 –

Fruitful Furlough
July 1967 to July 1968

Looking ahead toward furlough, I felt as if God had doubled in size during our years in Tsipirí as our margin of safety had been cut in half. We did not go to the States empty, wanting to be filled. Rather, we went hoping for chances to share what God had done as our faith had been stretched.

Our first furlough in 1957 was special—because it was the first! Our second furlough was just a brief interlude in 1961. Our third furlough, however, became a major event. We had been on the field continuously from late 1961 to the middle of 1967, almost six years. By then Marian and I were saying to each other, "It would be much easier just to stay here than to go home on furlough." But if we had been looking for ease, we would never have become missionaries!

Furlough was rushing upon us. I was now forty-five years old and Marian thirty-eight. We had six children and another on the way. With almost fifteen years on the field, we were "veteran missionaries." As we got older, the testings got progressively harder.

Who would guard our house during our furlough? The place was hardly safe to leave for a week's absence, let alone for a year. And where would we live while in the States? Our family was too large for us to stay with our parents as we had done the first two furloughs. The other hurdle we faced was the need for a better vehicle. With our extremely limited finances, we hoped to drive home rather than pay for eight plane tickets. We planned to use our vehicle during furlough and drive back to Costa Rica in it afterwards, but such a trip would be impossible in our old Jeep.

Once we got the final manuscript of Mark ready for the printer, we turned our attention—and prayers—to the complex web of problems facing us with furlough only six weeks away. One by one things fell into place. First, our neighbor Modesta—who as our maid had been a source of friction as well as of help—surprised us by asking if we would buy her house and land. We jumped at the chance, for her house would provide a place for a guard during our absence. Modesta's nephew Chepe, who was my peon, agreed to watch over our property.

The next matter solved was the vehicle. With the sacrificial gifts that Colgate Clark and his friend had sent for our jeep fund, we bought a used twelve-passenger Land Rover Safari. All the children—especially Steven—had prayed for the miraculous provision of this vehicle. The Land Rover had plenty of room for the kids plus space for luggage after I added a full-length rack to the roof. My tarp was large enough to protect our baggage from rain. While in San José to buy the Land Rover, we began the perpetual paperwork necessary for overland travel.

Our destination was Columbia, South Carolina, where I had reapplied to the Graduate School of Missions of Columbia Bible College—now Columbia International University. I wanted to finish the master's program I had started in 1952 before we went to Costa Rica. My interest, however, was not so much in a degree as in the chance to write a thesis.

Why Write a Thesis?

One day in Tsipirí while I was working on the road with a pick and shovel, an idea began to crystallize. I wanted to write a history of the organizational structure of my Mission. I wanted to know why we were the way we were. I wanted to find out how the organization had developed at headquarters in Dallas, and how field organizations developed. I had no agenda, nothing to propose. My real desire was to make a contribution to a Mission in which I was happy. Besides, I'd had a desire to write ever since I studied writing at Wheaton. My dream boiled down to a possible title: "The Organizational Development of The Central American Mission."

In preparation for my thesis, I corresponded with a member of the executive council of the Mission. He helped me narrow my focus. The general secretary promised full access to records in the Dallas office. I also arranged to research field records in each Central American country as we drove to the States for furlough.

My interest in the organization of the Mission had begun when I was unexpectedly thrust into field administration during the last year of our first term. For lack of available veteran missionaries, the Costa Rica field made an exception to our rule that a first-termer could not serve on the field committee. I was elected president of the three-member committee which conducted all business between the annual conferences. As president, I also represented Costa Rica at the annual field council of CAM missionaries throughout Central America.

After one year as president, I continued as secretary of the field committee. I took care of all correspondence, kept records, and wrote minutes and even a constitution and by-laws. Over time I discovered that the happiness of personnel was often related to mission policies—or lack of them—or else to local field administration. Relational problems sometimes led to defeated workers who lost the cutting edge of their ministry or even left the field.

Driving to the States

One event remained before we actually left for Columbia. Peter was to graduate from eighth grade at McConnell Academy—a bittersweet event. It was McConnell's first and last graduating class. Our hard-won school would be closing after only three years. Actually, we had already taken Steven out of the school when he got sick halfway through the term. The doctor advised bringing him home to recuperate from a virus. Once home Steven recovered immediately, for part of his problem was homesickness. Marian continued his second grade lessons at home, at the same time teaching Modesta's youngest son to read. Without help from a maid during this busy time Marian also typed the final copy of Mark and made advance preparations for furlough.

On July 5, 1967, we left our home in Tsipirí—so full of memories of our efforts to conquer the elements and to give the Word of God to the Indians. Then on July 10 we finalized the paperwork needed to leave Costa Rica and pass through five more countries on our way to the States, and then loaded up the Land Rover for the first leg of the trip. Peter, now fourteen, was a great asset with loading and unloading the baggage during the trip. Every piece—even the footlocker—had its own spot. We had to unload every night and again at each border for customs inspection.

In Nicaragua I started my research, going through an eight-inch stack of minutes. Most were about an unresolved problem that destroyed unity, led to loss of missionaries, and damaged the relationship between missionaries and the national church—a scandal that even made headlines in the newspapers. The chapter on Nicaragua turned out to be the hardest chapter of my thesis!

In Honduras I had all the cooperation I needed, but not enough time. In El Salvador, however, the person with the records would not release them—not very helpful to a researcher. Instead she asked, "What do you want to know? I'll tell you." At least I knew that two men of God had spanned the whole Mission history in that country. The second man was still alive. A wonderful spirit still prevailed.

In Guatemala the filing cabinets were in perfect order, with minutes of regular meetings since 1927 when all the fields were organized. I not only looked at records in each country but quizzed everyone, especially old timers. All such input was valuable. Unwittingly I asked one very successful missionary a question that revealed a deep hurt. "It's always just under the surface," she said.

While in Guatemala we left the precious manuscript of Mark at the Wycliffe center where their capable and dedicated typist would do the photo-ready copy. Her full-time job was typing languages she didn't understand. She did it as unto the Lord, making only two small errors in our manuscript. Leaving Guatemala, we began four grueling days of driving through Mexico, staying at night in cheap, hot motels—except for a night of great fellowship with colleagues in the city of Puebla.

Crossing into the U.S.

After almost two weeks on the road we reached Laredo, Texas, on a Saturday afternoon. We tried to avoid traveling on Sundays, so we hoped for a nice place to spend the weekend. All we found was an old run-down hotel with no air conditioning. Texas temperatures were close to unbearable. Mexicans were everywhere—we felt we were still in Latin America.

The next morning we looked in the phone book to locate a church. During the service we were introduced—a missionary family that had just traveled more than two thousand miles from Costa Rica. Afterward a man came up to us, a major at a nearby military installation. Gratefully we heard him say, "You must be tired after that drive. Come home with us for dinner. Our house is air-conditioned, and you can relax until time for church this evening."

We had a great meal and great fellowship with the major and his family. He loved the Lord and loved the Word. Our kids had fun playing with their children while Marian rested after helping his wife with the meal. The hotel wasn't so bad after that refreshing day. God had His angels at the end of a long drive, ministering to us at just the right place.

The "Two-bit Miracle"

From Laredo we drove to Dallas for a happy visit at the new headquarters of our Mission and then headed east toward Alabama. The second morning after leaving Dallas I asked the Lord for a "two-bit miracle"—just a small miracle. Our close friends and colleagues, the Ramalys, were on the way back to Costa Rica after their furlough. We had not seen them for a year and would not see them for another year unless the Lord worked it out for us to meet somewhere on U.S. 80.

All day our kids kept their eyes peeled for a Ford pickup with a camper shell on the back. The Ramaly kids were watching for our Land Rover. In the early afternoon we drove through Jackson, Mississippi, on a four-lane road separated by a wide median.

"I see the Ramaly's pickup," yelled Steven suddenly from the back of the Safari.

Really? In case it was true, I pulled to a stop at the side of the road. We kept our eyes glued on the pickup as it stopped at a light, turned left, then left again, pulling up just behind the Land Rover. What a reunion we had! We still remember the joy of it—joy at seeing our friends and joy at the Lord's kindness.

We happened to be parked by the entrance to a Holiday Inn. Our budget limited us to cheaper places, but this celebration called for splurging. It was midsummer and neither of our vehicles was air-conditioned, so we lingered over pie and coffee in the cool restaurant—the kids at one table having a grand time, and the four of us at another table catching up on a year's news. Refreshed, we continued east while the Ramalys headed west.

Soon we caught up with a VW bus at a stop light, noting that the license plate read "JESUS." As we drove along we wondered about that license plate. Several miles down the road we saw the VW stopped beside the road in a deserted area.

"Do you suppose they're having trouble?" commented Marian as we passed.

She persuaded me to turn around and inquire. The driver turned out to be a Dallas Seminary student traveling to Florida. He had run out of gas—the VW had no gas gauge. We took him to the nearest station where he filled up his gas can, then back to the VW. As we parted we exchanged addresses. He continued to write for many years and often sent gifts toward our support.

At the end of that memorable day we finally reached my father's house in Phenix City, Alabama. It was the first time I had seen Daddy since Mama's death four years earlier. Though it was good to see him again, things were different with Mama gone. From Phenix City we traveled to attend a two-day reunion of my siblings and their families—seventy of us talking, playing, talking, eating, and talking some more. We Joneses are talkers!

Where Will We Live in Columbia?

Before leaving Alabama we visited the little church in Montgomery that first began to support us. We were thrilled by their interest in our work in spite of our having been away almost six years. There at Cornerstone Mrs. Vines approached us with a question.

"Do you have a place to live in Columbia?" she asked.

Though the Lord had answered many prayers for a good trip to the States, we still did not have housing lined up in Columbia.

"When you get to Columbia, call this number," said Mrs. Vines, handing us a slip of paper as we parted.

We drove to Columbia in faith, arriving on August 16, more than a month after leaving Costa Rica. That hot afternoon we stopped at a pay phone on Main Street to call the number Mrs. Vines had given us. No answer. Soon we tried the number again. Still no answer. Again we called, but there was no response. The children sitting in the Land Rover grew restless. Finally we reached Mrs. Eich—the "number." The Eiches were close friends of Mrs. Vines, having attended Cornerstone before moving to Columbia.

Standing by the phone booth on Main Street, we waited while Mrs. Eich called her friends, the Millers. Mr. Miller had recently bought a used trailer as an investment. He graciously agreed to let us stay there rent-free until we found a house. In the morning Mrs. Eich invited us for breakfast and even served bacon—a once-a-year luxury for us in Tsipirí. The Lord's people were so kind.

This was the first time we rented a house for furlough rather than staying with parents. Mrs. Miller had a lead for a house through her friend, Mrs. Westervelt. Marian liked the little brick house, but we wondered if the owner would rent to a family with six children and one more on the way. Days went by as Mrs. Westervelt negotiated with the owner. At least the woman hadn't said no!

We prayed and waited. Finally, after hearing nothing for almost a week, we went back to Mrs. Miller.

"We'll rent the trailer once your husband gets it set up in his trailer park," we told her.

At this point we were desperate enough to cram into the old single-wide for the nine months that I would be studying.

1109 Denny Road

"Yes," phoned Mrs. Westervelt the next day, "the owner is willing to rent 1109 Denny Road to you!"

Praise the Lord! That house was the answer to Marian's prayers. For months she had been asking the Lord for a nicely-furnished place, convenient to public schools and to the Bible College. For a family our size the house, though not large, was more adequate than a trailer. It was well-furnished and carpeted, and even had drapes at all the windows. We borrowed a bunk bed and a youth bed to accommodate the three boys in one small room and another youth bed and a double bed for the girls' bedroom. Someone loaned us a crib for the expected new arrival. We bought a couple of stools so we could all crowd around the small dining table. There was even a washing machine—Marian's first automatic washer—in the little kitchen. What a delight to settle down in our first home in the United States.

The Lord also answered Marian's prayers for a convenient location. At the corner Peter and Priscilla caught the bus to junior high school. Susanna and Steven walked four blocks to the elementary school. For me it was a five-minute drive to the Bible College. Unwittingly, this house was the first step that eventually led us to make Columbia our stateside home.

Actually the house almost became a snare to Marian. Having the children at home rather than at boarding school, enjoying the life of a housewife in the States, she really settled in.

"I am never going to want to leave this place," said Marian one day as she contentedly hung out the laundry in the backyard. (Yet when the time came, she was ready and willing to return to Tsipirí.)

Columbia Evangelical Church

On our first Sunday in Columbia we drove downtown to Columbia Evangelical Church—the outgrowth of the Gospel Fellowship we had attended as newlyweds in 1952. At that time it was a storefront church on Main Street. Now there was a lovely new building near the university with a great pastor, Gerald Wheatley. Mr. Eich was an elder, Mrs. Eich was the organist, and Mr. Miller was a deacon. One of the members was Mrs. Prentice from Alabama, a friend of my sister Matred.

"You must be the Joneses!" exclaimed a military man after the service when he saw our Land Rover. He had recently been transferred to Columbia from Montgomery, Alabama, where he had attended Cornerstone Church. We felt so welcome!

This began a thirty-year relationship with Columbia Evangelical. We attended every Sunday morning and evening, the eight of us filling the eighth bench on the right. I paid my children a nickel for each point they could write down of Pastor Wheatley's beautifully-outlined messages. I had a deep respect for the spiritual quality of the elders who ran the church. On Wednesdays I took our children and the neighbor children to prayer meeting—there was a special prayer group just for the children.

At that time C.E., as the church was called locally, was still the only independent evangelical church in Columbia. It attracted many Northerners who couldn't quite handle the Southern "cultural Christianity" of that era, as well as many Southerners hungry for the Word. After our year at C.E., to our total surprise they began supporting us, eventually becoming our largest supporting church.

Our Hardest Year Financially

Each year we had served in Costa Rica the Lord provided more for us than the previous year, although we never appealed for money in our prayer letters. We had learned to pray for our daily bread. Yet costs were rising even faster than our support was, especially with the higher cost of living in the States, plus graduate school fees, and baby expenses. We never shopped for anything but bare necessities. One Saturday Marian stood in the grocery store crying because she couldn't afford twenty-five cents for a book for the kids. Most of the children's clothes were hand-me-downs from friends at church, except for Peter who grew out of his clothes twice that year.

New friends blessed us by inviting our family for meals. We were also blessed when one afternoon just before Christmas we came home to find a whole bag of new toys on the back porch. We never had a hint who had provided this surprise. "Providence has angels everywhere!"

Our backyard at 1109 backed up to the Clinton's backyard. Bobby and Marilyn, a new couple at CBC graduate school, had asked the Lord for playmates of the same age and sex as their four children. The answer to their prayer was found in four of our children. The Clintons gladly shared their phone—we couldn't afford one. If a call came for us, Marilyn would send her kids to get us. Marilyn also invited Marian to use her dryer when it rained.

We were moved by the sacrifice of the Clintons and other students who had left good jobs to answer God's call to prepare for Christian service. They had sold their homes and were living off the proceeds, finishing school with zero assets. I viewed Bobby as someone who was always getting the subject of the Lord into a conversation, as I try to do. He was always challenging, always discipling. Young men were in and out of his house, seeking his input. The Clintons' example encouraged us.

Grad School

My graduate courses in missions and Bible were more stimulating spiritually and academically than I had anticipated. I particularly liked Neil Hawkin's course on applied anthropology and his occasional chapel messages. He was the one man I most identified with, for he not only had worked in a tribe, but he knew the Lord. He would say with passion to us missionaries:

"Know your language! Know your culture! KNOW YOUR GOD!"

Neil Hawkins also moved me when he told how he and his wife experienced a new level of faith when they were assigned to work across a river that became uncrossable during rainy season. Furthermore, he once shared something that I later hung on to in many a crisis:

"Sometimes the Lord will lead you to the edge of a cliff—and let you fall," he said, "but He will catch you before you hit bottom."

Fellow students sought me out. One young missionary candidate came to me more than once with the same question:

"Mr. Jones," asked Bob, "how do I raise support?"

I always replied, "On your knees!"

Bob learned the lesson and is still on the field, but an older student who began seeking me out fared differently.

"I want to get to know you," yelled Fred as he honked to stop my car.

I soon learned not to expect to study at home, for Fred would appear in my driveway. He had been a stockbroker, then a mercenary soldier. Now he kept prodding me with questions, forcing me to disciple him. He grew like wildfire. Exciting, but intense. Then, near the end of the semester, he dropped out of school and returned to his old life. I have no clue as to why, not even a guess. Some fall away no matter how well-discipled and shepherded.

Our Seventh Child

On December 17, 1967, I left the children at Sunday School, then returned home to take Marian to the hospital. At noon I went back to church to let the children know they had a new baby brother. Philip Andrew was born on Timothy's third birthday. How the children loved him—they squabbled as to who would get to hold him. Priscilla, then twelve, did most of the cooking for several days, supplemented by meals brought by church ladies. The ladies even gave Marian a shower, the only one since her first baby.

We were aware of the social, economic, and practical issues facing a large family, but to us the children represented both a mighty potential for God, and a satisfying expression of our own love. As for the unknowns, the risks, the variables—we had the Lord. He was enough.

Second Semester

With the close of first semester I finished my class work. After semester break, I left for Dallas by bus for two weeks of research at the Mission headquarters. I had planned a twelve-hour layover in Phenix City to see Daddy. I asked, again, about his conversion and call to preach, as well as about people and books that had influenced him. Though I didn't find out any more than I already knew, I've always appreciated that day—the only one like it I ever had.

Then came the long haul to Dallas. Unfortunately, my suitcase never arrived, so I had to buy new clothes before starting my research. There at headquarters I spent days going through old files, as well as minutes of the executive council—records which throbbed with life. I was even given access to old personnel files in a back room. I wrote and wrote, page after page of notes on people and events.

Actually the first thirty years of minutes and records had been lost when a former building was sold. But the old copies of the Mission magazine were loaded with long, rambling letters that were full of interesting details. With the permission of the general secretary, I took a set of bound volumes of the *Bulletin* back to Columbia. I read them from cover to cover—like reading an encyclopedia—before beginning to write my thesis.

I had just returned from Dallas when we had a family emergency. A specialist diagnosed a lump on Susanna's ankle as a tumor and wanted to operate immediately. He was not optimistic. After a few hours before the Lord about it, and also enlisting the prayers of friends, the burden lifted. We had received no assurance of anything, except the confidence that "the Lord is good"—whatever the outcome. But there was no malignancy, not even a tumor, only "dense scar tissue." The doctor was mystified. Ten-year-old Susanna returned to school, as active as ever.

Writing the Thesis

Behind our house was a small unheated shed where I set up an office with a table for me and one for Marian who would type the manuscript. Day after day I'd hide out there to meet the Lord and then work on the thesis until midnight, with a small heater to ward off the chilly weather. As I finished each handwritten chapter Marian would type it, editing as she typed, asking questions to clarify an ambiguous point. She would reorganize material and suggest ways to handle sensitive matters. We were a team—Marian working when the older children were home to take care of the little ones and watch the baby.

Ever since I wrote term papers at Moody and Wheaton, I'd enjoyed writing—even winning a writing contest. While researching for my thesis I came across many touching stories from the early years. I felt the pain of Penzotti, when Clarence Wilbur died in his arms in Nicaragua. And the sorrow of a husband whose wife died in his arms in Honduras. And the pain of McConnell, the first missionary, when his son died of appendicitis, and when another son was killed in France in World War I.

I appreciated the compassion the Mission showed to the McConnells, allowing Mr. McConnell to go ahead to Costa Rica with a member of the council to get set up and then return to the States to bring his family. And I chuckled at the first missionary to arrive in Honduras, who quipped in his first letter back to the Mission, "And there was no one at the dock to meet me!"

As my research continued, I liked what I saw. I was happy with my Mission. I described the early days, then the organization in each country, plus final observations. The greatest blessing to me personally was to see how founder C. I. Scofield and the other board members bathed their meetings with prayer. They often felt themselves "in the very presence of the Son of God Himself." Before there were management manuals, strategy meetings, or brainstorming sessions, one member of the board dubbed their administration as "the administration of the Holy Spirit."

Al Ortiz

My course work was finished, but Mr. Petty, head of the Christian Service Department at CBC, was pressuring me to accept an assignment. A few times during the first semester, he asked me to preach at the Spanish services for Puerto Ricans in basic training at Fort Jackson. Now he asked me to pastor a Spanish group, meeting on Sunday afternoons at a Baptist church. Preaching occasionally was one thing, but pastoring was another story, when I was already putting in eighteen-hour days on my thesis and attending two services on Sunday with the family.

Mr. Petty—always gracious—kept coaxing me. He wanted an experienced missionary, not an undergrad, because the group was composed of Puerto Rican families who had settled in Columbia. Finally, after an undergrad promised to do visitation and take charge of the Wednesday night service, I agreed to lead the Sunday meetings.

To avoid preparing sermons, I planned to use the inductive method. I decided to work through the five chapters of I Peter, two Sundays per chapter for the ten weeks I would be leading. We read the portion aloud from the *Versión Popular*, each person reading a verse until we had read the passage three times. Then as we began interacting, asking and answering questions, one man stood out—Al Ortiz.

"Could you come over to the house?" asked Al after the first meeting.

I followed with difficulty in my underpowered Land Rover, as Al, who had once been a taxi driver in New York City, zoomed ahead. We talked until supper, and then he accompanied us to Columbia Evangelical. The next Sunday it was the same routine.

Actually, Al had only come to that first service to give Daisy, his wife, a chance to be with other Spanish speakers. They were relatively new in Columbia. Al worked two paper routes, plus his regular job as a mailman—"getting rich the poor man's way!" Weekends he went fishing with his brother. Lonely and unhappy, Daisy wanted to go back to New York. But it was Al whom the Lord was touching. Soon he began to appear in my driveway during the week, as Fred had done during the first semester.

"I have five thousand questions!" he kept insisting.

Sometimes he showed up at eleven p.m. and I'd be in the shed writing my thesis, but we'd talk. At one point he wanted to know why we missionaries got "so much money." At the time we were receiving less than $600 a month for a family of nine! Under the pretext of his "five thousand questions," he asked us to come to his house one night a week. He also continued to come to our house. His questions were masking a deep desire to know the Lord. My thesis was in his way!

Spring came, and Al went to the Spring Conference at CBC. Afterward he came to the house beaming.

"What a sermon!" he exclaimed. "Pilate said, 'What shall I do with Jesus?' and I, in the balcony, wanted to yell, 'Take him, take him!'"

By the weekend Al, without realizing it, was "taking" Jesus. And he no longer had "five thousand questions!"

"This week I was having my early coffee before starting my newspaper route when Daisy came into the kitchen," confided Al one Sunday night shortly after the conference. "For some reason, before I left I said, 'Daisy, let's pray.' I asked God to forgive me for not honoring Daisy as the weaker vessel"—the previous Sunday we had studied the passage in I Peter about showing honor to the wife as the weaker vessel.

Daisy was impressed! For a Latino husband known for being "macho," this was something new, but Daisy wanted more evidence. When Major Shanks, whom we had met our first Sunday in Columbia, was killed in Viet Nam, Daisy asked Al to go with us to visit the widow. Al didn't know the widow, so I couldn't figure why he wanted to go along—he hadn't told me it was Daisy's idea. When we got back to the Ortizes' house after a very special visit, Daisy was waiting with two questions for Al.

"Was the widow weeping?" asked Daisy.

"No."

"Was she wearing black?"

"No."

Again Daisy was impressed. How could a widow with three young sons face such a loss, if it weren't for the Lord?

Eventually not only Al, but about a dozen others came to the Lord. And finally, a few days before we left Columbia, Daisy came to faith as well. That night we had gone to visit the Ortizes for the last time. I was ready to leave, standing near the door. But Marian was talking to Daisy—pushing her to trust in Jesus. I felt that Marian was pushing too hard, but she stayed with it. And Daisy did pray to receive Jesus! She never wavered, nor did Al.

Finalizing the Thesis

While discipling Al Ortiz, I continued working on my thesis. The actual writing took four months, instead of the two months I had anticipated. As my deadline approached, Marian asked her mother to come from Pittsburgh to keep house for three weeks so she could type full-time. Mom Westling did the cooking and laundry and looked after the baby while the older children were in school. At nights she slept on the couch. She never complained. We couldn't have made the deadline without her gracious help.

For the final, perfect copy, Jeanne Chew, our colleague and lifelong friend, came for three weeks to type the final draft on an electric typewriter—a labor of love. Her knowledge of Mission history was much broader than mine, even with all my research. Jeanne helped edit some of the most sensitive material. To her credit, my thesis advisor declared the final copy to be the most perfectly-typed copy she had ever received.

We made the deadline, burning the midnight oil in the shed behind the house, substituting a fan for the heater as winter ceded to spring and then summer. Graduation was June 3. As I walked down the aisle to receive my degree, our neighbor Marilyn Clinton was teary-eyed—she and Bobby, more than anyone else, knew the effort we had put into that thesis.

Eventually the Mission published the thesis—at my expense—under the title "The Administration of the Holy Spirit." All CAM members received a copy. To my knowledge, it has not been widely used, nor has it profited anyone. Yet I am still glad to have rubbed shoulders with those faithful early missionaries—and to have had a glimpse into how an organization functions when the Holy Spirit is allowed to control.

My thesis was not the only matter we had to finalize. We had received the proofs of the Gospel of Mark. Marian set herself to proofread—while attending to closing the house and planning our summer itinerary. We needed to report to our supporting churches and say goodbye once more to our families.

Parting with fifteen-year-old Peter was a bittersweet experience. We had become accustomed to sending the children to boarding school, but this was different. We left him in Alabama to stay with my brother David until time for him to drive Peter to Ben Lippen, a boarding high school in North Carolina. As we pulled out of the driveway, Peter was crying disconsolately. Aunt Von put her arm around him and led him into the house to cry it out while Marian and I left for Costa Rica with our younger children, riding in total silence for the first hour, united by moist eyes!

− 15 −
Uphill Battle
August 1968 to March 1970

In the summer of 1968 on our way back to Costa Rica after furlough, we spent a couple of days in Houston with a family who regularly opened their home to missionaries needing hospitality— God has His servants everywhere! The heat in the attic room where we stayed was almost unbearable, but we stayed two days to have a winch installed on our Land Rover at a factory specializing in such items. After we crossed into Mexico, however, the Land Rover started giving us trouble on the first mountain. For two days it was "stop-and-start" driving until we reached the home of missionary friends in Puebla. There a new spark plug provided a simple solution to our problem.

When we reached Guatemala, we delivered the corrected proofs of the Gospel of Mark to the Wycliffe publication center. From there we traveled through El Salvador to Honduras where we left Priscilla, Susanna, and Steven in the capital to join an excited group of students waiting for the bus to Las Américas Academy—the M.K. school in Costa Rica no longer existed.

Leaving Honduras, we passed through Nicaragua and finally crossed the border into Costa Rica. After spending two weeks on the road, we felt like singing the national anthem of our adopted country! The Land Rover, with chains on all four wheels, made it over the badly deteriorated road to Tsipirí without the aid of the new winch. After a year of ease in the U.S., Marian was now back to life without electricity and I was back to pick-and-shovel work on the road. Daily we sought to maintain the proper balance between keeping the house going and the road open, while giving the Cabécar Indians our major attention. This meant keeping our eyes on the Lord for His direction.

Although I was happy to get back to translation, my efforts to translate the first verse of Acts seemed hopeless. However, the next day—after more prayer and study—five verses emerged. Célimo, who claimed he had come to the Lord while checking the book of Mark, returned to help with Acts. Though not sharp linguistically, he asked questions about the Scripture, and his smile of understanding was sheer joy. Yet he did not come to work regularly, and the translation progressed very slowly.

Since I had given hundreds of hours during furlough to my thesis on the organization of our Mission, I decided to gain time for translation by not accepting a job on the Field Committee that year. This would free me from trips to the capital for committee meetings and also from writing minutes. Of course, we still had to attend the annual missionary conference, as well as the conference of the association of churches.

After the missionary conference that November, I made the six-day round trip to Honduras to bring Priscilla, Susanna, and Steven, plus two other children, to Costa Rica for Christmas vacation—Peter spent his vacation with his Uncle David in Alabama. The kids kept up a stream of songs and chatter on the long trip. How many verses are there to "Found a Peanut" or "The Bear Went over the Mountain"? And then there was "We're Ninety-Nine Miles from Home," with its ninety-nine verses. Back in Tsipirí rain curtailed outside play during their vacation, but routine chores, familiar toys and games, and favorite books and magazines kept our children occupied. When they left, the silent house was loud with reminders. The tug at heartstrings upon parting does not lessen with experience.

Mark Published!

Early in 1969 we received the finished copies of the book of Mark, the first portion of Scripture ever published in the language of the Chirripó Indians! (The term "Cabécar" had not yet come into general use at that time.) The Gospel of Mark was an attractive book with clear type and several brightly-colored pictures we had chosen from the Bible Society assortment. This book represented the first step toward our vision to give the New Testament to an unreached tribe.

Both Marian and I were excited to finally hold the book in our hands, but wondered if the Indians would also be excited. We handed the first copy to Célimo without comment.

"*Iwashó,*" I said. (Read it aloud.)

He looked over the book, studied the colored picture on the cover, read the title page, and finally began chapter one. Although he was only a fair reader of Spanish, we thrilled to hear him read smoothly and with understanding. Then after almost an hour with only a few pauses, he stopped.

Célimo reading the Gospel of Mark

"*Jerä baasi,*" he commented. (It's really good.)

"Why did they bring John the Baptist's head on a plate?" asked Célimo a few days later. "Were they going to eat it?"

His question might seem absurd, but was actually encouraging to us. It meant he, on his own, had read beyond just the first pages of Mark. The question—which arose between him and his brother-in-law as they discussed the passsage—hints at the endless problems lying beneath the surface of a translation for an unsophisticated tribe that has no previous Bible knowledge.

We began using Mark for simple Bible studies, along with Chirripó songs and prayers. One Sunday six Indians showed up at our house for the meeting—a record number! In addition to the Gospel of Mark three new records made by Gospel Recordings provided another tool for ministry. Though these records were better than the original set, their usefulness was limited. However, overnight visitors to our house could at least play them for entertainment. Sometimes we lent a set of records and a hand-cranked phonograph to those with more interest.

We continued to have a steady stream of Indian visitors on their way to or from town. We fixed them a meal and then bedded them down on pallets in our living room after reading a portion of Mark.

"Is that for calling God?" asked an overnight visitor as she pointed to our piano.

Having heard that we used the piano during meetings, she, with her animistic background, assumed we needed it to contact God.

In addition to holding Bible studies and reading Mark to visitors, I continued working on Acts. It was the middle of 1969 before I finally finished translating the difficult discourse in Acts 7, one of the longest chapters in the New Testament. Another translation workshop was to start in September in Guatemala. Who would be willing to go with us this time? And who would guard the house in our absence? Célimo was too much of a family man to accompany us for three months.

Kitchen Modernized

Other things were going on beside translation. Most important to Marian was a "new" kitchen. The job took its toll in time as we fed the carpenter for almost a month, gave him a hand when needed, and lived in an upset house—but it was worth it! The old galvanized iron sink, the wood counter top, and open shelves in the unpainted kitchen were replaced by a stainless steel sink, a Formica countertop, and painted cabinets and walls. We had bought the sink with offerings from a Sunday School and shipped it in a barrel from the States. The Formica was perfectly installed, though the carpenter had never done such a job before. He was a detail man, not a contractor like his brother Emilio who had built our house six years before.

After the kitchen remodeling job was finished, I took the little boys with me to a country church where I gave special messages in Spanish, while Marian took Elizabeth and traveled with another missionary family to visit the older children at Las Américas Academy. At the end of May we all made the long trip to Honduras to attend Priscilla's graduation from eighth grade and then bring her and Susanna and Steven back to Tsipirí. The children's schooling involved not only the heartache of absence and the joy of reunion, but the headache of preparing their clothes and obtaining visas, plus the weariness of international travel.

Seven children, soon to be eight!
Back: Aziel, Marian, Susanna, Priscilla, Peter
Front: Philip, Timothy, Elizabeth, Steven

Circular from the Mission

Some time after I had finished my thesis, the home office sent a circular to all field missionaries, saying that the Mission planned to do some restructuring. The general secretary asked for suggestions from individuals and from field organizations. I was glad for the invitation, for my interest in administration continued.

My suggestions concerned Mission finances, relating to the disposition of funds deducted from each missionary for administrative costs. During our early years with the Mission there had been no such deductions, but by this point they had become monthly. One of my proposals was that part of the funds deducted in each field be returned to that field for local projects. The other proposal had to do with the payment of the Mission's part of missionaries' Social Security obligations.

In addition to my own letter in response to the circular, my local colleagues also voted at annual conference to make recommendations based on my suggestions. Perhaps the fact that other missionaries accepted my suggestions was part of the reason for the reaction to my letter. Probably I was naive, but at any rate I was totally unprepared for the response I received from the home office. I was informed that a delegation of three would be flying to Costa Rica from Dallas to talk with me, if I would receive them.

"Yes," I said, "if you will come to Tsipirí."

As the date approached, Marian and I fasted and prayed, assuming that on their agenda was the possibility that I would be asked to resign—my worst fear. I put all my fears into prayer, praying defensively. If I was asked to resign, we would lose our house, lose our residence permit, and lose the right to work with the Indians. Our house was actually owned by the Mission, a long-standing policy, although the funds had come from our donors and from the money we paid monthly in terms of improvements to the property. Our residence permit was dependent on an annual letter from the Mission representative, stating that we were still members in good standing. Mission regulations stipulated that any missionary who resigned would turn over his ministry to the Mission and leave the area.

We cried out to the Lord as we hashed over the issues. Marian reminded me that she had tried to talk me out of the letter I had written in response to the circular. The day before the delegation was to arrive, Marian showed me the verses the Lord had given her. In her regular reading that morning she came to Genesis 31. She said that it was as if the page turned gray and only verses two and three were visible: *"And Jacob noticed that Laban's attitude toward him was not what it had been. Then the Lord said to Jacob, 'Go back to the land of your fathers and to your relatives, and I will be with you.'"*

What did that verse mean for us? Just as Laban's attitude toward Jacob had changed, it was obvious that a couple of men in the home office — who had once been our colleagues on the field — had changed their attitude toward me. But what about going back to the land of my fathers and to my relatives? Did that mean we should resign and go back to the States? Marian knew that verse was from the Lord, but she put it on hold for years until its full meaning became more apparent.

For the moment, I could only see that Tsipirí — the property which we had "tamed" and where we had built our home — might no longer be ours. I saw our vision for the Indians threatened. I saw my colleagues as obstacles. I had become emotionally attached to The Central American Mission and to my colleagues. We had the strength that comes from being a team. Furthermore, it was through the Mission that I had first learned of the Indians living in the Chirripó Valley of Costa Rica. But now I was experiencing for myself what I had discovered while writing my thesis — that one's Mission could become a source of unhappiness.

Delegation Arrives

The day arrived. Our eyes were on the Lord. That morning a local colleague brought the delegation as far as Grano de Oro in his VW bus. From there I brought them the last five miles to Tsipirí, plowing through the deep ruts in my Land Rover. I wasn't even guiding the vehicle—the ruts were. I was glad my buddies—yes, colleagues are buddies—could see my world. I felt instinctively that if they were on my turf, I'd be safer, that I'd be at an advantage. Maybe they would think my ministry, my calling, was worth preserving.

Dinner was delicious. Then our local colleague spent the afternoon roaming the property with our children, now home from boarding school. His job was to keep the kids entertained and out of earshot while Marian and I met with the delegation. He knew the seriousness of the occasion; in fact, he had joked that if they made me resign, then he'd resign.

All afternoon Marian and I listened. At issue were the suggestions I had made when the request went out for ideas for restructuring. The leader said that I had crossed a line.

"You have too many ideas," he objected. "I don't know how many is too many, but you have *too many.*"

Later he told me, "You think more than any man in The Central American Mission"—a backhanded compliment.

"I just want the chance to be voted down," I commented later to one of the men on the delegation.

"You don't have that privilege," he responded.

After a break for supper all the family came to the living room for our usual family devotions—a time of good fellowship despite the tensions of the afternoon. The chapter we read that evening was from Acts. The children asked and answered questions about the text. Steven, then almost ten, asked one of the three men a question. The answer was obvious, but the poor guy couldn't come up with it at the moment—amusing to us, but embarrassing for him!

The $64 Question

"How's it going?" whispered our local colleague, heading for the kitchen to wash dishes with the children after the devotional time.

"Not good," I answered as I went back to the living room for more discussion with the men from Dallas.

In it all, Marian and I kept our cool—a calmness of the Lord prevailed. We had prayed for days. As the evening wore on, I sensed a change of direction when the leader paused and then asked the question I'd feared:

"Aziel, did you ever consider resigning?"

What should I answer? Out of nowhere, a thought came to me.

"Did *you* ever consider resigning?" I countered.

My question evidently rattled him, for he hesitated before responding.

"Yes, many years ago, early in my years here," he said slowly.

Somehow he did not follow through with the veiled suggestion that I should resign. Soon the session broke up, but in the letter I received after their visit, the leader referred to my question, as though I had been out of order, perhaps disrespectful. That certainly had not been my intention. I had been raised to respect all in authority. Although I differed with the direction—toward centralized decision-making—in which the Mission was moving, I had a great respect for the leader as a missionary and a man of God.

The Aftermath

Early the next morning I took the delegation back to "civilization." With chains on all four wheels I churned out of our valley—or "hole" as some called it. Halfway up the hill I plowed through some small landslides. I wasn't in the mood to use the winch, but by backing up a couple of times, I managed to push through the gooey, stony mess—letting my passengers taste the reality of Tsipirí mud.

Later as Marian and I rehashed the delegation's visit, she felt we should resign. I was not ready. Besides, we saw no alternative. In order to remain in Tsipirí we needed to continue as members of the Mission. Yet our relationship to the Mission would be in question for years. Only a few friends knew of our situation. We were deeply grieved at the change in attitude of the leader, whom we had loved and respected before we ever joined the Mission. Out of all this I came up with a new insight: the pain of a strained relationship is in direct proportion to the closeness of the relationship.

Before long one member of the delegation confided that the leader had come with a plan in his pocket to encourage me to resign and join Wycliffe. He was willing to urge our donors to continue giving to us as members of Wycliffe—a gesture of kindness on his part. Joining Wycliffe was what we had planned to do before we ever thought about The Central American Mission. However, when the board members of Wycliffe had delayed our acceptance until they could get to know us better, we had reviewed our previous doubts about joining a Mission that was primarily interested in linguistics and translation rather than church planting. Instead, we joined The Central American Mission because we wanted to "eat the fruit of the labor of our hands" by using our translation to disciple believers until a church emerged. CAM supported our desire to translate as a means to church planting. But if we left CAM, where would we turn?

For years we felt uneasy every time we saw a letter from the Mission. We continued to pray for the Lord's deliverance. A couple of years later a colleague from another field attended a meeting of the executive council in Dallas in which the leader asked the council to call for my resignation. My colleague told me that one of the council members asked for a reading of the correspondence that was the cause for asking me to resign. When my letters were read, the council reacted that those letters didn't back up the leader's contention. Again we were spared having to leave the Mission.

Preparing for the Translation Workshop

Our crisis with the Mission occurred as we were getting ready for a workshop, this time to hopefully finish the book of Acts. Furthermore, Marian was expecting another baby, due just days before we had to leave for Guatemala to attend the workshop. The older children had to leave for school at the same time we needed to leave for Guatemala. One more complication involved my need for a translation helper during the workshop.

One day my helpers, Célimo and Benjamín, came to ask me which helper I planned to take to Guatemala. As it turned out, they had gotten together and decided that Célimo would guard our house and Benjamín would go to Guatemala! Benjamín was already helping me with Acts on days when Célimo didn't show up. The problem was getting a passport for Benjamín, for he had a criminal record. Somehow our friend Emilio, who had brought Benjamín to me in the first place, was able to procure a passport for him.

Around the middle of August we closed the house and traveled to the capital to work on visas and permits, and to prepare the children's outfits for school, while we waited for the birth of our new baby. One day after Marian went downtown to buy last-minute items for school, she returned wearily to the Mission Home saying, "I'm not going anywhere again until I go to the hospital!" That day we celebrated Elizabeth's seventh birthday—not much of a celebration, with everything else that was going on.

Our Eighth Child

The next day, August 29, 1969, our fifth son was born. We named him David after King David, "a man after God's own heart," as well as for my brother David who was always such a help to us. The baby's middle name was John, after the beloved apostle. John also happened to be the name of Marian's brother. Although all our other children had been late, David was born five days before the due date—a mercy from the Lord to give Marian time to recuperate before we had to leave for Guatemala. We loved him as much as any of the other children, but his birth was eclipsed by the turmoil of preparing for the trip. On the way back to the Mission Home from the Clínica Bíblica, we stopped to have David's passport picture taken. That little photo is quite a treasure now, since we ourselves didn't take a picture of him until he was seven months old.

Although David was our eighth child and Marian had recently turned forty, we did not plan for him to be our last child. Even though Marian's faith wavered at times and mine did too, we knew God would provide for all the children that He gave us. The Lord had always proven Himself faithful. Yet, although we didn't know it at the time, David did turn out to be our last child. Marian still calls him "my baby."

"Our quiver is full"
Back: Peter, Priscilla, Susanna, Steven
Front: Elizabeth, Timothy, Philip, David

We had to get David included on Marian's passport before leaving for Guatemala on September 8. I took his passport picture and the Costa Rican registration of his birth to the U.S. Consul. As I sat in his waiting room, I was embarrassed at the way he barked at the Costa Ricans who entered his office. When my turn came, I didn't fare any better.

The consul looked at my papers and asked, "Where's your wedding certificate?"

"My wedding certificate?" I responded in surprise. "This is the sixth child I've registered at this Consulate and no one has ever asked for my wedding certificate." (We had left it in the States for safekeeping.)

"I can't put this child on his mother's passport without your certificate," he said with finality.

"But we have to leave for Guatemala in less than a week!" I replied. "There isn't time to write for the certificate."

"No way," he said, swearing at me.

All consuls are overloaded and pressured, but this was the only one who was ever discourteous to me. "Sir," I said, "you're not worthy of your office."

Finally he relented, stuck a sheet of official paper in his typewriter, wrote something, signed it, put his seal on it, attached the baby's photo to it, and handed it to me, saying gruffly, "Try this."

I took the paper and left, glad to have anything official. The carefully-worded document read, "According to evidence presented to me, David John Jones is the son of Aziel Jones and Marian Jones"—*not* of Mr. and Mrs. Aziel Jones. As I left the building, I wondered if the immigration officials at the borders of Nicaragua, Honduras, El Salvador, and Guatemala would accept such a paper.

The Exodus

"This is the most complex job I've ever done," our travel agent had remarked as he handed me a raft of documents for our family "exodus"—documents of all kinds for eleven people heading for three different countries! It was even more complex, he said, than the time he flew to New York to obtain a visa for a Costa Rican client traveling to Africa for a safari. *Don* Eloy, the travel agent, was a blessing to us during many years of international travel.

Peter and Priscilla left for Ben Lippen School before David was born. As we parted at the airport, Peter handed us a heartwarming note of appreciation. Priscilla looked poised and pretty in the white outfit she had worn at her graduation from Las Américas. While at Ben Lippen she wrote this poem:

HOME

A good book in an easy chair,
Laughter (and arguments),
Smell of fresh, homemade bread,
Bare feet thumping down the hall,

Dishes clinking as the coffee perks,
Snacks in midmorning
Gathering eggs from the chicken yard,
An occasional 'possum to liven things up,
Swimming in the ice-cold mountain creek,
This is home!

On September 4 when David was six days old, Marian accompanied Susanna, Steven, and Elizabeth on the train ride to meet the family who would be driving them to Las Américas. Elizabeth, though tiny for a first grader, was full of excitement—until that night. Then she cried for hours as Marian vainly tried to console her.

Early the next morning Marian—totally distraught—phoned me at the Mission Home in the capital, "What shall I do? Do I bring Elizabeth back with me, or send her on to Honduras?"

"Send her," I replied. "She'll be all right." Elizabeth did go to school. Praise the Lord, she had no further problems.

September 8 was our eighteenth wedding anniversary. Marian and I spent the day driving to Nicaragua, arriving that night at the Mission Home in Managua, along with Timothy, Philip, and ten-day-old David, as well as Benjamín. In spite of my fears, the official at the Nicaraguan border accepted the baby's substitute passport unquestioningly! Our dear friends, George and Anita Brower, were running the Mission Home in Managua at that time. We had met them while I was their Mission advisor during their time in Costa Rica for language school. They did their best to make our anniversary a happy time after all the turmoil we had been through.

The following day we passed through a small section of Honduras on our way to the Mission Home in El Salvador. At the time the two countries were at war.

"This land's not worth fighting over," said Benjamín looking out at the rocky, scrubby land. "It won't grow anything!"

Later when we reached a fertile area in El Salvador, his comment was, "I could live here. Corn will grow."

Arriving in Guatemala City the next day, we dropped Benjamín off at the SIL Center where the workshop would be held. Within an hour he had taken off his shoes and was playing soccer on the dirt road by the center. Though more "citified," the other Indians shed their shoes as well. With Benjamín happily settled, Marian and I went on to the Central American Bible Institute where we had rented an apartment for the three months we would be in Guatemala.

Workshop

This time I had no fear of a workshop. Much of the material covered in the lectures was review—but we needed all the review we could get. These principles had to become second nature. We learned to look for the "nearest *natural* equivalent" of unknown words. We studied how to translate figures of speech in a manner compatible with the target language. We learned to take a complicated passage, restate it in simple sentences, and then put it all together in a natural way. We studied how to make our translation sound as though an Indian were speaking.

While we translators studied principles, there were lectures on Biblical background for the Indians who helped us. Most of the time, however, was spent in actual translation. Benjamín was as easy to work with as Alfredo had been difficult. I spent all day at the center, except for a break for lunch at our apartment a few miles closer to downtown.

With three little ones to look after, Marian kept busy, but still found time to come by bus to the center a couple of hours each day. She was able to hire a local Indian woman to help with cooking and washing—a much better arrangement than bringing someone from Costa Rica to do housework as we had done for the first workshop we attended. In the evenings while I studied the next passage, Marian typed the draft I had worked on that day.

Often when Marian went to the center she took Timothy—now almost five—with her so that he could play with the children of other translators. His special playmate was a little girl named Nancy, who was born the same day he was and at the same hospital in Costa Rica!

The two were an inseparable pair—to the amusement of all the missionaries. Back at the apartment little Philip, almost two, amazed us with his symmetrical constructions made with colored blocks. He couldn't talk yet, but he had the skill of an artist or an engineer. And baby David was a special joy during those busy weeks.

On weekends we not only enjoyed the children but appreciated the fellowship of other missionaries and local believers. Benjamín also enjoyed his time off and learned to navigate the city of half a million. He and the other Indians spent most of their spare time at the zoo, marveling at elephants and other animals new to them.

We Finish Acts!

"Acts has lots of verses!" quipped a fellow translator. We had come to Guatemala with only a few chapters completed. Eight weeks into the workshop, we still had five chapters to go. Not too many for the remaining three or four weeks, but we had already pushed ourselves almost to the limit. Furthermore, by the end of the workshop we also needed to complete the verse-by-verse check with a consultant.

Benjamín was faithful. Though an outdoor man, he never complained about long hours at the desk.

"Let's get this done right," he said. "I might need it someday."

Translation is work—tedious work. Yet even translation was not our final goal. Our real goal was to see groups of believers meeting together to worship, pray, and study the Word.

In the final weeks Marian spent longer hours at the center. It was she who translated the last two chapters with all their nautical terms. She had already checked, revised, and typed the earlier chapters. Finally, a few minutes before five on the last day of the workshop, we finished everything, including the consultant approval. The Lord had helped us.

After we paid Benjamín he said, "As far as I'm concerned, you owe me nothing"—final proof of his dedication to the work.

Back to Costa Rica

Now for the long trip home—nine days including stopovers! At Las Américas Academy in Honduras we picked up Susanna, Steven, and Elizabeth, plus children of our colleagues. Their happy chatter and silly songs made the miles pass quickly. Every trip was a family event!

Benjamín was with us as well. He and our Steven—old friends— were excited to see each other again.

The side effects of a hurricane—rain, landslides, and washouts— made our return to Tsipirí interesting. In addition to the usual four-wheel drive and chains, we had to use the winch to get out of a bridge which broke under us. Near the house we found Célimo clearing a landslide. We had already passed several fallen trees which he had cut away. All was in order at home except for two fences damaged by floods. To relax from the tensions of translating and traveling, we cleaned the house and got some needed rest. With no electricity we weren't tempted to stay up late.

"Hung up" at Pashtắrí

During the children's vacation that year the Dillinger family came to visit us. Jerry and Ila Mae, who served at Las Américas Academy, were traveling to visit the homes of the students. I met the Dillingers in Turrialba for the drive to Tsipirí. Late that afternoon when we neared the edge of the Moravia Valley, a small wooden bridge over a tiny creek called Pashtắrí (-rí in the Indian language means "river or creek" as in Tsipirí) gave way under us. Since the water was shallow and the bridge was not high, there was no danger; but the Land Rover was "hung up," unable to move either forward or backward.

Marian was at home with the younger children, but twelve-year-old Susanna was with me. As Jerry and I struggled with the jack and the winch, Susanna started home with Jerry's wife and their three children. We had bought boots for all of them in Turrialba. Hopefully they could walk the three miles over the hill to Tsipirí by dark.

It had been raining for days. Now it started to rain again. Jerry and I worked in the torrential rain until long after dark when we finally were able to extricate the Land Rover. We drove on toward Tsipirí confident that Jerry's family and Susanna were snug and cozy at home. Unfortunately the Tsipirí was too swollen for them to cross. They shouted for help, but with the roaring of the creek Marian couldn't hear them. Jerry and I found them sitting beside the road in the dark, thoroughly drenched and chilled. The Dillinger's little boy was lying asleep in the ditch with water flowing around him. We took them across the Tsipirí in the Land Rover. Once home, we wrapped them in blankets as they sat by the stove. Marian lit the oven and left it open so they could warm up. After a cup of hot tea and something to eat, they recovered quickly. We had a happy visit together, celebrating Timothy and Philip's mutual birthday.

Christmas in Tsipirí

Though there were plenty of trees in the rain forest, none were the proper variety for a Christmas tree. Instead we went outside on Christmas Eve and cut some tropical greenery to decorate the walls. Our only other decorations were last year's Christmas cards which Marian taped to the walls in a pleasing display. This year's cards wouldn't arrive until January or February, or even later.

The little kids at Tsipirí — Christmas 1969

Our family Christmas Eve program was simple—just carols and Scripture and prayer. Gifts the next morning were *very* simple—just a book and a small toy for each child. We wrapped them in paper we had smoothed out and packed away after last Christmas. "We aren't poor," said Susanna once as a small child, "we just don't have any money." But we were happy, contented with what the Lord provided.

For Christmas breakfast we had our annual extravagance, a couple of slices of bacon to go with eggs from our hens. Dinner was fried chicken—always a treat. Then in the evening we wrapped ourselves in afghans and sat around the kerosene heater while Marian read *The Other Wise Man*.

Both Peter and Priscilla were absent that Christmas, staying with my brother David in Alabama during their vacation from Ben Lippen. We devoured their letters, as well as letters from Susanna, Steven, and Elizabeth once they returned to Las Américas in January. Although Marian shared my vision for translation and her involvement was vital, she paid for the separation from our children with occasional tears. But we still had three little boys at home to enjoy!

Back to Translation

With the children back at school in Honduras, I began in earnest to check the book of Acts with other helpers, hoping to finish checking by early May when the American Bible Society planned to hold a Translators' Institute in Costa Rica. We needed Bible Society approval for financing the publication of Acts. Finding men to check Acts was a constant concern. When no one was available for checking, I started translating I Thessalonians with Benjamín. It was slow going, because the epistles are hard to translate with their complex teaching and lack of narrative passages.

Now that the Cabécar Scriptures were beginning to emerge, I identified with a friend who wrote, "This has been the most exciting and satisfying work I've ever done," referring to his involvement in the revision of an English translation of the Old Testament. My own translation work was the fulfillment of the prayer I had recorded in 1950: "I'm Yours, that others might enjoy the privilege I've had today—the Word in their own tongue."

The goal of a New Testament in the Cabécar language, while still several years away, was no longer just a vision, but a possibility on the horizon. Yet we had to trust the Lord to keep us engaged in the uphill battle despite the clouds on the horizon.

— 16 —

Floods, Fasting, and Epidemics
April 1970 to April 1973

We thought we had seen it all! Rains and floods in Turrialba. Rains and floods in La Suiza. Then came the record-breaking twenty-five inches of rain on February 25, 1966—in the middle of "dry" season. But nothing prepared us for 1970, the "year of the floods."

In April of that year my attention was arrested during my morning quiet time by James 1:17: *"Every good gift and every perfect gift is from above, and cometh down from the Father..."* I was alone in Tsipirí with baby David and little Philip, for Marian and Timothy had gone to visit the children in Honduras. They were due home the next day, but torrential rains had persisted for three days.

Turning on the radio, I learned that the Caribbean side of Costa Rica—our side—had suffered the worst floods in history. Roads were closed—including ours. U.S. helicopters were rescuing the stranded and carrying supplies to isolated areas. I was cut off but had enough food for myself and the two children for another week, so felt no concern for my well-being. (However, I heard radio reports that I was missing or even dead!) But as I reviewed James 1:17, these words stood out: "good gift...from above...cometh down..." And I could only think, "The helicopter must be coming to rescue us."

Sure enough, before midmorning a small helicopter suddenly appeared. It landed nearby and the pastor of the CAM church in Turrialba jumped out. He took the kids, half-dressed, and returned in the chopper to Turrialba where Marian was waiting. Back alone in the house, a bit stunned, I read the verse again: "good gift...from above...cometh down..." I spent the rest of the day packing things the family would need, turning off the kerosene frig, and closing the house.

The next day I walked twenty-three miles with a thirty-pound pack, picking my way over muddy landslides, and around washouts and fallen bridges to a point where I could hitch a ride into Turrialba. There Marian and I were overwhelmed by the loving concern of the believers, who for years had been praying for our work with the Indians. The brethren even gave us financial help!

Those floods that had cut me off from civilization occurred in April, normally the driest month of the year. One year when I recorded daily rainfall, I noted that in April there were only thirteen days with some precipitation, quite a contrast to the later months when there were almost no dry days. In December of 1970 we were to experience twice the normal heavy December rainfall.

Translators' Institute

Back home in Tsipirí after the flood, Marian finished retyping the manuscript of Acts with the changes I had made. I used a different color ink for each helper's changes, so the draft from which she typed was a colorfully scribbled mess. In May we participated in a three-week institute sponsored by the Bible Society for translators from Mexico to Bolivia—many coming, as we did, to submit manuscripts for final approval. For us it was an easy trip, since the institute was held in Costa Rica.

We did get approval for Acts in Cabécar, plus a review of translation principles. In addition, we enjoyed the shop talk and fellowship with other translators, especially CAM colleagues from Guatemala, as well as the Mennonite couple, Ray and Susie Schlabach, who had come to Costa Rica to work among the Bribri Indians—closely related to the Cabécars. We also became friends with a German woman working with the Guaymí Indians just over the border of Costa Rica in Panama.

Marian missed the first week of the institute to be with Timothy during corrective eye surgery—the same surgery Priscilla had undergone eleven years previously. During the institute we took our CAM colleagues, the Ekstroms and the Sywulkas, to Tsipirí for a weekend visit. Ed Sywulka had been to Chirripó some twenty years before when he made the initial linguistic survey that was the basis for our joining CAM. Ed had also been our first teacher at the Summer Institute of Linguistics in 1951. Now retired after sixty-nine years of service, Ed and Pauline Sywulka are still role models for us.

Peter Returns from Ben Lippen

After the Translator's Institute I drove to Honduras and back, bringing Susanna, Steven and Elizabeth home from school. Then early in June, Peter and Priscilla flew back to Costa Rica from Ben Lippen School. Peter's return, however, was not a happy event, for we had just received a letter from the school informing us that he would not be allowed to go back for his senior year.

We didn't know what had happened, although we had sensed that something was wrong. For many weeks we hadn't gotten any letters from Peter. The school had a rule that the "ticket" to Sunday night supper was to drop a letter to parents at the door of the dining hall. Priscilla's letters arrived regularly, but not Peter's. We almost decided that Marian should fly up to the school. Instead I wrote his counselor, who answered shortly before the semester ended, telling us that Peter was in trouble and would not be allowed to return.

Later we learned that not only Peter, but a third of the rising senior class would not be allowed to return, and that another third could return only on probation. One issue was the new "electronic" music. The boys found ways to get around the rules, rigging their record players to turn off the prohibited music if someone entered the room. There were other issues that were more serious, for in those overwhelming days of the late sixties and early seventies, the school was struggling with the youth rebellion that took the whole nation by surprise. Furthermore, the headmaster was preoccupied with personal matters, as his wife was dying of cancer.

We wondered what we should do about Peter's schooling. Should we ask the school to reconsider and take him back on probation? One thing we knew that we should do was to pray! As we sought the Lord's leading, we decided to keep Peter at home to finish high school by correspondence. We wanted him to be "under our wings" during this difficult time in his life—and ours.

Fasting

We could do more than pray. We could fast. As a newly-married couple we had fasted every Tuesday evening. We had fasted on other occasions since then—most recently in 1969 when the delegation was to come from Dallas. But this crisis was even worse than the ongoing mission problem. We were desperate. We set aside periodic days to fast and pray, Marian in our bedroom and I in the study, while Peter looked after the younger children. In the late afternoons Marian joined me in the study. We shared what the Lord was saying to us and then prayed together.

Actually, it was good to have Peter, then seventeen, with us that year to help with landslides and washouts. We needed him. Once he and I walked thirteen miles to catch a bus to Turrialba to buy supplies. It was also good to be able to sense where he was spiritually, to read his attitudes, to observe his friendships.

Although Peter was not happy at home in Tsipirí, he enjoyed being with the young people at church conferences. We heard that he had become something of a showoff, and that he had a girlfriend—a Costa Rican pastor's daughter who was as far from the Lord as he was. Soon we learned that the girl was always present whenever Peter attended youth activities. We noticed that he spent a lot of time on the phone when in the city. We saw things and heard things that made us fear even for his life. He was always uppermost in our thoughts and prayers that year. We cried out to the Lord for the life and the soul of our firstborn.

Our children were an expression of our belief in the potential for God which is wrapped up in a human life. Over the years we had invested much time in reading the Scripture with them and praying for them. As they got older and lifelong attitudes and decisions were being crystallized, we were constrained to focus even more prayer on them, for only as they followed the Lord would they continue to be a joy to us and an honor to our Lord.

Other Trials

Our normal life and work taxed us to the limit. It was taxing, to say the least, to walk two hours each way, over tricky, wet trails crisscrossed by myriad roots, just to have a Bible study with two Indians. And it was taxing to drive three hours to Turrialba thirty miles away, spend a day buying food and fuel, and then return home with the help of chains and winch, only to repeat the routine two weeks later.

It was something of a crisis when our gasoline-powered washing machine broke down. Peter and I took it to town in the Land Rover, with the usual help of chains and winch, and had it repaired. We returned to Tsipirí days later, but ten miles from home something in the differential broke. We drove seven more miles with only the front-wheel drive, then parked the car, hired men to help carry supplies, and arranged for an oxcart to haul the washing machine. The breakdown was a kind of last straw, for only two weeks before that we had broken the rear axle. And that was preceded by an engine overhaul, new clutch, new brakes, and work on the gears—to say nothing of frustrations over a defective spark plug and a faulty carburetor.

Repairs on our Land Rover were constant and costly. One day as we drove along, I vented my frustration:

"I just wish that for once I'd have a brand-new car that didn't give me trouble."

Peter rebuked my impatience, only to have Timothy—eleven years younger—pipe up from the back seat.

"Now Peter, when you're a daddy, you're going to fuss about your car, and *your* son is going to fuss at *you!*"

Rainy weather was the norm, bringing down new landslides and creating a sea of sticky mud that stained everything. An avalanche thirteen miles from home affected our only annual family outing—a trip to the 4th of July picnic at the U.S. Ambassador's residence. We had to return home when we found the road closed. Another time landslides detained visitors at our house for three extra days—fortunately we had enough food on hand.

Crossing on the Beams

The rains created a new trial for our recurring supply trips to Turrialba. On our way home from town we had to cross the Moravia Valley—an extensive, relatively flat swampy area crossed by several small creeks. Perhaps the valley had once been a lake, before some earthquake opened an outlet and drained it. The last creek in Moravia before starting up the hill toward Tsipirí was called Jukri by the Indians.

A flood at one time washed away the planks on the makeshift bridge over the Jukri, leaving only the beams—two pairs of parallel logs. The width between the two sets of logs was exactly the width between the wheels of the Land Rover. From the bridge it was six feet down to the water. One slip and the car would be totalled—perhaps not in the fall but in extricating the vehicle without a crane! Yet I had to try. Otherwise we would have to walk the last three miles to Tsipirí and later find carriers for our luggage and supplies.

Peter got out and crossed to the other end of the bridge to guide me across. Marian pleaded with me to let her and the other children get out so that they could navigate the beams on foot. With Peter signaling from the other side, I inched across. They all got back in and we continued on to Tsipirí.

Several times in the following months before the bridge was finally repaired, I crossed the Jukri on those beams with no one to guide me. I would drive a few inches, get out and check my wheels, then drive a few more inches, check the wheels again, and eventually make it safely to the other side. We were on a narrow margin of safety, but we knew that some accidents *must not happen*. That was part of our mindset.

We faced many trials during these years, even threats to our very presence in the area. We were accustomed to going forward in the face of trials, but sometimes we felt that our prayers were like exhausted sighs. Yet as we continued to wait for the Lord to work, we were encouraged by Abraham who "staggered not at the promise of God through unbelief." We were also encouraged by the many friends who prayed for us.

Bright Spots

Amid the trials, the Lord brightened our lives with blessings. A very literal bright spot in our lives was the day the lights came on in Tsipirí! We were given money for a generator and finally were able to hire workmen to build a shed for it and to wire the house—after I'd made the extra effort over a period of months to bring in the materials. At last in September of 1970 we ended seven years of filling kerosene lamps and lighting candles. The lights were a special blessing to Marian as she typed manuscripts in the evenings—her only free time.

Peter and Steven uncrating the generator

When the generator was installed, the children—who'd prayed so long for it—had already returned to school. Elizabeth—who had cried so pitifully the year before as she left for first grade—went off happily, saying, "This time it's Steven's turn to cry!" Leaving home was increasingly difficult for him. During their vacation all the school children had enjoyed the three little boys. Timothy had recovered from eye surgery, but was soon to have another corrective surgery. Philip had fun playing rough-and-tumble with David, who was now walking. The children always brightened our lives.

Weekend ministry was another bright spot. Translation occupied my weekdays, but I gave most Sundays to Bible studies in Chirripó huts. What little interest I'd found among Spanish-speaking neighbors had evaporated, but interest seemed to be increasing among the Indians. Usually we studied a passage from Mark as we sat in hammocks or else on low benches around a small table.

Early Bible study using the newly published Mark

During one of my early treks to Chirripó I had guided an Indian teenager's clumsy hand, already calloused by using a machete, as I tried to teach him how to hold a pencil. Now Rafael was a family man in whose home I held Bible studies. My own teenager, Peter, helped Rafael improve his stumbling efforts to read. Peter was quickly picking up the Cabécar language during his enforced absence from boarding school. Once on the way to a Bible study Peter's machete slipped as he cut away a branch hanging over the steep, slippery trail. He gashed his leg so badly that, though it was not an emergency, I took him to town for stitches. The stitches were to no avail, for the cut later opened up, taking two months to heal.

A few Indians, like Célimo, seemed to feel the force of God's Word.

"I am progressing in God's Word like one climbing a tree!" he said.

Others observed the change in Célimo, for when I asked Virgilio what new life in Christ meant, he answered, "It's what Célimo has."

One day Célimo was visiting a man who pulled out the Gospel of Mark, asking, "What does this passage mean?"—a significant indication of emerging interest.

Translation was also encouraging. Marian was nearing the end of typing the changes I had made in the book of Acts following the Translators' Institute. I had forged ahead with the Pastoral Epistles whenever I had a helper—without helpers I'd study or do correspondence. On my desk were nine Bible translations open to the current passage. Within reach were five more translations, six commentaries, Bible dictionaries, a Greek lexicon, and other helps. After weeks of concentrated translation, I stapled together the first handwritten draft of I Thessalonians. By the end of 1970 I also finished drafting II Thessalonians and then started I Timothy.

The Second Flood of 1970

Late in November we put away books and papers and left for San José, where the mechanic took a week to do two days' worth of new repairs on the Land Rover. Then I drove to Honduras to bring the children home for Christmas vacation. In spite of overheating, loss of water, a slipping clutch, jumping gears, a faulty starter, a broken main spring, and two flats, I made the round trip in the time I had scheduled.

Damaging flood rains had begun not long after we left Tsipirí. Getting home after the trip to Honduras was difficult. Ten miles from home we got stuck on what was normally an all-weather gravel road. Then three miles short of home, where the gravel ends and where we always put on chains, we discovered that a bridge had washed out. Seeing the bridge out again, after it had been replaced only recently, left us with a sickening sensation, for we knew the odds were against its being fixed for many months.

We managed to ford the stream, but got stuck five hundred yards further along, getting out with the help of the winch. Then after two more miles of mud, we sank to the bottom of the last mud hole only half a mile from home. When the winch cable snapped a second time, we gave up and walked the rest of the way home.

Constant rains continued throughout December. The Tsipirí stayed at flood stage, cutting us off from the outside world. For twenty-one days the children could not play outside, but they were happy to be home, playing with Matchbox cars on simulated roads on the linoleum, building block cities—no Legos then—or draping the table with blankets to make a "tent" for a playhouse. They sometimes put one of their little brothers in a cardboard box and gave him a wild ride around the house. Sometimes they made a train out of inverted chairs. Their noise was a happy sound to Marian and me. Occasional squabbles did not spoil their fun. When they tired of active play, they did puzzles or read books or looked at old copies of *The National Geographic*.

Evacuated by Helicopter

During that rainy month Peter and I walked several hours before we finally caught a ride to Turrialba to replenish supplies. Peter went out to town again on December 19 to mail some documents, but when he didn't return after two days, we became concerned. Finally on December 23, he awoke us at 4 a.m., after walking twenty-three of the thirty-one miles from town. He announced that we would be evacuated later that morning by helicopter. Authorities had no hope of repairing the road before we had to leave December 29 to get the children back to school, so friends arranged for a chopper.

Somewhat flabbergasted, we began packing frantically—gifts for Christmas and clothes for school. We still weren't quite ready when we heard the roar of a large U.S. helicopter. The pilot waited impatiently for us to board.

"Missionaries!" he complained in disgust. "More baggage than Carter's Little Liver Pills."

We were whisked to Turrialba in fifteen minutes, as the kids excitedly watched the road beneath us. Friends awaited us at the improvised landing pad as we arrived in unkempt clothes and rubber boots with our motley assortment of muddy boxes and suitcases. We'd forgotten little David's shoes, so he was barefoot.

We had a lovely Christmas at the Mission Home in the capital before the children left for school in Honduras with another missionary family—we took turns making the long drive. In January we returned to Tsipirí during a respite from the weather. The newspaper confirmed the excessive rainfall, announcing that 220 inches fell in 1970, in contrast to 93 the year before. During December alone 51 inches fell, in contrast to 20 the previous December! Our Canadian "neighbor," who at that time owned the huge cattle and logging operation in Moravia, once commented to me about the effect of the weather.

"Nothing is impossible around here," he said, "but everything is more inconvenient"—quite an understatement!

Priscilla was not home that Christmas to get in on the excitement. At Ben Lippen she wrote the following about the contrast between Christmas in Tsipirí and Christmas in the States:

DREAMS

Construction paper chains hung carefully in the dining room window.
Greenery collected on Christmas Eve afternoon nailed all over the house—

giving it a more-rustic-than-usual appearance.
Simple, family Christmas program;
  followed by the rush to get the stockings hung.
Bounding up the next morning to empty them —
  an apple, a tangerine, a box of raisins, maybe a comb or a whistle.
Unwrapping the loving, homemade gifts
  and refolding the already twice-used paper.
But:
No stockings here. An artistically decorated artificial tree
  surrounded by perfectly-wrapped presents.
The elaborate choir cantata two weeks before.
Somehow this isn't quite Christmas.
"Wish I were home!"

Epidemics Devastate the Indians

In January of 1971 the rain finally stopped. In fact, in March a VW bus made it to our house—the first vehicle ever to arrive without four-wheel drive. Fortunately, no emergencies had arisen while the roads were closed at the end of 1970, but now I made one emergency trip after another. There was a devastating epidemic of measles, plus an epidemic of whooping cough, and also an epidemic of *gastro* among the Indian children in the Chirripó Valley—thirty children died that season. Among those I took to the hospital were Benjamín's children. Our own Timothy and Philip had serious cases of measles.

It was at this point that Paul and Doris Lloret, CAM missionaries in language school, drove out to Tsipirí in their VW to ask how they could help, for Doris was a nurse. For years we had envisioned a monthly clinic ministry. With encouragement from the Llorets we set a date for the first clinic. I went to the capital for vaccines and medicines. Peter and Benjamín left on an overnight trek to notify as many Indians as possible. I feared that the rains might start again and close the road or keep the Indians from coming, but the Lord heard our prayers and prospered our plans.

Doris and another missionary nurse treated almost one hundred forty Indians. In April they returned and treated over one hundred fifty people! While the Indians waited their turn, we played a cassette with portions from the Gospel of Mark, or else Marian read passages to the people when she wasn't busy cooking. Peter served as pharmacist, doling out the pills the nurses prescribed. By the end of the day we were exhausted, but happy to have helped.

The epidemics eventually slacked off. In June on her last visit, Doris treated forty Indians before she and Paul finished language study and headed for their new field. Without the Lloret's help it was more difficult to procure medicines and personnel, but we envisioned more clinics in the future.

Peter Starts Bible College

During his year at home Peter kept talking about going to the University of Costa Rica. Although he knew we had always planned for our children to go to Columbia Bible College, he kept dragging his feet about sending in the application.

"We'll send you to Bible College," we insisted. "After that you may study where you will."

Peter's continued resistance was wearing Marian down.

"Let's give up and let him go his own way," she said to me one day.

"No," I said. "We'll keep nudging him—and go as far as we can."

When he filled out his application to CBC, what he wrote regarding his salvation and Christian life sounded fine. Privately we were uncertain of his spiritual condition; however, he was accepted, PTL! He still had to finish his high school correspondence course. At the end of July he took his last exam. We still wondered if he would actually get on the plane, but thankfully he did.

With him flew Priscilla, returning to Ben Lippen as a junior. Susanna, who had graduated from Las Américas in May, asked to study ninth grade by correspondence, which would be much less expensive for us than having all three of them studying in the States. In the end, we also decided to keep Steven and Elizabeth home, rather than sending them to Honduras to school. Susanna and Steven did most of their studying on their own, while Marian helped Elizabeth, as well as Timothy who was beginning first grade. Philip and David rarely got bored with so many siblings around!

Seeing Peter and Priscilla off to school:
Back row: Peter, Priscilla, Susanna, Marian, and Aziel
Front row: Steven, Elizabeth, Timothy, Philip, and David

Six weeks after Peter entered CBC, he wrote that he had thrown way "her" picture. Breaking with his girlfriend marked a complete turnaround in his spiritual life. From then on Peter never wavered in his faith. He committed his life to serving the Lord. We kept on praying for him, but our hearts were at rest. The Lord had heard our desperate cries; in the future we would fast again as we faced other pressures.

More Clinics

We continued to hold clinics as often as we could find nurses or doctors. Medical students, although quite willing to help, proved slow and indecisive. Then a doctor who had grown up in the CAM church in Turrialba offered to help us. Juan came several times to Tsipirí to hold clinics. As a doctor, he was a very practical man. Having worked in the area, he was quick to size up each patient, treating only obvious symptoms.

Doctor Juan treating patients in our living room

A problem arose when non-Indians got wind of the free clinics and began walking to Tsipirí from Moravia or even from Grano de Oro. We asked them to wait until all the Indians had been treated, for many of the Indians had to trek hours to get home. The "whites" felt slighted, but we knew that they could easily catch a bus to Turrialba for medical attention. Once when I took Juan back to town, a woman in Grano de Oro hailed us. Her house was in front of the bus stop. Juan calmly told her, "I'll be glad to see you Monday morning at my office in Turrialba."

Actually, some patients—especially the men—were in excellent health, toughened by hard work in the open air. But in those days the women and young children tended to be undernourished and susceptible to disease. Respiratory diseases and intestinal parasites were common complaints. Yet all had excellent teeth, for their diet did not include sugar.

In all we held eight clinics between March of 1971 and May of 1973. Each time we faced the same risks. Would the doctors show up? Would the road be open? Would rains hinder the Indians from coming? Only once were we rained out. Peter and Benjamín had raced over the hills, up steep inclines, down the ravines, taking every shortcut, notifying everyone about the upcoming clinic. But the morning of the clinic it rained and rained and rained. Not a single Indian showed up, praise the Lord. Why praise the Lord that no one showed up? Because the doctor didn't show up either!

Translation Continues

In between clinics I continued to translate. As I checked the crucifixion story in John with Célimo he commented, "I feel sorry for Jesus suffering so." But some did not believe.

"No one can take away the wrong we have done," a friend said to Célimo. "No one can raise the dead."

"I don't know much," responded Célimo, "but that is what the Word of God says."

"What is said in the Gospel of Mark was said to others, but it is also for us," commented Virgilio, another of my translation helpers.

But Benjamín, our main helper, was not growing in faith.

"There are more demons than gods," he told Virgilio, expressing a view consistent with the demon-centered religion of the Cabécar Indians.

By January of 1973 I had finished not only the Pastoral Epistles but the Gospel of John. Of course, each book was "finished" many times: the first draft, the second draft, the third draft, the initial typing, the consultant check, the final draft, the final typing, the initial proofreading of the printed copy, then the final proofreading. Part of this process was Marian's work, squeezed in at odd moments between teaching children and looking after the house.

As for the book of Acts (which had been approved by the Bible Society consultant during the Translator's Institute in 1970), it took us months—in between other work—to finish checking the consultant's suggestions. When Marian finished typing the final draft, we mailed the manuscript to Guatemala in 1971 for typesetting. The first set of proofs eventually arrived by slow mail from Guatemala to be proofed and returned, followed by the final proofs, which Marian finished correcting in May of 1972. However, it was not until March of 1973, as we were anticipating another furlough, that we finally received the published copies of Acts.

Our thrust among the Indians in Chirripó up to this point was captured in a poem written by Paul Lloret, the colleague who had helped us start the clinics in 1971:

WORDS WE LEARNED AS CHILDREN

When first he came,
We thought him such
As many who had come.
Our fathers told
Of men who came with weapons,
And who walked throughout
Our land.
And now they pass in birds
That grind and clatter
In the sky
But he has stayed.

At first it was not often
That he came.
He talked to us at first
As others talked,
In Spanish words we'd gathered
From the market-place as men.
But always did he ask
For words we learned as children.
He stopped us on the trail
To ask, and ask, and ask again
Until we wondered why
His mind forgot so quick.

Days he walked
And nights he spent
Within our houses
Tired, but always asking.
Then he built his house
Beside our trail
And we would visit him
And talk—we always talked.

And he would ask of things
Our fathers said—

Of spirits, and of rains,
Of sickness, and tigers,
Hogs and corn.
And as we talked,
He marked the papers full
Until he had
An overflowing treasure-box.

Others come
And asking questions,
Taking pictures, leave.
But he has stayed,
And now he talks to us
In words we learned as children.
He talks to us of one
Who orders evil spirits out of men,
Who stops the water
In its deadly course,
Who stops the sicknesses of men.
He made a book for us to read
And walks to us again
To read and talk.

He is the strangest sort of man.
He does not want our land,
He totes our zinc to make our roofs
And wire for pasture land,
And cleans our wounds
And helps us with our pain.
He stops his work
To listen to us talk,
And talks to us
Of one who made the earth
We walk upon…
In words we learned as children.

− 17 −
Pivotal Furlough
May 1973 to July 1974

Our 1973-1974 furlough meant leaving our work for a year. The books of Mark and Acts were now in the hands of many Indians. Part of Mark and all of Acts were also on cassette tape. We trusted that these books, scattered about in homes throughout the Chirripó Valley, would be like seed that would sprout—even though my helper Virgilio lost the very first copy of Acts when he got drunk. For three years I had been holding simple Bible studies all over the area, but now we were flying back to the States.

"Where are we going?" asked little David, three years old, as we boarded the plane in May of 1973.

"I didn't know an airplane was like *this*!" exclaimed Philip—now five years old.

"Looks like the world is tipping!" shouted eight-year-old Timothy in his unending torrent of words, as the four younger children had their first plane ride.

Our first stop was Honduras for Steven's graduation from eighth grade. Then when we arrived in New Orleans my brother David met us with a '67 Oldsmobile he had bought for us to drive while on furlough.

"Miles aren't so long in this car," said ten-year-old Elizabeth— jeep roads were much slower.

"There aren't any hills here!" observed Timothy with amazement. (Years before as we drove the serpentine roads to Tsipirí, Steven had looked up from the book he was reading and exclaimed in surprise, "We live in the mountains!")

Soon we reached Mobile, where we said good-bye to my brother David and went on our way to Ben Lippen for Priscilla's graduation from high school. From there Priscilla and Susanna traveled with us to South Carolina to get Peter at Columbia Bible College, and then back to Alabama. At last we were a family again!

Phenix City, Alabama

We enjoyed being near some of my sisters in Phenix City for a few weeks and then gathered with all my siblings at our annual two-day reunion at Kolomoki. That July, however, Daddy was missing, for he had died in February at the age of eighty.

The day that my father, Rev. R K Jones, died, Marian and I happened to be in San José where the news could reach us. In order to get to the States in time for the funeral I needed an exit visa, but getting one normally required a few days. However, I learned I could get a visa quickly for a family emergency, so I flew standby the morning after I heard the news. I arrived in the midst of the heaviest snowfall ever recorded in the Southeast. Daddy's funeral was special— marking the end of an era. Somehow I felt sad that he had missed this great event. We thirteen siblings alternately laughed and cried at the funeral, as we had done at Daddy's house while his body lay in state. Family and friends from far and near, past and present, honored him after forty-seven years in the pastorate.

Daddy's empty house was available to us for our furlough year. However, Priscilla—who was to start Bible College in the fall— suggested that we spend our furlough in Columbia. Her desire was the deciding factor which put us in South Carolina on a furlough for the second time. Before settling in Columbia, we visited friends along the east coast. Peter was working and ministering in Baltimore that summer. While visiting him, we celebrated Steven's fourteenth birthday, and also took the children sightseeing in Washington, D.C. We wanted them to see the capital of the nation of which they were citizens but not residents!

From New Jersey we headed west to Pittsburgh where we visited Marian's parents, and finally reached Chicago before turning south again. As we spoke in churches during that summer, we always focused on what God was doing—and on our vision of what He would yet do. We basked in renewing relationships from past years and making new friends. To us, deputation did not mean "beating the bushes" to raise support, but enlisting prayer for ourselves and our ministry. Our trust was in the Lord!

Settling in South Carolina

A house was waiting for us in Columbia near the one that we had lived in during the previous furlough. Other furloughing missionaries also lived in the neighborhood. The house was adequate in size, but not nearly as pleasant as the former house. We were praying for a local ministry during furlough, but for a study project I planned to write up the grammar of the Cabécar language, while Marian wanted to brush up on her Greek. However, neither of those projects materialized. Instead, I became heavily involved in ministry, and Marian was busy keeping the family going and typing my ministry notes, as well as a short article I published on Cabécar verbs. She didn't even have time to type the final manuscript of the Pastoral Epistles.

Peter and Priscilla lived with us but studied at the Bible College two miles up the road. Priscilla had lived in a dorm from first grade through high school—except for furlough. She missed dorm life and wrote a paper titled "Dorm Sickness" for an English course. Susanna studied again at Ben Lippen, one hundred sixty miles away. I cherished the time I spent with her, driving her home for occasional weekends and then back to school. Steven was in ninth grade at a local Christian school, but Elizabeth and Timothy attended public school two blocks from our house. Only Philip and David were still at home.

With the children going to different schools on different schedules, it was quite an operation to keep our home moving as an orderly unit, eating meals as a family and praying together daily without hectic hurry, but the Lord helped us continue our family life much as we had done in Tsipirí. At Peter's urging, we read the missionary classic *Behind the Ranges* aloud as a family on Sunday nights after church—the first of many missionary stories we read over the years during family devotions. The constant flow of friends in and out of the house—our friends and the children's, as well as students interested in missions—was an inspiration rather than a frustration.

Home Bible Class

In answer to our prayer for local ministry, a couple at church who had recently come to the Lord asked us, "Would you lead a Bible study for our neighbors one night a week?"

A good group gathered in their living room, most ready with pen and notebook. "I'm sorry," I began, "but you won't need to write anything. I don't plan to lecture. Instead, we'll be looking together at the book of John to see what it says."

I used the same method I had used years before at the Bible study for professors in Turrialba and later used with unschooled Indians in their dirt-floored huts. As we began the study each one read a verse or two aloud to get everyone focused, then one person reread the whole passage for coherence.

"What does it say?" I asked after the reading. "What grabs you?" "What impresses you?"

We were off to a good start. Slowly they caught on and began to listen to the Word, figuring out what it said, not just listening to what I said.

"What does this verse mean?" someone would ask me.

"Reread the passage and then tell me what *you think* it means!" I'd answer. Or I'd say, "Will someone else answer that question?" Very simple, yet so effective and powerful!

Once when a newcomer asked about a certain passage, I responded as usual, "What do you *think* it means?"

"The problem is," she answered, "that if I answer you, I'll have to change my thinking!"

These "cultural Christians" in the Deep South were learning to hear what God says in His Word. However, if they didn't embrace the message, God stopped speaking to them.

Lessons on the Christian Home

Another answer to our prayer for opportunities to minister came when I was asked to teach a series of lessons on the Christian home. Someone evidently thought that since we had a large family, we had earned the right to share! From October through December I taught an adult elective in Sunday School at Columbia Evangelical Church, the same church we had attended on our previous furlough. What I ended up doing was sharing how Marian and I had raised our children. Before each session I prepared an outline, which Marian typed for the group.

In regard to discipline, what I emphasized was that it must be *early enough, soon enough, firm enough, and consistent enough.* "Early enough" in the child's life to forestall patterns of disobedience. "Soon enough" after an offense so that the young child's mind connects the discipline with the offense. "Firm enough" to be effective— halfhearted discipline breeds resistance. "Consistent enough" to establish a pattern—we must not overlook later the same offense for which we disciplined earlier. I used the word "enough," to indicate that though we parents are not perfect in our exercise of discipline, we must discipline regularly, not sporadically.

As to the purpose of discipline I pointed out that godly discipline is *didactic* as well as *punitive*—that is, for teaching as well as for correcting. Discipline is intended to train the child to control himself, rather than merely punish him for offenses. The object is prompt obedience without defiance or sullenness. All this requires parents to be careful not to give commands thoughtlessly, for commands must be obeyed—they are not suggestions open for negotiation on the part of an astute or reluctant child.

Perhaps what was most appreciated in my teaching was the section about devotional life in the home. I shared what Marian and I had developed over the years, starting with a very simple song and prayer when our first child was a baby. Then we added a simple Bible story and a short memory verse as he grew. By the time he was ready for school we changed to a book of more detailed Bible stories, but kept up the simple story book for the next child and the song and prayer for the baby.

Eventually we added a short reading from the Bible itself before each meal—Proverbs at breakfast, Old Testament at noon, Psalms at supper. Then after supper we gathered in the living room to read a chapter from the New Testament in an easy-to-understand version. Each of the children read a verse, even if an older child had to whisper the words to him. Then each one was given a missionary letter. We knelt and each of us prayed, at least mentioning his missionary. I expected the older children to apply or mention the Scripture passage in their prayers. We prayed in order of age from oldest to youngest—the children wanted to get the longer prayers over with first!

Sunday evening devotions were different. In Tsipirí there was no church to attend, so we each chose a hymn to sing while Marian played the piano. Then we would listen to a sermon on tape, or Marian would read a short sermon, perhaps from Spurgeon, which the kids enjoyed. Finally I prayed a pastoral prayer for the week. On Fridays we later modified our devotional time. Instead of the New Testament reading, Marian would read a chapter from a missionary biography and only she would pray. This saved time for a family game night, the suggestion of our daughter Susanna. Occasionally we varied the daily format, worshipping the Lord at length with Steven leading, after he learned to play the guitar.

Family devotions were for everyone in the house including visitors. Even though it was difficult to maintain our practice during furlough, we felt we must experience the Lord together. Everyone was also present for Bible reading at the table even at breakfast. If a child was tired he was allowed to go back to bed afterward—but none ever did. Mealtime Bible reading proved to be the simplest, least time-consuming way to get a lot of the Word into the children.

We were not doing all this just for the children! Marian and I needed the Word as much as they did. In addition to the family times she and I maintained our own personal devotions early in the morning before the children got up. If they were awake they were to stay quietly in their room, perhaps looking at books. As they grew older, they started reading the Bible and praying on their own in the early morning.

More Teaching on the Home

I was asked to repeat the series on the Christian home during the spring quarter. At that time I prepared new handouts each Sunday. These were not just outlines but full lessons which Marian edited and typed. Eventually all the material was put into a manual. However, I did not include a chapter on teenagers. I felt we had not yet earned the right, since several of our children were still young. I wish now that I had, because the teen years are crucial to preserving whatever good patterns are set during childhood. Furthermore, the way we deal with our teenagers affects the younger children as well. At the heart of the matter of teens is: "Parents, capture your child's will by the age of twelve through discipline and training. Don't release your authority as long as your teen lives at home. Even though he may challenge you, you can maintain what you won by discipline before the teen years."

In spite of what Marian and I had learned by that time about raising children for the Lord, we now see areas where we could have done better. We've been asking God to fill in the cracks that we left in their training—and to help them train their own children. But at the time I taught the series, my class was very appreciative. They even bought me a new suit to replace the old one I'd worn every Sunday that year!

Another Opportunity to Teach

During the winter quarter from January through March I was asked to teach an elective on "The Triune God." I was given a manual to teach from, but didn't find it helpful. Instead I made my own lessons, studying up to sixty and eighty hours a week. My biggest blessing was to get a handle on the ministry of the Holy Spirit.

For a couple of years Marian and I had been wondering about the Spirit. I kept asking, "If all I have is in Jesus, then why the Holy Spirit?" I read commentaries and theology books from the CBC library, for I had left all my own study books in Tsipirí. Slowly, as I studied for each Sunday's class, my thoughts began to crystallize. I realized that each person of the Trinity had a role: the Father as initiator, the Son as mediator, and the Spirit as energizer, although other terms could be used. Each respected the role of the other, yet all worked together, even though one might be in focus (as the Father in creation, the Son in salvation, and the Spirit in regeneration).

The first few Sundays I focused on the Father and on the Son. Then I spent several Sundays on the person and work of the Spirit—a very current topic at the time. As background I read many of the new books then being published on the subject. The final three sessions I gave to the Holy Spirit's ministry in the earthly life of the Lord Jesus, followed by a lesson on the Spirit's work in the lives of the apostles, and finally one on the Holy Spirit in our lives today.

As I did original study from the Gospels, especially Luke, I was amazed to realize that *all* that Jesus did was through the power of the Spirit, who first came upon Him at His baptism. What He knew and taught was revealed to Him by the Spirit. For me, the capstone of the accumulated evidence was Acts 10:38: *"How God anointed Jesus of Nazareth with the Holy Ghost and with power: who went about doing good, and healing all that were oppressed of the devil; for God was with him."* Later as I scanned the whole book of Acts in preparation for the lesson on the apostles, I was surprised at how often the work of the Spirit is mentioned.

Before the last lesson I scanned the whole New Testament for all the passages on the Holy Spirit in our lives, then late on Saturday night I spread out my notes on the table, praying through them point by point, hour by hour, throughout the night. I had done the same before the lesson on the Holy Spirit in the life of Jesus. Both times when I taught I was hardly aware that I was speaking. Rarely have I had so much power, nor seen God work in so many lives. People were moved—and so was I.

I concluded that just as we must receive Jesus Christ for pardon from sin, we must receive the Holy Spirit for power over sin *and power to minister*. Since then, I have found that this is what A. W. Tozer says in one of his books. Teaching those lessons put theological underpinnings to what God had already been teaching me and Marian personally.

Al Ortiz is Ordained

Al and Daisy Ortiz were now living near our furlough home. This special couple had come to the Lord through our ministry with Hispanics on our previous furlough. In the intervening years Al had graduated from Columbia Bible College—we'd been present at his graduation when we first arrived on furlough. He and Daisy were now appointed as missionaries, but to earn a living until they left for the Dominican Republic, Al was working as a mailman. He often stopped by our house for a good time of fellowship at the midpoint of his route!

In September Al performed his first baptism at a lake near Columbia; our son Steven was the first person he baptized. Soon Al asked me to preach at his ordination on October 23, which I considered a great privilege. As I mulled over what I would say, the Lord gave me a message, clear and simple: "The Three Resources of the Man of God"—the Word of God, prayer, and the Holy Spirit.

My thoughts flowed together well, growing out of my experience and convictions. Yet as I reviewed my notes the day before I was to preach, I didn't feel satisfied with my last point. Marian and I had always been open to the Spirit and desired all that God had for us, but I kept snagging on that last point. So I started praying, along with Marian.

"Holy Spirit," I heard myself saying, "forgive me for not giving You the same importance as the Father and the Son." Never before had I addressed the Holy Spirit directly except in a hymn, but that night I felt I should.

When I went back to my notes, I added a few lines: "Appropriate the Holy Spirit, and don't assume Him. Ask for the power that He gives." I was satisfied. When I preached the next night, I was, as it were, carried along by the Holy Spirit. I knew that the Spirit was in my message.

"It took you twenty years to write that sermon," commented Al.

He was right, but I had had a dealing with the Holy Spirit the night before. Later while teaching on "The Triune God," I crystallized my understanding of the Spirit's ministry.

New Fire

In the following days, I began to listen to the Holy Spirit. I asked, "What do *You* want me to pray in this situation?" As I ministered one on one, instead of using "stock" formulas for counseling, I started listening for the whisper of the Spirit, "What is *Your* word for this person?" For another person with a similar problem, I'd do the same—*His* word for *this* person. Things changed for Marian also. The Word became a new book. She had new liberty in prayer.

Steven had also been touched by the Spirit a few months before this time, while finishing his last year at Las Américas Academy. A volunteer teacher held after-school classes on the book of Romans for those who cared to participate. Steven, always hungry for the Lord, experienced new victory through studying Romans 6 to 8. This was the beginning of a new era in the spiritual life of our family.

"I don't know what would have happened to us as a family if the Lord hadn't touched us," remarked Steven one day near the end of that furlough year in Columbia. It was indeed a pivotal year!

One of the final events of that year was my own ordination. Although we had been duly commissioned in 1952 by The Central American Mission and also by Moody Church, I had never been ordained. I had held back, preferring not to accept the title of

"Reverend" but to reserve that title for God alone, in accord with Psalm 111:9, *"...holy and reverend is his name."* However, now in June of 1974 I wanted to be ordained as a seal of the fresh work the Lord had done in our lives that year. I also desired ordination as a recommissioning for the work that still lay ahead. So I was examined by the elders of Columbia Evangelical Church and formally ordained to the ministry. Even so, I prefer not to use the title "Reverend!"

Family Transitions

Not only was this furlough in Columbia our last year together as a family, it was Priscilla's first Christmas at home since David's birth four years earlier. We bought the "perfect" tree—especially to Priscilla's taste—with money given toward some "American extravagance."

Peter, our firstborn, was now engaged to Deborah Bayuszik, whom he met at the Bible College. We had all attended her graduation from CBC very early in our furlough. How excited we were to meet her, as well as her family who had driven from Butler, Pennsylvania, for the graduation. Debbie was a wonderful match for Peter, and we liked her family too. Both we and they had prayed fervently for the Lord's choice of mates for our firstborn. Marian and I were thrilled with the prospect of Peter and Deb's eventually joining us in our ministry in Chirripó.

"Daddy," Peter had said to me, "you can put some slides of us in your slide show because we expect to work with you."

Although Peter and Debbie were now engaged, Debbie soon left for Italy for a two-year term with a church-planting team—a commitment she had made before their engagement. The separation was hard for them both, but we admired her for following through with her commitment. As Peter and Debbie looked ahead to marriage, they asked if I would perform the ceremony, but at the time I was not yet ordained.

"Is it right to get ordained just to perform a marriage ceremony?" I questioned Peter.

"Don't you think that performing a wedding is a spiritual service?!" he responded. Peter's words added another reason for my ordination at the end of our furlough.

Not only were our children transitioning, but Marian's parents made a major change as well. Her father finally retired at the age of seventy-five and bought a lovely piece of property in Costa Rica. There they would be near their two daughters and the grandchildren. Rather than fly to Central America, Dad Westling wanted to travel overland from Pittsburgh. Marian and I would lead the two-car caravan, driving our furlough car back to the field.

Peter also headed to Central America—not with us, but with a summer evangelistic team from Columbia Bible College. We would cross paths with him in El Salvador on our drive down. Afterward, he planned to fly to Rome to visit Debbie before his senior year. Only Priscilla remained in the States, where she worked and studied linguistics that summer.

Our drive to Costa Rica as a two-car caravan was quite a feat, but it went well. The four younger children rode in our car, but Susanna and Steven—both teenagers—rode with Dad and Mom Westling, who spoke no Spanish. In case the two cars became separated, the grandchildren could at least speak the language well enough to ask directions! In the heart of Mexico City on a limited access highway, we noticed Dad Westling exit the maze of traffic. We pulled over and waited. Sure enough, after about fifteen rather tense minutes, they turned around, reentered and found us!

By mid-July of 1974 after over two weeks on the road we arrived at the Westling's place in the suburbs of San José. There we spent a couple of weeks helping the folks get settled. They seemed to adjust well to their new surroundings, especially considering their age. Marian and I, however, were the ones who found it difficult to readjust to life in Costa Rica. What we missed most was the satisfying ministry and rich fellowship we had experienced in Columbia during that pivotal furlough year.

— 18 —

The Family Grows Up
July 1974 to June 1979

Returning to Costa Rica in the summer of 1974, I went to the dealer who had promised me a more powerful Land Rover. Inflation had set in and prices had skyrocketed. Furthermore, he didn't even have a secondhand vehicle of the type I wanted. I ended up selling the Oldsmobile we had driven from the States and buying a used Toyota station wagon. Although it was more powerful than my old Land Rover, it was not as comfortable, nor did it have a winch.

On the first trip back to Tsipirí we got stuck and had to hire a team of oxen to pull us out. I also discovered that the four-wheel-drive mechanism was defective. Once it was fixed and we bought a winch, we had very little trouble with that vehicle—a mercy from the Lord.

"I Want Fellowship"

Isolated once more in Tsipirí, Marian was lonesome after the furlough which had marked such a pivotal time in our spiritual lives.

"I need fellowship," she complained. "You're responsible to minister to me."

"Someday," I replied, "when there's a church among the Cabécars, you'll have fellowship with other believers right here."

My off-the-cuff answer didn't satisfy her. We both knew that day was still far off. "Now what?" I wondered. The solution that emerged as we talked it over was to set aside a few minutes at bedtime, after the children were asleep, just for ourselves. We would read a few pages from a spiritually stimulating book—for we'd already read the Bible during the day. Then we'd pray together.

When we got engaged, we began praying and reading the Word every evening. Then on our wedding night we spent an hour in the Word before praying. Our nightly time together with the Lord continued until we started family devotions once the children were old enough. But we had lost the time together, time for just us. Fellowship—Marian had used that word. The two of us began reading and praying again each night. It was refreshing and renewing. It was "quality time."

To this day we continue the practice. When under pressure or tired, we don't read. But pray together we do—always. We also talk, bringing up what's on our minds, sharing blessings, sharing news, talking about what's bugging us or about some situation with the kids. There's always something to pray about! We found that ongoing spiritual fellowship is basic to marital harmony.

Home for Christmas

Priscilla came home for Christmas that year—her first Christmas in Costa Rica since eighth grade. Torrential rains were falling as we traveled from the airport to Turrialba to buy groceries before heading toward Tsipirí. At the bus terminal in Turrialba I checked with the driver of the bus to Grano de Oro about the condition of the river there. (We knew we would have to ford that river because the bridge was too damaged for vehicles to cross.)

"No," he said, "the ford is not passable."

That meant a night in Turrialba as we waited for the water to go down. We always had an open door there at the home of *don* Emilio, the friend who had built our house. Emilio was away from the Lord, no longer living at home, but his wife, *doña* Flora, always took us in. We were a crowd with Priscilla home from CBC, Steven from Ben Lippen, Elizabeth and Timothy from Las Américas, plus Philip and David and the two of us. It didn't matter, we were still welcome. Flora offered her "cup of cold water in the name of the Lord."

"The river's still too full to cross," said the bus driver when I checked again the next day.

The following day he assured us we could cross, so we loaded up and left. Two hours later when we reached Grano de Oro, we discovered that the water had not yet gone down enough to ford. Now what should we do?

"Let's walk!" we all said in chorus.

The children were anxious to get home—especially Priscilla whose Christmas break was short. Local friends helped us make packs out of gunny sacks and rope—tying a rock in each "ear" of the bottom of the sack and uniting them at the mouth. It made a nice pack for perishables: meat and vegetables. We put on our rubber boots, crossed the river on the damaged bridge, and headed home. As we walked the two hours across the Moravia Valley and up over the ridge to descend to Tsipirí, we noticed with concern that Priscilla was limping.

The next day when I walked back to Grano de Oro to get the car with the rest of our baggage, I found the water still quite deep. I drove too fast through it, but fortunately, the fan didn't touch the water. If the fan had thrown water on the distributor, the Toyota would have sat in the river for a day.

Priscilla limped all during her vacation. She had no pain, but Marian sent her back with instructions to have friends in Columbia take her to a doctor. Among the new friends we had made during furlough were Ronald and Sandra Barber, to whom we had become especially close. They had been in the classes I had taught at church and we had met with them often for fellowship and prayer. Now Sandra took Priscilla to an orthopedic surgeon.

Priscilla's Surgery

During her quiet time early one morning, Marian had decided to choose a verse to write on a bookmark she'd been given. From that morning's passage she chose Matthew 15:28, *"O woman, great is your faith; be it done for you as you wish."* No sooner had she finished than we heard someone knocking at the front door.

Who could be knocking so early? It was just getting light that morning in January of 1975.

At the door stood the pastor from the church in Turrialba, three hours away. He greeted us with news that Peter had phoned the previous night, saying that Priscilla needed surgery. We hurried to town to phone Sandra Barber who reported that Priscilla's limp was caused by a cyst that was resorbing the bone inside the top of her hip. She needed a bone graft as soon as possible. Her hip socket was almost gone. If it crumbled, a pin wouldn't help.

We authorized the surgery but asked that it not be scheduled until after the prayer meeting planned for January 31 to pray for us and for the Chirripó Indians. While we were on furlough, seventeen people had signed up at the missions conference at Columbia Evangelical Church to pray for us daily. We had asked Ronald Barber to call those friends to a meeting at his home. Much prayer went up for Priscilla that night.

Marian very much wanted to go to Columbia to see Priscilla. Her trip, made possible by an unexpected gift, was a special reward from the Lord.

"Thank you, Lord, that I can go," she prayed the night before leaving, "when so many times I've had to stay."

Marian left with the promise, *"Open thy mouth wide, and I will fill it."* She returned exuberant. The timing of the details was so perfect that a friend declared that no human hand could have planned her trip.

Actually, Priscilla's surgery was even more serious than anticipated, but her healing was complete. It was just as the Lord had assured Marian through that verse in Matthew even before she learned that Priscilla needed an operation. During her hospitalization Priscilla was showered with love. My brother David drove all night to be there for the operation. Two pastors visited her, as did the president of the college, a couple of faculty members, and many fellow students, as well as friends of ours. The Barbers, who had made all the arrangements, took Priscilla into their home for several weeks until she was able to return to school on crutches.

To the States for Peter's Wedding

Peter's graduation from CBC was coming up in May, but we didn't attend, preferring to wait until August and go to his wedding. Even for a wedding it was difficult to obtain mission permission to leave the field, especially since we asked for two months. Only by driving could we afford to take the whole family, but the round trip itself would take almost a month, leaving us little time for the wedding.

Our Toyota station wagon was a good vehicle for the trip, but mid-afternoon on our last day through Mexico we had a blowout. The tire had been recapped shortly before we left Costa Rica, but the road to Tsipirí was hard on tires—recaps never lasted. Hour after hour we drove on with no spare. We would have bought a new tire if we'd seen any for sale in the small towns we passed in the semi-desert of northern Mexico.

Finally around eleven at night we reached Monterrey and stopped at a large gas station, hoping to find a tire so we could drive the last hundred twenty-five miles to the Texas border.

"Can I help you?" asked a young Mexican who pulled into the station behind us.

"We need a spare," I explained. "We don't know whether to drive on to the border without one or try to find a motel this late at night."

"Go to that place over there," said our new friend, pointing to a used tire shop nearby, "then come and sleep at our house on the edge of town."

While I bought a tire and rolled it back to the gas station, Marian got acquainted with the fellow's wife—an American, named Jones! They were believers, serving the Lord in a music ministry. We followed them thirty minutes on a deserted road to their modest home. Marian and I were given their bed—and a fan on that sweltering night. The couple slept on the floor, as did our girls. The boys slept in the Toyota in the enclosed patio. We were to leave early in the morning, but as we loaded, the young wife made us pancakes for breakfast. Somehow we failed to get their mailing address, so we couldn't even write a thank-you note!

"If you went back, there'd be neither house nor people," insisted Ronald Barber when we got to the Barber's home in South Carolina a few days later and told him about the incident. "That fellow was an angel sent by God!"

In South Carolina we spent a few days with the Barbers, for I needed time to prepare for my part in the wedding. Peter had given me specific guidelines: I was to preach on the permanence of marriage, then perform the Bible-based ceremony Peter and Deb had written. While I studied, the kids all had a great time with the Barber's children.

"Wouldn't it be nice if our kids married yours and we had grandchildren in common?" remarked Ronald as Marian and I chatted with him and Sandra in the living room while the kids were enjoying themselves in the den. The four of us committed it to the Lord in prayer—a prayer He was to answer several years later!

Soon we were on our way to Pennsylvania for the wedding. We had written to a supporting church in Pittsburgh, asking if anyone would be willing to give us hospitality for a few days. Jack and Mary Jane Hoey, who had six children of their own, volunteered to take the ten of us into their home! It was the beginning of another long-lasting friendship. Jack even took a week off from work to help his wife manage the expanded household. Mary Jane and a friend helped Marian prepare a special surprise for Peter—Costa Rican *arroz con pollo* (chicken with rice) for the rehearsal dinner.

The Wedding of Our Firstborn

Peter and Debbie were determined to make their wedding a God-honoring event. I felt privileged to be officiating. As part of the ceremony on August 22, 1975, they signed their marriage certificate and I presented to them our gift, a family Bible, symbolizing their desire to base their marriage on God's Word. The photographer later posed the new couple with their joined hands laid on the open Bible. He commented that he had photographed hundreds of weddings, but this one was different.

The wedding was a family affair. Deb's four sisters and our three daughters were bridesmaids, all wearing dresses they had made themselves. Debbie also had made her own beautiful gown with material she had bought while in Italy. Marian's brother-in-law was on hand to provide music—Irene and Dick were on furlough from Costa Rica. Even Marian's mother was present—she surprised us by flying up alone from Costa Rica for the wedding of her first grandson!

Leaving our older girls at Columbia Bible College for Priscilla's third year and Susanna's first, we began the long drive back to Costa Rica with the five younger children. (Peter and his bride had gone to Illinois for ministry in a small church there.) Steven, who had finished his sophomore year at Ben Lippen, would be studying eleventh grade at home by correspondence. Marian would teach Elizabeth in seventh grade, Timothy in fifth and Philip in second—while David waited to play with them.

As I stood in line at a border crossing along the way, I noticed a station wagon out front and a young man talking to Marian. He handed her something and drove away. When I got back to our car, Marian showed me a five dollar bill.

"He gave me this and said, 'This is to bless you with!'" explained Marian, saying that the young man was part of an Hispanic team from Florida on a ministry trip to Central America. Since then we have used those words whenever we have felt led to give a spontaneous gift: "Here's something to bless you with!"

Santa Ana

Once back in Costa Rica after a trip of almost ten thousand miles, our first stop was Santa Ana, where Marian's parents had retired the year before. Their home near San José had become our "mission home." For several years Marian and I had been praying for a place near the capital. The CAM Mission Home had been rebuilt and was quite adequate for our housing when we needed to be in San José. However, with a family our size we wanted a place of our own. Never did we imagine that the Lord would answer our prayer through Marian's folks!

When Marian's sister had first proposed the idea of their parents' retiring in Costa Rica, we wondered how a couple their age could adjust to a new country. Irene and her husband Dick, who lived in San José, bore the brunt of helping them get established. Our friend *don* Emilio, who had built our house in Tsipirí, spent months remodeling the Westling's house. Emilio and Dad Westling got along very well even though neither knew the other's language! Dad drew the plans, Irene helped interpret, and Emilio did the work.

With Marian's parents living in Costa Rica, we began to spend one weekend a month with them, just to be near them. We wanted our children to get to know their grandparents. Besides, the warm sunny weather in Santa Ana gave us a nice break from the damp chilly days in Tsipirí. Furthermore, we needed to come to the capital once a month for Elizabeth and Timothy to have their teeth braced—Peter had had his braced during the years that McConnell Academy was in operation near San José.

Our most special memory of weekends with the Westlings was the Sunday evenings after supper when Dad would ask Steven to get his guitar and lead us in praise songs before we had prayer together.

Westling's Fiftieth Anniversary

By the time of Marian's parents' fiftieth anniversary in October of 1975, they were well settled into life in Costa Rica. A maid helped with the housework and a gardener took care of the fruit trees.

Marian and I introduced her parents to an English-speaking Baptist church where they made new friends and Mom found fellowship with the ladies. With the good weather Dad's health improved to the point that he was able to attend church regularly after years of listening to radio preachers in Pittsburgh.

Not only did the Westlings have new friends and new health, but even their house was new. "It's strange," Marian said. "The old, termite-ridden wooden house is now rebuilt with cement, but using the same floor plan as before. The old house was aging and decaying, but now it's new and permanent like the resurrection body—the same body, yet new."

For the Westling's anniversary celebration, Marian and Irene invited all their parents' new friends from the Baptist church. Our missionary friends also joined us at Santa Ana for the happy occasion. We were so glad that Marian's folks had come to Costa Rica to end their years near their daughters!

Enlarging Our House

A few months after *don* Emilio finished remodeling the Westling's house, he came to Tsipirí to build an addition to our house. The bigger the children, the smaller the house—or so it seemed! We had originally thought of enlarging the dining room window into a bay window to give the kids a nice place to sit and read. Soon the plan evolved into removing the window and adding a small sunroom. Finally we decided on a good-sized den rather than just a sunroom!

The den became a great blessing, but the construction involved an agonizing month of unending tensions with Emilio. He was not the same man who had built our house in 1963. He had left his wife and was now far from the Lord. He was like a tiger ready to pounce whenever Marian or I made any suggestion about the construction. His outbursts of temper reminded us of King Saul's outbursts against David.

Our Bible reading in Proverbs at the breakfast table was what irritated *don* Emilio. The chapter for the first day he was with us dealt with adultery. A month later that passage came up again, for we read Proverbs according to the day of the month. *Don* Emilio felt we had chosen the passage on purpose to speak to his sin. He simmered all day as he poured fresh hand-mixed concrete in the ping-pong room, a bonus room under the new den. Leaving the concrete unfinished, he quit in a huff and packed up his tools. I took him to Moravia where he could catch a bus back to town.

Emilio's sudden departure left us in a bind. The rough concrete needed to be smoothed by hand as it dried and as the final coat of red ocher was applied. The job fell to Steven, who was now sixteen. Early in the month of construction he had volunteered to help Emilio. Steven learned framing and discovered a real interest and aptitude for construction. He and Timothy, then eleven, stayed up all night finishing the cement.

During the month *don* Emilio was with us, he not only built the den, but finished some of the interior walls, as well as the garage we had started in order to protect the car from the unceasing rains. Behind the garage he built a new shed for the generator. Originally I had housed the generator near the house for practicality, but I could hardly stand the noise it made. The old generator shed became a playhouse for the kids, much to Marian's delight.

In the years since 1970 when we installed the generator, we had rebuilt the back stairs, adding a roof to keep them from rotting out again. Then we cemented the laundry and drying area under the house—Marian had long since quit hanging clothes outside, only to have to rescue them from the rain by noon. We also cemented the shop I fixed up under the house. With all that cement downstairs, the kids no longer tracked mud up to the house.

Tsipirí was becoming much more livable, even though we had no furniture for the new den. That didn't matter to us; we were just glad for the extra space. We moved some trunks into the den and covered them with quilts as makeshift couches. Soon a friend sent us a check large enough to purchase a sofa bed. Marian sent her a happy thank-you note, and Margaret responded by promptly sending a similar check with which we purchased a second sofa bed. Later Marian's mother bought me a platform rocker for my birthday. We moved the piano in from the tiny original living room. Now our family room was set up for daytime play, devotions in the evening, and sleeping space for occasional guests. The old living room became the place to entertain Indians who were spending the night in increasing numbers.

The Tsipirí house with the new den at the right

Soon after we built the den, my older brother came for a short visit. Haniel had been a missionary to Burma, but was currently assistant dean of engineering at Auburn University. I had him check my latest engineering project. Haniel helped me figure out how high on the hillside I needed to place my water barrels in order to have enough water pressure to fill the automatic washer we'd bought from fellow missionaries. Unfortunately, though I did get the needed pressure, we discovered that the washer had a tiny filter which quickly got clogged with the leaf trash in our rain water. Marian ended up continuing to fill the washer by hand for each cycle. Even so, that machine was a blessing in that it spun so much more water out of the clothes than our old wringer washer—important in our constantly damp weather.

Our Twenty-fifth Anniversary

We celebrated our Silver Anniversary early, with a party at Santa Ana with Marian's parents, her sister and family, and our missionary colleagues. All our children were there except Peter; he and Debbie were living in Dallas at the time. For the guests Marian fixed a big pot of *arroz con pollo*, and the children prepared a program of songs and Scriptures. We even played—for the first time—the tape of our wedding ceremony twenty-five years before.

Soon the children returned to school—Steven to Ben Lippen for his final year, Susanna and Priscilla back to the Bible College. Then Marian and I headed for Honduras, taking Elizabeth and Timothy to Las Américas. Knowing that we would be there for our anniversary, the staff decorated a room for us. Crepe paper streamers hung from the ceiling and a huge poster hung on the wall, depicting us and our eight children!

On the morning of September 8, 1976, our actual anniversary, we found our Toyota decorated for the return trip to Costa Rica. From the back bumper hung tin cans and toilet paper streamers. All the windows were written on with shaving cream. One said, "*¡Recién casados—hace veinticinco años!*" (Just married—twenty-five years ago!).

As I started to clean the writing off the windows before leaving the school grounds, the teachers shouted, "No, no, leave it on; let the people along the road enjoy it!"

We drove off laughing, tin cans clattering—grateful for such loving colleagues at this special school. Once we left the campus, I did take off the tin cans but left the signs. All day we drove through the mountains and on down toward the Pacific coast. That day was even more special than we had hoped. The last two hours after dark were unforgettable. The full moon rose as we drove along, talking at length and in depth—sharing many things very close to our hearts. That day was better than a second honeymoon. Truly the Lord had fulfilled the verse inscribed in our wedding rings: "*And they that know thy name will put their trust in thee: for thou, Lord, hast not forsaken those that seek thee*"—Psalm 9:10.

Dad Westling's Death

Back home in Tsipirí, Marian began teaching Philip third grade and David first. David was an eager pupil. Philip, as the oldest boy at home, had earned the cherished right to accompany me to Chirripó homes on Sundays. Financial burdens, with five in boarding school, weighed heavily on us, but our supporters remained faithful and Marian's parents also helped. The Lord was good.

For several years I had been under treatment from a urologist, who now suggested surgery for an enlarged prostate. So in February of 1977 I was operated on at the government hospital in San José. After the first miserable night in the recovery room, I spent several more days in the hospital, with Marian staying in the other bed in my room. We read together and enjoyed visits from fellow missionaries, as well as national pastors. I had asked my missionary colleagues to come with a Scripture for me, so each conversation began with a verse—great fellowship! For Marian the time was restful. Grandma Westling took good care of Philip and David, and Grandpa read Narnia books to them until Marian and I returned to Santa Ana.

God's timing in my surgery was perfect. Two days after the doctor gave me permission to drive again, we rushed Dad Westling to the Clínica Bíblica, the hospital where most of our children had been born. For four days Mom Westling stayed with Dad while doctors tried to diagnose his problem. Marian and Irene were with her. Visitors came and went. Dad was alert, even asking for a Miami Herald so he could read the stock market report, but the doctors concluded that a cancerous tumor had ruptured.

"How long does he have?" I asked the doctor. "Weeks? Days?"

"No," said the doctor gravely, "hours."

Soon the Baptist pastor arrived, as well as other friends. Dick, Marian's brother-in-law, was the one delegated to communicate to Dad what the doctor had said, but we couldn't tell if he had heard. We all stood around his bed and spontaneously began singing song after song between our tears. We read Scripture and prayed. Marian and Irene stayed on with their mother, but I had to return to Santa

Ana to relieve the missionary who was looking after Philip and David.

At three the next morning, March 17, 1977, the nurse alerted Mom that the end was near. She and her daughters watched while Dad's breathing got weaker and then stopped altogether. By daylight I was out with Dick choosing a casket, for by Costa Rican law the body had to be buried that day. Then we and the pastor planned the funeral as we sat around Dad Westling's hospital bed where his body now lay in state.

More than a hundred people packed the church that afternoon. Dick, who was not only a missionary but a concert pianist, played his favorite number, "Jesu, Joy of Man's Desiring." The pastor's words were a blessing. I ended the service by reading all fifty-eight verses of I Corinthians 15—the resurrection chapter. We sensed the presence of the Lord in those powerful words!

After the burial, we went back to Santa Ana where Mom and Marian rearranged the furniture in the large living room. Lonely days would be ahead for Mom as she continued to live there, but at the moment she was buoyed up by the prayers and presence of family and loving friends. In fact, she even exclaimed, "This has been a wonderful week!"

Three Graduations!

In May of 1977 we drove to Honduras for Elizabeth's graduation from eighth grade. It was fun watching her excitement, as she entered heart and soul into the events of the week. She had even made her own graduation dress during Christmas vacation, with Grandma to fix up her mistakes. Marian had made some of the girls' clothes when they were young, but Priscilla became the real seamstress of the family. Elizabeth's first and only attempt was that fancy full-length dress—an ambitious project for a beginner.

Heading back to Costa Rica, we left Marian at the airport in Tegucigalpa, the capital of Honduras, to fly to the States in time for Steven's graduation from Ben Lippen School. He received the Bible award and the award for Christian character, even as he had during furlough at Columbia Christian School. The Lord had used him at Ben Lippen to help other boys who were struggling in their spiritual life.

"There's a small group of kids in each school who follow the Lord without wavering, and another small group who have no desire to follow Him; in the middle there's a large group that is susceptible to the influence of either one of the small groups," Marian had concluded after years of having our children in boarding school.

A few days after Steven's graduation from high school, Priscilla graduated from Columbia Bible College. Marian especially appreciated being there, since she had missed Peter's graduation. Actually, Marian attended all three of Priscilla's graduations—grade school, high school, and college. We didn't take this privilege for granted. Each graduation involved different circumstances, as well as our financial state at the time. In each case we had to make a decision in faith.

Comings and Goings

Following the graduations, Marian visited my family in Alabama and then was given a plane ticket to Dallas where Peter and Debbie were working. Priscilla spent her summer at the Summer Institute of Linguistics, and then came home to spend a year before continuing her studies. Susanna spent her vacation keeping Grandma Westling company before going to Honduras to help out for a year at Las Américas Academy.

All our family, including Peter and Debbie, was in Costa Rica for two special weeks in August. Then Steven started CBC and Philip went to Las Américas for fourth grade. Elizabeth started high school by correspondence and Timothy studied seventh grade on his own, while Marian taught David. Priscilla was a great help.

In October of that year came the exciting news of the birth of our first grandchild, Jonathan Edward Jones. Our children in Tsipirí took delight in showing Jonathan's picture to everyone—even to visiting

Indians. It was a joy to hear them pray that he would become a man of God. That same month Marian made another trip to the States, but not to see the baby. Her mother invited her to accompany her to Seattle for a visit with Dad Westling's sisters and then to Pittsburgh on business—Mom had arthritis and needed help traveling.

Fresh Trials

After our trials in 1969 when it seemed we might need to resign from The Central American Mission, we had spent several uneasy years, facing subtle changes in the Mission as leadership became more centralized and less field-focused. There was a new philosophy in the Mission. The past was over. I kept out of local office and Marian and I continued to pray. Each missionary was now required to write a job description to be reviewed annually, not by the Field Committee as a whole but by the local field president. To me, writing a job description was just one more chore.

"I don't understand why you don't want to write a job description, when you are the most organized missionary here," commented the field director for Central America.

Inwardly I smiled, because I really had no plan except to translate the New Testament and plant the church. My strategy was to seek guidance from the Holy Spirit each day.

Although I had not accepted any office on the Field Committee for several years, there came a time when only three missionaries were eligible for election—the others were too new to hold office, or had gone on furlough. I was one of those eligible and was elected president. This meant that I would need to represent Costa Rica in August of 1977 at the council meetings for CAM leaders in the various Central American countries.

Field Council Meetings in Nicaragua

After the week of discussions in Managua, all the council members went out to a restaurant. On the way the field director had shocking words for me. My mind was whirling as he spoke.

"Aziel," he said. "'Dallas' is not happy with the new Field Committee of Costa Rica. We want you to resign and to ask the other two members to resign as well."

Dazed, I didn't even taste the supper. When we resumed our discussion after the meal, the matter of the Costa Rica Field Committee was discussed from ten in the evening until five in the morning. I was told that although there had been nothing amiss about the election process, the committee was to resign en masse as requested. With supernatural calmness and no sleepiness, we continued our discussion all night.

All angles were discussed. Their preconception of "the problem" in Costa Rica slowly emerged. The top leadership sensed resistance to new policies and wanted to root out opposition. I'd always said, if only to myself, "I'll never resign, just fire me." But sometime in the wee hours I heard myself saying, not "if I step down," but "when I step down." Instinctively I knew I would, for if I didn't, I probably would be told that I could not keep working in Costa Rica—as the previous president, now on furlough, had already been told, even though the association of CAM churches and the Field Committee had given hearty approval to his return.

The discussion ended at five a.m., for I needed to catch a bus for the twelve-hour ride back to Costa Rica. As I rode along, my mind kept whirling. To bring focus to my thoughts, I read Psalm after Psalm until the Lord gave me a word from Psalm 62. Then I made a decision: Not only would I resign from the committee, but I would resign from The Central American Mission as soon as we found a way to continue our work in Costa Rica. That meant three questions had to be faced, the same questions we had faced back in 1969 when we first considered the possibility of resignation: How could we maintain residence in Costa Rica without the sponsorship of CAM? How could we obtain ownership of our base in Tsipirí? What organization would extend tax-deductible receipts for donations to our work?

Marian's Reaction

Back in Santa Ana that night, I waited until Marian and I were alone in our bedroom to tell her what had happened. She broke down in tears, releasing years of tension and uneasiness. I knew she was ready to resign. She'd been ready in 1969, but I wasn't ready then. After Marian dried her tears we began to pray, pouring out our souls. We felt hurt by our Mission and by some of our wonderful teammates. Yet we were faced with an unfinished task.

With Marian's mother still living in Santa Ana, we were spared having to stay at the CAM Home when in the capital. We could be at peace in Santa Ana without being surrounded by colleagues at this difficult time. There was no one we could confide in but the Lord. He was refining us.

We continued to attend the required meetings of the local missionary body. The Lord gave us grace. I resigned from the Field Committee, as did the other two members. The Mission transferred a man from another field to take charge in Costa Rica, a man who knew nothing of the history of our field operation nor of our relationships with national churches. A special friend of ours became the new leader of the Field Council for Central America. He asked me to keep on for the time being as power of attorney for CAM in Costa Rica, a post I had held for many years. For his sake I agreed to do so.

Lessons Learned

Soon I was applying all I knew about forgiving, releasing resentment, and extending blessings to those who had hurt me. I had to make a choice. The key was in *unilaterally* releasing the ones who had hurt us to the Lord, for Him to deal with them in His way. Victory came when I thanked God for what had happened. I knew the Lord had a purpose in everything that touched me. It helped me to forgive when I realized that those who had hurt me were not intending to do so, but were doing what they thought was best for the Lord's work.

Within a few months I was not only thanking the Lord for lessons learned, but I discovered a new ministry—ministering to others who had been hurt.

Light in the Tunnel

Sometime after the fateful meeting in Managua, Marian was waiting her turn to speak to our travel agent when she overheard him talking to another client.

"Now that you've had residence in Costa Rica for five years, you no longer need a letter from your mission for me to renew your residence." said *don* Eloy to a missionary from a sister mission.

A light went on in Marian's mind, for we'd already had residence for over twenty-five years! I checked out the matter at the immigration department and found it was true. We only needed to apply, and to present a good conduct report from the proper department. Soon the condition of mission membership was removed from our residence visa.

The next hurdle to be cleared was the matter of ownership of Tsipirí. The Mission had always required that all properties be titled in the name of The Central American Mission. The reason was to keep missionaries mobile, not tied to a residence they had built. Now, however, some missionary residences were no longer in use and had become a headache to the Mission. The Mission announced that missionaries would be allowed to buy homes, and that those living in mission-owned residences could buy them from the Mission.

We jumped at the offer. Even if we hadn't been thinking of resigning, we would have offered to buy the Tsipirí property. It was home! Most of the money we had invested in it had come from personal gifts and from the rent we paid monthly, but some funds had been channeled to us through the Mission. We asked to buy the property for that amount, requesting that the money go into the lending fund for construction of CAM churches—a popular project of the Mission. Our offer was accepted, and Marian's mother provided the money. So the new field leader, now having the power of attorney which I had formerly held, sold me the Mission property in Tsipirí.

We still needed a sponsoring agency. One that we looked into was not able to take on any more missionaries. We considered another, but did not feel comfortable with its stance. So we continued to pray. Then in the summer of 1978 the Barbers, our special friends from Columbia, came to visit us in Tsipirí. I confided to Ronald our desire to resign and our search for new sponsorship. He responded, "If there's anything I can do for you, let me know." Ronald would later provide the answer to our need for a new agency.

Years of Growing and Sowing

At the end of that summer Priscilla returned to the States for further linguistic studies. Susanna, having finished her year volunteering at Las Américas by directing the graduation musicale, resumed her studies at CBC, as did Steven. Elizabeth and Timothy continued to study at home, but that year we sent Philip and David to Las Américas. Each year we sought the guidance of the Lord about the children's schooling.

First, however, David had a routine eye exam. He'd already had eye surgery, as Timothy and Priscilla had. The ophthalmologist now discovered that his optic nerves were swollen and sent him to a pediatric neurologist, who recommended a brain scan. We gathered from his concern that he suspected a tumor. Scans were not available in Costa Rica at the time, so Marian took David to South Carolina. No tumor was found, praise the Lord. The diagnosis was that the swelling was due to an insignificant condition which sometimes occurs in far-sighted children. Although the Lord spared us life-threatening emergencies, He did not spare us chronic problems with eyes and teeth and other matters. For these He gave grace!

Peter, our oldest, had been in the States since his graduation from CBC, but in September of 1978 he and his wife Debbie finished their linguistic studies and headed for Costa Rica. They hoped to begin literacy work among the Cabécars as they served under a small funding agency based in South Carolina. Their determination to stick it out was ironically symbolized by their driving from Dallas in a car that had no reverse gear. Deb's parents accompanied them on the long trip so that they could see where their daughter would be serving. And, of course, Peter and Deb brought baby Jonathan—our first chance to see our grandson! The little family settled in with Grandma Westling for several months so that Deb could study Spanish at the language school in the capital. They provided companionship for Mom in her loneliness, while living inexpensively with her proved to be a boost for them, since they had almost no regular financial support.

Now that we had a grandchild it was obvious that our family was growing up, even though our youngest child, David, was only eight years old when little Jonathan was born. During these years that the family was growing up, we were also occupied with translating the Word and sowing the seed. Both Marian and I were involved, and increasingly the children as well. As we continued to pray for the Spirit's working throughout the Chirripó Valley, we hoped for a harvest. But first we had to plant the good seed. The period from 1974 to 1979 was a season of sowing, using what we'd translated— and continuing to translate.

– 19 –

Sowing the Seed
1974 to 1979

"Did you print John yet?"

This was Virgilio's first question when we saw him upon returning from furlough in 1974. Since our return several Indians had bought copies of Mark and Acts and I had resumed Bible studies on Sundays. However, the Gospel of John was not even typed, much less published. Virgilio's question, however, spurred Marian to get back to typing manuscripts.

While slopping over a muddy trail on the way to a Bible study, we met a young Indian woman. On an impulse Marian invited her to come and work three days a week. Gladys, our first Indian maid, worked sporadically, but often enough to free Marian to finish the final copy of the Pastoral Epistles and begin the final typing of the book of John.

With Benjamín again as my main helper, I began translating James, the first of the General Epistles. One day Benjamín inquired about radio programs.

"Who makes them?" he asked. "Who pays for them?"

Benjamín didn't tell me what he had in mind, but appeared a couple of days later with his copy of Acts, prepared to tape Bible readings! He envisioned regular programs in the Cabécar language at 4:00 a.m.—prime time for Indians who sit around the fire in the morning chill, drinking quantities of black coffee while they talk and listen to their battery-powered radios. Actually the idea of a radio program had already been suggested by the friend who initiated our clinic ministry. Marian had it on her prayer list, and still does.

Bible studies in homes were becoming exciting, at least in contrast to the blunt indifference of satisfied paganism which we'd faced in early years. Twice Virgilio, one of my helpers, appeared unexpectedly at a meeting and helped me explain a passage.

"Peddling My Wares"

Since early in 1970 I had been holding regular Sunday meetings in Indian homes. Before that we had held services in our home in Tsipirí for anyone who happened to appear, but then Rafael invited me to come to his house to study the recently-published book of Mark. I hesitated to commit myself to such a long trek on a regular basis, until the Lord spoke to me through Jesus' command: "*Go into all the world.*"

On most Sundays I left right after breakfast and walked two and a half hours up and down exhausting hills on wet, slippery trails. Once I arrived at Rafael's house, I chatted awhile as I rested in the hammock and drank coffee. I would even take a short nap until my host and probably his wife and children would gather in a circle, sitting on logs or crude stools. If visitors came and the group was large, they sat on the sleeping platforms around the edge of the hut. A cooking fire burned nearby on the dirt floor—the pot balanced on the smoldering ends of three green logs radiating out from the fire.

Each of us in turn read a verse. Some needed much coaching as they stumbled along. Often it was syllable by syllable. But there was no rush—they had all the time in the world! Furthermore, they were highly motivated to learn to read. My personal motivation was to get them hooked on the Word they were reading. After a lengthy time of reading through a passage, a good reader would reread the whole unit before I asked simple questions to check their understanding. I wanted them to know that the text had a message. Reading wasn't just a ritual. Besides, I didn't have a good enough command of the language to preach a sermon! I called my method "Bible Study Evangelism." I wanted to saturate the Indians with the total Word of God, even as I was systematically saturating my children with it.

Bible study at Moisés' home

The meetings at Rafael's house began a twenty-year pattern of trekking to various huts on the weekends. In my earlier years of trekking as I was becoming acquainted with the different Indian areas, I had tried to share simple truths: God is holy; we are sinful; Christ died for us. But now with the publication of Mark I had a book! Even though I had no master plan, no defined strategy, at least with a book I had a tool. Even without a literacy program, people were learning to read. Many learned with the help of the alphabet book we had produced in 1964. Later I also began making simple blackboards out of plywood that I painted with dull black paint. I made dozens of them, sold them at cost, and kept a supply of chalk for sale. In every home that had a blackboard, people learned to read!

Without realizing it, I was creating a demand for the Word by going out and using the book of Mark. Years later I submitted an article titled "Translator, Peddle Your Wares," which was published in a journal for translators. The idea that the translator himself should sell people on the translation—peddle his own product—was built on my experience. I didn't want to create a museum piece, as some translations unfortunately are. The translator may be the key to its being used.

Not only did we start home Bible studies with our translation but we used it with Indian visitors at our home. Increasing numbers were coming to sleep, for our house was a good stopover point on their way to or from the outside world. We often talked to more Indians in our living room than during a Bible study in a hut. They listened by the hour to Scripture that Benjamín had recorded on cassette tapes. One night three of Virgilio's brothers pounded on our door at bedtime. They came to sleep, but asked to hear a tape first. Our discussion after the hour-long tape of I and II Thessalonians was outstanding. Another night an Indian couple listened to the tape twice, as the man followed along with the typed text. Almost every day passing Indians listened to the tapes. When we had an Indian maid, we would read the Word and pray with her at lunch time.

Drowsiness

One Sunday in January of 1975 I climbed the short hill to Célimo's house—with its beautiful view—for a Bible study, only to have it dulled by my drowsiness. For months I had tended to become sleepy while teaching the Indians. Now I fought sleep, even pacing the floor while I answered Célimo's questions about Acts 15. Then as I prayed briefly to end the meeting, I fell sound asleep—all this in spite of leaving home rested and later napping while Célimo attended another visitor. We concluded that this could be a subtle tool of the enemy. In my diary I wrote: "The enemy seems to put me in a sort of physical stupor (ineffectiveness) which parallels the Indian's spiritual stupor (indifference)."

When I communicated this in a prayer letter, I received an unprecedented response. My condition was diagnosed as diabetes, hypoglycemia, abnormal blood pressure, overwork, or a lack of sleep. To please my friends I had a checkup. It showed nothing. But a missionary friend also in pioneer work wrote that the enemy will surely attack, whether by sleepiness or otherwise. And in my rereading of *Pilgrim's Progress* at that time, I noticed that Hopeful, Christian's friend, was "very dull and heavy of sleep" and severely tempted to take a nap on the forbidden "enchanted ground."

I was not the only one troubled with sleepiness. Virgilio would now have to take short naps while helping me translate. Benjamín had trouble with sleepiness when reading the Bible. Marian and I would now be plagued with extreme weariness when we prayed. Yet sleep was no problem at other times. Satan's work is often covert. If we were not told that Satan was back of the disasters which struck Job, would we recognize the sinister hand behind them? The attacks of drowsiness eventually ceased, to be replaced by other types of attacks.

Bible Studies at Reigildo's

Several homes were opened to me for Bible studies, but after a while interest would lag. Then early in 1975 I began going monthly to the home of Reigildo, a prosperous farmer by Chirripó standards. He had an inquiring mind that attracted me. His teen-age sons, Isaac and Alexis, joined us for the studies. Sometimes the whole family would meet with us around their Formica-topped kitchen table with its matching chairs—an unheard of luxury that seemed out of place on the dirt floor.

"Why do we love our children?" asked Reigildo one Sunday.

"Because God loves us like children," I answered.

From there I contrasted the Cabécar concept of a god who loves us as we love our animals and who fattens us to be eaten by the demons.

Reigildo (at the right) with his family

By November of 1976 I was going twice a month to Reigildo's house. Isaac and Alexis, his oldest sons, had learned to read fluently.

"What does this mean?" asked Isaac one day, pointing to a picture in Acts 8 of Philip baptizing the Ethiopian eunuch.

His understanding of baptism seemed as clear as the Ethiopian's, for he had read the passage in preparation for the Bible study.

"When are you going to be baptized?" I asked him.

"Next time you come," was his quick reply.

When I returned, however, he had gone to a wake for the dead. Instead I baptized Alexis that day—the first person in Chirripó to be baptized as a believer. Reigildo, however, was not ready to take such a step, although his interest in the studies was outstanding and his wife could see changes in his life.

By January of 1977 Reigildo began to absent himself frequently from the meetings. In March he got sick, and still was not well by May even though he had consulted two witch doctors and spent ten days in the government hospital in the capital. When I arrived for the Bible study, I noticed that around his neck were fetishes to be seen by the demon which had caused his illness. I saw blood on Reigildo's chest and knew that a witch doctor had put a still-beating chicken heart there to divine his health.

"What did the *jawá* say?" I asked.

"That I'll get well slowly and not die," he answered.

The witch doctor had also treated Alexis. I was told that he was not going to sit with us for the Bible study because he was restricted as to food and activity by order of the shaman. Whether the order was aimed at keeping him from the study or not, it was another affront to our God.

I suggested to Reigildo that they were giving the demons the respect that only God deserves.

"Don't you obey your doctor's orders?" he retorted. "We have our ways of doctoring and you have yours."

He also insisted, as did all Indians, that the witch doctors act on God's authority.

Disturbing Events

The Alcoa helicopter flew over Tsipirí regularly in the early seventies on the way to a bauxite exploration camp in the heart of Chirripó territory. A producing mine would radically affect the Indians' lives. Disconcerting activity was also developing in the hills behind us where a logger was exploiting the lumber. It hurt to see trees fall before the chain saw. The logger eventually left when he found no market for his lumber. Nor did Alcoa find bauxite in Chirripó. But our most serious concern was that these efforts had narrowed the already narrow protective barrier of woods between the white man and the Indians. Their shrinking lands were protected by unenforced laws.

Year by year we had seen white men's farms push closer toward the heart of Cabécar territory. Yet the Indian population was steadily expanding. I could foresee the day when they could not support themselves on the steep mountains with their unproductive soil.

During a day of prayer in September of 1971 I prayed that Indian lands would be protected from intruders. I also prayed about the possibility of a reservation, and even that someday only we and the Indians would live east of Tsipirí, the creek on which our house was located. I knew that I was praying against the local tide and wider history, but I jotted down the requests and kept them before the Lord.

Chance Visitor

One day two hikers appeared on our front porch. One was a Belgian named Claude. We chatted awhile before they went on to Chirripó. When they returned, Claude wanted to talk. He had observed that Chirripó was isolated and relatively unimpacted by Latin culture. As a geographer serving at the time with the United Nations Food and Agriculture Organization, he had a vision of protecting the Indians from uncontrollable outside influences. He was particularly concerned that they not lose their lands and their stability as a tribe. He saw the need for a reservation—but of the right kind.

As we talked, I found myself agreeing in principle. I, too, wanted the Cabécar territory to be protected from being overtaken by outside encroachment. In essence, the concept of a reservation was born that day on our front porch.

Claude became a frequent visitor to Tsipirí on his treks to Chirripó. A pleasant, handsome fellow, he seemed to enjoy our home. We heard his woes and triumphs. Even he himself could not understand why he worked so hard to promote the Indians' welfare. We knew God was in it!

"It always seems like Christmas at this house," said Claude one evening as praise songs reverberated through the house from our stereo.

"As Christians we're happy, but not just at Christmas," responded Marian.

When we read the Bible at the supper table, we pulled out a French version for Claude to follow along—we kept versions on hand in various languages. He spoke excellent English, but we wanted to maximize the impact of the Scripture. Often we talked with him about the Lord, but he never let us get personal. He managed to dodge the issue, but we kept him in our prayers.

Previous Efforts to Protect Indians

Thirty years before, among Indians who lived in the Pacific watershed of Costa Rica, there had been reservations. The whites were encroaching faster in that area than in Chirripó which was much less accessible. Yet there had never been an officially defined and decreed reservation. Even so, Indian lands in Chirripó and elsewhere in the Caribbean watershed where most of the Indian population lived were considered protected.

In some countries reservations were unpopular—keeping people in, rather than protecting them from outsiders. On some reservations native people were not allowed to buy and sell land. In reaction to that, pro-Indian movements advocated giving them titles. Titled land could be sold. Many Indians not only sold to whites but became peónes of those who bought their land. Some pro-Indian movements were idealistic, unrealistic, and anti-Christian. Missionaries were maligned as destroying the culture. In Costa Rica a book was later published denouncing our ministry as being dangerous since we used the indigenous language.

The Presidential Decree of 1976

Claude was not of that persuasion—though he himself was a secular European. Soon he founded CONAI, an acronym for the

National Commission of Indian Affairs. He was determined to push through a reservation decree. He made friends in government offices, even in the president's office.

In March of 1976 over two hundred Chirripó Indians—the largest group we had ever seen—listened to Claude read the president's decree. I thought that they, who live so scattered over the mountains, felt like a nation, perhaps for the first time ever. Plans were laid for a visit, by helicopter, from the president of Costa Rica to celebrate the inauguration of the reservation. The decree, to be put into effect, required the creation of a local government—a totally new concept. Benjamín and others who were responding to the gospel were named to key positions in the new association. Claude felt that I had prepared the men he needed to serve on the first board. Reigildo became the president and Benjamín the secretary.

The unique concept incorporated by Claude into the decree was that the land would be owned by an Indian association, a legal entity run entirely by Indians but with CONAI oversight. The land would not be owned by the government. Indians could buy and sell land to each other with the approval of the association. But they could not sell to outsiders, for the title to the whole reservation was held by the association. Individuals did not hold titles, but that didn't matter. They had never held titles. They were a closed society and everyone knew who owned each piece of land.

Claude—with his training in geography and cartography—drew the limits of the 66,000 hectare Chirripó reservation, one of five in the country. The Tsipirí was one of the boundaries, which left us inside the reservation. Actually, the decree had been written to allow the presence of outsiders serving the Indians: medical personnel, teachers, and others, including us. Even so, Claude later excluded our land by redrawing the boundary in another area in order to preserve the original number of hectares. In recent years, however, the reservation has been extended farther toward Moravia, leaving our property an enclave within the reservation.

The President's Visit

Hundreds of Indians gathered in April of 1976 at Reigildo's pasture to await the president's helicopter. The appointed hour passed but no helicopter, then another hour but still no president. Any disappointment they felt at not seeing him seemed to have been compensated by their amazement at realizing they were so numerous! Some had walked two days to get there. Seeing so many people caused me to revise my estimate of the population of the tribe. Instead of about eight hundred in the Chirripó Valley, I estimated twelve hundred—about half the total number of Cabécars as they were beginning to be called. The tribe had grown significantly since we arrived at the end of 1952, and continues to grow. Yet we were not effectively touching more than two hundred.

Finally, the Indians began to disperse. As they passed through the gate of the pasture, I counted more than six hundred fifty. Reigildo invited me to eat the president's meal!

"I'm going to pray there will be seven hundred Indians waiting for the Lord Jesus when He comes—*and He will show!*" said Marian excitedly—and prophetically—when I told her that the president didn't show up.

Seven hundred was far beyond my faith, certainly not seven hundred *baptized* believers. At the time there were none. Would I live to see that many in my lifetime? A staggering thought!

"I believe there are already seven hundred believers—and perhaps even that many baptized!" said one of my sons several years ago. The reservation decree is still in force today, despite serious threats over the years, including at one point cries via the media to remove "the foreigner who is disturbing the Indians in Chirripó." But the first step toward the implementation of the reservation decree was the major one—compensation for non-Indians who would lose land. Eight local Latin families and many more elsewhere would have to be relocated. In spite of generous compensation from the government, they were upset. As the assessors arrived to lay the groundwork for removing our Latin neighbors, Marian and I were praying that the expropriation would proceed as peacefully as possible, with a minimum of tension and resentment. Our particular concern was the effect that the decree would have on those attending the Spanish services that we had recently started in Grano de Oro, the village closest to the new reservation.

Meetings Begin at Victor's

The meetings I had begun holding at Reigildo's house in 1975 would continue biweekly for seven years, but I was also searching for a place to hold studies on alternate Sundays. By September of 1977 I started monthly Bible studies at the home of Victor, who was as poor as Reigildo was prosperous. Interest was so great that I soon began going to Victor's twice a month. Now all my Sundays were committed and I was reaching a triangle from Tsipirí to the Chirripó River three hours from home. Yet Scripture portions were also selling across the river, and there were repeated calls for me to go to the Pacuare River, still further away.

Victor reading the translation

At one meeting Victor's wife, who sat with us when not tending a crying child or a boiling pot, responded to my query as to what she had gotten out of the study.

"We're supposed to live straight by the power of the Holy Spirit," she said—the first question any woman had answered.

Less than a month before that, I had made a hurried trip to Victor's house to pray for his wife. She lay dangerously close to death after giving birth to a premature, stillborn child. Huddled outside the hut under a dirty blanket, she was lying on a sheet of plastic over the damp soil, with just a makeshift roof of banana leaves between her and the damp sky, as was customary in those days. Now she was interested in the Lord "because He raised me up" in answer to prayer.

Another day, Victor prayed for the Lord to make him holy. Later on his way to the store, the first source of legal liquor, he prayed that he would not succumb to drink. He didn't! Victor began actively inviting people to his house for the Bible studies. Some from Reigildo's group began going to Victor's, and vice versa. Both groups were not only growing—now averaging twelve adults instead of three—but even meeting in my absence!

Isaac and Alexis

On Palm Sunday of 1978 I baptized Isaac, Reigildo's oldest son. After the baptism, Isaac, and Alexis (his younger brother whom I had baptized sixteen months before) and I celebrated the Lord's Supper—the first ever in Chirripó! The three of us sat around a crude table of hand-hewn lumber while Reigildo and the family watched. It was a joy to lead, but I was primarily concerned with how to say, "Lord's Supper," "Symbols," "This is my body...this is my blood," "In remembrance of me," "Show His death." All are conceptual problems which, although everyday experiences in translating, were annoying when trying to lead a meaningful act of worship! And I was aware of the American Bible Society statement that translators help to fashion the religious language of many generations.

Reigildo's sons, Isaac and Alexis

By this time Isaac and our Steven, who were about the same age, had become close friends; once they were almost swept away while crossing a swollen river. Alexis was memorizing Scripture, and also asked for Scripture portions to sell on trips. (We did not normally give away Scripture portions, but sold them at a subsidized price. If an Indian wanted the books enough to pay for them, we knew he would value them; otherwise they might even end up as toilet paper—better than dried banana leaves.) Of their own accord, the two brothers were teaching the Scripture to a cousin who lived across the Chirripó River. In addition, Alexis began traveling regularly to the Pacuare River area to conduct Bible studies. He said the Lord had taken away his fear of sharing the gospel with those steeped in their old beliefs.

Indians Learn to Pray

An Indian's first response to the gospel was usually a willingness to pray, praising God for material blessings. Slowly I was figuring out terminology for prayer, hopefully with grammatical correctness. Since the Cabécars never prayed, I had no pattern. I had to figure out how to say, "Bless...," "Grant that...," "We pray for...," and much more. I never became highly proficient, yet Indians did learn to pray fervently.

One day Reigildo prayed for Steven and Isaac as they were about to cross a swollen river. They had already waited a day for the water to go down. Steven made it home safely but admitted that they could have been swept away when they fell and were almost carried down the roaring river toward the boulder-filled rapids.

Steven and friends crossing a river

Reigildo prayed for his horse which had been bitten by a snake. I sold him some anti-venom, but he returned it unused—the horse had recovered after prayer! Alexis prayed that Eliécer would forgive his enemies, saying he'd learned to forgive through reading in Acts about Stephen's forgiving those who killed him. Virgilio prayed about his sins after we translated the story of Zacchaeus. One Sunday at a meeting Antonio asked us to pray for his three-week-old baby who wouldn't take nourishment. Alexis and Isaac laid hands on him and I prayed. That same afternoon the infant began eating—"coffee, chicha, everything!"

Guilty? Who? Me?

One morning my translation helper didn't show up, so when Antonio came to see me after breakfast, I had time to try to press Biblical truths upon him. After two hours of reasoning with him, I was impressed at how impossible it was to penetrate the heart of the Cabécar religious system. The apostle Paul when preaching in Athens spoke of the resurrection of Christ in relationship to man's judgment. Later as Paul reasoned with Felix of *"righteousness, temperance, and judgment to come,"* he again spoke of the resurrection. I found myself relating Paul's preaching to Jesus' saying that the Holy Spirit would convict the world of sin, righteousness, and judgment.

The whole significance of Jesus' death and resurrection is tied to these basic themes. But with the Chirripó Indians, sin is not a moral offense against a holy God. If there is any sense of guilt, it is not with God but with man. Therefore, to the Indian, the work of Christ, which frees from guilt on the one hand and makes us holy on the other, seems irrelevant. Also, since the Indian equates ultimate judgment with physical death, then heaven, hell, and eternity are not serious issues. This is particularly reinforced by the Cabécar belief that the body never rises—only the soul lives on, either in a sort of limbo or in the "place of the boa." However, because Jesus arose, the Indian will also arise bodily, as a whole person, to face the man Christ Jesus—in person—as his judge.

Thus, as I reasoned with self-righteous Indians—like Antonio that morning—*"of righteousness, temperance, and judgment to come,"* I was struck anew that conviction of sin does not depend as much on my saying the right thing as on the Holy Spirit's convicting them *"of sin...of righteousness...and of judgment to come."*

Did Jesus Rise?

The resurrection—Christ's and ours—continued to be a major talking point.

"Do you believe that?" asked an Indian, incredulously.

"Jesus arose, but we won't," said another with finality.

If they rejected the truth of the resurrection, they usually rejected the gospel completely. Romans 10:9 took on new meaning for us: *"If thou shalt confess with thy mouth the Lord Jesus, and shalt believe in thine heart that **God hath raised him from the dead,** thou shalt be saved."*

"How did the Lord comfort you when your mother died?" I asked Reigildo.

"By the resurrection," he answered.

His sons Isaac and Alexis had encouraged him by reading passages about the resurrection, one of which we had studied the day they heard of her death.

One year we were hoping to come up with a new song for Easter, but it wasn't until the night before that an idea came to Marian during family devotions. After prayer, she reached for a hymnbook and walked over to the piano. Within minutes we had a one-stanza adaptation of "Christ the Lord is Risen Today." (We did not normally translate hymns, but usually took the core idea and adapted it, or else wrote totally new lyrics. Music was not a feature of Cabécar culture. It was not until much later that Indians themselves were inspired to compose original tunes and lyrics.) The next day I used the new song in the Bible study in a hut with a dirt floor and a tin roof—no organ or stained glass windows! Another adaptation was from the praise song, "He is Lord, He is Lord, He has risen from the dead and He is Lord."

Marian's Sunday School

A few times Marian accompanied me to Bible studies when someone was available to watch the younger children and cook the evening meal. I liked having her with me, for she would catch comments I hadn't and would add her own comments. But the trek would wear her out for a day. However, in 1976 she developed a ministry of her own. Just as in the original Sunday Schools for poor children in England, she taught more than Bible. In those days when there were no schools in the Chirripó Valley, she invited Benjamín and Célimo to send their children for a three-hour session. After singing and praying and telling a Bible story, she began teaching them to read and write and do simple arithmetic.

On Sunday afternoons Marian would spend another three hours preparing material for the next Sunday's lesson. With housework and homeschooling, along with checking and typing translation for me, she had no time during the week to prepare new material. Marian had majored in elementary education in college and specialized in teaching reading, so she enjoyed her Sunday ministry. In the course of the years and in answer to prayer, she developed some simple primers, plus a reader to go with our alphabet book.

Though Célimo's children were dull and unmotivated, Benjamín's showed interest. Bright little Edwin, the youngest of all, was the fastest learner. Célimo's children dropped out, but others came, including some teen-age girls. They were fun to teach, especially when Elizabeth was home to play the guitar for the class. During the year Priscilla was home between college and grad school, she taught literacy classes in conjunction with my Bible studies. At Victor's there were many children to teach, plus Victor's wife. At Reigildo's, Priscilla taught his teen-age daughters to read well enough to take part in the studies. When Priscilla left for school, Timothy, then thirteen, decided to keep up her classes since he always accompanied me on Sundays anyway. He had as many as twelve students in the makeshift schoolhouse Victor built for the classes. With Marian's Sunday School, my Bible study, and Timothy's literacy class, we had three meetings going every Sunday.

Seed Sprouts—and Withers

Not all the seed fell on good ground. Célimo actually said, "I can't give up my customs for Christianity."

Two of his little boys then died within two weeks of each other. Soon Célimo was drinking contraband liquor—distilled by a local "white"—and failing to show up for work. Even so, he told me that he prayed every morning and that his wife had trusted Christ—Marian had been focusing prayer on the wives of our translation helpers. Yet Célimo never made a commitment to Christ;

he seemed "bewitched." Eventually he moved away and we lost track of him.

Benjamín, on the other hand, was burdened about witnessing to fellow Indians. He took Scripture portions to sell and tapes to play to others, yet only once did he ever come to a Bible study. Once he participated in the five-day trek with the group traveling to the home of a revered diviner to pay the annual head tax for each Cabécar. He came back perturbed about the Indian religion, saying it was "not complete—only pieces," whereas the Bible "made his liver feel pretty."

At one point Benjamín was considering baptism, but when he got involved in the new association in charge of local Indian affairs, he became hard to deal with and irregular as a translation helper. Little by little his interest in the Scripture waned, and his old religion took precedence.

Others showed what seemed sincere interest, yet cooled off and fell away. Reigildo was up and down, double-minded, yet he talked of building a chapel so that the Bible studies wouldn't be interrupted by the noisy chickens inside his house. Victor continued to show much interest, but saw nothing incongruous about participating in the annual trek to consult the diviner to learn whether "our end"—the end of the world—would occur that year and whether there would be good weather for crops.

Syncretism

In spite of growing interest in many places, a basic problem persisted—syncretism. Syncretism is the mixture of new truth with old beliefs and practices. Benjamín tried to hide it, but Reigildo tried to justify it. One Sunday at a Bible study we discussed, *The son shall make you free.* All agreed that one who practices sin is in bondage to sin. But no one agreed that their practices to protect themselves from demons constituted bondage.

"Our practices are just customs," retorted Reigildo.

Yet back of each custom—whether a ritual bath or the wearing of a fetish or a host of other practices—was the intent to appease some demon.

"What about that?" asked Steven, pointing to a post on which was a crudely-drawn stick figure of their god, left from the ceremony for the protection of Victor's new house. We had just studied I Thessalonians 1:9, "...ye turned to God from idols to serve the living and true God." Victor acknowledged his inconsistency. He was more open-minded than others.

Unfortunately, the fetish necklaces were worn, and purification rites and witchdoctor's healing ceremonies were performed in good faith that they were the means that "god" gave the Indians to protect themselves from demons. In fact, the core of their religion was built around the fear of demons as the cause of sickness and death. Those who now believed in Jesus needed to replace the fear of demons with the fear of the true God, yet it was hard for them to understand that their pagan beliefs and practices were incompatible with their new faith. It would take more than twenty years before these issues were dealt with definitively.

Counterattacks

Those coming to faith began to feel the sting of opposition.

"Why do you pray?" asked Eugenio's father as he prayed before eating. "God isn't here. He can't hear you,"

"When do you start getting paid for all that studying each Sunday?" was his father's next question.

"Why do you study in your own language?" a local white man taunted Victor. "You should use Spanish. Besides, why doesn't Aziel leave?"

Other attacks were not so obvious. They seemed like coincidences, but when so many things happened in July and August of 1978, we began to wonder. Victor's wife almost died. Isaac and Steven were almost carried away in a flooded river when returning from teaching and selling Scriptures. Two of my translation helpers, plus the hosts of both Bible studies, as well as the two baptized believers all suffered bad machete cuts. I myself had three minor cuts which took weeks to heal. The pain in my knees after a trek became increasingly severe, and the pain in Marian's side was still unexplained after exams by a specialist. Worst of all, the eye doctor feared that our youngest child had a brain tumor.

In addition to all this, a group of Indians, spurred by two whites, asked the president of Costa Rica to remove us. They also falsely accused Benjamín and Reigildo. Another community leader who attended our meetings was beaten up. Finally, we had unprecedented problems with erratic translation helpers. Yet that year ended on a very optimistic note. We knew many were praying for us. And as we prayed and persisted, the Lord kept working.

Still Translating

On Sundays I continued to hold Bible studies, but weekdays were always dedicated to translation. Indians throughout the area were buying and reading the three published portions of Scripture, totaling eight books—Mark, Acts, and the Pastoral Epistles (I and II Thessalonians, I and II Timothy, Titus, and Philemon). Four more portions, totaling ten more books, were in various stages from the first draft on my desk to the print shop in Guatemala. These books were: The Gospel of John, the General Epistles (James, I and II Peter, the three Epistles of John, and Jude), Romans, and the Gospel of Luke.

One Sunday in May of 1978 I had just bathed in our icy creek and was stretching out to rest after my weekly trip to a Bible study. The exhausting trek involved ascending from Tsipirí at 3700 feet to 4500 feet, then down to 2900 feet and back home again—two and a half hours each way. I was fifty-six years old and feeling the effect of years of trekking. As I lay down to listen to a praise record—my first step toward physical and spiritual renewal—Marian handed me a book.

"Look what came in the mail we got last night!" she said. It was the first copy of the Gospel of John, finally printed after almost three years since we sent it in for publication. As I rested on the couch paging the attractive portion, I felt like I was holding a sorely-needed new tool!

First Bible Conference

Encouraged by Marian, I invited the regular attendants from the Sunday Bible studies to our home for a conference during Holy Week of 1979. Peter and Deb, along with friends of theirs from language school, handled the logistics of feeding everyone. During the three days of the conference we studied the book of Romans morning, afternoon, and evening. From the manuscript that Marian was preparing to mail to Guatemala for printing, she and a colleague typed copies of chapters one through eight.

Six Indians—Virgilio, Isaac and Alexis and their sister Rafaela, Victor and his nephew Porfirio—came for all twelve sessions. Six others came for part of the time. Three years before, only one of them could even read, but now they were all "with it." The message got through!

For a while it seemed as though their conceptual saturation point had been reached, but then God seemed to stretch their capacity as the Spirit-directed logic of the apostle Paul built to its climax. The concentrated dose also gave Marian and me a richer appreciation of the power of the book of Romans.

While I grappled with how to talk in their language about identification with Christ, they grappled with understanding the concept of being in Him. Yet they were already aware of the liberating truth of daily victory over sin through life in the Spirit, and they rejoiced that if God is for us, nothing can overpower us. We ended with a new song of praise to the Father, the Son, and the Holy Spirit. As we sang, Marian and I were not just teachers, but fellow believers worshipping God together with the Indians.

When the conference was over, Virgilio, the sharpest of the group, said that the strongest impression of those present was that "we are guilty." They realized they were guilty of moral offense against a holy God. The Romans conference was special to us, for it was the cumulative result of twenty-five years of work and prayer. Seeing God do so much in three short days, with people of so little background, stirred us to stretch our faith in the God-potential of all creatures—Indians, our children, and ourselves—made in the image of God, enlightened by the Word of God, and illuminated by the Spirit of God.

Even so, there were some tense moments during the conference.

"If God is *really* like this, then our Chirripó god is *not* the same God," blurted Benjamín, who attended a few sessions.

I knew Benjamín felt this, though he'd been hiding his true feelings for a decade. His passionate remark should have been a signal to us that something was not right, but we were blind.

Benjamín and family in 1980

All along we had been using the native term for god in our translation. We had been advised to use the local term rather than one borrowed from the trade language, unless the native term had particularly negative connotations. It was assumed that usage in the context of the Bible would redefine the term.

Obviously, this had not happened for Benjamín. What he saw was that the God of the Bible was drastically different from his god. Why couldn't we see it? More than two decades would pass before we came to our senses and realized what an awful mistake we had made in using the native term.

The Holy Week conference was the last major event of our fifth term of service among the Cabécars. Soon we would return to the States for another furlough. For the first time Indians came to the house to tell us goodbye. Our last Sunday was very special. Benjamín and his family came to the meeting at Victor's. It was our biggest attendance ever. Patricia, Victor's niece, was baptized, along with our Philip. Then we celebrated our fourth communion service in a Chirripó hut. We felt the communion of the Spirit and the fellowship of the budding saints.

Departure Date—June 1979

Never were we less interested in furlough! We were enjoying watching a church begin to emerge, rooted in Chirripó soil! We were encouraged to see Scripture portions translated and in use! Although we were part of the "conflict of the ages" between God and Satan, as Luther expressed it in his hymn, "For still our ancient foe Doth seek to work us woe," yet we were confident that God would win the battle as Luther concluded, "We will not fear, for God hath willed His truth to triumph through us."

But ready or not, it was time for furlough. We left Costa Rica, knowing we had established a firm beachhead in enemy domain. While we were gone, Peter and Debbie would be living in Tsipirí. They would have a chance to try their wings. The work would not stop as it had on our previous furloughs. For years we had asked the Mission to assign another couple to help us. Now the Lord had answered our prayer by sending our own son! We were blessed!

— 20 —

Transitional Furlough
July 1979 to July 1980

Our fifth furlough was due, but neither Marian nor I were excited about leaving. By now we had lived in Costa Rica more than twenty-five years. The thought of "home assignment," as it's now called, was not very appealing. Yet it was time to touch base again with our prayer partners and supporting churches. They were our lifeline! We wanted to let them know how the Word—the seed we had sown—was impacting Cabécar hearts. Our friends had backed us faithfully. We wanted to interact with them face to face.

Goodbye, Mom Westling

Pulling back from our work and packing up for furlough never was easy. This time it involved getting our house in Tsipirí ready for Peter and Debbie to occupy during our absence. Then we drove to Mom Westling's home in Santa Ana, near the capital. There we helped celebrate her 80th birthday. Life in Costa Rica after Dad's death was lonely for her, but on her birthday she was surrounded by friends and family. That evening we sang together, shared Scripture, talked of what we were thankful for, and each one prayed—a nostalgic evening climaxed by a family slide show that Peter had prepared.

On June 22 we and our four younger children waved goodbye to Grandma as she stood alone on the porch in the early dawn. Marian's sister Irene lived across town only a phone call away. Peter and Deb would be in Tsipirí and would visit Mom every month or so. Mom also had her friends at the International Baptist Church. Even so, we felt sad leaving her. I wondered if we would ever see her again.

Missionary friends came to the airport to say good-bye even though our plane took off at sunrise. We all enjoyed the flight, even Timothy who hadn't wanted to leave Costa Rica. Beneath us as we flew over Nicaragua—newly engulfed in a civil war—we saw a solid cloud cover, white in the sunshine. On the clouds we saw the shadow of our plane, encircled by a rainbow! In fact, a second faint rainbow surrounded the first one. It was the first time Marian had seen a circle rainbow. To her it seemed like a sign of the Lord's blessing on our furlough.

Back in the United States

My brother David, along with my brother Lael, and his wife, met our plane in New Orleans. From there David—always so helpful—drove us to Alabama. After a weekend of transition with his family, we all drove to Kolomoki, the state park in Georgia which is the site of the annual R K Jones Reunion. Reconnecting with my twelve siblings and their families after a five-year absence was something we looked forward to each furlough, though to our children their cousins were strangers.

Still in culture shock, we spent the next two weeks traveling around Alabama. Driving an automatic transmission on U.S. highways was too abrupt a change for me after years of driving a stick-shift in the mountains of Costa Rica. Our base in Alabama was Phenix City, where Daddy and Mama had retired after spending many of his ministry years there. Although they were now with the Lord, Phenix City was still a center of family life. Five of my eight sisters lived in the area. We enjoyed visiting them, as well as most of my other brothers and sisters in the Deep South. As we also reconnected with many friends and supporting churches, we were encouraged to see how the Lord had answered prayer in several lives.

On to South Carolina

In the months preceding furlough Marian and I had been praying for a rental house in Columbia. Then in May, Priscilla had written from South Carolina to say that the house we had rented on our previous furlough was available again. She planned to phone us when we were in the capital—we had no phone in Tsipirí—for our answer. Marian's first reaction was, "Not *that house!*" She had endured that house for a year and didn't want to face it again. Though it was adequate for our needs, it was poorly furnished and renovations had not been well-designed. Yet since less than a month remained until our flight to the U.S., she didn't want to refuse, for it wasn't easy to find affordable housing for a family our size. She wished she could say yes and no at the same time!

As we discussed the matter with the family and prayed about it, Marian began to feel that she should say yes. Then when we read the Daily Light selection that evening, we were both struck by the first verse: "I will go and return to my place!" Her answer to Priscilla was, of course, yes.

When we reached 1504 Denny Road in Columbia, the condition of the house was rather disconcerting, but the Lord gave grace. After a night's rest, Marian felt better about the place, though no improvements had been made since we lived there before. She was determined to rise to the challenge. Furthermore, she had a glimmer of hope that the Lord would soon answer our long-standing prayer for a place of our own in Columbia. On previous furloughs there we had noticed that missionary families owned homes in the neighborhood that they could return to on furlough. Since the area was close to Columbia Bible College, there was a good source of student renters for the time when the missionaries were overseas. Of course, we had no money even for a down payment; but just before we left for the States, Marian's mother confided that she would be willing to help us buy a place.

Returning to Columbia gave us a chance to reconnect with our older daughters. Priscilla and Susanna were studying and working in Columbia. They would be living with us during our furlough. So would Steven, but he was currently on tour with a music group from the college.

A few days after settling in, we celebrated Marian's 50th birthday. By then we had hung pictures and decorated the house as best we could. Even Marian thought it looked good! She had asked the girls to invite our friends to come with a verse of Scripture to bless her at this milestone in life. The party was memorable, thanks to our daughters. Then after a family celebration the next day, we left David, our youngest, with friends and headed north on a three-week trip.

Furlough Travels

From Columbia to New Jersey to Pittsburgh to Chicago and points between, we visited supporters, churches and friends—sharing, interacting, being entertained, answering questions, listening to what others were learning. Everywhere we reported what God was doing among the Indians in Costa Rica. We always asked for prayer, never for money although our needs were many. We ministered publicly and privately—over coffee, and from the pulpit. Few missionaries feel they are given enough time to share their hearts, but we considered that whatever time we were given was from the Lord.

Over the years we had realized that interest, prayer, and support is a response not so much to what we do—even though our ministry is interesting and challenging—but to our walk with God. That is what attracts.

For us such travel was a time to be enriched as we saw what God was doing in individuals and churches that supported and prayed for us. Yet at times we became aware of needs in friends' lives. One friend gathered a group to pray for us, but privately spoke with bitterness at how he had been treated by an organization. I was now thinking of resignation and asked myself, "What is *my* spiritual condition? Am I usable?" I wanted to stay usable.

Our trip—a "deputation trip"—was not just ministry. There were picnics with friends, chances for the kids to swim and play games, and time for a bit of sightseeing between meetings. We even connected with Steven at a church in New York. There we were blessed as we attended a concert in which he was singing. The Lord met our needs, even though we had left Columbia without funds to return.

Our final day on the road prepared us for what lay ahead. As we drove south, Marian passed the time by reading a book called *The Happiest People on Earth*. A Scripture message on the car radio spoke to both of us about the Lord's blessing on our ministry this furlough. The miles clicked off so quickly that we decided to drive further than planned, hoping to stay with friends in Asheville. Since they weren't home, we then drove three more hours to Columbia even though I was very tired. It was a long, long day, but before we reached home we providentially stopped at a pay phone—the phone was not yet installed at our house. We needed to let our friends, the Barbers, know that we had arrived a day early and would pick up David the next day.

Sad News from Costa Rica

The next morning we were awakened by a neighbor with a message from the Barbers. Costa Rica had called, asking us to phone that morning at eleven. If we hadn't called the Barbers the previous night, they wouldn't have known we were in town. Not wanting to make an international call on the local pay phone, we drove half an hour to the Barber's house to phone, only to learn that Marian's mother had just died unexpectedly after a day's illness. Miraculously, on an hour's notice, Marian got to a waiting plane and flew standby to Costs Rica for the funeral—held the following morning, according to local law.

Not only did the Lord use that unexplained urge to call the Barbers to allow Marian to learn about her mother's death in time to get a flight, but Peter and Deb, in the jungle, miraculously found out and joined Marian and her sister for the funeral. Even Steven, who had finished his concert tour and had gone to Costa Rica, was present to sing at the service.

In the following days the two sisters took care of their mother's belongings, and then Marian spent a weekend in Tsipirí. An Indian friend had heard the news and came to pray for her.

"Lord," he prayed, "we know that Marian's mother has arrived at your place. Take good care of her and comfort Marian."

Later another Indian came and prayed, "Lord, Marian is an orphan now. But you are our father and Jesus is our elder brother, so you help her."

When Marian and Steven returned to the U.S. they brought back letters from Indians: Reigildo, Alexis, Isaac, Virgilio, and even Rafaela who had recently learned to read and write. Then German, a young man in the group across the Chirripó River, wrote, "I am following the Lord." This was his first expression of faith! They also brought back news of Peter and Debbie who were settled in our house and continuing the Bible studies. However, government backing for Peter's proposed literacy program was slow to materialize.

Family Life on Furlough

The comings and goings of Priscilla, working at her job; of Susanna and Steven at Columbia Bible College; Elizabeth, Timothy and Philip at Columbia Christian School; and David at the nearby public school, soon became organized—with the help of a car pool, three cars and three bicycles! The whole family ate together each day at breakfast and usually at supper. We prayed together, and even sat together for the third consecutive furlough in the eighth row at church each Sunday. Yet we asked prayer for continued oneness.

Our house was the center of much activity and, at times, commotion. The children brought in their friends from school and church. Steven was courting; he and Cameron, daughter of our close friends the Barbers, were always frustrated with CBC dating rules and some of our own. At church we found that our family standards were questioned, if not challenged. I clashed with a youth pastor over his youth activities. As a result, he asked for several months of weekly discipleship classes! Together he and I went through a book of A. W. Tozer's writings!

Our own friends often came by. Our spiritual son, Al Ortiz, who was now a missionary himself, spent precious time with me early in our furlough before he and Daisy returned to the Dominican Republic. My older brother and his wife visited; even Marian's sister and her husband stopped by on their own furlough travels. Once a month we prayed with the special friends who had been meeting faithfully for four years to intercede for us and the Chirripó Indians. Almost every week we visited Ronald and Sandra Barber to pray and fellowship with them. After the years of isolation in Tsipirí, the opportunity to renew friendships during furlough was a special blessing.

Each week I wrote to Peter and he sometimes sent us cassette tapes full of news about the Indians. He wanted help in learning the Cabécar language, so my letters were stuffed with reams of data. Marian began typing the final manuscript of Luke from the handwritten copy we had brought from Costa Rica. We mailed the manuscript of Romans to Guatemala for printing, even as we waited for the proofs of the General Epistles to reach us from there.

During our furlough we made other deputation trips to churches and individual supporters and participated in mission conferences, as well as family reunions. On furlough our children were getting acquainted with the land of their citizenship. Children of missionaries—now sometimes called "third culture kids"—live in two worlds, yet are part of neither. Even so, Costa Rica was home to our kids in a way it was not to us.

Women to Women

We had hardly arrived in Columbia when Marian was asked to teach a class of "Women to Women"—classes taught by various women at different locations in the city. Though I encouraged her, she was dubious until she found that the topic that year was the Christian home. Then she learned that the supervisor of the classes had also been dubious since she didn't know Marian. However, none of the other prospective teachers accepted and four ladies called suggesting Marian. That was a confirmation not only to the supervisor but to Marian. Yet she accepted with reluctance, knowing she was not one of those special "out-front" speakers who are popular with women, as the previous teacher had been.

Sure enough, after the first week many of the women dropped out! But the Lord had assured Marian that if she would depend on Him, she would not be disappointed. Her close friend Sandra Barber came each week to drive her to the class. Sandra's encouragement buoyed her up, and the group settled down to a faithful core of around three dozen ladies who were serious in their desire to follow God.

For Marian, teaching involved many hours preparing her heart and her mind, all in addition to watching over a large family's daily needs. The Lord sustained her and gave her a message for each week. Comments from the class encouraged her. Gradually, she filled a notebook full of material.

My Class on Prayer

After we settled into our church routine in Columbia, I was asked to teach an adult Sunday School class on prayer. That was not surprising, for on the previous furlough I had been asked to teach on the Triune God for one quarter, and on the Christian home for two quarters. I wrote a manual on the home as a result of teaching about the family, while the lessons on the Triune God set in concrete my concept of the Trinity. Particularly impacting to me was my study on the ministry of the Holy Spirit in the life of Jesus, and also the work of the Spirit in the lives of the apostles and in us. Now I approached this series on prayer with the same enthusiasm: spending many hours each week studying, reading, thinking and writing. As the weeks passed, my convictions about prayer crystallized.

Unconsciously and unintentionally, I reflected in my teaching what Marian and I as a couple had been hammering out on the anvil of reality, as we translated the New Testament and tried to establish the church in an unreached group, while at the same time facing the unending challenge of life in the jungle, as we raised eight children and dealt with tensions locally and in our Mission. We were constantly cast upon God. I sometimes referred to all this in my letters as "working in the context of multiple impossibilities." As for reaching the Indians, I spoke of the "blunt indifference of satisfied paganism." We, of necessity, had learned to pray in order to survive.

The Intent of Prayer

To our amazement, forty people crowded into the first hour-long class on prayer. This continued Sunday after Sunday for thirty weeks. I began with what—to me—was an obvious assumption: "When we pray, we are asking God to do something we would not expect Him to do if we didn't pray." We don't pray for things we expect to happen. We don't pray for the sun to rise, but we do pray for rain!

The thought that prayer is intended to move God sent a shock wave through the group! Yet in the Scripture, God is portrayed as a personal being who responds to His children. Frequently I quoted Psalm 103:13, *"Like as a father pitieth his children, so the Lord pitieth them that fear Him."* In many cases He will do nothing if we don't pray. Yet as a Father, he enjoys giving "fun things" just to make us happy. Yes, He is sovereign—sovereign enough to adjust the universe, if necessary, in order to answer prayers. He acted sovereignly when Joshua prayed and the sun stood still, or when Hezekiah prayed and the sun's shadow went backward on the sundial. Furthermore, as I now ask, "Would the fire have fallen if Elijah had not prayed?"

Reaction was strong and frequent.

"We can't pray that God would change man because that would mean violating free will," said one man.

A CBC professor who was attending the class reacted in shock to such comments, saying, "They seem to take a fatalistic attitude."

Other reactions were more positive:

One person said, "I learned to *ask for things*, not just to trust." He also said, "I believe God brought me to Columbia to learn to meet the Lord each morning."

Another commented, "That Sunday school class is the shortest hour of my week."

Someone told our daughter Susanna, "What a wonderful class your Daddy has." Marian and I ourselves were spurred to pray more, as we pondered the Scriptures on prayer.

One matter that I brought up in the class was that prayer may even move God to change or modify or postpone a decree. The classic example is when God said He would destroy Israel and make Moses' descendants into a great nation, but then answered Moses' prayer asking Him *not* to destroy Israel. God is sovereign, yet He is *not* like the ancient kings of Persia whose decrees could not be altered. This means He is not merely doing, fatalistically, what He will, regardless of us. Instead, He is a personal God working from eternal purposes, and often our prayers are strategic in His plan. He works through the prayers of His people—and often only through them as He did through Daniel when he prayed. We don't pray just to have the privilege of having a part in God's work. Rather, we are a responsible part of His fighting force, part of a regiment which has a place in His war.

We must be true to Scripture. We need to adjust our thinking to the totality of His Word. He has given directions for praying but has not explained how it all works or answered all our questions.

Questions from the Class

Some questioned praying about small or unimportant matters. Yet the heart of personal prayer is desire, *our desire ("what things soever ye desire, when ye pray...")*. We also pray *His desire, "thy kingdom come, thy will be done,"* but our God is big enough to run the world without panic and still take care of the small details of our lives—and even take care of the sparrows. However, we must always pray with passion and persistence. Even though God cannot be forced to grant a petition contrary to His will, Jesus makes a big point of persevering in prayer. The Biblical focus is on fervent prayer, not lackadaisical praying.

Many questioned my saying that no is not an answer to prayer. Actually, it is a denial. Jesus taught, *"Ask, and it shall be given you; seek, and ye shall find; knock, and it shall be opened unto you."* He taught us to expect a yes answer to our prayers. We must be honest with God and ourselves. We are linguistically and semantically dishonest when we say that a denial is an answer to a request. However, God's silence is not necessarily a denial—timing may be involved. We may just need to persist. (However, if we ask God, "Do I, or do I not, do this?" then no is an answer.)

We tend to be simplistic about unanswered prayers. We are quick to quit praying when we don't see an immediate answer. Not only is God's response related to our faith, His will, and our persistence—or lack of it—but we must realize that we have an enemy. There is often supernatural opposition to some of our praying—not just our failure or His unwillingness. Daniel had fasted for three weeks, praying for what was the revealed will of God, but the Prince of Persia held up the messenger sent to answer the prayer.

In the class some snagged on my saying, "You don't have to tack onto every prayer the phrase, 'If it be Thy will.' When Jesus prayed this in Gethsemane, He knew His Father's will and asked to avoid it, if possible." A pastor friend from Costa Rica once made this observation, "We always add 'If it be Thy will' in order not to *comprometer nuestra fe* (not to put our faith on the line)." In our walk with the Lord, we should learn to sense His will, recognize the nudges of the Holy Spirit and be sensitive to His subtle signals so that we can ask with confidence.

Our ability to discern His will is in direct proportion to our walk in fellowship with the Lord and our sensitivity to His Spirit in a personal ongoing relationship of *knowing our God*. We shouldn't just latch onto whatever Scriptural promise seems to suit our situation. His promises are not like tickets cheaply thrown out to any passersby to be redeemed for the asking, but are for His loyal family to appropriate as they walk in obedience and fellowship with Him.

One lady in the class, an old friend and missionary colleague of ours, told me of her fears as she was about to enter the hospital.

"What do you want God to do for you?" I asked her.

"I just want Him to do His will," she answered.

Again I questioned, "What do you really want Him to do?"

"I want Him to heal me," she confessed.

"Then ask Him," I said, "without saying, 'If it be Thy will.'"

She couldn't bring herself to do so. But in the hospital as she was getting ready for her examination, she made herself pray for healing—without adding "If it be Thy will." When they examined her, not only did they find no significant problems, but her usual sky-high blood pressure was normal—and stayed down!

"The class on prayer made a permanent change in our lives," she said later.

After preparing for each class, I usually prayed several hours before teaching. I wrote in my diary, "I feel I'm moving to a higher level of praying, like another stage of a rocket launch." At some point in this era I learned to pray *after* ministry, nailing down or sealing in what I had taught—like putting in a new grease seal after replacing a wheel bearing.

Other Prayer Ministries

During the year I began to encourage men to pray daily with their wives, apart from devotions with the family and the blessing at meals. I had read an article on this subject by Harold Burchette who was currently teaching a short course at CBC. He had discovered that missionaries and pastors rarely prayed with their spouses and that most men have a problem doing so. For Marian and me as a couple, praying together had become the most important thing we did together on a daily basis—quality time!

One man in the class arranged for me to teach about prayer to some of the workers at the Christian school where he worked and where three of our children studied that year. This class turned out to be a very special time with believers hungry for more of the Lord. These down-to-earth ladies who served in the cafeteria were so appreciative and responsive.

There were always people coming and going to our house, some asking for informal discipleship, others just wanting to relate or to pick our brains. Often we would ask as they were leaving, "Do you have any prayer requests?" and pray together before they left. We already maintained an ongoing ministry of corresponding with many who received our prayer letters. We picked up comments in their letters or we asked in our letters the same type of questions we asked visitors, "What is the Lord impressing on you?" or, "Where are you reading in the Word these days?"

Although this approach opened the door to ministry and to rich fellowship, it sometimes backfired. One young woman recounted her troubles, heartaches, and divorce until she finally ran down.

"Have you had to forgive some people?" I questioned.

"Now you're meddling!" she objected.

Home Owners!

Now that Marian had received an inheritance from her parents, she was hoping to buy a house that we could return to on subsequent furloughs. We expected to have children studying at Columbia Bible College for several more years; they would be able to put the house to good use. Eventually we hoped to retire in Columbia. By this time we had lived in Columbia longer than in any other city in the United States since our marriage in 1951. We found it easier to come back to the same place each furlough—we already knew how to get around. Or as I like to say, "I know where to buy a nail!" We had forged many friendships in Columbia, and were happy at Columbia Evangelical Church, though we never formally joined.

Each week Peter's old friend Ed, who was now a budding realtor, came to show us houses all over the area. Nothing was ever just right, not even a beautiful place at the edge of the city that Marian referred to as "Green Pastures." She was beginning to lose hope of ever finding the right place, when one day in February, Ed told us about a house for sale only a few blocks from where we were living. The next day he came to take us to see the place. Such a pretty setting, with a larger yard than we had expected. The house was attractive from the outside, and though the rooms were arranged rather unexpectedly, our general impression was that it would be suitable, in spite of some drawbacks. In fact, it would probably be better than what we had originally envisioned.

The next day after Marian taught her weekly "Women to Women" class, we went to see the house again. This time the children were with us. We all knew this was it! Marian especially liked the large, sunny kitchen—just what she had hoped for. We all kept talking about how we would fix up the house. That evening Marian and I talked far into the night, discussing possibilities with Steven. He was now twenty years old, and already interested in construction. The next night we talked late again with him about whether to go ahead immediately with the purchase or wait for the Lord's confirmation.

As a fleece, we decided to wait a week to see if our interest was still strong and if the Lord would keep the house available that long. In the interval, Marian and I talked and prayed with the owners, a Christian couple who had raised seven daughters in that house. Marian had asked the Lord for a "hallowed house," a place hallowed by the presence and prayers of God's people, so meeting the owners was a confirmation to her—not that we needed much confirmation! The owners themselves felt that our desire to buy the house was a confirmation of their decision to move.

After an anxious week, we signed a contract. The price was lower than most of the places we had looked at, so we didn't try to bargain. We had been blessed with Marian's inheritance and wanted to bless the Christian owners by paying their full price. In the earlier years of our ministry, owning a stateside home would have been a distraction, but at this point it was a blessing. Such is life in the will of the Lord, as we walk with Him.

Resignation from The Central American Mission

Ever since the meetings in Nicaragua in 1977, we had been considering resigning from CAM International, as The Central

American Mission was now known. As we prayed about it, we realized that administrative differences could be solved by our seeking a different sponsorship. We also realized that our Indian work in Costa Rica did not really mesh with CAM's Spanish work there. At this point we realized, too, that the future of our work now seemed to lie in the hands of our own sons, who were already actively involved.

However, as the months of furlough rolled on, our plans didn't materialize as quickly as we hoped. Our friend Ronald Barber had offered in 1978 to do whatever he could to help us. Now he asked a couple of friends from church to join him in establishing a new board; his wife would be the bookkeeper. Ronald himself chose the name "Christian Missions, Inc." as being appropriate for any eventuality. Nine months of our furlough passed before all the legalities of establishing a new mission and obtaining the right to issue tax-deductible receipts were finished.

Our decision to resign was firm, yet we found ourselves hesitant to "take the leap." We would be ending twenty-eight years of happy, personal relationships. Even those whose actions precipitated our resignation were still our friends, for a mission body becomes like an extended family. Our children called our colleagues "Uncle" and "Aunt," and their children did the same to us. Finally we set a date late in March to mail our letter of resignation, which would take effect on May 31, 1980—two months before our return to Costa Rica.

Just before we mailed the letter, we were involved in a missions conference with Dean Lewis—the missionary who first had the vision to reach the Cabécar Indians. When I told Dean about our upcoming resignation, he seemed sad and disappointed, but made no comment. Yet in revealing to him our plans, I felt the "die was cast." I had reached the point of no return. We then mailed our resignation to the mission and also sent letters to our friends so that everyone—mission leaders, colleagues, donors and prayer partners—would get the news at the same time.

Resigning from CAM when we still had several children dependent on us was a real test of our faith. We felt the force of Larry

Christenson's words, "Faith always trembles when it comes to the brink of that step where everything depends on God alone." We wondered if our supporters would continue. All but one did! Their loyalty was a great encouragement, as well as a confirmation that they gave because they were interested in us and our ministry, not because of the Mission sponsorship under which we served. Most of all, it was a sign of the Lord's continued favor.

"The Principles and Practice of The Central American Mission" stated that missionaries who resigned must turn over not only Mission moneys and properties but the work as well. How could we turn over our ministry? One field leader in his response to our resignation reminded us of that statement but then admitted, "We have no one to take over your work." He encouraged me to shepherd the flock that God had given me. The only other reaction from a Mission leader had to do with our having waited until our furlough was almost over to resign, when according to Mission policy we should have resigned at the beginning of furlough. We regretted that the process of establishing a new sponsoring board had taken longer than we anticipated.

Final Months in Columbia

Winter was almost over by the time we signed the papers on the house at 6315 Winyah Drive in February and mailed our letter of resignation to CAM in March. In Columbia winters are mild, sometimes passing without even a flurry, but Marian and the children prayed for snow. The Lord answered their prayer twice—with a day off from school each time! The first time it snowed, the kids, even the older ones, were more excited than even at Christmas. All seven were outside right after breakfast, throwing snowballs and making a snowman.

Although not too old to enjoy fun in the snow, the older three were now adults. Living in a household structured for younger children was difficult for them, and adjusting to life with adult children was not easy for us. Priscilla had resumed her studies after Christmas, taking classes needed for beginning a graduate degree in linguistics. Steven had traveled to Illinois for the Triennial Missions Convention at Urbana over the Christmas break, and then to Costa Rica during his spring break from the Bible College. He was still courting Cameron, also a student at CBC. Marian's concern for life companions for our older daughters kept her praying!

Spring brought the news of our first granddaughter, Joanna May Jones, born April 5, 1980. Our daughter-in-law, Debbie, had come to the States to await the baby's birth; then after Peter joined them, the little family, including two-year-old Jonathan, visited us before returning to Costa Rica. For Marian it was special to see and hold the beautiful, bright-eyed newborn and to see the beginnings of another generation of Joneses following close after our youngest, David, who was now ten years old.

After the former owners of our new house moved out, we spent weeks working there during our spare time, repairing and renewing. My specialty was yard work, Marian planned, Priscilla and Susanna painted, Steven did carpentry and even the younger children helped. The kids did a huge amount of work. Many friends at church also came to our aid. Furniture was donated or loaned. The previous owners left us their old appliances, but out of Marian's inheritance we purchased a piano and a set of encyclopedias—two essential items without which no house of ours could be complete.

Moving day at the end of May happened to fall on the same day that our resignation from CAM became effective, so it was a time of new beginnings—a "new" house and a new sponsoring board. From that day on, our energies were concentrated on preparing to return to our work among the Cabécar Indians. Marian did manage to correct the proofs of the General Epistles and Romans as well, a job she'd put off for most of furlough.

In anticipation of leaving, Marian and I made a ministry trip to Pittsburgh, one to New Jersey and another to Alabama. At the churches I shared the fruit of my year's study, speaking on "The Nature of God as related to the Nature of Prayer." The Alabama trip included the annual Jones Reunion at Kolomoki State Park—it would be five years before I saw my brothers and sisters again. At the church in Columbia I finished my series on prayer; I also concluded the series I was teaching to workers at the Christian school. One-on-one ministry and correspondence continued to the end.

In between trips and ministry we took care of details left to finish as we set up our permanent stateside residence, like hanging curtains and family pictures, and buying a striking clock—another "essential" for our home. Our friends blessed us with a housewarming party and prayer time. The local group praying each month for our work with the Indians continued to meet throughout our time in the States.

Not only were Marian and I busy that summer, but Steven was on tour again with the college musical group. Elizabeth and Timothy were enrolled in summer school, seeking to get ahead since they would be studying by correspondence after we returned to Tsipirí. David also went to summer school and Philip continued piano lessons. Priscilla and Susanna were busy with jobs and managing the household while we were away on ministry trips.

As we contemplated leaving the older children in Columbia, I needed reassurance from the Lord. With their increasing independence, I was concerned about how our family values would continue. The Lord spoke to me through some phrases from Isaiah 44: "Do not be afraid, you are my servant...I will pour out my power on your children...They will thrive like well-watered grass..."

Another passage the Lord brought to my attention was for me personally: "Man of God...strive for righteousness, godliness, faith, love, endurance, and gentleness." These words from I Timothy 6 reinforced the conviction that I needed to stir myself up to love and gentleness. My own frustrations during furlough, even as I was teaching others about prayer and the Holy Spirit, proved that I needed not only the Spirit's help but my active participation in the process.

To Costa Rica under Christian Missions, Inc.

It had been a full year for both Marian and me—extremely full. From then on, we never again took a one-year furlough. When we returned to Costa Rica early in August with the four younger children, the three older ones remained in Columbia to continue their studies while living in our new house. One unexpected blessing of buying the house was that it gave our children a place of identity in the States—an antidote for the rootlessness often experienced by missionary kids.

By the time we left for the field in early August, our new board, Christian Missions, Inc., was functioning smoothly. The flight to Costa Rica—a fun trip on a noisy, crowded old plane—hurled us once again into the Latin world. One of our former colleagues from CAM met us at the airport and took us to the CAM Mission home to spend a few days while we made preparations to return to Tsipirí. Some time later we deliberately attended a devotional meeting of the local CAM missionaries—we wanted to "break the ice." Though Marian and I were very conscious that we "used to be with the Mission," their welcome quickly put us at ease. We felt comfortable, and evidently they did too. We still enjoyed seeing our former CAM colleagues and appreciated CAM's kindness in our separation.

The end of furlough marked a significant transition for us as missionaries and as a family. We were under new sponsorship and would now be known as independents serving with our own board. We had purchased a home that would provide a permanent stateside base for our family. Furthermore, during the months of teaching, I had solidified my stance on prayer. Now we would return to Costa Rica not only to continue sowing the seed but also to see the Cabécar church emerge at last—in answer to prayer.

– 21 –
The Birth of the Cabécar Church
1980 to 1987

Returning to Costa Rica for our sixth term among the Indians, we expressed our heartbeat with a quote from a missionary in a resistant field: "Prayer is both our program and our strategy, it is both our offense and defense. Effective persevering prayers remain our number one priority." We remembered the Scripture that says, *"Not by might, nor by power, but by my spirit, saith the LORD of hosts."* We realized, however, that the Spirit of God works in proportion to our prayers. We knew that the Spirit's activity is "triggered" or "activated" by prayer. We didn't just *assume* His activity, but rather *asked* for His working to bring about the birth of a church among the Cabécar Indians.

A House for Peter and Debbie

During our furlough Peter and Debbie had stayed at our house in Tsipirí. Peter kept the road passable and our old Toyota repaired. Debbie was a great sport, taking jungle life in stride. Their presence in our house kept the books from being eaten by roaches and the blankets by mice during our year in the States. Peter led Sunday Bible studies in Chirripó—one at Victor's and the other at Reigildo's on alternate Sundays.

By now Peter, serving as a volunteer, had developed a literacy program for the government's newly created system of Indian reservations. The Indians in the Chirripó Valley, as well as in the Pacuare, Estrella, and Telire Valleys, and even in distant San José Cabécar—their place of origin—all had the same language. All called themselves *ditsä si,* "the true people." The government had now instituted the term "Cabécar" as a unifying name for our target group.

Anticipating our return from furlough, Peter had phoned while we were still in Columbia. He and Debbie needed their own place, but the new location they hoped for had not yet materialized. Now he asked if we would allow them to fix up our "other" house for their use. Several years previously, we had purchased an adjacent plot with a tiny, rustic house behind our place in Tsipirí. The owner, our former maid Modesta, sold it to us in 1967 when she left the area. Her son, then a teenager, had built it from rough boards that he and his brother had made with a crosscut saw. The house provided a place for a caretaker when we were away.

We arrived back in Tsipirí to the sound of skill saw, router, sander, and hammers. Steven had flown to Costa Rica for a month in order to help Peter remodel. Together they transformed the four little rooms into a nice home according to Deb's design. After our arrival Timothy and Philip became part of the work crew. Elizabeth helped Debbie with baby Joanna, while David entertained young Jonathan. My part was to install a sink and a local-style water system—a hose leading from a spring on the hillside down to a fifty-five gallon drum at the house. It was a family project in true Jones' style, with much discussion and some squabbling.

In September, Steven returned to Bible College, Philip and David left for boarding school in Honduras, and Peter and Deb moved into the still-unfinished house. I resumed trekking each Sunday to Victor's house or to Reigildo's, so Peter began probing for interest in the gospel elsewhere. For us it was a joy to have Peter and Debbie serving with us as colleagues.

Back to Translation

Soon I was back to my schedule five days a week: translation from 8:00 to 2:00, correspondence or other writing from 2:00 to 4:00, and then physical work until it got dark at 6:00. This was my time for fix-it-jobs such as servicing the diesel light plant, working in the shop, filling the kerosene refrigerator, or repairing the road. After supper was the time for family devotions, reading, and writing.

Marian was back to typing manuscripts, checking commentaries, and writing in her suggestions. She checked for content, meaning, spelling, punctuation, word division, and general accuracy. I was always discussing translation and linguistic matters with her. Of course, she also resumed helping Elizabeth and Timothy with correspondence courses, as well as cooking three meals a day with Elizabeth's help—all from "scratch." The children had their jobs, lifting the load of manual labor needed to maintain life in the jungle. Certainly they gave us much joy and companionship in the isolation of Tsipirí.

In translation we never worked on just one book at a time. Usually three books were in process. We would be working on the first draft of a new one, while checking the proofs of another. Or we would do the first draft with one man, but the second or third draft with others. I constantly juggled my helpers according to which one came to work or what book we were focusing on.

By the summer of 1981, a year after we returned from furlough, I was finishing the first draft of Matthew with Célimo, while Marian typed the final draft of Luke. Benjamín participated with us in the prepublication check of Luke by the Bible Society. The General Epistles had arrived from the printer and were for sale. At this point we had only eight books of the New Testament left to begin translating.

Ongoing Process

After Marian mailed the final typewritten manuscript of Luke to Guatemala in May of 1982, it was two months before the proofs came back. Unfortunately, there was an error in almost every paragraph. By the time Marian corrected the printout, mailed it back to Guatemala, and received a new set of proofs, a few more months had gone by. Mail service between the Central American countries was painfully slow. The new set of proofs contained many fresh errors. And the next set as well. Each proofreading took several hours of Marian's time. By the time we received the published portions of Luke, three years had gone by since Marian first mailed the manuscript. The problem? Apparently the keyboarder—during the switch from typewriter to computer—depended too much on the ease of correcting mistakes on the computerized draft. Fortunately, never after that did the process take so long as it did with Luke.

Translation was my primary work five days a week. Furthermore, language analysis never really ended. Once while preparing a Bible study in the book of Romans, which by then was already published, I noticed a predictable order in the verb suffixes, a very important discovery. Translation and linguistics were a means to an end, for we were creating our own tools. My prime time during the week was given to *finishing* the Book; Sundays were for *using* the Book. We made our schedule, but accepted interruptions, and took time for family celebrations and trips to the States, never forgetting our double vision to reach a tribe for God and to raise a family for God.

Cabécar Lessons

Every pioneer linguist needs to prepare a dictionary and write a pedagogical grammar, a series of lessons to help others learn the language. With Peter and Debbie now living in the little house, and with Timothy already fifteen years old and increasingly involved in the ministry, we scheduled classes for them from 4:00 to 5:00 P.M. five days a week. That meant that after my translation helpers left at 2:00, I quickly wrote a short lesson pointing up one feature of the language. Marian devised homework to reinforce the lesson.

Our three "students" learned, especially Debbie, who was starting from scratch but studied faithfully. Timothy, who already spoke the language quite well, later said, "I don't know how it happened, but after the lessons I could understand how the language functioned." Actually, I myself learned more in the process. The lessons continued for a number of months until Peter and Debbie moved to Estrella. With this simple, practical approach—not trying to "plug all the holes"—I eventually prepared almost eighty handwritten lessons. Later I also wrote a comparison of the Cabécar and Bribri languages, to point out the similarities of the key features.

Sowing Seed amid Opposition

The meetings continued at Reigildo's and at Victor's. Peter often accompanied me but also began a new Bible study at the home of Ambrosio, a cousin of Victor's. The younger boys went with me on Sundays, but Timothy sometimes would go across the Chirripó River to a new Bible study that Alexis had started. This was Timothy's first involvement on an individual basis. (Alexis combined the Bible study with a literacy class he taught—under the sponsorship of the government literacy program that Peter had developed.) On some Sundays three different Bible studies went on simultaneously!

On my way to Victor's one Sunday, just ahead of my foot I spotted a deadly fer-de-lance, called the "true snake" by the Indians. In all my years of trekking I'd rarely seen a snake on the trail, never a poisonous one. Did that fer-de-lance just "happen to be there?" To the Indians, a poisonous snake was an arrow sent by the demon owner of the snake to cause death. Now I was invading Satan's territory with the message of Jesus who came to destroy the works of the evil one.

We continued to pray defensively for physical, mental and spiritual protection from the devil, as well as against opposition to the gospel from local sources. The media voiced its opposition at times. The literacy program developed by Peter was challenged by organized forces. The communist newspaper mentioned my name more than once, asking for my removal. A government anthropologist published a book in which he appealed to the legislators to remove us. Local "whites" whose land had been expropriated for the reservation questioned our presence in the area. One spread the lie that we were getting rich by selling our knowledge of the Cabécar language. The possibility of a hydroelectric project on the Chirripó River also concerned us, for it would lead to devastating social repercussions.

Some of the Indians involved in the Bible studies were opposed by family members. Victor's sister attacked him for allowing meetings at his home to study "those books in our language." The family even hired a witch doctor to curse Victor. Though they expected him to be "dead within six months," he did not succumb to the severe chest congestion that plagued him.

Conflicting Religions

Those who were being exposed to the gospel were slow to see the implications for their long-held practices. Benjamín insisted that their harvest festival, a drunken orgy involving homemade corn beer, was "only a custom." Yet on the trail to a meeting Isaac voluntarily pointed out to me a small handful of corn lying at the edge of a field, placed there for *Tami*, "the mother of the earth" and her male counterpart, *Blu*, "the rich one." Célimo told me that observing the harvest festival kept them from getting lazy. Evidently this meant that it made them able to work and consequently to become rich.

As I worked with my helpers on the translation of the Scriptures, I spent time discussing with them the implications of Christianity. Yet one of my helpers came to me without any embarrassment, asking for a chicken "to pay a man for his services." He needed to pay the shaman who had spent a few days "purifying" his family—performing ceremonies to prevent demon-caused sicknesses. Even Victor, when I discussed with him the highly secret burial practices needed to get the departed soul to its proper place, reacted with surprise and indignation to my suggestion that he reject such customs.

"If I give up those practices," he said, "then who would bury me when I die?"

Holy Week Conference

We had celebrated the first Holy Week Conference in 1979 before going on furlough. Now in 1981 we called another conference at our home in Tsipirí. This time twice the number came as for the first conference, a total of twenty-four Indians, with around nineteen in each session. Lots of kitchen work goes into feeding two dozen people, plus our own family, for three days! To our disappointment neither Reigildo nor Victor came at all. Yet Benjamín attended some sessions even though he never came to our Sunday meetings. Happily, several young men came from the new group started by Peter.

In the Sunday Bible studies at Reigildo's we had been using photocopies of Luke as a sort of trial run before publication. I had enjoyed watching the group learn for the first time about Jesus' birth, as recorded in Luke 2. Now in preparation for the conference Marian hurriedly finished typing the final draft of the last three chapters of Luke so each person could have a xeroxed copy. The trial, crucifixion, and resurrection of Jesus would be an appropriate passage to study during Holy Week.

Emotions began to peak when the group saw Jesus praying in Gethsemane. A greater emotional peak came the next day as we saw Jesus nailed to the cross. Virgilio said that to die for one's enemies is a "hard thing." Benjamín cried during the long prayer time following that study. Alexis realized the implications of Jesus' promise to the repentant thief; he saw that—with Jesus—one can get to paradise *the same day* without a Cabécar-type feast when pigs and chickens are eaten so that the souls of the animals can help the dead person's soul get past the place where writhing snakes obstruct the path to the nether world.

Easter was no anticlimax! These Indians, emerging from paganism, identified first with the unbelieving disciples and then with the two who walked with the resurrected Christ on the road to Emmaus. Finally, they identified with the eleven as they touched the scars from the nails and saw Jesus as victor over death. We then turned to the gospel of John and heard Thomas say, *"My Lord and my God."* It was only natural for us to pause and sing "He is Lord," using the newly expanded songbook which Debbie typed for the conference.

In the conference sessions we focused on reading, as we did each Sunday. Thus, the new readers—many were newly literate—were able to practice and also learned to answer questions like, "What does it say?" "What does it mean?" We often picked up one of the five other portions already printed and compared Scripture with

Scripture. One night we had an extra session at their request to study Romans 12:1,2.

We also celebrated the Lord's Supper with the three baptized believers—Isaac, Alexis, and Patricia. For the service we used the lovely pewter plate and goblet given by the prayer group in Columbia. On it were these words: *"Jiwa bas jer jano Jesús duáwaska."* (With this, remember Jesus' death.) We had used this Communion set only once before, seated on crude benches in an Indian hut, with our feet on the damp floor muddied from weeks of rain. In spite of the surroundings, we had worshipped the Lord, one in Him.

The following year we called a third Holy Week conference at Tsipirí. It was another good one—session after session, with breaks only for meals and refreshments. The Cabécars, so isolated in their scattered huts, enjoyed and needed the social times of such protracted meetings. Previously this isolated tribe had experienced social gatherings mainly in their traditional house dedications, wakes for the dead, and harvest celebrations. During the decade of the eighties we averaged one conference a year. Each was intentionally heavy on teaching—sowing the knowledge of the Word.

"Second Front" in Estrella

Peter and his family eventually moved to the Caribbean lowlands, opening a second ministry front about six hours by car from Tsipirí. Their new location gave them access to the Cabécar Indians living in the Estrella River area where Marian and I had once considered locating. It brought us great satisfaction to have them reach this needy area.

Since they would no longer have access to our vehicle, they bought a used Land Rover. While getting acquainted with the area, they were allowed to use one of the workers' houses on the banana plantation established by the Dole Fruit Company. On my early trips to this area in the late fifties I learned that the fruit company was beginning to buy nearby lands from Latinos who had staked claims there. The Company, known locally as *La Bananera*, drained miles of swampy lands and cleared useless second-growth. For their employees the Company not only built simple, adequate housing, as well as dispensaries, schools, and soccer fields, but also paid attractive wages with benefits. Many enterprising workers who saved their money for a number of years were able to buy land and become independent.

A banana worker who became friendly to Peter and Debbie eventually sold them a piece of his land claim. Early in 1982 my brother David and his son Mike came from the States with men from their church to build a house for Peter and his family. Steven—on break from college—and Timothy were part of the work team, along with Deb's dad and uncle. Elizabeth helped Debbie cook for the crew and look after the children. I helped transport the men, as well as worked a bit on the water system. Another extended family building project!

Soon Peter and Debbie were walking the trails along the Estrella River, crisscrossing the tributaries, looking for interest in the Word of God. Once as Debbie crossed a river with the baby on her back, Peter watched horrified from upstream as the unexpectedly swift current pulled them under. In the Lord's mercy, Debbie managed to hang onto a large boulder until an Indian helped her and the baby to safety.

Peter continued developing a literacy program for the government, training literate Indians to teach others. He also established a friendship with an Indian whom he visited frequently, and from whom he learned more about the Cabécar world of demons and witchcraft, while at the same time teaching the Word to this man week after week. Sadly, Peter's pupil eventually lost interest. Now Peter experienced the numbing impact of satisfied paganism that I had earlier felt.

Chapel in Chirripó

After Peter and Debbie left for Estrella, I continued the Bible studies at Victor's and at Reigildo's on alternate Sundays. I was encouraged with the long-sustained interest at both places. Reigildo's older sons, Isaac and Alexis, would usually know the contents of the chapter by the time I arrived for the class. Their sister Rafaela also participated in the studies—Marian had taught her to read—and was thinking about being baptized as her brothers had been. Victor's group was lively and stable. They had seen healing in answer to prayer. Victor, too, had talked of being baptized. Furthermore, Peter felt that the group he started before leaving for Estrella would be willing to unite with my two groups, thus forming a single group that would meet every Sunday.

Building a chapel in a central location would serve as a means of unifying believers who lived on scattered farms dotting the steep hills. No one would be able to say, "I don't know where you're meeting this Sunday," or "I didn't come because I don't like the host."

"He's proud, he's rich," said several who wouldn't go to Reigildo's house. (He owned five horses and three farms!)

"He's fighty, he's critical," claimed those who wouldn't attend meetings at Victor's. (He had no horses and was a poor farmer.)

Both of my groups were already showing interest in building a chapel. Of course, each group wanted their own chapel! Reigildo—a key man in Chirripó—had pointed out a spot near his house that I thought would be ideal. Yet I wondered if some from Victor's group might be unwilling to go to a chapel on Reigildo's land. Somehow he and I never finalized anything. Victor assumed all along that we would build on his land. I knew Alexis and Isaac would be willing to go there, but would Reigildo humble himself to meet with Victor's group?

In the end Antonio, a man from Victor's group, offered a spot half an hour from Victor's house. This land was more central to the total area. Although I had questions about the compatibility of the mix of clans and family relationships—practical realities of those involved—we finally accepted Antonio's offer.

"This Is My Money"

At both of my meetings we were taking up offerings toward the construction of a small building. Each week we collected the money in a tin can. (Actually, my primary object was to teach them to give and to be responsible for their funds.) Alexis, the treasurer of Reigildo's group, willingly turned over to me the funds they had been saving up for three years toward the purchase of tin roofing—the only significant expense in an Indian building. Victor, however, refused to release the money that his group had supposedly been saving.

"But you were going to build here! The money is mine! I won't give it! I need it to feed those who come," he protested.

Apparently Victor had spent the money. Furthermore, I learned that he was hoping to use the proposed chapel for storage.

The joy of birthing a church is tempered by the travail of the process. Victor's refusal dampened my excitement at the prospect of uniting the two groups. I thought of the Apostle Paul who spoke to the Galatians as "my little children, of whom I travail in birth again until Christ be formed in you." Like Paul, I travailed in prayer, hoping to see Christ formed in Victor and others emerging from paganism.

Inauguration of the New Chapel

On our first workday Peter, Steven, Timothy and I set out from Tsipirí, while Isaac and Alexis came from Reigildo's group. From Victor's group only Antonio showed up. Within a few hours we had used up all the poles that Antonio had prepared for framing the building. On the next workday I leveled the dirt for the floor while the others hauled more poles—the ridgepole and smaller poles onto which the roofing would be nailed. On the final workday they nailed the sheets of roofing that Benjamín and his sons had hauled over the ridge from Tsipirí. (I had purchased the roofing in town, taking it as far as I could in my Toyota, and then had paid an oxcart to take it the rest of the way to Tsipirí. At the time a washout prevented my driving all the way home.)

During the weeks of construction I was suffering from a heavy cold, my third major cold that year. My left ear was ringing again, "rattling," one of the first signs that I was losing my hearing in that ear.

Inauguration day was October 4, 1981. Timothy and I arrived soaked, for it had begun raining halfway to Suékicha, the local name for the spot where the chapel was built. Antonio had done a good job of finishing the final details, such as making simple cane benches and a table for books. He had even nailed the extra roofing as walls on two sides of the building, to shield the "weather side." Yet we still shivered in the cold as the fog closed in the beautiful valley below. And the only ceremony was a short discussion of the purpose of the building, followed by prayers from the group.

The special treat for Timothy and me that day was that Peter and Debbie walked in unexpectedly during the meeting! They had left Estrella at four that morning, arrived at Tsipirí at nine to leave the children with Marian and Elizabeth, and then trekked more than two hours to the chapel—undaunted by the rain.

Hopes Begin to Dwindle

We built the chapel in faith—faith that weekly services there would eventually prove to be better than meeting in homes on alternate Sundays. Yet it was mostly downhill after the first meeting. Things never "took off" at the chapel. The weekly attendance was less than the combined attendance at the home meetings, even though some from both meetings were represented, plus a few new ones who lived nearby.

Sometimes only one person appeared, but I taught that one, always sowing the seed. Only one or two from Peter's old group ever came. Reigildo came only once, although his nephew Eugenio came often despite opposition at home.

"Why do you go to the chapel?" nagged Eugenio's father. "They don't pay you to attend."

Nevertheless, a teenage girl named Zoila, whom Marian had taught to read, came several times from Súfu, José Gilberto's place an hour away. Once she brought her common-law husband, Franklin, and he liked the Word. (Finding Franklin may have been worth the chapel effort. We would later discover that he was a good translation helper.) Mayela, who also lived near Súfu, attended a couple of times. To add to my concern about the low attendance, I soon found that Antonio was using the chapel for a storage shed.

A building is not a church. We knew that. Though we hoped to move a step beyond home meetings, the chapel was not producing the results I expected. Had I, in effect, been trying to "make" a church happen? Timothy had thought that the time was ripe, but was it *God's timing*? We kept on praying and hoping.

Ongoing Renewal

Each Sunday afternoon I returned from the Bible study in Chirripó totally exhausted physically, mentally, and spiritually. After an icy bath in our cold creek, I turned on the generator so that I could listen to a joyful, contemporary praise record. I was too tired to pray and too tired to read, but I turned the volume up high, lay on the couch, and absorbed the refreshing sound. This was my first step toward renewed strength.

After Marian's good dinner of meat and potatoes—no rice and beans on Sunday—we each chose a song from the IVCF hymnbook, with Marian playing the piano. As a family we expressed our deep devotion and commitment to the Lord in worship. We sometimes sang missionary songs like "Ye Christian Heralds," or "We Rest on Thee, our Shield and our Defender," the song the five missionary martyrs sang before going, unknowingly, to their death at the hands of those they sought to reach in Ecuador. One of the songs I often chose was, "Jesus, Wond'rous Saviour." Though tired, I was refreshed as I expressed my love for Him in song. Then we listened as Marian read a sermon by Spurgeon. Sometimes we listened to a sermon on tape. Finally, we all knelt as I prayed my weekly "pastoral prayer." Over the years, our Sunday night family worship was a time of renewal—the highlight of our week.

The next morning it was back to the translation desk with an Indian helper. But first, as always, Marian met the Lord at daybreak in the living room, and I met the Lord in my study for a couple of hours before breakfast. I had to hear from God, feed my own soul, and out of the overflow, minister to my wife and my children, yet still have enough spiritual reserve to reach an Indian tribe—while coping with the stress of life in the jungle.

II Peter 1:3 says: *"Seeing that his divine power hath granted unto us all things that pertain to life and godliness through the knowledge of him that called us by his own glory and purpose..."* We drank from His waters, tapped His resources, and banked on His sufficiency, always, in all things. We learned that He is adequate! Through His Word and His Spirit, God's provision was as available in the jungle as in the States. We grew in the knowledge of God. And we ministered out of the overflow. Appropriating divine resources was a *way of life* essential to establishing the church, and a part of the dynamics we tried to communicate to the believers and to our children.

"Take Down the Chapel"

Several months after the inauguration of the chapel we went to the States for a few weeks, leaving Alexis in charge of the meetings. To our dismay he reported that nobody came to the chapel while we were away. Following our return from the States, at least one person usually came, although we never had good attendance. However, in our November '82 prayer letter I wrote: "As I trudged home from the chapel recently when, for the first time, no one had come, I cried out to God again, 'We have given our lives; we have no more to give! We have prayed to the hilt; what more can we do?' We are not discouraged, just puzzled, and waiting. For we are strengthened by an overriding conviction that God is building His church; that we will reap; that our labor is not in vain. So we continue, on our knees, in faith."

In 1983 at Easter we celebrated another great Holy Week Conference in which we studied the First Epistle of John at our home in Tsipirí—an encouragement, yes, but not really a church. There were many who showed interest, but no "critical mass."

In July of that year I arrived at the chapel one Sunday to find six young men: Isaac, Alexis, their cousin Miguel from across the river, one man from Peter's group and two of Benjamín's sons. This was the way it should be. Exciting!

The very next Sunday, however, as I trekked to the chapel with Timothy and Philip, I was reflecting on the previous night's tension during a meeting with Latin believers in the village of Grano de Oro, and also recalling pessimistically my recent confrontation with Antonio concerning his relationship with his wife's daughter. As I mulled it over, I thought to myself, "After what happened last night in the Spanish service, today should be the day when Antonio tells me not to use the chapel any more."

Ever since we built the chapel, Antonio had needled me for favors. Recently he'd been asking me to take him and his common-law wife and stepdaughter with me when I went to town for supplies. When this happened three months in a row I began to wonder what was going on. The jungle grapevine soon informed me that he was taking them to the hospital for birth control shots, for he was sleeping with both of them — scandalous even to animistic Indians — and didn't want his already large family to increase still further. That news ended his trips to town with me. I suspected that he would eventually react by asking me to move the chapel. In fact, I'd already been been wondering if I should do so.

When I reached the chapel that dreary Sunday, crippled Margarita, another stepdaughter of Antonio's, handed me a neatly written note in which he had said: "You may no longer meet on my land. Take your building away, or I will tear it down. They pay you for having services, but you have paid me nothing for my generosity in letting you build on my land." (In Grano de Oro a similar lie was circulating among the unbelievers: "*Don* Aziel is getting rich with the extra bonus he receives for each baptism.")

This was a real blow, though at least it brought closure to a bad situation. But who would even be willing to carry away the tin roofing of the chapel? We had no truly cohesive group. To his credit, Benjamín — always loyal though not responsive to the gospel — sent his older children to remove the thirty-two sheets of galvanized iron. (By this time metal roofing was fast replacing thatch for roofing in Indian territory.) They tied it with vines into several rolls and carried the heavy bundles on their shoulders—even his wife helped. Soon the tin was stored in my garage.

Our Lowest Point

The chapel episode, coupled with tension in Grano de Oro, was perhaps the lowest point of all our years among the Cabécars. For a time I was dazed. I asked myself, "Where do I go next Sunday?" The chapel had failed, but worse than that, we had also lost the two exciting Bible studies which had previously met twice a month for seven years. Furthermore, I had lost my relationship with my friend Reigildo, a quality person who was by then the head of the association which administered the Cabécar reservation. I wrote in my diary in October 1983: "We are basically starting again in planting a church. I still have no sense of despair, rather a real sense of moving in the Spirit. God will build His church though we can't see how." Maybe this is what the Apostle Paul felt when he penned II Corinthians 4:8: *"We are perplexed, but not in despair."*

However, it was during this time that three Americans then living in Costa Rica came to know the Lord through our witness. First it was a butterfly collector and his wife. Then another man, a construction engineer, got saved and was discipled by the first man. Soon the Latino church in Grano de Oro also "took off." All this was like an emotional tonic, a confirmation that we were still in a spiritual condition to touch lives—if not Indians, at least "other sheep." The Cabécar church had not been birthed, but the pain of the failed chapel eventually proved to have been the initial "birth pangs" of the church that emerged.

Soon I felt a fresh anointing. This happened after all five of my sons prayed over me as we celebrated my sixty-first birthday. In a prayer letter I wrote about overhearing their conversation later that same evening: "That night was special to me as, at a distance, I heard our sons talking, dreaming, and planning—how to establish the church of Jesus Christ in those mountains. It was now *their* thing, *their* vision. Some of them will be walking those hills when I can't walk them any more." That comment proved prophetic. And where did their vision come from? From walking those hills with me as they grew to manhood.

We Build on the "Ashes" of the Chapel

"When I get my own house built, you can meet there," said Eugenio after we tore down the chapel.

"If no one wants the chapel, your Daddy could build it on my land," said Juan, our loyal caretaker, to our youngest son, though he was uninterested in the gospel.

Benjamín, always loyal and dependable, also offered to let us build on his acreage, but we hesitated since he had no stated commitment to Jesus.

Alexis and I hoped to rebuild at his father's other farm, located just down the hill from our house in Tsipirí, but Reigildo was no longer interested.

"Did I ask you to leave?" he objected. "You used to meet at my main place, but then you built a chapel on Antonio's land. Why do you come to me now?"

Soon Reigildo formed a friendship with the Catholic priest who had recently begun work in Chirripó. Furthermore, Alexis eventually studied to become a shaman. (Years later I found out that Isaac tried to learn also, but he said, "I could never remember all those incantations.")

In the end, we had to leave our useless "what ifs" with the Lord. We had built the chapel in faith. We would move on in faith. We would begin again. In a way, I was relieved. I was free from having to go to the chapel every Sunday. I resumed meetings at Tsipirí, but was free on alternate Sundays to respond to interest in other places.

An even wider door was about to open. Shortly before we took down the chapel, Alexis and Isaac had begun teaching the Word to their cousins, sons of a man called Mundo. One day Peter and Timothy decided to check out the interest at Mundo's, a few hours away. On their return we heard them shout from the trail above our house, announcing their arrival. Hurrying to the front porch, we watched as they ran down the driveway, tired and sweaty, breathless and excited. They had found "serious interest" at Mundo's home in a "strategic location" at a sort of crossroads of trails, ridges, and rivers on the far side of the Chirripó River.

Soon a man named Florentino, a cousin of Benjamín's, came by to see me on his way to a meeting of reservation leaders. He was pleased with the copy of the Ten Commandments I gave him, and the result was an invitation to his house in a totally unreached area. Florentino lived near the Pacuare River. To get to his home, I drove for an hour—ten miles—along the road toward Turrialba, then turned on a side road to Paso Marcos where I parked the jeep, found the trail and walked for an hour.

Crossing the River

"Daddy," said Timothy to me one day in response to my dilemma about where to go after losing the chapel, "why don't you go to Mundo's?" (He had been helping teach Miguel, Mundo's son.)

Going to Mundo's would mean packing for an overnight trip and arranging for a lay pastor from Turrialba to substitute for me at the Saturday night meeting in Grano de Oro. Since I wasn't sure of the last part of the trail, Timothy—who had gone ahead—waited for me at the new vine bridge over the Chirripó River and led me to Mundo's house. Near the house, I came to a small stream. Trying to cross such a stream by stepping from one big rock to the next was tricky at best, as I well knew. I slipped on a wet boulder and arrived thoroughly soaked.

At Mundo's I could sense the serious interest that Timothy had reported. I, too, was drawn to this happy, close-knit family—like Reigildo's and like our own. I liked the bright-eyed, responsive children. I continued to make overnight trips once a month, often with one or two of my younger sons.

Timothy crossing a vine bridge

Once when Timothy slept on a narrow bed there, sharing a thin bedspread with Miguel, Mundo's son, I expressed my concern for his comfort. "No problem," replied Timothy, "he's my brother." My sons were becoming "Indians!"

Each Sunday morning a neighbor of Mundo's named Efraín came with his family down the steep, thirty-minute descent from his house to attend the meeting. I was particularly encouraged by the interest shown by Efraín, a natural teacher then working with Peter's literacy program. Yet as I returned home from these monthly visits, retracing my steps until I reached the Chirripó River, I then had to face the daunting *Raíz de Hule* hill from the river at 1000 feet to the *Camino Real* at 4,000 feet. Weary and bored, I once counted my steps during the two and one-half hour climb; I took 10,500 steps up the muddy horse trail crisscrossed by countless roots! In dry season I quenched my burning thirst at one of two Indian huts near the summit, drinking water from a seep hole. Like the Indians, I never carried water—it was heavy. Even when I reached the crest, I still faced an hour's descent along the *Camino Real* (the main trail) to Tsipirí.

A typical meeting

On the way home from another of these weekend trips, I came upon a local Latin selling clandestine liquor to an Indian who occasionally worked for me.

"God sees what you're doing," I remarked quietly to the Latin.

"Let's settle accounts right now," he threatened, pulling out his machete.

I kept on walking and he did not pursue.

On another Sunday as I drove out of my gate on the way to a Bible study at Florentino's, this same man again threatened me—in front of three other Latinos doing business at the spot where Indians and "whites" often met to buy or sell.

The Tide Turns

As I continued visiting Mundo, his interest waned. Nor did he like for other people—particularly Efraín's family—to attend the meetings. Earlier I had stated that I would continue my visits only if others were welcome. By now it was apparent that Mundo's real interest was for his sons to learn to read. Yet soon an even bigger door opened.

In mid-December 1983 Peter, who was visiting after he moved to Estrella, and Timothy, home for vacation from Bible College, accompanied me to Mundo's. After the study from the Epistle of II Peter, Efraín asked us to go with him to visit Carlos Luis, and then go to his own house so we could pray for his sick baby. The day was too short for that, so I returned to Tsipirí as planned. Peter and Timothy, however, went with Efraín to return home the following day.

At Efraín's, the sick baby was lying listless in the hammock, wearing a crude fetish necklace that the grandfather, a shaman, had put on the child in hopes of appeasing the demon behind the illness.

"Take it off," commanded Peter, knowing that unless the fetish was removed, Jesus would not get the credit for the healing.

Efraín grabbed the necklace, broke it, and threw it in the fire. Then Peter and Timothy prayed for the child's healing. The next morning the baby awoke normal.

A week later Peter was involved in a major accident. Was the accident a coincidence? Or was it a counterattack for his having angered the demon behind that sickness?

The healing of Efraín and Adelina's baby opened the door to begin a new Bible study at their home. It precipitated our younger sons long-term involvement in the Cabécar church: its establishment, its nature and its future. In the process they set the direction of their own futures. Their involvement escalated as rapidly as Efraín's interest. We did not plan it or foresee it—it just happened. However, I had once asked the Lord during a day of prayer for one of my sons to be my successor.

"I Feel Sorry for You"

A few months after we tore down the chapel, crippled Margarita brought me another note, a note that would open the door to begin another group on the "ashes" of the chapel. This note was from José Gilberto and Patricia (Margarita's half sister) inviting me to begin a Bible study at their home in Súfu. (Every piece of Cabécar land has a name.) Although not so far from Tsipirí as Mundo's place, it was still a rather difficult hike to Súfu. Actually, there aren't *any* easy hikes in the Chirripó area! To get to José's house I had to climb to the crest above the Tsipirí Valley, then descend almost 2,000 feet to Victor's house before climbing another forty-five minutes to Súfu.

"*Don* Aziel, I feel sorry for you," José Gilberto had told me after the chapel was taken down. "You ought to be able to teach *somewhere!*"

In January 1984 I went to Súfu (Porcupine House) for the first time. Timothy accompanied me, reinforcing what I was trying to teach. He felt it was an "anointed" meeting—probably the first time we ever felt *that* way about a meeting. When I first began meetings in Indian homes more than a dozen years earlier, I called them Bible studies, but the people saw them as reading classes. Yet my goal was far beyond just giving them reading practice. I intended to change their worldview, their value system and their lifestyle. Here at Súfu the Lord gave me a glimpse of the goal toward which He was working.

At this first meeting several young people were present—José Gilberto and Patricia, José's sister Zoila and her husband Franklin, and another sister named Mayela. All of them had previously visited the chapel at least once and had liked the Word. José and Franklin, brothers-in-law, were already *de facto* elders. By midyear I was going to Súfu twice a month, and we had absorbed most of those left from Victor's group. The new group was stable, often with twenty or more in the circle. After some months, José built a little chapel at the bottom of his long hill so that I wouldn't have to make the final ascent. This became a pattern: any head of a household who invited us and showed long-term interest, would usually build a little chapel nearby.

Our Younger Sons Begin Trekking on Their Own

As the younger boys grew and the work developed across the Chirripó River, they would often leave for a few days in Chirripó to lead a meeting or a conference across the river or up in the headwaters. Sometimes they just wanted to spend time with the Indians or explore territory new to them, yet evangelism and discipleship were always on their minds. Timothy was eighteen at the time we tore down the chapel, Philip was fifteen, and David thirteen. By this time Peter and Debbie were living in Estrella, reaching Indians in that area. Meanwhile, I continued my three monthly commitments—twice a month at José's, once a month at Florentino's, and once a month at Mundo's. If the younger boys were home, they accompanied me. In fact, once when I went to Florentino's all five sons and even Peter's young son were with me!

In my earlier trekking days I had traveled with a heavy pack. These boys traveled light. They left Tsipirí with only a thin cotton bedspread for a blanket, a square meter of plastic sheeting as a raincoat, a flashlight, and a portion of the Cabécar Scriptures—all in a little Indian tote bag. Philip usually carried a guitar as well. They always wore rubber boots, wonderful footwear for trekking muddy trails and crossing rivers. (Even Indians who formerly went barefoot now wore loose-fitting rubber boots—locally made and relatively cheap. I myself had long since given up leather boots, which had to be unlaced and removed each time I crossed a river.) Instead of wearing heavy jeans, David preferred lightweight trousers which dried quickly after he crossed rivers. They all ate what they were served, and carried no food or medicine.

At home in their absence I was always at the desk translating and checking, traveling only on weekends. But as I translated, I always watched the weather, knowing what rains did to the rivers. Once as Timothy was being swept away while crossing a swollen river, he grabbed an overhanging bough but wasn't able to pull himself to safety because his boots were filled with water. Only when he shook off his boots was he able to pull himself out of the current. On another occasion Philip and David were being ferried across a wide, flat spot in the Telire River on a makeshift balsa raft. The raft fell apart, but they made it to shore safely. Further up the Telire they would need to cross the river at a dangerous spot. There a makeshift bridge made of two parallel logs spans the treacherous *Shakabao* ("Rainbow") rapids, crashing through the vertical rock walls of the gorge below. Yet in spite of swollen rivers and other obstacles, the boys always reported, "No problems." Only later as I heard them talking to each other, did I learn of their close calls. I had suspected it all along, for I had trekked those same trails in the same bad weather before they were born.

Bad weather was not the only threat to their safety. In distant Telire, the hinterland of the Cabécar people, armed drug runners occasionally plied the trails. They had taught the Indians in remote areas to grow marijuana. Under cover of darkness the *marijuaneros* carried their illegal merchandise down to the lowlands where it brought them a good income on payday at the port city. The Indians appreciated the cash and barter items they received, but didn't understand the legal implications of the trade.

The drug runners, however, surely realized that our sons might report them. The mere presence of our sons was like a silent voice, pricking their conscience. Peter told us about the *marijuanero* who appeared with an AK-47 one dark night in a hut where he was staying in Telire. And once when Philip was in remote Telire with a group of Indians, government agents appeared suddenly in a helicopter to hunt for armed drug runners. The Indians disappeared in the bush as the helicopter descended. Philip—with no identity papers—was left alone to try to prove that he was not a drug runner. A harrowing incident for young Philip!

Risky Ventures or Spiritual Adventures?

In May of 1983 Timothy, then eighteen, made an eighteen-day exploration trek from Tsipirí to the upper Chirripó Valley and across the Matama Ridge to the upper Telire Valley. From there he continued until he reached Sa Ká ("Our Place"), the ancestral "homeland" of the Cabécar people close to the border of Panama. For Marian— and even for me—it was an act of faith to give our consent for the risky venture. In fact, we delayed so long that rainy season was beginning before we had peace about letting him go. True, he had been to Chirripó many times on his own, and had crossed the ridge to Telire before—which involved a twelve-hour trek from the last hut in Chirripó over the 7,000-foot ridge to the first hut in Telire. But the final stretch from Telire to Sa Ká (San José Cabécar) involved a few days on a rarely-used trail that he had never before traveled—a total wilderness with no huts at all. Timothy was never far from our thoughts those eighteen days as we prayed for his safety and for the Lord's purposes to be accomplished.

Timothy did return safely, reporting that the lonely trail, where he could easily have lost his way, had providentially just been reopened by a group of Indians traveling from Chirripó to take the annual head tax to the prophet-priest in San José Cabécar. This trail was normally used only once a year by those transporting the money to pay for the services of the *sakichawí* who guarded the sacred stones that determined the fate of the Cabécar people—and of the world itself. As Timothy reached the unfamiliar trail, he was greeted by the group on their way back to Chirripó. Before continuing home to spread the news of the prediction made by the *sakichawí* as to next year's weather and harvest, they gave Timothy the advice he needed for navigating the trail.

Two months later Timothy made a short trek through Telire, this time with Peter, learning new trails and making new contacts. In the evenings they would sing and share a passage of Scripture with their host and then pray for the family. If there seemed to be interest, they would plan to return on a later trip. At one home in Telire, they even found a tattered copy of the Gospel of Mark that Steven had sold to an Indian two years previously in Estrella, a day's walk away! (By then hundreds of copies of the six Scripture portions already published were scattered all over the Cabécar Indian territory.)

The following year Timothy, Philip, and David—now 19, 16, and 14—trekked together from our house through Chirripó to Telire and on down to Estrella. This trip was sparked by a new understanding of the spiritual opposition we faced in reaching the Indians. Timothy's inspiration came from a pastor in the States who had never been to Costa Rica. This pastor had drawn a rough map of Cabécar territory, indicating a few points where prayer needed to be focused against the demonic forces that controlled the area. Timothy recognized these places as sites that were important to the Indian religion.

The boys set out from Tsipirí planning not to minister at various homes but rather to travel quickly to the key points where they planned to pray. Few people gave them food along the way; in fact, they went four days without finding anything at all to eat. When they arrived in Estrella nine days after leaving Tsipirí, we were there to greet them. In fact, as we drove around the last corner, we spotted them just ahead of us on the road. They hopped on the back of the Toyota and rode the last hundred yards to Peter's house! Marian was overjoyed to see her "three little boys"—grubby and skinny, but safe and sound.

The Family Develops in Ministry

Our sons were growing up among the Cabécars and unwittingly being trained of God for the future. Marian once remarked, "We established a beachhead and held it until our sons grew up and established the church." This was an oversimplification, but it held some truth.

Although our older sons eventually developed different roles, they were one in heart and soul with the younger boys and us in our desire to reach the Indians. Yet it was our three youngest—"the three little boys"—who would ultimately take the lead among the Cabécars.

In reality, our sons were building on our shoulders. They had more time, and were traveling farther than I could. They knew the trails and the river crossings. They were also more advanced in the Cabécar language, especially the younger sons. They understood the culture, and were well acclimated to the Cabécar diet and lifestyle. They knew the people, their clan structure, their kinship relationships and their beliefs. They themselves were well-known all over the Cabécar territory. However, their involvement was not part of some master plan. In fact, we had not even anticipated it.

Peter kept probing in Estrella, looking for people interested in the gospel, as well as trying to establish a literacy program in that area. He also made occasional trips to Chirripó, traveling by car to Tsipirí and from there on foot to the Indians. Occasionally he trekked overland from Estrella up to Telire and across the ridge to Chirripó. More and more, however, he was drawn into training others for cross-cultural ministry.

Steven would come and go from the States, helping with building projects and participating in ministry trips. His visits greatly encouraged and strengthened not only us but the believers as well. Often the Lord would give him a new song that ministered to us all, or he would lead us in powerful prayer. He talked of returning to Costa Rica on a permanent basis, but those desires never became a reality. More than once he said, "It's time to return to Costa Rica." Yet as we look back, we can see that the Lord had other plans for him.

Although we lived in a "man's world," our three daughters also played a role in fulfilling our vision. They helped in the ministry as they were able, at times trekking with me or their brothers. In Tsipirí they helped Marian make our isolated base into a real home and haven. In the 1980s, however, Priscilla was beginning her own missionary career, and Susanna was continuing preparation in the States, but Elizabeth was still with us part of the time. Once when a group of Cabécars arrived at our door as night fell, she cheerfully prepared fifteen meals and served forty-five mugs of coffee within the next hour.

Elizabeth preparing a meal at Tsipirí

Inching Forward on the Translation

Over the years a steady trickle of Scripture portions we sold to the Indians went to the remote corners of the tribe—each book potential "dynamite." Meanwhile, I kept on translating. At the end of 1984 I was doing the final revision of I Corinthians and working on the first draft of II Corinthians. I was also completing the final revision of Matthew, which Marian had begun to type—a job she enjoyed.

We had just made the switch from manual typewriter to computer. Once Marian learned to use it, she loved it. Previously she didn't start typing a book until I had made three handwritten drafts. Now she began to type my first draft. Clean, corrected copy was easy to come by—but we used more paper! And with multiple translation helpers, paying the rising minimum wage sometimes stretched our finances.

Reading the Gospel of Luke

All translation was done with Cabécar helpers. Benjamín was a loyal and dependable helper for the most part, but Célimo had not showed up for work in months. Victor Manuel was talking of leaving the area. As a helper, he was picky and critical but that made him valuable, though difficult to work with. I had one new helper, Isaac, the son of Reigildo. Though young and inexperienced, he was beginning to develop spiritual insight. It was a pleasure to work with a committed believer. Actually, he had asked to be in on the translation process.

In May of 1985 we received word that the Gospel of Luke was finally published—three years after we originally submitted the manuscript. The copies were waiting for us at the office of the Bible Society in San José. With the publication of Luke there were now eighteen books of the New Testament available in seven separate volumes. The second reprint of the Gospel of Mark was also ready to be picked up. Supplies of the original run and the first reprint had long since been exhausted.

When I had first tried out the draft of Luke at Bible studies before submitting the manuscript for publication, the passage we looked at one Sunday was from chapter eleven, where Jesus referred to Jonah's preaching in Nineveh and to the Queen of Sheba having traveled to hear the wisdom of Solomon. At the end of the discussion, I asked the sharpest man in the group for a summary.

"When Jonah preached in Nineveh," he responded, "the Queen of Sheba heard and told Solomon!"

His answer illustrated a very real problem for people who haven't the foggiest notion of the time span in the historical allusions in the New Testament, or of the geography of the Bible lands. Furthermore, he totally missed the point of the passage—that people should heed Jesus' wisdom for He is greater than Solomon, and should repent at His preaching for He is greater than Jonah. So I continued praying for comprehension on the part of the readers, as well as for clear, accurate translation on our part.

New Beginning across the River

The healing of Efraín's daughter late in 1983 proved to be the turning point in the birth of the church. At the time I wrote, "God may have begun to answer our prayer for a breakthrough." Why did I feel that? Was it prophetic? This was also a turning point for our sons. They were the ones who took the initiative in following up Efraín's interest.

For the first year and a half after our initial contacts with him, Efraín was on his own, with very little discipleship. His home was too far from Tsipirí for me to go regularly, but our younger boys continued visiting occasionally.

In July 1984 Peter, Steven, and Timothy went on an overnight trek to Efraín's. We wrote, "Efraín is eager to know the Word, so they taught him until exhaustion overcame them. Efraín gives evidence of being a true believer and willingly renounced his pagan beliefs and practices. He is active in teaching others to read and encourages them to study the Scriptures."

Three months later when Elizabeth and Philip went with me to Efraín's, I had a chance to see for myself that something truly spontaneous was happening. By this time Efraín often gathered a group of extended family members and neighbors for meetings. Philip was moved by their singing; he felt it was the first time he ever really worshipped with Indians. I was very impressed with Efraín's hunger for the Word of God. He had acquired copies of all Scripture portions published up to that point. However, although he was a natural teacher, he was a poor farmer. Furthermore, his house was flea-infested and falling down, the worst Indian house I ever slept in. Yet what mattered was that the Lord was at work.

In a prayer letter in January 1985 we wrote, "In Chirripó the focus is on Efraín's group. He continues to lead a sizable group of Indians in Bible study, prayer, and singing. They are reaching out, evangelizing, and praying for the sick. Our sons always come back thrilled by the intensity of their victory over old fears and beliefs. Now Efraín is planning to build a chapel. Is this a breakthrough?" (We had watched too many beginnings "fizzle" not to be cautious!)

Timothy Links with Efraín

Timothy's contacts with Efraín happened when he was home on vacation from Bible College. After he finished school, however, he became totally involved in ministry there across the Chirripó River, staying at Efraín and Adelina's home for weeks at a time. I was impressed with Timothy's ministry, but was puzzled when he said he was praying for a fresh calling. He wasn't himself, for he had left a girlfriend in the States.

All five of our sons were present in September 1985 for a weekend conference at Efraín's, complete with portable generator and sound system! And the following month there was a second conference, this time to inaugurate a chapel there, using the tin roofing from the old chapel at Antonio's. Shortly, however, Timothy left to spend a month in South Carolina, only to find out that the girl on his mind apparently wasn't up to facing life in the jungle. (Certainly it would be no picnic!) Soon the "old" Timothy was back in Costa Rica, speaking of his "new commitment."

By January 1986 Timothy reported that two dozen adults plus several children were meeting regularly at Efraín's. The believers were reaching out to others and visiting sick neighbors to pray for healing. One resistant neighbor dropped his opposition after God touched his sick children.

Holy Week 1986

Action continued to intensify across the river at Jamárítábá, Efraín's place. For the four-day Holy Week Conference in 1986 about fifty adult Cabécars were in attendance, representing eighteen families. Timothy had helped Efraín build a substantial house so that there would be room to accommodate visitors.

"This conference was when the Cabécar church was born," said Philip when I discussed the conference with him years later.

The relationship of our younger sons with Efraín and his family was a two-way relationship—a strong, personal, impacting friendship, stronger than some would recommend. (An older missionary once counseled me concerning missionary relationships with the locals: "Friends with all; intimate with none.") Yet at the time we very much liked what we saw in Efraín and were happy for our boys to be involved.

Late in May of that year Timothy took a team of five Indians, including Efraín, on a two-week trek to the remote Telire Valley. (On this trip Timothy discovered some old men who still remembered meeting me when I explored the area twenty-five years earlier.) The team found food, lodging, and open doors for the gospel—plus marijuana runners. They also received a warm invitation to return soon.

By July a literacy thrust was going on at Efraín's. Marian had worked extra hours, producing materials. Philip helped teach reading there, but his main ministry was music. Like Steven, he hauled his guitar over the hills and through the rains and across the rivers. The Lord gave him new songs, as He so often did for Steven. For Marian and me, it was exciting to follow the rapid developments at Efraín's as Timothy and Philip and David returned to Tsipirí with their reports. Efraín himself occasionally came to Tsipirí to visit. On one of these visits he had professed to receive Christ as Savior. Things kept happening in such quick succession that it made up for all the years of weary seed sowing.

"Shake the Dust off Your Feet"

Around this time the pastor of one of our supporting churches wrote that he was coming for a visit, saying he hoped to be an encouragement. We were excited that he was interested. Few pastors ever visit their missionaries. When I picked him up at the airport, we drove directly to Tsipirí, for I wanted to give him the greatest possible exposure during his short stay. The next morning, after working together on the road awhile, he talked with Timothy at length and heard all that God was doing across the river at Efraín's. His reaction surprised us; he felt that Timothy was too independent and that our new mission did not give us adequate field supervision. He also was concerned that we seemed to be building an 'empire.'

The next day he trekked with me to Súfu, where we met with the thriving group that had arisen out of the "ashes" of the original chapel. More than twenty Indians were gathered for the Bible study at José's house that Sunday. The pastor watched as the happy group worshipped and interacted; then they listened to his testimony as a meal cooked on the fire at the center of the hut.

After the meeting we ate and then made the long, tricky descent to the stream at the bottom of the hill. Before we began the 1900 foot climb up the other side—too steep for horses—we paused to get a second wind.

"Since the Indians have not responded, don't you think you should shake the dust from your feet and leave?" asked the pastor as we rested.

"I can't leave now!" I blurted out. "I'd lose everything I've done!"

Actually, the Cabécar church was already born, but not even we realized it at the time.

Decisions at Súfu

The interest at Efraín's was exciting, yet at the same time the yeast of the Word was working silently but powerfully at Súfu. In the Bible studies I never made a public appeal for decisions, trusting rather the accumulated effect of reading the Word of God. However, I did check out people one-on-one as to their understanding and commitment. Yet it was during a meeting at Súfu late in 1986 that crippled Margarita spontaneously made a clear confession of her sins, claiming forgiveness through the blood of Christ. She cried as she did so—the first Indian I ever saw cry. Margarita, who had learned to read in our meetings and who had been faithfully hobbling over the hills to our Bible studies for ten years, also pardoned her enemies that day!

After Margarita's confession, José Gilberto's sister Mayela also confessed her sins and prayed for forgiveness. Mayela, a young wife, had been ailing for years because of the curse of a witch doctor. Other, more powerful witch doctors had not been able to break the curse, but after her confession we prayed for her healing. She gradually improved to the point that she resumed household duties, though she still couldn't work in the fields. Her husband noticed the change in her, but it would be many more years before her full deliverance.

Though blessings increased, the monthly trek to Súfu remained a challenge. One Sunday as I faced another three-hour trek to José and Patricia's house, everything in me rebelled at the thought. My knees had been bothering me for several years already. Timothy, still recuperating from a trip, kindly offered to go in my place, but I declined.

"If Caleb could conquer a mountain at eighty-five," I said, "I can go to Súfu at sixty-four!"

We did have a good meeting that day, for although few had blessings to share, most admitted they had sins to confess. That was new!

By the time Margarita and Mayela prayed to receive Christ, a score of other Indians had also confessed their sins and trusted in Christ. All this happened in 1986, although in our previous thirty years among the Cabécars no one would even admit guilt! The core group at Súfu continued faithful in attendance, but it was not until more than a decade later that the Holy Spirit brought victory over sin in certain individuals.

Testings

September 1986 marked the first anniversary of Timothy and Efraín's group. Even I went to the celebration, though I had to walk twice as far as to Súfu. However, Efraín himself—ten days overdue from a trip—did not appear. Peter went to look for him and found him a hundred miles away in a hospital, deathly ill with complications from measles.

After Efraín returned home, the disease spread through his whole family, involving us in more hospital trips. My Toyota still served as ambulance for the Indians. Timothy initiated a vaccination program, obtaining help from public health workers. We failed in our efforts to secure a helicopter to evacuate one very sick young man from Timothy's group, but some new believers went to see him, laid hands on him and prayed. He took a turn for the better, but the epidemic continued to spread.

It was crisis time in Chirripó with serious illness in every home. The Indians had no natural immunity to this disease from the outside world. For us it was a relief—when the epidemic subsided—to spend a week in Santa Ana, away from the constant rains, the sea of mud, the pressure of translating, the weekend commitments, the interruptions from Indians asking for favors, and the commotion of Red Cross and public health workers trying to help Timothy control the spread of epidemic.

Opposition Again

In addition to local testings, opposition cropped up again. Demonstrators in 1985 accused us of buying up Indian lands, building a military base, and of being linked with the CIA. Our presence in the area had been challenged before, but this demonstration was carried on nationwide TV. Our Indian friends later defended us against the false charges.

The following year our names appeared again in a certain newspaper accusing us foreigners of "bothering the Indians" — not to speak of other charges. Changes in the Bureau of Indian Affairs brought unrest in some Cabécar areas, where I continued to meet each month with a small group interested in the Scriptures. Our own presence on the edge of the reservation and our freedom to move about in Indian territory was in question. Even the use of the alphabet we had created was in jeopardy, due to the recent creation of a new alphabet by linguists at the university. Furthermore, anthropologists resented our impact on the religion of the Indians.

As excited as we were about reaping the fruit of the labor of three decades, we were sobered by the opposition, just as the Apostle Paul when he wrote, *"For a great door...is opened unto me, and there are many adversaries."* We needed wisdom, discernment, and humility. Prayer was our recourse. We continued to move forward on our knees, seeking to establish the kingdom of God, doing battle in the name of Jesus.

Still Plugging Away on the Translation

Though the weekends were packed with ministry, translation still dominated my weekdays. Late in 1985 I reported, "Currently, my helpers are working with me on I Corinthians 12-15, a challenge to any translator. My three 'steadies,' Benjamín, Victor Manuel and Célimo are usually here, and an old helper, Virgilio, has returned. Isaac, a trainee, comes infrequently. Last week, after working over the verse, *'If Christ be not raised...ye are yet in your sins,'* Benjamín, for the first time in over fifteen years of translation work, prayed, 'Thank you, Father, for loving us enough to send your son to die for our sins.' More recently, he admitted to Virgilio, 'The religion that the old people taught us is just not true!'" Yet Benjamín still often functioned as "burier," a key person in rituals aiding the departed soul to get past the demons on the road to the nether world.

Benjamín correcting a manuscript

Soon we mimeographed a handout of I Corinthians 15, the resurrection chapter. The idea of a person rising again was an incredible thought to any Cabécar. Those who rejected this truth never came to faith in Jesus, but those who pondered the idea and considered the Scriptures about the resurrection of Jesus usually became believers.

With some trepidation, I asked Victor Manuel, my most capable helper, to attempt a first draft of Ephesians—a very difficult book. His work proved a good starting point for checking with other helpers, although he was not always happy to see his work tested. Around this time, Timothy began trying his hand at translating passages from Genesis. I had done a preliminary translation of the first three chapters of Genesis a year or two before this time, in order to teach my translation helpers the Biblical view of the origin of things.

Genesis later proved to be crucial to the Indians' understanding of Scripture as a whole.

By the middle of 1986 Victor Manuel had started to draft Hebrews and Benjamín had begun a draft of Revelation. This meant that every book in the New Testament had at least been started. (Eighteen books were already for sale.) Furthermore, Timothy had translated several more chapters of Genesis; printouts of chapters one through eleven were already in use. I myself was working over the first draft of Galatians with Benjamín and experiencing what J. B. Phillips felt after doing his Modern English translation; he said that Bible translation is like working on an electric line without turning off the current! Even in the tedious process of checking translation I felt the power of the Word. Marian felt it, too, as she double-checked the translation during the process of keyboarding.

Besides continuing translation, I kept making more copies of the alphabet book—a very popular item. From time to time Marian worked on literacy. We also kept expanding our hymnbook, another popular item. A new edition in 1986 contained thirty songs, including a number of new ones written by Steven. A year later Marian and Philip were working on an edition with fifty songs!

Outreach Expands

Invitations to hold Bible studies started popping up all over. Though interest had waned at the home of my original contact in Pacuare, a new door opened to me there, at the home of Gumercindo. Pacuare was a difficult area, but very needy. Furthermore, changes in the leadership of the Bureau of Indian Affairs brought on much controversy there. Besides Pacuare, I also made trips to Blori and Chofuitey checking out new contacts that Timothy found through Efraín. At least these places were relatively close to Tsipirí.

No longer could I trek as far as my sons! Early in 1987 I turned sixty-five, but Timothy (twenty-two), Philip (nineteen), and David (seventeen) spent much time on the trail. Philip made a survey trip to a distant area of upstream Pacuare where I hadn't been for twenty-five years. David spent three weeks in Telire with Efraín and his son Israel. Although the drug traffic was increasingly serious in Telire, they had no problems. They were able to hold meetings in two areas, with more than two dozen in attendance in each area. Their host and his daughter both made a profession of faith—the first in Telire.

We sensed the pulsation of interest throughout the mountains. Young Indians now went out on their own to teach the Word. Efraín continued to spearhead outreach in several areas. In addition to the chapel on his property, the believers planned to build a more centrally located chapel on "our" side of the Chirripó River on the spot where Efraín's grandfather once lived. That man had heard the gospel through an interpreter from Mr. Jamison, the missionary who lived among the Indians for a short time in 1895.

In January 1987 Efraín and Adelina were legally married, after Timothy helped them obtain the necessary paperwork. We all went to the county courtroom in Turrialba to witness the civil ceremony. (Protestant marriage was still not legal in Costa Rica.) Later we had a small celebration at Tsipirí and blessed their union. Their marriage, after years of living together, was a victory, as well as a precedent for the emerging church—at least in my eyes. Not that anyone was anxious to follow their example!

Dean Lewis Returns to Chirripó

It was Timothy's idea to invite Dean Lewis to the Holy Week Conference in 1987 at Efraín's place. He wanted Dean to come and see with his own eyes the result of his early vision to reach the Indians in Chirripó. Thirty-seven years had passed since Dean's first trip to investigate the need for a missionary. In the meantime he had gone on to serve the Lord in various Spanish-speaking countries. Now the Cabécar church was blossoming.

Dean and his wife Colista came to our house at Tsipirí, by the creek where Dean and I had rested when I first trekked with him to Chirripó in 1953. After a night's rest, he and I said goodbye to our wives and set out for the ten-hour trek to Jamáritábá, twice as far as Dean and I had traveled on our first trek together. As we walked, he begged me to be easy on him. I jokingly reminded him that he hadn't been easy on me on my first trip! However, I assured him, "Yes, I'll go easy on you; this trip is hard on me too." (Actually, I was a month older than Dean but in better health.) Along the way we greeted people who remembered him. That afternoon as we crossed the Chirripó River, we still had to face the 45-minute climb to Efraín's—so hard for Dean, though he never complained.

To the left: Efraín and Timothy leading the meeting
To the right: Aziel, Dean, and Peter

Sixty Filled the Chapel

More than sixty Cabécars filled the chapel at Jamárítábá that evening, three times as many as had ever attended one of my Bible studies. Timothy and Philip had gone ahead to make preparations for the conference—including arranging for a horse to carry a portable generator so there would be light for the meeting. David was there as well. Peter and Debbie and their children came all the way from Estrella to attend. Indians came from the various groups that Timothy and Efraín were by then overseeing. A few came from my Bible study groups.

What excitement! What praying and singing! Philip and five Indians accompanied the singing—he had taught them to play the guitar. As the believers sang, Dean pulled out a tiny tape recorder and asked cautiously if it would be culturally acceptable to record the singing. Of course, there were already three battery-operated recorders, including a big "boom box," on the table—all belonging to Indians! The meeting lasted well past midnight as several Indians "preached." Timothy and I, as well as Peter, shared in the ministry of the Word. Dean was asked to give a greeting, as Timothy translated.

Five Baptisms

The next day we all went back down that 45-minute hill to a spot where I baptized Efraín and four family members. (It never occurred

to me at the time that I should have given Dean that honor.) Near the baptismal site lived a man who thirty-eight years before, had been named for Dean as an infant. Dean had brought a nice gift for him. The man had been a friend of mine, but the family ' had been poisoned against us by the Communists. When we got to his house, an older man came out threatening me with his machete, so Dean's thoughtfulness was thwarted. (Never before had I been threatened with a machete in a Cabécar hut.) However, before I turned away, I was able to slip to the man's wife a picture which Dean had taken of her when she was a child. Then we trudged slowly back up the hill to Efraín's.

The Awful Trek Back

The following day Dean and I stuck together as we slowly trekked the ten hours back to Tsipirí. First, down the hill again from Efraín's and across the white-water Chirripó, bracing ourselves with walking sticks cut from a canebrake at the edge of the river. On the other side the trail climbed steeply up from the river for three hours until it led through a pasture sloping more gently upward for another hour or more. Finally, we sloshed for a couple of hours along the more level, but muddier, root-laced trail along the shady summit.

When we reached Reigildo's house, Dean was given a refreshing drink which revived him somewhat. By this time Peter had caught up with us, although he had started later and was carrying a large pack plus his youngest child. Then Peter also took Dean's small pack in order to conserve his waning strength for the last stretch. Soon it was downhill, but slippery and full of holes and roots. Resting frequently, Dean continued with the aid of a walking stick in each hand until we finally reached Tsipirí. Totally exhausted, he staggered up the driveway to our house.

Dean's Vision Fulfilled

What a privilege it was to take Dean to Jamáritábá! There he saw with his own eyes the fulfillment of his vision thirty-seven years before when he stood looking across the Chirripó Valley and asked the Lord if he should take the gospel to these Indians. Looking up, Dean had noticed a rainbow arching across the deep valley and had heard the Lord say, "I love these people. Someday there will be a church among them." Marian and I had responded to the need to reach the Cabécars. Dean's vision became ours.

Now with my own eyes I was seeing our own vision fulfilled. Here was what Timothy had tried to tell the pastor who visited us in 1986. My mind raced, reviewing all the years of mud, sweat and tears, the years of translating and checking, the years of trekking, teaching and praying. Though the emerging church was yet to be tried by fire, we did have a church—by some definition—thanks to José Gilberto and Efraín and my sons.

Dean's rainbow of promise - 1950

– 22 –
A Church for Grano de Oro
1975 to 1987

As the Lord was building His church among the Cabécars, He was also touching the lives of the Latins who lived in Grano de Oro near the edge of Indian territory. Grano de Oro had once been part of a vast ranch called *Hacienda Moravia*, developed in the 1940s by a Costa Rican coffee grower. The legendary Fernando Alvarado Chacón had established his own "Shangri-La" in a high, hidden valley about thirty miles southeast of Turrialba. To access the valley he had built miles of one-lane gravel roads and even a suspension bridge over the Pacuare River.

When I first arrived in Moravia in 1953, I found a sawmill, a dairy farm, and beautiful coffee groves amid the timberlands on the hills at the edges of the ranch. At the center of everything was a school, a church, and a large home for the owner. The workers' houses were well-constructed and neatly painted. A hydroelectric plant provided lights. Unfortunately, the owner had overspent and the creditor had foreclosed, leaving an administrator to oversee his affairs. Soon, another creditor foreclosed in Grano de Oro, a mile or so west of Moravia.

The night I arrived in Moravia on my first solo trip after language school, two of the farm workers sought me out to inquire about the gospel. How did they know I was an evangelical, I wondered? For the next ten years I passed through the area almost every month as I trekked to Chirripó. I got to know most of the workers and talked to some of them about the Lord. One man became interested and bought a Bible. His young son, Javier, enjoyed winding the gospel phonograph I loaned them. The father eventually lost interest, but the boy never forgot the message of those records he listened to so often.

The administrator of Moravia replaced no workers, made no repairs, neglected the coffee trees, and let the cattle die. We watched the sickening decline as "Shangri-La" gradually became "Ichabod." By the the time we moved to Tsipirí, located beyond the ridge to the east of the ranch, even the bus service had become erratic. When a new bus driver, a professed evangelical, moved to Moravia, he asked me to start a Bible study at his house. He himself did not attend, yet some of Javier's family did. The bus driver soon organized a *turno,* a local fair, to revive this dying community, and then absconded with the money that was raised. His departure was another dead end for the gospel.

Grano de Oro Becomes a Center

As Moravia declined, Grano de Oro absorbed many of the former workers. However, with an absentee creditor and no overseer, it became a village of *precaristas* (occupants with a "precarious" legal basis). A man named Moisés, who ran the local general store and bar, was the chief *comerciante* (trader), buying corn, beans, and pigs from the Indians, and selling salt, sugar, boots, machetes, and other items to both Indians and local Latins. Moisés had been brought to Grano de Oro by the original owner and had now moved into the vacant house of a creditor who foreclosed. With several capable grown sons, *don* Moisés was an important man in the community.

Grano de Oro had been a coffee farm, with the name "Grain of Gold," based on a wordplay reflecting the economic value and color of the dried coffee bean (called in Spanish "grano de café"). Gradually, all the land was claimed and boundary fights began. Other stores opened, with more Latins acting as middlemen for Indian produce. Most Latins had small farms, with Cabécar Indians working as day laborers. Grano de Oro eventually reached its potential of about 450 scattered inhabitants. By this time we had established our base in Tsipirí, four miles east of the center of Moravia and almost six miles east of Grano de Oro.

Javier, the boy who loved to crank the gospel phonograph, had grown up, married, and grabbed his piece of land. One day he stopped my jeep.

"When are you coming to my house to teach me?" he asked.

Surprised, I went to visit him. Several times I took my family with me, providing a Sunday afternoon outing on the weekends when I didn't teach a Bible study in Chirripó. Though Javier and his wife professed faith in Jesus, they seemed slow to grasp the Word. Their house was not up to local standards nor did he have a good standing in the community.

A Chance Meeting

One Sunday in June of 1975 as I was on the trail to Chirripó for a Bible study, I met Elena, an older, married daughter of *don* Moisés. (Like her brothers, she also traded with the Indians.)

"Oh, *don* Aziel," she said excitedly, "two missionary ladies came to Grano de Oro last night on their way to Chirripó. They had a meeting in Papa's house. We loved it!"

A light went on in my mind. Did I feel a bit of "competition?" After all, these missionary ladies—Costa Ricans from the capital— were on "my turf." Yet I had been praying for Elena's whole clan— albeit with very little faith. Marian, too, had been praying for the extended family ever since a grown son of *don* Moisés and his family had lived near us in Tsipirí.

"Elena," I responded, "I'd be glad to lead a Bible study in Grano de Oro if you would like!"

"Fine," she answered.

When I asked where we could meet, she said, "At Papa's house."

Elena agreed to ask him, but I couldn't believe he would be interested! The next day, however, she came to Tsipirí to buy a Spanish Bible. She had asked me the previous day if I could get her a Bible. Even at our remote location, I always kept a stock of Bibles for sale. With some trepidation I then asked what her father, *don* Moisés, had said about a meeting the following week.

His Answer? "Yes!"

Amazing! I couldn't believe that *don* Moisés had said yes! Actually, I had planned to start going to Chirripó on Saturdays for a Bible study that evening, and then have another Bible study the next morning at a house an hour away. Was I willing to give up my plans for more time in Chirripó? I never forgot that my first calling was to the Cabécars, yet I knew that Jesus had "other sheep" besides the Indians. Elena and I agreed that I would come the following Saturday. At least I could still go to Chirripó on Sunday.

When Saturday came, Grano de Oro was on my mind. Later I wrote in my diary: "At eleven I settled down to fast and pray primarily for the service we'd have in Grano de Oro tonight. I never did feel like I prayed well. A pain in the back of my head made it hard to pray. In fact, neither Marian nor I had any desire to go."

On that first night we waited over an hour in Elena's father's living room. The gloom was alleviated only by a couple of candles. Finally, Moisés closed the bar, brought home the pressure lantern, hung it on a nail over the doorway, and then went to the kitchen to eat his supper. We felt awkward, not only because we didn't know what response we would get, but also because I had once clashed with *don* Moisés.

The room was full. Our whole family was there. Many from the extended family of *don* Moisés were there. Javier and his family were also present. None of them had ever been in an evangelical church, yet the overall response was encouraging. In the meeting we followed an inductive Bible study format, using a modern version. Elena's father knew more Scripture than we thought. We even sold two Bibles and two hymnbooks that evening.

Before we left, Moisés's teenage daughters served us dessert and coffee, good Latin style. As we chatted with Elena, we found that both she and Filomena, her aunt, had made a profession of faith the night that the two Church of God missionary ladies had preached. Never did we have any reason to doubt the genuineness of their faith.

"And what about next week?" I asked cautiously as we left.

Yes, we would meet. We retuned home to Tsipirí about eleven P.M., greatly encouraged! The next week we had another good meeting with the group, but as we left, we had to tell them that we were leaving Costa Rica to drive, overland, to the States for Peter and Debbie's wedding.

Upon returning to Grano de Oro two months later we faced the nagging question: Would we be able to continue services? Once more the answer was yes!

So every Saturday evening at five o'clock we loaded the family in our Toyota and "plowed" out of our "hole" in Tsipirí, often with all four wheels spinning and mud flying. About an hour later—five and a half miles—we arrived in Grano de Oro. After greeting people, we sat on the old, worn-out easy chairs in the dark *sala,* waiting for *don* Moisés to close the *cantina,* bring in the lantern, eat his supper, and then give us permission to start the service. The meeting was set for 6:00 P.M., but sometimes we didn't get started until 8:00.

Open Bible Approach

Interest increased. More and more people took turns reading the Scripture we were studying. After a few meetings Moisés's wife, *doña* Chala, and her sister, *doña* Filomena—women who had minimal education and had never done much reading—pulled out their glasses and deciphered a verse. More and more of the group answered questions and commented on the passage we'd read from the Spanish *Versión Popular,* the original model of *Good News for Modern Man.* As the group grew in knowledge of the Word, they began to internalize the Scriptures.

When visitors from a well-established rural church came for a weekend, we discovered that the group in Grano de Oro had a better understanding of Scripture than the visitors, who had been brought up on preaching rather than inductive Bible study. We were blessed to see how our "open Bible approach" had opened up the Word to the new people in Grano de Oro. Their response was worth what it cost us—a commitment every Saturday night, fallen trees, landslides, and flooded creeks, notwithstanding. Often on a stormy night the group would greet us, saying they didn't think we'd come!

My Friend the Campesino

The Costa Ricans I knew best were these rural people— *campesinos*. No doubt my Spanish today reflects the local country talk. All Indian areas are surrounded by Latin *campesinos*, so I related to them regularly, a natural for this barefoot boy from small-town Alabama. In fact, I felt more comfortable in rural homes in Costa Rica than in those in the capital city. Even though Grano de Oro was populated by rural folk, storekeepers like Moisés and his family were on a level above the machete-swinging *peón*. We saw this and built upon it. Yet when any person, anywhere, of any social strata, has an encounter with the living God and His Word, his heart is transformed, gifts are released, and that person's "God-potential" is sometimes amazing. We had seen it when we ministered to the professors at the Agricultural Institute in Turrialba; we saw it again here among rural *Latinos*, and eventually in Chirripó among the Cabécar Indians as well.

A Fresh Touch

During the Christmas holidays in 1975, a few months after we started meeting in Grano de Oro, CAM missionaries Mark and Barbara visited us. During the service they introduced new songs, accompanied by Barb's guitar. The people loved it! Back in Tsipirí that night, although it was late, Mark and Barb poured out their hearts to God with us in fervent prayer for the Lord to work. From that night on, we sensed a fresh touch on the little group in Grano de Oro. It seemed as though God had put His seal of blessing on our ministry there.

When I needed to be away on a Saturday, I sometimes invited a lay preacher from the rural CAM church in San Joaquín de La Suiza to take charge of the service. Marco Tulio had been an old "drinking buddy" of the men in Grano de Oro, but was now a joyful evangelist. On another occasion I invited the men from the CAM church in Turrialba. One of them did come out to Grano de Oro on the bus and spent the weekend. Later I heard that he had been rather undiplomatic. However, *doña* Chala, Moisés's wife, got saved under his ministry. We were cautiously optimistic.

Javier's Baptism

Javier and his family had all come for our first meeting and subsequent meetings. He was from one of the other large families in the village. In 1976 he asked for baptism. As I questioned him, I knew his testimony was weak, yet I felt I should proceed.

"I want my baptism to be public, for everybody to see," said Javier. He chose the most central spot in the village. It could not have been more public!

As we went down to the water, forty sets of local eyes were watching. I suddenly felt very self-conscious: I was no longer the *gringo* working with the Indians back in Chirripó. Instead, I was now an evangelical pastor—a new public role for me. I was breaking into a solidly Catholic community. I had put *my* reputation on the line for Javier's faith. If he failed to live up to his profession, I would feel like a fool. I wondered if other missionaries ever felt that.

"Someday Chala and I hope to be baptized too," confided *doña* Filomena quietly to Marian as we walked away from the river after the baptism. She and *doña* Chala were the only two from our group of around twenty who had the courage to watch the baptism. Not even Javier's wife was there—only curious onlookers.

More Baptisms

Early in 1977 two teenage girls from the group—Chala's daughter Pércide and Filomena's daughter Alcira—made professions of faith.

On Christmas Day of that year we had our family celebration in Tsipirí, then hurried to Grano de Oro for our first group baptism. Not only did I baptize *doña* Chala and *doña* Filomena and the two teenage girls, but also Filomena's husband, as well as our own teenagers, Elizabeth and Timothy.

All gave good testimonies, including Felo, Filomena's husband. He had once hit me in the face on a pitch dark night—hit me with a rubber boot, in which he had hidden a liquor bottle. Yet now he spoke boldly to his drinking buddies present. In her testimony Alcira told how she had sat week by week in the Bible studies waiting for me to invite people to receive Jesus. Finally, in desperation, she went to her room, got on her knees, and asked the Lord to save her. Pércide spoke of wanting to be ready for the Lord's return.

As the crowd at the river dispersed, those who were baptized went to Felo and Filomena's house for the Lord's Supper—a less public location than *don* Moisés's house. Before the Supper I laid my hands on each to receive the fullness of the Holy Spirit and then asked each to pray. I had done the same with Javier the previous year, before celebrating the first Lord's Supper with him.

Marian was especially happy about *doña* Filomena's baptism, for she had been praying for the family for several years. At that time they were living near us in Tsipirí and one of Filomena's older daughters worked for us. We always read the Bible and prayed with her at the noon meal; she, in turn, told her mother about the Scripture. Furthermore, Filomena had heard the Christian radio station as she passed by the house of one of our helpers. We learned from the grapevine that Filomena had expressed interest in the gospel even then.

On Good Friday of 1978 there were three more baptisms. That day I baptized Felo and Filomena's son, Rafael Moisés, who was named for both his father and grandfather. "Moisecito," as he was usually called, was our Steven's close friend. He had promised Steven he would accept Jesus and later his sister Alcira led him to faith. Another of those baptized was Lourdes, the youngest daughter of *doña* Chala. She was now a teenager and had professed to receive

Christ. During the baptismal service Mireya, Javier's wife, appeared and asked to be baptized, so I included her as well.

What about the "Saints?"

In those days rural homes in Costa Rica were decorated with pictures of the heart of Mary or the heart of Jesus or the Holy Trinity. These pictures were called "saints." We never mentioned the pictures nor spoke against Roman Catholic doctrine unless a question came up in the Bible study.

The *sala* where we met at Moisés's house was almost filled at Christmas with a huge *portal*—manger scene—in front of a large Christmas tree. At midnight on Christmas Eve a doll representing the "Infant God" was added to the manger to be worshipped. During the first few years we held Christmas services in Grano de Oro, we squeezed into one side of the room and some sat in the hallway as we sang and read the Word. The family would hold their ceremony later. After some years the *portal* disappeared. So did the "saints." The believers no longer needed these images to bolster their faith. However, we learned much later that *don* Moisés had kept the saints in a box under his bed.

From Moisés's House to Felo's House

After meeting for five years at the home of Moisés and Chala, I worked it out with Felo and Filomena to hold the weekly meetings at their home. There I could begin the meetings on time rather than waiting for *don* Moisés to close the *cantina*. However, I failed to clear my decision with the group. This bothered Moisés, as well as his family who hoped he would get saved if we continued meeting at his house. Because I had not been diplomatic, I received a lot of flack. I feared the worst, but within a few weeks everyone was cooperating. Felo's house proved to be a peaceful meeting place.

Spontaneous Response

As the believers matured they began reading the Word daily on their own. During a meeting I often asked, "What has the Lord impressed upon you in your reading?" Often they related what they had read to events of the week. After a few years both *doña* Chala and *doña* Filomena began to respond with references not just from the New Testament but from the Old. Each eventually read the whole Bible through more than once, though reading was difficult for them. I never tired of seeing the power of the Word of God at work in the believers' lives!

We wanted to instill not just knowledge of Scripture but response, both verbally and in changed lives. The believers edified and exhorted one another, talking about the Lord naturally both in the meetings and at other times. Although none of our group had previously attended an evangelical church, many learned to hear God speaking to them personally through the Scripture!

"If You Can, You Ought To"

One rainy Saturday night we were late leaving for the service in Grano de Oro. It was already dark when we drove away—darkness comes early in the tropics. When we reached the creek, I waded in to test the depth. The creek was swollen, but not too deep to cross if I took off the fan belt. (I had asked my mechanic to remove the catalytic converter, which was not legally required. Without it, I only had to loosen a single nut in order to take off the fan belt.) I opened the hood to loosen the nut, but it was already late and I was wet to the knees, so I slammed the hood and got back in the Toyota, saying, "We're not going."

Elizabeth, by then a teenager, responded, "Daddy, if you *can*, you ought to." Where did she learn that? So I got out again and loosened the fan belt. After crossing the two little creeks bordering our property, I stopped, tightened the belt, and proceeded. We had a good meeting and got home with no problem. However, a few times we had to abandon the jeep on the way home from a meeting when we encountered a newly-fallen tree and had to walk down the muddy, slippery hill to the house with the aid of flashlights.

The Washout

Our greatest test for getting to Grano de Oro began late in 1980 when heavy rains washed out a culvert a mile from the center of Moravia (which by then was owned by the Kibbey brothers from Ohio). When Timothy tried to detour around the washout by driving through a pasture, our old Toyota bogged down in the mud, so he walked the remaining miles to Tsipirí. The Kibbeys helped us by extricating our vehicle from the muck with their tractor and driving it to their house for safekeeping. They even changed the oil, since the Toyota had sat in water for two days. For seven long months until the road was repaired, we walked three miles to the washout, crossed on a plank, continued another mile to Dale Kibbey's house, and then drove the last stretch to Grano de Oro for the Saturday night meeting.

Supplies delivered by oxcart during the washout
(Note propane tank amid boxes of groceries. Also note banana plants in the background.)

After the meeting we drove back to Moravia, left the car with Dale, and walked home from the washout, usually arriving at Tsipirí around midnight. The next morning I had to leave early to trek to my Cabécar Bible study. Looking back now on those walks to and from the washout, I remember only the lovely moonlit nights, the cry of night birds, and the noisy insects—not the mud or the rain. Marian usually went with me, as well as the younger children, who were then teenagers.

For seven months while the road was washed out, we had to walk the same three miles from Tsipirí to the washout in order to get our car for a trip to Turrialba for supplies, or to the capital for meetings or doctors or planes. Bringing our baggage and supplies home from the washout reminded us of our early days in Tsipirí, when there was no road to the house. Now again we had to hire an oxcart to take the diesel fuel, kerosene, propane, lumber, and groceries. Often we remembered the words of the Canadian who had lived in Moravia before the Kibbeys bought it: "Nothing is impossible out here, but everything is more inconvenient!"

The new Toyota at work
(Note winch on bumper, chains on the tires, mud splattered above the back wheel, and Indian standing on back ladder.)

Not long after the road was repaired we were given a special gift which enabled us to buy a thirteen-passenger diesel Toyota—the only new vehicle I ever owned. The donor had firsthand knowledge of the condition of our road and our need to replace the old Toyota. We had been praying for a new vehicle for three years. The Lord provided the ideal vehicle for hauling passengers and supplies on a less than ideal road.

The Kibbeys and Grano de Oro

We had first met Dale Kibbey and his wife Joan when they appeared at our house during a visit to Costa Rica before they bought Moravia. As we conversed with these strangers, we soon discovered that they knew the Lord! They had met and married while serving with the Peace Corps in South America. After their return to the States they came to faith in Christ and later were filled with the Spirit. Piggybacking on an investment their father had made in Moravia, Dale and his brother ended up buying the ranch. That we would be their "neighbors" factored into Dale and Joan's decision to move to Costa Rica—with their six children and Joan's mother.

During the seven months that the road to Moravia was washed out, Joan Kibbey invited us to supper on Saturday nights, knowing we'd be tired after our walk from Tsipirí. Following the meal, Dale and Joan usually went with us to the meeting in Grano de Oro. Even after the road was repaired, they continued to attend the meetings. In fact, on New Year's Eve they hosted a special service at their home in Moravia. More than sixty came, half of whom were unbelievers.

Not only did the washout bond us forever with Dale and Joan, but the Kibbeys earned the love and respect of every person who worked for them, or who lived in the area. Among other things, Dale gave each family in the valley a Spanish Bible, the *Versión Popular*. When the Kibbeys sold the ranch and returned to the States in 1982, I had occasion to go to town about fifteen minutes after Dale and his family drove away. At every house people were standing along the road even as far away as the Pacuare River, after saying *adios* to the Kibbeys.

Noribette's Baptism

Don Moisés and his whole family were capable people, though they blended in well with the community, where only a primary school was available at the time. Noribette, one of the younger daughters of *don* Moisés and *doña* Chala, had left Grano de Oro to work in the capital while continuing her studies. She eventually finished high school and started classes at the university, but sickness and lack of funds caused her to return home. Before she left the capital, however, she talked with a priest about her concerns. Knowing that her relatives were now evangelicals, he cautioned her about their influence.

Marian and I did not meet Noribette until she returned to Grano de Oro. By that time she was actively seeking God. She saw the effect of the gospel in her extended family and talked with her cousin Rafael Moisés, who led her to trust Christ alone for her salvation. When she got saved, others began coming to the meetings. There was a depth, a strength, a mystique about Noribette. Furthermore, she soon developed a very strong devotional life.

Noribette's baptism on Christmas Day 1981 was touched by the Lord. In my diary I gave five lines to our family celebration in Tsipirí, then wrote the rest of the page about her baptism that afternoon before a large crowd in Grano de Oro. "After her testimony of faith in Jesus, I led Noribette to the water and baptized her. As I did so, I was very conscious of the presence of the Lord. Back at Felo's house, we celebrated the Lord's Supper, which was preceded by sharing verses with Noribette. Then I laid hands on her to receive the fullness of the Holy Spirit and she prayed after I had prayed. After the Lord's Supper the group had a round of prayer. Then everyone gave Noribette a kiss or a hug." I knew her baptism would prove significant, but I did not yet see how.

In my diary I wrote that following the service "we all celebrated by eating the traditional Christmas tamales. On our way home we stopped in Moravia for Christmas dinner with the Kibbey family. Later that night as we drove home to Tsipirí, Elizabeth bubbled happily about Noribette. I was very happy to see all this excitement come out of Elizabeth. Our children *were* learning about life in the Spirit! Then before we got out of the car, Elizabeth prayed a long solid prayer. PTL for a *great* day in the Lord. This one will stand out."

The "Nica"

Around the time that Noribette returned home from the capital, a stranger came to work on a farm near Grano de Oro, a Nicaraguan refugee named José Isaac. Soon he began attending our meetings. At each service I asked those present what they wanted us to pray about. One night when I asked for requests, José Isaac answered: "To be saved!" Everyone noticed the change in his life after he prayed to receive Jesus that night. He wanted the whole village to come to his baptism, which was early in 1982, two weeks after Noribette's baptism. A light rain was falling as I baptized him, with a complete rainbow arching over the whole Moravia Valley. Seventy people, most of them unconverted, gathered at the river to witness the event. This was our largest crowd ever at a baptism. At the Lord's Supper which followed, all eleven of the baptized believers were present.

Others Come to Christ

The Holy Spirit continued to move in Grano de Oro throughout 1982. Two more men, Hernán and Luis, made a profession of faith. Although Hernán, who was Felo's brother, kept stumbling and Luis did too, at least Luis now allowed his wife Elena to come to the services. (He had prohibited her from attending during the seven years since her profession of faith led to the start of the meetings.) Four other men were attending the meetings as a result of the testimony of José Isaac and of Noribette.

That year Jeanette, an older sister of Noribette, who had been working in the city for several years, returned to live in Grano de Oro. Jeanette, a single mother with two children, soon came to Christ. So did Ana Lía, a daughter of Luis and Elena. Later in the year Ramón, another Nicaraguan refugee, made a profession of faith. Watching the growth of the believers was a joy!

When Jeanette asked to be baptized, she added that Ana Lía, her eleven-year-old niece, also wanted to be baptized. A week later I learned that Luis, Ana Lía's father, opposed her baptism, even though he himself claimed to be a believer. Her godparents—an aunt and her husband—were violently opposed.

"She'll go to hell if re-baptized," they argued, "and we're responsible for her."

The new priest nagged them on, "Who's this foreigner teaching this false religion?" And, "The Bible doesn't say we have to be baptized in the river."

"But Jesus was!" said *doña* Chala, Jeanette's mother, an uneducated woman but wise in the Scriptures.

A storm had broken loose, putting the whole clan, already split by the gospel, in turmoil. I went to see Luis, asking for permission to baptize Ana Lía. His refusal was courteous but final.

On New Year's Day 1983 Jeanette was baptized in the presence of about seventy local people, including Luis. Forty-two came to the service which followed, when the twelve baptized believers celebrated the Lord's Supper with us—a very special occasion. Afterward *don* Moisés, who occasionally harassed his family about their new faith, reportedly said that he wished all his children would get baptized! He had seen the changes in their lives. Jeanette was the fifth of his many children to be baptized, along with his wife, sister-in-law, and two grandchildren.

Still Increasing in 1983

From week to week a spirit of praise and prayer continued as we met in Grano de Oro. Some weeks there was hardly time left for Bible study. During Holy Week four more believers were baptized. Fifty-five came to the service which followed—the largest number ever. One of those baptized was young Ana Lía, with the blessing of her father, who had refused permission before. (This time Luis told me that since I had respected him and hadn't baptized her against his wishes, he now gave his consent. However, it would be several more years before he would allow his wife to be baptized.) Ana Lía's cousin Wagner, the son of Hernán, was baptized after giving a forceful testimony. Moisés and Chala's youngest son, Johnny, was also baptized, along with his wife Maritza.

Before their marriage, Johnny and Maritza had not attended the meetings. In fact, Maritza was an outsider from another rural community. After their wedding in the Catholic Church in her village, Johnny brought his bride to live in Grano de Oro. When they arrived after the marriage ceremony, we were in the middle of our meeting with the believers. At the time we were still meeting at *don* Moisés's house where our services were often interrupted by the arrival of visitors. We just waited and enjoyed the interruption as everyone greeted the newlyweds.

"Just a minute," called our son Steven as the couple was leaving, "I have a song for you."

Picking up his guitar and his Bible, Steven sang the classic words on marriage from Ephesians 5:22-33. Johnny and Maritza later began coming to the services and eventually came to trust in Christ alone for salvation.

As the gospel spread through the extended family of *don* Moisés and *doña* Chala, a new lie began to circulate in Grano de Oro:

"Aziel is getting rich with the extra bonus he receives for each baptism!"

Perhaps that rumor had arisen when a large gift from a supporter enabled me to purchase a new vehicle. However, in spite of opposition the group grew. In addition to the Saturday night meetings, Noribette initiated a midweek prayer meeting which rotated among the homes of the believers. The first week they met, she led a newcomer to the Lord. She also had an influence in the life of Gladys, a girl who had once worked for Marian. Although Gladys was the daughter of a woman of ill repute, she was seeking the Lord.

When Ramón, the second Nicaraguan refugee to make a profession of faith, asked for baptism, I hesitated due to his interest in Jeanette. Although he attended the services faithfully, I questioned whether he was truly trusting in Jesus or was trying to impress Jeanette. I finally baptized him late in August 1983, but by faith. During a driving rainstorm that muddied the waters, he and our youngest son, David, were baptized in the Moravia River which traverses Grano de Oro. Ramón's faith did prove genuine; he never wavered.

Trained for Service

After we had been meeting in Grano de Oro for a few years, the young people began to show interest in formal Bible training. "Moisecito" was the first to study. With financial help from his father, Felo, who sold a piece of property, Rafael Moisés left early in 1979 for a year at the Guatemalan Bible Institute—three countries and four bus days away from his tiny rural community. Felo cried when his nineteen-year-old namesake boarded the bus. As I put my arm over Felo's shoulder, I thought, "This is a long way from the time Felo struck me in the face that dark night nine years ago."

Three years later when Moisés returned to Guatemala in 1982 to continue his studies, he was accompanied by his cousin Pércide, with the blessing of her father, *don* Moisés. En route to Guatemala they were detained four hours in Nicaragua for questioning because of their Bibles and books. Afterwards Moisés wrote, "We felt like Peter and Paul before the authorities! The Spirit filled us and we weren't afraid of anything or anybody." Their interrogator, noting their defense, said, "Man, you guys just don't give in!" Their Bibles and books were confiscated but were returned the next day.

That same year we sent Lourdes, the younger sister of Pércides and Noribette, too young to leave Costa Rica, to Elim Bible Institute in the western part of the country. Alcira, a sister of Moisés, went with her to study. With four young people at Bible school that year, the expenses mounted. The Lord provided through their families. We helped, and so did some of our supporters.

When Moisés graduated in 1983, he and Pércide had to return to Costa Rica by plane since bus travel in Central America was interrupted by the war in Nicaragua. The following year she went back alone and finished her studies, as did Lourdes and Alcira. By then Noribette was interested in formal Bible training and was investigating seminaries in Venezuela, Guatemala, and Costa Rica. The Bible schools where we had sent her sisters and her cousins were geared for sixth-grade graduates, but Noribette was qualified for a higher-level school.

After Pércide graduated, she began serving in a country church a couple of hours from Grano de Oro, while the two girls who had studied at Elim helped out in Grano de Oro. Moisés often led the services in my absence but was reluctant to serve regularly. In fact, sometimes he didn't even attend the services. There were periods when he was more loyal to the soccer team than to the church.

Our teenagers became friends with the teens in the Grano de Oro congregation, particularly with those who went to Bible school. Occasionally, our kids drove to Grano de Oro to attend the young people's meeting. For a time there was even a romantic interest between our teens and theirs.

New Blessings

At the end of 1984 Moisés, Pércide, Lourdes, Alcira, and Noribette planned and carried out impressive programs on Christmas Eve and New Year's Eve, while we sat back and *"enjoyed the fruit of the labor of our hands."* What a joy to be with a house full of believers when a decade before, there were none. Our own children were very much a part of the celebration—adding two guitars, a bass, a drum set, and a tambourine to the other three guitars.

At a meeting early in 1985 Moisés sang a new song which the Lord had given him. As he sang about being prepared for the Lord's coming, his sister-in-law, Marita, prayed aloud, asking the Lord to save her. Then Alberto, her husband, made his first public declaration of faith.

A few days later, Moisés, along with his father and three other men from the group, walked the two hours to our house, saying, "We came to pray for you and share Scripture verses for your upcoming trip to the United States!" Later that evening as I drove them back to Grano de Oro, I marveled at the difference from my first trips through Grano de Oro in the 1950s, trekking to Chirripó with pack on my back while everyone—including some of these same men—stared suspiciously at this *gringo*, this *misionero evangélico*, when I stopped at the local bar for a soda! Now when we reached Grano de Oro, Moisés handed me a paper with his final prayer request: "That the Lord will enable us this year to put a chapel on the site of my grandfather's tavern." His faith and vision blew our minds!

Problems, Disappointments, and Setbacks

Over the years, several who made professions of faith did not follow through. Furthermore, not all the baptized believers maintained a good testimony. Javier, the first man baptized, had various problems and eventually dropped out of the church, but most of his family remained faithful. Felo, the second man to come to Christ, did well at first but disappointed us when he later reverted to his old ways. He was not the only man to have trouble with drink in this small village with its three bars.

Occasionally there were problems with the young people. One young man started a youth group, which was gratifying, but when he announced plans to put up a stand in a local carnival to raise money for the congregation, I put my foot down. Another young man wanted me to change the hour of the services so as not to conflict with the local soccer game, the biggest weekly event in every town in Costa Rica. For some of the young people the temptation to marry unbelievers was a serious problem.

There were times of discouragement in the lives of the believers—until the Spirit touched them again. There was a sense of loss when some of the believers moved away from the village in search of more steady work elsewhere. Most of them sought out evangelical churches near their new home, but some no longer followed the Lord.

The excitement of growth in the congregation was often tempered by major challenges, personal clashes, and deep disappointments. There was a popular chorus in the churches of Costa Rica: *"En las luchas, y en las pruebas, la iglesia sigue caminando, y solo se detiene para predicar."* (In the midst of struggles and trials, the church keeps on moving, and only pauses to preach.) These lyrics expressed the struggles we all felt. Yet as Christ's "called out ones," we experienced a oneness that bonded us.

Elders Named

On occasional free Sundays in Tsipirí, I often spent the afternoon praying. As I prayed one Sunday in January 1986, I had a strong impression from the Lord that I should name two elders for the Grano de Oro congregation. During the service the following Saturday I named Johnny as elder in charge of the meeting in my absence and Ramón as elder in charge of the midweek cottage prayer meeting. These men functioned well.

Due to the small size of the congregation we never formed a legal organization for the church; the legal procedures would have been very complex. However, we did write a document defining the relationship of the church to us.

Building the Chapel

For several years the believers in Grano de Oro had wanted a building of their own. Meeting in homes was not suitable long-term. At one point the younger daughters of *don* Moisés even fasted and prayed, asking the Lord for a building site.

Around the time that I named the elders in 1986, I talked to *don* Moisés about selling us part of a convenient lot that he owned—the only titled land in the village.

"I'll donate a part of it for the church," he replied.

Amazing! I decided to "go for broke" and responded, "We'd like to buy the whole piece"—about an acre.

"Well, I'll donate a part," he said, "and you all can buy the rest."

We had been taking offerings for several years in order to teach believers to give. They had already saved up the amount needed for the purchase, so in a village where no one had a clear title, the church got a titled property! What a blessing from an unexpected source.

Grano de Oro chapel under construction

Rafael Moisés designed a simple building and got the lumber cut locally, the exact number of pieces. Our son David got the men together to clear the site and to split posts for a fence around the property—he also helped with his chain saw. The following year my brother David came with a team from the church he pastored in Alabama. In five days they put up the shell of a chapel! Each day Noribette cooked the noon meal for the men. The team did the carpentry, but Felo was the boss. One of the men on the team was a contractor. On previous building projects overseas he had been the boss, but this time he had to submit to local leadership. The team slept at Tsipirí, so we took turns driving back and forth on our miserable excuse of a road. One day as we bounced and jolted along during the forty-five minute ride, they jokingly complained, "Aziel, your driving would be all right if you'd just drive on the road."

Our Own Place

About sixty local people—double our usual number—joined the work team for the inauguration of our chapel in March of 1987. What excitement in the community! Even *don* Moisés was there. Most of the crowd had to stand, although Timothy had designed and built several simple, but comfortable benches. As Marian and I sat there, we felt like an old couple at a family reunion viewing all their extended family—the fruit of their marriage. We were looking at our extended spiritual family, twelve years after our first service in Grano de Oro. The ministry there had always been a "fun" thing for us.

The chapel had no windows yet, just large openings where Felo later installed the frames. Moisés worked on the finishing details and his brother built a pulpit and platform—a bit too "churchy" for me! The believers eventually painted the chapel and made a concrete sidewalk and a nice gate. The ladies kept the floors waxed and polished. We all felt good about having our own place—a "home" for the church. The same week that we built the chapel, the Catholic faithful, who met in the community hall, began construction of a large cement church.

The Aftermath

Having "our own place" continued to be a blessing. Furthermore, soon after we began meeting in the new building, two young men in the congregation asked to be baptized. One was a son of Javier, the first man I baptized in Grano de Oro. In addition, a new couple had come to the Lord early that year. The believers encouraged them to be baptized as well. I planned to baptize all four during Holy Week, a good time for such an event. As we waited at the river for people to gather, we noticed a Land Rover leaving the village. We didn't think much of it until the new couple failed to show up. Finally, I went ahead with the baptism of the two young men.

Only later did we learn that the godfather—whose responsibility and authority in religious matters was well respected—had whisked the couple away. Perhaps the believers had pushed the new couple too hard, before they were firm in their faith. They never did get baptized and eventually dropped out of the group. Yet a church was born and has survived. Yes, the church has had the normal problems, plus those of a frontier town with Indians on the fringe. Indians occasionally came to the meetings, but in those days they didn't fit in, although they were always welcome.

Why Did the Church Survive?

For us, the ministry in Grano de Oro was always an "extra"—a "crumbs-from-the-table" effort, like Jesus' ministry to the Syrophenician woman's daughter, who was healed with the "crumbs" from His ministry to the people of Israel. Since the Spanish ministry was an extra above and beyond our work with the Indians, we could not devote much time to it. In the early years we were absent one weekend a month to visit Marian's parents when they lived in Costa Rica. Occasionally, I was absent for a weekend of ministry in Chirripó. When we went to the States we would be gone for several months or even a year, yet the church did not die. I really wanted the CAM church in Turrialba to take responsibility for Grano de Oro, but it was just too far away. Yet there were laymen like Marco Tulio, who came many times to minister when I was away. Eventually, the believers themselves began to share in the leadership.

Even though we did not give much time to the ministry in Grano de Oro, the church did survive. I like to think that crucial to its survival was our strong Biblical emphasis, both in the meetings and in getting people personally into the Word. We used a Bible study format which they could easily follow, whether individually, as a family, or as a body. Another factor in the survival of the church was prayer. Not only our prayers and the prayers of friends in the United States, but the prayers of the believers themselves. They developed their own weekly prayer meetings and monthly days of prayer. Above all, the Lord himself fulfilled His promise: "I will build my church." Even in a place like Grano de Oro there was "Golden Grain" in His harvest field.

— 23 —
The Family Expands
1980 to 1988

During the 1980s we witnessed not only the birth of the Cabécar church and a church in Grano de Oro, but we watched the family mature and expand in ways beyond our imagination. Children finished college and went on to serve the Lord. Five of them married, and nine more grandchildren were born. For our oldest son, the 1980s included a serious accident and a career shift. Meanwhile, as I began to realize that my trekking days were over, the three younger sons started shouldering our work.

After three decades in Costa Rica, we were totally at home in our adopted country. Marian's parents were buried there; her sister and husband were seminary professors in the capital. We had our favorite doctors, dentists, mechanics, and stores. We had friends in the capital and in Turrialba, which was like a hometown to us.

Budding Romance

A few months after our return from furlough in 1980, Susanna was alone in South Carolina—or so we thought. Yet early one sunny morning in Tsipirí as Marian was fixing breakfast after a night of torrential rain, she heard a slight sound. Glancing toward the front door, she screamed, "Susanna!" Yes, there was Susanna, standing on the front porch. Homesick, she had borrowed money to fly to Costa Rica for Christmas. In Turrialba she found a ride with the Kibbeys, our neighbors from Moravia. The next morning she walked the four miles from their house to Tsipirí. What an unexpected joy!

A few months later, a rather startling letter came from Susanna in Columbia. Marian read it aloud to me as we drove to the capital from Turrialba where we had picked up the mail at the post office.

Susanna wrote of a young man from India whose family had immigrated to America. She had met Prem Shastri at church, where they both sang in the choir. He had come to Columbia to pursue a Ph.D. in chemistry at the University of South Carolina, but was now headed toward missions, specifically Bible translation.

Their interest in each other was serious; but Susanna, knowing we might have a problem with his being Indian, said they wouldn't marry if we opposed. As she wrote that Prem was attracted to her spiritual qualities, her interest in missions, and her family background, I found my heart overruling my initial concern. Furthermore, I learned that not only was Prem a believer but his parents, Percy and Shantha Shastri, were Christians as well. In fact, he was a fifth-generation Christian on both sides of his family. Before immigrating to America to teach in a college, Prem's father had been an officer in the Indian Air Force; now he was serving as a lay pastor. Prem's mother was the daughter of an English professor. English had always been the language of Prem's home.

We felt positive about Prem, yet I needed a confirmation from the Lord. The next morning I was arrested in my regular reading by Psalm 2:7, *"Thou art my son; this day have I begotten thee."* That verse spoke personally to me. My heart leaped in response. I didn't just "grab that verse out of the air." Years before at Moody Bible Institute, I had learned from Stephen Olford to listen to the Lord's voice as I read His Word in my daily quiet time.

Prem later visited us in Tsipirí, after surviving a visa hassle due to his Indian passport. He was detained four days in Honduras while I went from one government official to another until I obtained permission from the head of the Immigration Department for him to enter Costa Rica. During his visit we grew to love him; he left with our blessing on his upcoming marriage to Susanna.

Two Weddings in Two Weeks

A few days after we received Susanna's startling letter about Prem's interest in her, Steven and Cameron flew to Costa Rica—she wearing her new diamond! Their romance had been developing since they were teenagers. In fact, Marian and I had once prayed with her parents about the possibility of a marriage between their family and ours. Now, several years later, Steven and Cameron were planning a June wedding. Susanna and Prem also announced plans to marry in June.

Steven was to graduate from Columbia Bible College in May. Cameron would receive her associate degree in the same ceremony. (Susanna had finished her B.A. there at the end of 1980. Elizabeth and Timothy were still with us in Tsipirí studying high school correspondence courses, but that year Philip and David had returned to Las Américas Academy in Honduras.) On our way to the United States for the graduation and the weddings, we stopped over in Honduras long enough to attend Philip's graduation from eighth grade. Then in Columbia we settled down in our own home—the house we had bought during furlough in 1980—to enjoy the hustle and bustle of preparing for two weddings.

On June 12, 1982, Steven and Cameron glorified God in a beautiful ceremony. Following their vows Steven sang to Cameron an original song of testimony and gratitude. After the pastor pronounced them man and wife, they knelt and prayed—their first act as a married couple—asking that they would be *one...to the praise of His glory.*" Each of the fathers gave a charge to the couple. One of the groomsmen was Steven's friend Moisés from Grano de Oro, who flew in from Guatemala where he was attending Bible School.

Susanna and Prem's wedding on June 25 was just as special. The bridesmaids were dressed in traditional Costa Rican outfits, while Prem's mother and sisters each wore a beautiful wedding *sari*. The groomsmen each wore a *guayabera,* the classic overshirt of tropical America. As Susanna came down the aisle between Marian and me—typical of Costa Rican weddings, Prem sang to her. When she reached his side, she responded to him in song. I gave a short message based on Genesis 12:1,2 showing that *children are the vehicle for communicating divine revelation from generation to generation.* Prem's father also had a good word for the couple.

Priscilla to the Field

Less than two weeks later, we drove Priscilla to the airport in Charlotte for her flight to Papua New Guinea as she began her missionary service. By this time she had finished her M.A. in linguistics, joined Wycliffe Bible Translators, and was assigned to Malaysia following orientation in New Guinea. Marian and I were accustomed to family separations, but this one was different. We each felt a lump in our throat—our first daughter, still single, was going a very long way off for a very long time. Priscilla, who had never cried when she left for boarding school and had loved dorm life, wrote in her first letter from New Guinea, "As my plane taxied away from the terminal, I could see you all watching from the window of the waiting room and there were tears."

More separations followed. Marian and I flew back to Costa Rica with the three younger boys, leaving Susanna and Prem to stay in our house while he studied at the grad school of Columbia Bible College. We left Elizabeth in Greenville, South Carolina, to study at the Evangelical Institute.

Soon we were back in Tsipirí, back to translation and revision, weekend meetings in Cabécar and Spanish, road maintenance, visitors, as well as trips to town for supplies or to the capital for doctor appointments or other business. How we missed Elizabeth's happy spirit and practical help! Timothy and Philip were studying by correspondence, and David had a tutor for his sixth-grade studies, a friend who came from the States to relieve Marian of supervising his lessons that school year. Our days revolved around books and papers. In fact, one day when two translation helpers were at the house, I suddenly realized that each of the eight people on the premises was at a desk!

Slow Plodding

On December 30, 1982, I wrote in my diary, "Marian and I still can't figure out why we have no breakthrough." We were at a low point. The chapel services in Chirripó were not prospering. Timothy had described the situation as a "stalemate." In my diary I added,

"This on the eve of our *thirtieth* anniversary of arriving in Costa Rica!" The next night—New Year's Eve—Marian and I and the three boys, along with Elizabeth who was home in Tsipirí for the holidays, joined Peter and Debbie to share what the Holy Spirit had been doing in each of our lives in recent months. We ended the year with more than an hour of solid prayer. With little to show for our thirty years among the Indians, Marian and I were, nevertheless, refreshed in spirit and encouraged by the spiritual development of our children.

As we plodded on, translating and producing literacy material, as well as leading services on Saturday nights in Grano de Oro and on Sundays in Chirripó, we were soon to be surprised by the conversion, not of the Cabécars we had come to reach, but rather of "other sheep."

"Other Sheep Have I"

To reach our house in Tsipirí, visitors can drive to the point where the rustic jeep road ends and the main trail to Chirripó—the *Camino Real*—begins, and then turn left into our long driveway. To our front door came government agents, Peace Corps workers, botanists, anthropologists, doctoral students interested in frogs, snakes, or spiders, as well as hikers wondering where the road went and hippies looking for a place to get away. We learned a lot from our visitors, especially the scientists.

Surprised visitors often greeted us with, "What are *you* doing *here?*" From answering that question it was a short step to asking where they were from—and then finding out where they were spiritually. They were on our turf, drinking our coffee, and sometimes in need of a place to spend the night. One cold, rainy night a German stepped in out of the rain and found us gathered in our living room for family devotions. When he sat down, I handed him a German New Testament so he could take part in the reading. "Wherever did you get this?" he asked. When he had first come seven years previously, I was not prepared. Now, however, I had on hand New Testaments in English, Spanish, French, German, and Chinese.

One Saturday night late in 1982 as we drove up the hill from Tsipirí, we noticed a jeep parked beside the road with a large sheet attached to the side of the vehicle. A noisy generator provided power for a light focused on the sheet to attract bugs. Two men were picking beetles from among the many bugs and moths gathered on the sheet and then dropping them into "killing jars." The men were still at it when we returned from our meeting, so we invited them down for coffee the next morning.

Only one of the men responded to our invitation, Jim, a collector from Ohio who had moved to Costa Rica hoping to earn a living by selling specimens to collectors worldwide. In addition to collecting in rural areas like Tsipirí he raised butterflies at his home in the capital. When our boys showed Jim a collection of six scarab beetles, each a different color, he excitedly pulled out his collector's guide.

"You've already found six out of the series of ten!" exclaimed Jim, realizing he had come to a productive area.

"I knew there were missionaries living down the hill," admitted Jim on his first visit, "probably hanging up Indians by the ankles and beating them till they converted!"

When he returned early in 1983 for a second visit, he brought a recent copy of *Time* magazine with an article entitled, "The New Missionary." The article concerned a friend of ours and had a positive slant which probably broke the stereotype Jim had of missionaries. At any rate, he took a New Testament home with him.

Each month at new moon—when there was no moonlight to interfere with his bug light—Jim came back to collect. At night he set up for beetles, but during the day, after putting out his butterfly traps, Jim sat in his jeep reading literature we had given him. He and our David, both outdoor men, became friends. Timothy also talked with Jim and eventually lent him a copy of *Mere Christianity* by C. S. Lewis.

"I have a question before I go," said Jim one night as he was leaving Tsipirí, "If I died now, where would I spend eternity?"

"Jim," I answered, "I hate to tell you, because I like you whether you get saved or not. But I have to say you'd go to hell."

"I knew you'd say that," said Jim with a smile, "but I wanted to hear you say it."

My Special Sixty-first

We had finished translation for the day and my helpers had already gone home when our translator friends, the Schlabachs, drove into our front yard. They had come to help celebrate my sixty-first birthday. It was February 22, 1983. Peter and his family had come from Estrella; Steven and Cameron had arrived from the States, bringing Elizabeth. All the children were at home except the two older girls. While we were still at the table after a supper of southern fried chicken, Peter wanted to pray "for the work." I said, "Fine, but first I want y'all to pray for me"—a common practice at our family birthday celebrations.

Peter stood up, laid hands on me, and began releasing some things he felt he needed to confess. As he continued praying, Ray Schlabach joined him, and soon Steven, Timothy, Philip, and David gathered around me as well. Peter kept praying. How he prayed! Forty-five minutes later my shirt was wet with my sons' tears. I felt bathed in prayers and tears! For me, it was like a fresh anointing.

Years before, I had taped a copy of Acts 2:39 to my study door: *"The promise is unto you and to your children."* For years also, Marian's aunt had sent us a subscription to a magazine that exposed us and our children to exciting testimonies of life in the Spirit. A month after my birthday I wrote in my diary, "We began to see what the Lord has been doing in the various family members in the realm of life in the Spirit."

A couple of months later David's tutor returned to the States. Marian was grateful for her help teaching David and creating artwork for literacy materials. However, it had proved difficult for her to live with us, and for us to live with her in the very close proximity that life in Tsipirí demanded. By the time she left, the school year was almost over. Marian was able to take over as tutor without undue pressure, especially now that Elizabeth was home again doing her happy thing—housework!

"We Considered the Evidence"

On our trips to the capital each month we stopped at Jim's house for coffee. We enjoyed him and his wife, Sue. Both had been reading the New Testament I'd given Jim. Eventually they invited us to come for supper the next time we went to town. That evening Jim spoke excitedly about a certain paragraph in *Mere Christianity*. Sue had read the New Testament thoroughly and asked for a copy of the whole Bible. She had a good grasp of the Gospel of John; we were amazed when she enumerated for us what was in each chapter.

"Are you ready to tell God something?" I asked Jim later. He hesitated but said no, nor did Sue pray.

A few days later, we stopped briefly at Jim and Sue's house to leave them a Bible. While Marian chatted with Sue at the car, I talked with Jim in the house. Suddenly he changed the subject.

"After you left the other night," Jim said, "Sue and I talked a long time, considering the evidence for Christ, and…"

At that point my heart sank, thinking he was going to say that they didn't accept the evidence. But Jim continued, "…we've come to see that Jesus is the way. Sue and I both knelt and received Christ as Savior!"

"Jim," I said, "I want you to tell Marian what you just told me!"

We hurried to the car where Marian and Sue were talking. After Jim told Marian the good news, he added that they had a lot to straighten out but that "now life has purpose and perspective." Before we left their house, we phoned the pastor of the Union Church, an English-speaking congregation. Soon Jim and Sue were involved in a Bible study group there.

That night Marian and I had an anointed time praying for Jim and Sue and then for each other. We prayed for an even greater touch of the Lord on our ministry. (We had learned to take advantage of a spiritual high to reach out in faith for even more.)

Proposed Trip to the States

Our family memories are punctuated by many three day drives to Honduras to take the children to boarding school. Each trip was preceded—and aggravated—by getting clothes and bedding ready, including the tedious task of sewing labels on every piece, even socks and hankies. The flip side of each painful goodbye was the warm "welcome home."

When our four older children were ready for high school in the United States, however, they flew to New Orleans where my brother David met their plane and drove them to North Carolina. What a blessing his help was in getting them settled in the dorm at Ben Lippen School! Now in the fall of 1983 Timothy, who had done all his high school studies by correspondence, had been accepted at Columbia Bible College, as had Elizabeth. Marian wanted to accompany them and help get Elizabeth settled into the dorm—a mother's "thing."

On August 31 we arrived at 4 A.M. at the SAHSA ticket counter for our flight to the States. "Sorry, today's flight is canceled," the ticket agent said nonchalantly. Seeing our shock, she offered, "We can book you for tomorrow."

After phoning my brother David to wait a day to meet us, I turned to Marian and said, "We have a free day! What do we do?"

"Let's go to visit Jim and Sue," she suggested immediately. They excitedly responded to our phone call with an invitation to supper.

The timing was right. Jim and Sue had both been impacted by books we had lent them. Sue was ready to burn their esoteric books, and Jim had begun to question his belief in reincarnation. We referred Jim to several Scriptures. Then as he saw the light, he renounced in prayer his former pattern of thinking. After that he handed me a long, carefully written list of more esoteric books that he had planned to buy on his next trip to the States.

"They'd only have made me go nowhere faster," exclaimed Jim, before we ended the evening with a wonderful time of prayer.

"Now we know why Aziel and Marian's flight was canceled," prayed Sue.

With great effort Jim prayed, formally rejecting reincarnation and his other old beliefs. Then it was time to talk about their need to be baptized. Jim agreed but said he wanted to burn the books first.

Later Jim and Sue boxed up the books, including the writings of Edgar Casey and an expensive set of theosophy books, and traveled to Peter's house in Estrella where they could burn them without being noticed by neighbors. After the bonfire, Jim became deathly ill. As he lay in bed, he remembered some valuable Indian relics he had bought on the black market. He was planning to take them to the States although it was illegal to export such treasures. His thought was to sell them—he knew where—in order to build a house with the proceeds. Now he felt the Holy Spirit telling him to turn the relics over to the museum. Following that decision, he recovered. After careful examination, the museum experts concluded that the relics, maces used as authority symbols, were worthless reproductions.

Stateside Interlude

The day after our "divine appointment" with Jim and Sue, we left Philip and David in the care of Peter and Deb, and flew to the States with Elizabeth and Timothy. Marian did see Elizabeth settled in the dorm at CBC. We also got acquainted with Timothy's roommate, Noel Sánchez from El Salvador. The son of a pediatrician from El Salvador and a nurse from Rhode Island, Noel was truly bilingual. He and Timothy became close friends and soon they and Elizabeth found a Spanish church in Columbia. Not surprisingly, a romance began to develop between Noel and Elizabeth. Even less surprisingly, Timothy, sitting in classes after trekking the trails in Chirripó, was not at all excited about classroom studies!

Marian and I enjoyed a few days with Susanna and Prem at our house in Columbia before spending the rest of the month traveling.

On our way to see Steven and Cameron, who were working and studying in Dallas at the time, we visited nine of my siblings. We enjoyed our time together on the road driving a quiet, comfortable car provided by my brother David, but Marian confessed, "It's lonesome traveling without the children!"

While we were in the States, the pastor of a supporting church asked to see us. He was troubled by a report from someone present at my 61st birthday celebration that one of our sons had spoken in tongues that night. This was a very sensitive issue at the time. Supporting churches were even sending questionnaires asking our position on spiritual gifts, particularly tongues. We assured the pastor that no one had spoken in tongues that night. Puzzled, he responded, "Now I don't know who to believe!" Fortunately, we were learning to let the Lord defend us, and He did. We now enjoy a happy relationship with this brother!

Another "Other Sheep"

Not long after we returned to Costa Rica, we found another "other sheep." Or more exactly, he found *us*! One Saturday afternoon as I was readying my pack for a weekend across the Chirripó River, a messenger arrived asking me not to come that day. I was glad to have a break from the five-hour trek and especially the return trip the next day, when after recrossing the river—no bridge over the swift current—I'd face the hill that took me 10,500 footsteps to climb. However, I was upset by the thought of a weekend with no ministry opportunity. I never wanted to miss seeing God at work!

Early that afternoon I heard a jeep roaring in low gear down the steep descent to the Tsipirí Valley and stopping at my gate. Soon a tall lean *gringo* strode across my front yard.

"I'm John Slaughter, Birmingham, Alabama," he said. "I know your niece Debbie—organist at my church."

Working on an engineering contract on the Pacific coast of Costa Rica, John managed to cross Costa Rica and locate us with only the return address on a letter we had sent my niece. After I walked down and unlocked the gate, John roared in, driving a company car, a long-bodied diesel Toyota like my own "work horse."

We wondered what had driven this man to cross the country looking for us—asking directions from a pastor and even from a priest, and wondering desperately, "Will Aziel be at home?" After we got acquainted, I asked David to give him a tour of Tsipirí while I "changed gears" mentally and began to prayerfully listen to the Lord, trying to sense what God was doing. By this time, John had told me that he and his wife were youth leaders at their church and that there was a group in Birmingham praying for him.

Later at supper he mentioned that his pastor's wife had written him: "John, in a vision I saw you in the greenest, lushest valley in all the world, and there, where the valley starts to go up the hill, you met Jesus." That letter had spurred his search for us.

"John, do you realize where you are?!!" Marian asked when she read the letter.

After supper we invited John to join us for family devotions, but he said, "You go ahead; I need to go to the truck for something." Marian, Philip, David, and I began praying—hard!

"Now, tell me again," asked John when he strode back in, smelling of cigarette smoke, "what did you say I have to do to be saved?"

To myself I thought, "Since he's asking, I'd better cover all the basics: sin, repentance, and faith in the atoning work of Christ." After doing so, I knelt with John by the coffee table. He began praying silently.

"Pray out loud," I said.

"Why?" he queried.

"You got married publicly, didn't you?" I asked. "Do you want to shack up with Jesus or get married to him?" He laughed and started praying a good prayer of confession, repentance and faith.

"Praying out loud isn't so bad, once you get started," he said in the middle of his prayer as he looked up and laughed again. A bit later he stuck out his hand to me, saying, "Hold my hand," as though he needed reassurance.

When we finished praying, Philip, always sensitive to the Spirit, began strumming his guitar and singing an appropriate chorus, then another and another as David and Marian and I joined in. John knew the songs from his time with the youth at his church. As we continued worshipping, he was ecstatic. Finally we opened the Bible to the book of John and read the first chapter, then showed him a bed where he could sleep. He had come prepared to spend the night in the back of his Toyota.

The next morning, as I sat in my corner meeting the Lord, I heard John striding to the front of the house in his heavy work shoes.

"Last night you reaped where you hadn't sown," he blurted out. "The people in Birmingham did the sowing; you did the reaping." (The passage to which he was referring occurs at the end of John chapter four. Obviously, he had read three more chapters from the Bible we'd lent him!)

"According to the vision, you have to go up the trail, John," said Marian after breakfast.

"Yes, I know," he responded, "but I want to borrow your Bible again."

Back after an hour or two up on the Chirripó trail, he referred to the parable of the sower which he'd just read and asked with concern, "Will I be good soil?" ("Time will tell," Peter later said.)

As he left for the Pacific coast, we lent him a cassette by Phil Driscoll, one of our favorite contemporary worship tapes. He played it full volume as he roared up our bumpy hill. (With a company car, he didn't need to pay for any springs he might break.) Later he told us, "I was bawling like a baby as I listened to that tape."

Passing through the capital on his way to the coast, John stopped at Santa Ana to leave something Marian had sent to Peter.

"I've just been to your parent's house; I got saved!" announced John as he strode into the house.

Peter and another missionary counseled him and prayed for him to be filled with the Holy Spirit. That night John roared down the narrow, serpentine highway, praising the Lord all the way to the Pacific. He claimed he drove it in an hour; it took me three. The next morning he blurted out to his boss, "I got saved!"

John was in and out of our house and our lives for the next several months. Each time he came with his guitar and sang a new original song, capturing what he was experiencing of the Lord. Once he arrived at Tsipirí with camping gear and went to Chirripó alone for a spiritual retreat.

Our house was too distant for John to visit often, so we introduced him to Jim and Sue who provided the fellowship he needed. They became close friends. During early visits to their house, John drank and smoked with Sue, whereas Jim had simply dropped these habits, was growing steadily, and was discipling John.

When John's contract ended, he went back to Birmingham but sent his sister Ellen "to experience Costa Rica." Ellen found a job teaching at the International Christian School in the capital and stayed several years, enjoying fellowship with our extended family and friends. As John hoped, God also touched his sister in Costa Rica. Through the church we attended when in the capital she grew and was filled with the Spirit. I had the privilege of baptizing her in Tsipirí before she returned to the States, permanently impacted by Jesus. For some, Tsipirí became a symbol of a spiritual encounter. So much drama was squeezed in between tedious years of translating!

Just What We Needed

Jim and John's response, coupled with response in Grano de Oro, boosted our morale tremendously at a time when we had seen little visible response among the Cabécar Indians in spite of much sowing over many years. The conversion of these "other sheep" provided objective evidence that we were still in a spiritually usable condition. Actually, the Cabécar church was already on the horizon but we didn't yet recognize it.

Not all of the "other sheep" who appeared at our door in Tsipirí heard a full witness, but most heard something of Jesus. A Peace Corps girl responded as enthusiastically as John and Jim. She hurriedly completed her project in Chirripó, then returned to Tsipirí, asked for a Bible, and lay on the couch for two days while she read the entire New Testament. We talked, answered her questions, and then she made a firm confession of faith. She began attending an English language church in the capital, but sadly, she went down spiritually as fast as she had gone up. Later we found out that she had been hiding an immoral relationship she was unwilling to give up. We grieved over her.

Through the years we discovered that out of our ministry came many special friends: Jim and Sue, and John in the '80s; some from the agricultural institute in Turrialba in the '50s; Al and Daisy in Columbia in the '60s; and in the '70s and '80s those in the Latino church in Grano de Oro—where some contacts had even begun with conflict. I was once challenged when I said, "If we carry out the Great Commission we will find many physical, mental, social and psychological needs met," but for me and Marian, ministry—talking about Jesus—has satisfied many of our own social needs.

Our needs were met not only by converts but also by other missionaries. Now that we were no longer serving with CAM, we related more to our Mennonite colleagues working among the Bribri Indians, a tribe closely related to the Cabécars. Ray and Susie Schlabach had been in Costa Rica twenty years by this time, and one of their daughters was studying at Columbia Bible College with Elizabeth and Timothy. A young Wycliffe couple, Paul and Linda Williams, had come early in the '80s to assist the Schlabachs in the Bribri translation. These two couples and a few others—all serving with different organizations—formed part of what Marian and I called our "Inner Circle." Peter and Debbie were, of course, part of this circle. Whenever our ministry responsibilities allowed us time together, we related both spiritually and socially. Without a mission organization to relate to locally, we valued this fellowship.

Peter's Accident

One rainy night the sound of a jeep grinding down the hill toward Tsipirí woke us from a deep sleep. It was Peter, coming to announce that Debbie had given birth that day, October 29, 1983, to our third grandchild, Luke Aziel! What fun we had talking and drinking coffee until long after midnight. Peter left early the next morning, his jeep barely able to ford our swollen creek. Seven weeks later, as Peter and Debbie and the baby were driving to our house for Christmas, they had an accident. Luke was in serious condition, with two fractures of the skull. Peter was knocked unconscious for a time and spent two days in the Turrialba hospital. He required fifteen stitches on his forehead and a cast to protect his badly bruised knee. Debbie had minor cuts and bruises. Their jeep was totaled and several items were stolen. The other two children, Jonathan and Joanna, were in our car, so they escaped injury.

Ray Schlabach viewing Peter's jeep

Luke and Debbie were sent to the Children's Hospital in the capital. There the son of our dear friend Flora from Turrialba, who was now an orthopedic surgeon, met the ambulance and contacted a neurosurgeon. Luke did well the first day, but the next night Debbie's phone call awakened me: "Luke just had a seizure." I hit the floor on my knees and cried out to God. Luke was transferred to intensive care. The following day while we were praying at the hospital, our doctor friend checked the intensive care unit and found Luke in grave danger. The subsequent days were tense, as friends all over Costa Rica prayed, and reports went out internationally by phone and ham radio. That Sunday a friend remarked, "Luke is the most prayed-for person in the world today."

In spite of Luke's crisis, our family had a wonderful Christmas, although we celebrated a few days late. All eight of our children were together for several days, as planned before the accident, but near the Children's Hospital rather than at home in Tsipirí. We had the use of the house which Marian's parents had remodeled when they retired in Costa Rica. Susanna and Prem arrived before the accident, in spite of being delayed two days in Miami while we went from one government office to another, resolving difficulties due to his Indian passport. They brought the exciting news that even Priscilla would be coming, arriving just after Christmas with Steven and Cameron. We still missed her, ten time zones away from us in Malaysia.

Prayer took on a new dimension when Steven, Cameron, and Priscilla landed at the airport and went straight to the hospital. As Steven prayed with holy boldness, the name of Jesus resounded down the long halls of the renowned pediatric hospital. No one objected. Spiritually, we were at a peak as we prayed over each new crisis and concern. Back at Santa Ana each evening, weary with watching and praying at the hospital, we vented our emotions in exuberant worship, as Steven led with his guitar. Those times were long, loud, and joyful. Peter observed, "When you're 'prayed out,' what else is there to do but worship the Lord!" I was moved by our children's love for the Lord and for each other. I cannot quite capture the intensity of those times of family worship night after night, as various ones of our inner circle of friends joined us—friends like Ray and Susie, Paul and Linda, Bob and Janet, George and Gail. One friend said, "Let's go to the Joneses. It's the best church in town." The bonds between us all were strengthened by the saga of Luke's accident.

To add to the strain of Luke's condition, Peter had to "upfront" cash at the hospital every three days. Friends stepped in with gifts and loans. One family drove six hours to the capital "to help in any way we can." Many came repeatedly to the hospital to pray. Others brought food to Debbie as she stayed with Luke. Our memories are full of the Lord's blessings during those tense days.

As the doctors continued draining fluid off Luke's brain and installed two shunts, his condition eventually stabilized enough that he was released from intensive care. He spent a total of twenty-four days in the hospital. Then came the "final straw." At Luke's discharge, Peter faced a court case! According to Costa Rican law, he was accused by the government of child neglect because Luke's injury resulted in more than twenty-one days of hospitalization.

Six months after the accident the doctors removed Luke's shunts and—after a final CAT scan—declared him normal. However, the case against Peter dragged on for almost a year. During the trial three mechanics testified that a locked steering mechanism had caused the wreck. What a relief when Peter was absolved of all charges, and a woman of means in Turrialba paid his defense lawyer.

Several months before Luke's birth, we had been listening to a series of tapes on signs and wonders with Peter and Deb on Sunday nights in Tsipirí. Yet, as the drama of Luke's injuries unfolded, Peter said, "Nothing weakens my belief in what we have been learning about healing." He wondered if his wreck was a satanic counterattack. Later, back in Tsipirí, Marian fell and broke her arm, painful though just a hairline fracture. Only an accident? *The possibility of counterattack intensified our ongoing, conscious emphasis on defensive praying as we sowed the seed of the Word among the Cabécars.* We were taking enemy territory for the Lamb—and we needed protection.

As a family we were already reading books about life in the Spirit, and this carried over into our ministry. We began to minister with more expectation. This *level of expectation* is part and parcel of life in the Spirit. Not only did we look for supernatural gifting, but for more results from our ministry and our faith. We also began to realize that the discipling of the Cabécars should include not only basic *doctrines* and *disciplines,* but also the *dynamics* of life in the Holy Spirit.

Another Wedding Approaching

In the summer of 1984 Elizabeth and Timothy were home from Columbia Bible College, joining Philip and David in Tsipirí. We all enjoyed Elizabeth's joyful spirit as she moved about the house on her tiptoes to the rhythm of music—and dreamed of marriage. Her singing and her guitar intensified our daily family worship. The children kept us up-to-date on electronic equipment and contemporary musical tastes. The joy and reality of the Lord made Tsipirí a happy home!

During that summer Timothy's roommate Noel Sánchez came to visit, having obtained our permission to pursue Elizabeth. While he was at Tsipirí, her brothers took him across the Chirripó River to Efraín's place at Jamárítábá. For Noel, the trek was a sort of "bridal price" extracted by her brothers. They expected him to prove that he could handle their tough world! He did, and when he left for the States, Elizabeth was sporting a pretty little diamond.

We never received any special word of confirmation from the Lord for the marriage of these two. However, as always, we asked the Lord, and then listened to what the Holy Spirit was saying to *our* hearts. We had asked Elizabeth what she wanted in a husband. On her twenty-first birthday she answered, "A man who has a real heart for the Lord, who is of one mind on important things, and who is musical." Noel was trained in classical guitar. Furthermore, both had grown up in Central America, and both were bilingual and bicultural. Elizabeth said, "At the first sight of Noel, I knew I was going to marry him!"

We were encouraged to find out that Noel's parents, Hugo and Kathy Sánchez, were known by our missionary friends serving with CAM and were serious about the Lord, active in a CAM church in San Salvador. Most parents reproduce themselves in the children. In the core of the child, though it may not be apparent, are the *parents,* hidden in the child in the foundation laid by them—unless there are significant overriding factors. That Noel himself desired to study for the Lord's service was encouraging, along with the fact that his church in El Salvador thought well enough of him to help finance his Bible training.

Elizabeth remained at home in the months approaching the wedding. She and Marian enjoyed plenty of mother-daughter talk. Elizabeth's help with housework gave Marian more time for editing and keyboarding the book of Matthew. It also lightened Marian's overall load in our somewhat tough "man's world" on the frontier. With Elizabeth home, Philip—very helpful in the kitchen—was more free to minister to the Indians and to speed up his high school correspondence courses from the University of Nebraska. Marian supervised David's studies, but his spare time was devoted to caring for his pig and his coffee and banana plants. He also had a corn patch where he was almost bitten by a deadly fer-de-lance.

The deadly fer-de-lance that didn't get David

Transitions

Early in 1984 we bought our first computer for keyboarding the translation. Peter, and later his friend Eduardo, helped us transition into the computer world. However, the new technology initially took more time because Marian had to redo what she had already finished on the typewriter. In changing tools, we had to change our way of thinking and working. For those like us who began with a pen and

3x5 slips of paper, filing drawers, and manual typewriters, this was difficult. Still, we made the change and then gave our typewriters to Timothy to use in teaching Cabécars to type.

At the end of 1984 Timothy said to me, "I want to help you—you have been faithful." Was this the "front edge" of a call, albeit subtle? At the time what he had in mind was to take a year off from college to help in outreach to the Cabécars. Already he and his younger brothers excelled me in speaking Cabécar, yet I never once heard a negative word about my ability in the language. Only once did I even *feel* threatened by their grasp of Cabécar. The transition to the sons' leadership had begun already, unplanned—and unnoticed.

During the Christmas holidays that year Timothy installed low-voltage lights that functioned with battery power—another improvement to life at Tsipirí. Now we had light in the house even when the generator wasn't running! We enjoyed the holidays with the four youngest whom Elizabeth had dubbed: "the foursome." The foursome were different from our first four children in that the older ones all went to the States to study at Ben Lippen High School while the younger four all completed high school by correspondence at home in Tsipirí. Furthermore, each of the four eventually married Latins. Marian and I foresaw that they might want to marry locally. Our main concern as each child faced possible marriage was to discern what the Spirit was saying.

Mr. and Mrs. Noel Sánchez

Our upcoming six-month furlough was planned around the wedding of Elizabeth and Noel on March 23, 1985. By the end of January we were closing the house and looking for a guard—the usual wearisome routine before going to the States. Yet we left Costa Rica greatly encouraged by the love of the believers in Grano de Oro who walked two hours to our house to tell us goodbye. As for the Indian believers, Efraín and his family walked all day to Tsipirí to say goodbye! In fact, it was hard for us to leave the believers, and once we arrived at our house in Columbia it was difficult to adjust again to life in the United States.

Our entire family was able to attend the wedding. Peter and Debbie, who were on a study furlough, drove from California with their children; Priscilla flew in from Malaysia; and Susanna and Prem came from Dallas where they were studying linguistics. Steven and Cameron by this time were living in Columbia where they had built a house. Their first child, David Steven, born May 11, 1984, was almost a year old.

For the ceremony Elizabeth chose to wear Marian's wedding dress. I had the privilege of performing the ceremony, which included a short message. During the service, a nervous Noel set aside his written vows and exclaimed sincerely, "I'll try to do what I'm supposed to do." Not surprisingly, happy guitar music was the order of the day. For the moving recessional, Steven's deep voice resounded as he sang:

> "Now unto the King eternal, immortal, invisible,
>
> the only wise God,
>
> Be honor and glory forever and ever,
>
> Amen, amen,
>
> Be honor and glory forever and ever.
>
> Amen!"

After their honeymoon, Elizabeth and Noel moved into our Columbia home, while Marian and I spent several weeks traveling to missions conferences and visiting supporters and family. On that trip we also visited John, the engineer who had come to the Lord in Tsipirí the previous year, and Jim and Sue, the butterfly collectors who had come to Christ a year before John's conversion. John was back in Alabama, while Jim and Sue had returned to Ohio. Before they left Costa Rica I baptized Jim and Sue in the creek at Tsipirí and they had renewed their marriage vows.

We were back in Columbia in time to see Noel receive his B.A. degree and Timothy receive his A.A. Timothy's plan was that after spending a year working among the Indians in Costa Rica, he would return to complete his B.A. However, as he became more and more deeply involved in ministry, the subject of further schooling was shelved. The harvest of the "first fruits" among the Cabécars had come—and *that* needed attention!

Before the end of July, Marian and I were back in Costa Rica. Our children in Columbia had prayed that as we took up the yoke again, we would find it light. That was the recommissioning we had wanted as we returned for our seventh term. Then when we landed in Costa Rica, we were met by our colleagues, the Schlabachs and the Williams, as well as Peter and his family who had returned earlier. All of us gathered for a noisy reunion at the house where Marian's parents had lived. The exciting news we shared with them was that just before we left Columbia, Marian's sister, Irene, had called to accept our offer for this house—our base near the capital. She had inherited it but had no need for it herself. This was a special ending to our furlough and an encouragement as we returned to take up the yoke once more.

Family Expands Again

Three more grandchildren within fifteen days! At the end of 1985, Ruthanne Elizabeth was born to Elizabeth and Noel on December 17, and Joseph Isaac to Steven and Cameron on December 31. Then on January 1, 1986, Sara Elizabeth was born to Peter and Debbie. Marian called them her "triplets." By this time we had seven grandchildren, being raised by parents with a vision for the "God-potential" in children.

As the family expanded, Marian and I still enjoyed life in Tsipirí with Timothy, Philip, and David. Actually, Timothy spent much of his time out among the Cabécars—and while at home began to try his hand at translation, drafting the first few chapters of Genesis. He also made trips to faraway Indian areas,

David picking his coffee

includeing a visit to Paul Williams among the Bribris, coaching Paul on the verb system common to both Cabécar and Bribri until he could conjugate any Bribri verb on his own. Philip continued his correspondence courses, as well as helping Marian with cooking and washing. David worked hard on his studies too, so that he could have time outside to work on his coffee and cacao trees or with his new chain saw. He was now sixteen; Philip had turned eighteen the day Ruthanne was born, and Timothy turned twenty-one that same day.

Missions Movement in Costa Rica

All during my earlier years as a missionary I often wondered: How is it that we missionaries have communicated our *message* of salvation, but have not communicated to the emerging churches the *motivation* that moved us to come? However, in the 1980s the maturing churches in Central America began to look beyond their borders. God's time had come! The first missions conference was held at the CAM seminary in Guatemala in 1983, sparking vision in young men who soon became pastors. A large CAM church in El Salvador—the church where Noel was raised—held a major missions conference the following year. Then in 1985 FEDEMEC—the nascent Costa Rican missionary society—sponsored an exciting missions conference for young people from the churches in the capital. That same year Peter was invited to speak on missions in a new CAM Bible School in Costa Rica.

The wind of the Spirit "bloweth where it listeth." Costa Rican churches were now asking, "How can we get involved in world missions?" Young men began to seek out Peter for counsel regarding their part in missions. We struggled to relate to these "winds of the Spirit" blowing through the Spanish churches and still not neglect our work among the Indians.

The Turrialba Missions Conference

We as a family became increasingly involved in the missions movement when the new CAM pastor in Turrialba sponsored a missions conference, attended by four hundred young people late in 1985. Peter and I both led workshops on tribal work. Dr. William Taylor, who had so impacted the infant CAM church in Turrialba in the 1940s, was the keynote speaker. Another speaker was a Venezuelan medical doctor turned missionary, who had learned in Amazonia that he didn't need blond hair and blue eyes to qualify for service! His colleague from South Africa, Peter Ward, also serving with Operation Mobilization, and Peter's fiancée, Barby, a Costa Rican-American, brought their burning vision for the Muslims.

God used a slide presentation on Nepal to give me a personal burden for Central Asia. However, I was most powerfully impacted by the bold, one-line banner strung across the auditorium of the local high school:

"LET US WIN FOR THE LAMB THE REWARD OF HIS SACRIFICE!"

After Dr. Taylor's final message to the conference, I was called upon to pray for him, my friend and former mission leader—our past conflicts long forgotten—as he ended his last visit to Costa Rica. What a privilege to bless this veteran in whose tracks I had so often walked in Turrialba and nearby rural areas and of whom his converts so often spoke fondly!

Later I had the even greater privilege of driving him to a rural village so he could say goodbye to his spiritual son, Miguel Córdoba—a barefoot farmer and spiritual giant, saved back in the 1930s. What a sacred privilege to see these two stalwart warriors in their final embrace!

After the Turrialba conference Timothy said to me, "You came home different!" Soon a book about Nepal lay on the table in our den and pictures of Nepal graced my study. And as I write this over two decades later, my new passion *still* burns!

Cross-Cultural Realities

Soon after the conference we heard that a young man named Luis and a group of local believers were trying to evangelize a small settlement of Cabécar Indians near our area. Luis had been inspired by Peter's message at the Bible School a few months previously. Though I do not like to admit it, I felt this as "competition."

"Daddy," said Peter, "people like this will come, whatever you do. Would you rather they come with cross-cultural training or without it?"

When Peter learned that a group, including Luis and leaders of the missions movement, were planning a trip to evangelize the Cabécars living in Estrella, he invited them to his home nearby for an introduction to cross-cultural realities. They listened to him and humbly embraced what he had to say, the roots of which he had learned by observation and table talk growing up in Tsipirí. The group never even saw a Cabécar Indian but the encounter launched and defined Peter's future—training Latins for cross-cultural missions.

The Berea Conference

As the missions movement expanded, other CAM pastors, including the pastor of a church called Berea, conducted their own missions conferences. Our family was invited to minister at the Berea Conference early in 1986. The early morning prayer meetings were moving. In the evenings I watched all five of my sons interacting with the pastor, often praying together in a football-like huddle. Steven ministered powerfully with his guitar. In fact, he ministered with unusual intensity even though he had not actually come to Costa Rica to participate in the conference. The reason for his trip was to renew his residence, since at the time he and Cameron were still thinking of joining us in the work among the Indians.

As we said good-bye to Steven at the airport after the conference, we sensed that something was wrong. After he got home, there were calls from Columbia, asking what had happened to Steven in Costa Rica? Did we cause a breakdown? Mystified, we sent Peter to Columbia to be with his brother and to assess the situation. Steven slowly recovered and eventually got off medication. Still, it was a very difficult time for everyone. We cried out to the Lord in desperation, sensing a damper on family joy and unity, a quenching of the spiritual excitement in the family. We wondered if this could have been a counterattack by the enemy. Opposition and counterattacks were bound to come, but we had to keep moving forward—in faith.

Missions Movement Solidifies

In 1986 FEDEMEC sponsored another youth missions congress with about fifteen hundred young people filling the large Templo Bíblico in the capital. A procession of flags from around the world initiated the three-day meeting. Peter was on the program, and Marian had been asked to give a message, in order to inspire young women interested in cross-cultural missions. She received a standing ovation after she shared our twofold vision of reaching a tribe for God and raising a family for God. Afterwards several girls asked to speak with her, requesting prayer about their role in missions.

On the final evening of the 1986 conference Carlos Chacón's powerful, hour-long message challenged the youth to commit their lives as missionaries, trusting God *alone* to supply their needs. After over thirty years on the field, I was finally hearing a Costa Rican preacher-turned-missionary express my convictions.

"Young people," exclaimed *don* Carlos, "God alone is enough. God has more money than they do in the United States!"

Believers in other Central American countries had also begun to wake up to the Great Commission. Peter went to Honduras in 1987 to challenge young people for cross-cultural missions. Timothy and his Cabécar disciple, Efraín, accompanied Peter and assisted in the ministry. Later that same year Peter was part of the large Costa Rican contingent that flew to Brazil for the first Ibero-American Congress on Missions—known by the acronym COMIBAM. Excitement about reaching the world with the Good News was mounting throughout Spanish and Portuguese-speaking countries.

The First Etno

At the end of 1986 Peter invited five men—including Luis and FEDEMEC president, Randy—to his first *Etno*. He based the name of his training program on the Greek term used in Scripture for ethnic groups. For a week torrential rains fell as the little group lived in the Estrella jungle, experiencing Cabécar culture, eating Indian food, and studying their language. They were totally immersed in another world, a "hands-on" experience. Each night, using *Operation World*, the worldwide prayer guide and almanac, they prayed for strange peoples in strange lands. The guys returned with their worldview greatly expanded.

Just over a year later, a dozen outstanding new *Etnistas* attended the second *Etno*. Modifications were made: a *Pre-Etno* screening weekend was added, the time was lengthened; girls were welcomed, and our three youngest sons—all recovering from hepatitis—came on staff. Peter's own unique ministry was now firmly established.

Praying through the Eighties

The year 1987 was our thirty-fifth in Costa Rica. The previous September we had celebrated our thirty-fifth anniversary, and in February 1987 I celebrated my sixty-fifth birthday. As the years passed, our concerns increased and so did our prayers. We were praying about how best to use the next few years wrapping up our work—Timothy was praying for a "nice transition." Finishing the translation was our top priority, but opposition still threatened us.

During the 1980s Marian spent extra time fasting and praying—especially for the Spirit to work among the Indians. Once she did a "Jericho Fast," fasting one meal a day for six days and then all day on the seventh day. Her main focus at the time was prayer for the establishment of churches in Chirripó. Another of Marian's special prayer concerns was for a life companion for Priscilla, our oldest daughter. Both Marian and I prayed and fasted on several occasions in the wake of Steven's breakdown. We also focused prayer on the translation and on opposition to our work.

Priscilla's Aquila

Early in 1987 while on furlough from Malaysia, Priscilla was working on a master's in library science at the University of South Carolina. Most of her work in Malaysia had centered in the library of the linguistic office in Sabah. Now, at the suggestion of her supervisors she was taking further training, and was also asked to take a short course in desktop publishing—new at the time. Among others who attended the course at the Wycliffe center in Dallas was Jonathan Kew, a young man from England whose mother was from Sweden. Priscilla reported that Jonathan spent quite a bit of time helping her with her project. Susanna and Prem—in Dallas while Prem finished his M.A. in linguistics—made it very convenient for her and Jonathan to pursue a friendship.

When Jonathan went back to Asia, where he was doing surveys for Wycliffe, Priscilla admitted that he "walked in and stole my heart"—this from our girl who controlled her emotions so well! In August, Jonathan's parents invited her to their home in England. At the time we happened to be in Santa Ana where we could be reached by phone. One night we were awakened from a sound sleep by Jonathan's call asking me for our "permission and blessing" to marry Priscilla!

"Well," said Marian when I paused to tell her, "you're going to say yes, aren't you?"

Without time to listen to the Lord—for we had already sensed that their relationship was from Him—I responded with a hearty "Yes." A mother's prayer answered!

Priscilla wanted to celebrate her wedding in Costa Rica where she had grown up. Jonathan's parents, David and Ragnhild Kew, as well as his Swedish uncle and aunt, all came for the occasion. (We since have discovered that Jonathan's mother is distantly related by marriage to Marian's father's family in Sweden!)

The complications of arranging a marriage in a Spanish-speaking country with legal documents from England were daunting. All documents had to be authenticated by the Costa Rican consulate there, before being officially translated into Spanish and then authenticated by the Costa Rican government. Later the marriage certificate was officially translated back to English since the couple would not be remaining in Costa Rica. In addition to the complications of the legal documents, there was the necessity of a civil ceremony, for Protestant marriage is not legally valid in Costa Rica. We arranged with *don* Ricardo, our lawyer from Turrialba, to perform the ceremony at his office in San José a few days before the church wedding.

On January 23, 1988, Priscilla and Jonathan were married in a beautiful, God-honoring ceremony at the Union Church in San José by Jonathan's pastor who came from England with his wife. Our family provided music and I preached a short message. All our children and grandchildren attended, as well as Marian's sister and family. Many missionaries and Costa Rican friends shared the joyful occasion. At the reception Steven's song, a takeoff from Scripture, made a great hit: "Every Priscilla Needs Her Aquila!"

Mr. Chipper Tastes Missions

As the newlyweds honeymooned in Costa Rica, Tom Chipper, Jonathan's pastor, wanted to get a taste of missions. He and I trekked from Tsipirí to the chapel at Súfu. We found forty-six Indians present—the largest crowd ever.

As a not-so-chipper Mr. Chipper and I slowly climbed the steep, nineteen-hundred-foot hill on our return to Tsipirí, he moaned, "I can't make it."

Rather bluntly I replied, "You will."

"But I am shattered," he groaned. I too felt rather shattered after each bimonthly trip to Súfu.

We kept resting and I kept reassuring him, "I never lost a case."

"But you will this time," he protested.

Yes, Mr. Chipper did survive! My trek across the Chirripó River with Dean Lewis the previous year had been much longer, much more difficult, and much more risky.

Timothy Marries an Etnista

Around the time of Priscilla's wedding the seeds of another romance began to germinate. In January 1988 I took a jeep-load of *Etnistas* to the *Pre-Etno*. As we unloaded at dusk, Timothy's eyes met those of Keiry Sánchez. Each felt attracted to the other. However, for the whole month of jungle camp, nothing was said or passed between them. Back at Tsipirí after serving on staff at the camp, Timothy wrote her and showed us the letter before he mailed it.

"If you don't approve, *this is off,*" he said. We deeply appreciated his desire for our input!

Marian and I had an overriding conviction that the Lord was in their relationship. At *Etno*, Keiry had proven her ability to live like a Cabécar woman—an ability Timothy wanted in a wife. Her cultural adaptability also extended to our culture and language, for she had spent a year living with an American family as an exchange student while in high school. Even her name, Keiry, sounded similar to "Katie" in English. She had committed her life to the Lord's service during the youth missions congress in 1986 at which Marian gave a message. In fact, when Marian reviewed the list of girls who had spoken privately with her after that message, there was Keiry's name!

Timothy worked out a trip to the capital for our whole family to attend a concert by Steve Green. Keiry joined us, their first—and only—real date! We mingled with hundreds of English-speakers, mostly missionaries, gathered in one of the largest churches in San José to be blessed by the singing of Steve Green, himself a "missionary kid" raised in South America.

While we were in the capital, Keiry's mother, Yadira Quesada, and her stepfather came with her to Santa Ana for dinner. Timothy and Keiry said little while we two sets of parents discussed their relationship. Concluding that God was in this, we, together, gave our approval, set the wedding date, and then committed them to the Lord. It was like a Hebrew betrothal! As a part of the *Etno* program, Keiry was already scheduled to stay with us at Tsipirí as an intern. During that month, Timothy would be coming and going to and from Chirripó. We would get to know her and she us.

My personal reservations about cross-cultural marriages were readily overcome. I really liked Keiry, and even felt a strong love for her. Marian remarked, "I think the Lord gave you that love to move you to heartily approve their marriage." True, but even so, we were always listening to the Spirit and moving in faith.

"We Want a Celebration!"

Timothy and Keiry wanted their marriage to be a real celebration. And celebrate they did! Led by a contemporary band, we worshipped at length. There was special music by Steven and testimonies by the bride and groom. I preached and so did Peter, who also performed the ceremony. Efraín and his family were there in their boots, fresh from the jungle, and he was one of several who laid hands on the couple and prayed for them after their vows. The almost three-hour service was followed by an even longer reception—a sit-down meal for five hundred guests in the patio of Keiry's church in the city of Heredia. Most of our children were there for the occasion, as well as Timothy's close friend from Bible College days, Joseph Crump.

The church wedding—their "real" wedding—on July 23, 1988, was preceded on July 4 by the civil ceremony performed by a young Christian lawyer at our place near the capital. I was impressed with the instructions to husband and wife which she was required to read. Actually, the occasion served as a private family ceremony, complete with a small reception. A week after the civil wedding our family was back at Tsipirí for a Cabécar-style "wedding." Dressed in everyday clothes and rubber boots, Timothy and Keiry had a Christian ceremony as a testimony to the many Indians who gathered.

After honeymooning in Costa Rica and spending a month in the United States, the newlyweds went to Chirripó to live with Efraín and his family for two months. Keiry quickly learned to speak Cabécar, while also learning the role of a Cabécar woman. Timothy helped Efraín's family with the bean harvest and also built a large, sturdy Indian-style house for them—including a room for him and Keiry.

Timothy and Keiry's marriage did not split the unity of our three younger sons. In Santa Ana, Timothy enlarged the cabin the three boys had built in the backyard of the house where Marian's parents once lived, adding a nice bedroom and kitchen for him and Keiry. On our property in Tsipirí they fixed up the little house which Peter and Debbie had remodeled for themselves before building their own place in the Estrella area. They were close to us and to Philip and David, although Philip left for his freshman year at Columbia Bible College soon after Timothy and Keiry's wedding.

Family Expands Again

No, not another wedding, at least not yet, but we rejoiced as new grandbabies were added to the family. Andrew Noel Sánchez was born on April 1, 1987, a brother for Ruthanne Elizabeth. Now Elizabeth and Noel each had a namesake! Susanna and Prem Shastri's first child arrived that same year on December 19. Her birth was an answer to five years of prayer. They named her Irene, from the Greek word for peace. Her middle name, Ilenya, came from Hindi.

Daniel John Jones was born to Steven and Cameron on November 4, 1988, his mother's birthday. A month later Elizabeth and Noel had a second son, Santiago Emilio Sánchez, born on December 19, 1988. They called him "Santi."

Visits Back and Forth

Even with our heavy responsibilities in the 1980s we still took time for family visits with kids and grandkids. We were busy with the translation and the emerging Cabécar church. Our extra time went to the Spanish church. But when the children came to Costa Rica, their visits provided pleasant interludes. Each came with their firstborn, as they had come with their spouse-to-be. We treasured those times. Steven and Cameron took the prize for the most visits! They always brought blessing not only to our family worship, but in practical ways as well. In fact, they brought blessing to others beyond our family, even spending two months in 1987 helping a missionary friend with a building project.

In 1987 Marian and I went to the States for our very own family reunion. We rented a lodge at a retreat center in the mountains and spent three days with all the children and grandchildren. We worshipped together, shared our hearts with each other, prayed and talked. Our celebration of the Lord's Supper the last night was truly special. After our reunion at Ridge Haven in North Carolina and the two-day annual reunion of my siblings at Kolomoki in Georgia, we also visited our spiritual children who had been born again in Costa Rica: Jim and Sue, the bug collectors, and John, the engineer. Along the way, we saw friends and supporters.

Vision and Faith

We ended 1988 with not only our original eight children but with three wonderful daughters-in-law and three great sons-in-law. By this time Peter and Deb had four children, Steven and Cameron had three, as did Elizabeth and Noel, while Susanna and Prem had one—eleven grandchildren in all. What a joy they all were to us! Years before, we had faced social pressure against a large family, but God was now vindicating the vision and faith of earlier days. As the family nucleus expanded, we prayed that the spiritual life of the family would intensify and not degenerate. Developing a godly heritage was as important to us as establishing a church among the Cabécar Indians.

Family reunion in 1987
Back row: Peter, Steven, Timothy, Philip, and David
Front row: Priscilla, Susanna, Elizabeth, Marian, and Aziel

— 24 —
The Final Push
1989 to 1993

As we began the final push toward the publication of the Cabécar New Testament, we were greatly encouraged. On all sides churches were emerging. Three or four vibrant groups met regularly in the Chirripó Valley. The believers were anxious for the completed New Testament. Young Indians crisscrossed rivers and mountains with the printed and spoken word. We had a toehold in the Pacuare Valley and even in the remote Telire Valley.

Up to a hundred Cabécars gathered for Christmas or Easter meetings. New people expressed repentance and faith in Christ. A friend asked if I felt excited when a Cabécar made a profession of faith. "Not really," I answered, "for each must be tested. But every time I see a hundred Cabécars in a three-hour service, singing, praising, giving testimony, sharing Scriptures, drinking in the Word taught by Cabécar leaders, I get all choked up. For in such moments I see, in a flash, the fruit of a lifetime of plodding and praying."

However, we had been duly warned by other translators that as we approached the final push to complete the New Testament we could expect all kinds of delays, hindrances, and hassles. Three weeks into 1989 we hit the first of these delays. One Sunday morning in January as I was driving to Pacuare for a Bible study, my left foot began to hurt—for no apparent reason. Since I was expecting to walk only half an hour after reaching the end of the road, I was not concerned about the pain. Yet it became so intense by the time I parked the jeep that I sent José Gilberto, my companion, to tell my host not to expect me. When José returned an hour later, I was writhing in agony. Not since I caught my hand in Daddy's printing press when I was seventeen years old had I experienced such pain.

As I drove home, I could hardly push in the clutch on my heavy Toyota. Back at Tsipirí, I crawled from the jeep to the house and crashed on the bed. I did not sleep that night. The next afternoon at one, the time of our daily radio schedule, Marian turned on the new two-way radio that now linked us with our inner circle of missionary friends. Hoping someone would answer her calls, she waited and waited. Then, praise the Lord, our friends the Wilmarths responded. No one else! Marian—who does not drive—asked them to come and drive us to the capital.

Ironically, I was the one who had resisted buying a two-way radio. Yet only a few days after putting up the antenna, I was the one who needed the radio to call for help! I had resisted because I did not want to be a slave to a daily radio schedule. Fundamental to my thinking was to make sure that every appliance was a *servant* and not a *master*. By deep conviction, I jealously pursued a lifestyle which would protect my calling to reach a tribe and raise a family. My feeling that I had limited abilities drove me to avoid diversions which might threaten my "this-one-thing-I-do" mindset.

Daily radio contact is especially helpful during emergencies, yet we cannot prepare for every emergency in life. It seems to me that the Lord lets each of us decide our own "level of faith." That is, if we prepare for an emergency, we might have an emergency—and vice versa. Nevertheless, we must be sensitive to the Spirit as to where we set our "level of faith," which is probably affected by our level of spiritual maturity.

During the twenty-six years we had lived in Tsipirí, we had never had a family emergency. Yet even so, we realized that it was time for a radio—just as five years earlier we had realized it was time for a computer. Our friends the Schlabachs, who worked among the Bribri Indians, had had a radio for years. Over the 1988 Christmas holidays Ray Schlabach came to Tsipirí and installed our new equipment.

Now three weeks later, the new radio was our lifeline! Several hours after Marian's call, the headlights of the Wilmarth's Mitsubishi pierced the darkness in Tsipirí. Marian had packed our bags and readied the house for a lengthy absence. Soon we were on our way to our base in Santa Ana near the capital, where in the morning we contacted my doctor, but the prescribed painkillers and antibiotics provided little relief.

A staph infection had traveled through the bloodstream from a boil on my side, settling in my foot and then spreading up my leg. Eventually I was hospitalized for surgery, during which the doctor extracted thirty cc. of pus from a four-inch incision in my foot.

"You could have lost your leg—or your life," he commented later. After my release from the hospital, a nurse came daily for several weeks to debride the incision. My doctor, who was a personal friend, would not let me return to Tsipirí.

"Any other doctor," he said, "would have sent you home, but I know you. I know where you live. I don't trust you to stay off those trails!"

While I recuperated, Marian and I enjoyed life in the capital, where we attended a good church and were blessed by fellowship with friends of our inner circle. Peter and his family usually spent much of their time at our base there, but during my recuperation they, along with Timothy and Keiry, were running another cross-cultural training session. David was helping them, but Philip was studying in the States. Priscilla and Jonathan, however, came for a visit in March, and Jonathan gave us help with computer problems. Elizabeth and Noel and their children also came for a working visit and he did some remodeling for us. We even had a visit from Jim, the bug collector who had come to faith while collecting in the Tsipirí area six years before.

Our house there in Santa Ana, which had belonged to Marian's parents during their retirement years in Costa Rica, had a small apartment attached During my recuperation, Marian and I moved into the apartment, which not only gave us our own quarters but freed the main house for Peter's family and for guests. We very much enjoyed our own little "pad" complete with a kitchenette. Actually, our taking over the apartment was the beginning of longer stays in the capital. I was now sixty-seven years old and starting to think about the need for gradual withdrawal from Tsipirí.

Publication Pending

By 1989 the whole New Testament was in at least second draft. Twice we had ordered reprints of Mark and once of Acts. In addition to the New Testament books available for sale, we had distributed early drafts of half of Genesis, a brief version of the Ten Commandments, two chapters of Job, some Psalms, and the book of Jonah. Our most sought-after handout was not actual Scripture, but a simple drawing titled "The Two Ways," depicting Indians trudging along the path of life. A few turned aside at the cross to follow a new trail to heaven; others continued along the broad road which dropped off into the fire. After viewing that drawing, more than one Cabécar came to faith in Christ, saying, "I'm afraid of the fire!"

In February 1989 while I was recuperating from my foot surgery, we arranged for two of our translation helpers to come to the capital for a day to check the Gospel of Matthew. With my foot propped on a chair and my walker at hand, I met with the Bible Society consultant, my two helpers, and Marian. The day was a total contrast to previous checking sessions. The new consultant assigned to us was a young man whose only experience had been with sophisticated, educated Indians, markedly different from our naive, unschooled Cabécars. My helpers didn't understand his questions and comments. We never even finished the short passage he had selected from the Beatitudes. He spent much time discussing one of our renderings with which he disagreed—even though our rendering of the verse agreed with one suggested by the Bible Society translation handbook on Matthew. Our helpers sensed the tension but were not able to answer his questions. For years afterward they talked about that session!

No final decision came out of the session, but we realized we would need to look for a different publisher. Although the director of the Bible Society of Costa Rica had always been very supportive of our work, he did not have authority to publish translations unless approved by a consultant appointed by the United Bible Societies. With the shortage of consultants, the process could take years. Furthermore, there were unsolved problems of compatibility between our computer programs and those of the Bible Society. We had no illusions about the possible difficulties facing us.

Our investigation was to last more than a year as letters went back and forth. The International Bible Society did agree to publish for us, but only if the United Bible Societies would release us. We were greatly relieved when the UBS—publisher of most of our portions—passed the decision down to the Bible Society of Costa Rica. We then contacted *don* Alberto, the local director, who readily agreed to release us.

"We don't care who publishes your New Testament," he said. "We just want to be a part of it."

Once we were released, the IBS agreed to publish our New Testament, but with the understanding that we would have to bear the cost of the camera-ready copy. Their other stipulation was that the Summer Institute of Linguistics would approve our translation. For us, that would mean traveling to Guatemala to check with consultants, but we were happy that things were progressing!

Back to Work at Last

By late April, three months after my surgery, the incision in my foot was almost healed. I was allowed to drive again and to do some walking, even though my foot and leg were still swollen. Finally in May the doctor approved our return to Tsipirí with orders that I do no unnecessary walking; no treks to Indian huts for services—not that I felt like trekking! Instead, my "little flock" hiked to our house every other Sunday for a time of singing, prayer, and Bible study. Even before the problem with my foot, the group from Súfu had sometimes come to our house for services.

"*Don* Aziel, we feel sorry for you having to trek to Súfu," José and Franklin had once said. "Next Sunday we'll go to your house in Tsipirí."

By their standards, I was getting too old to walk that far! At first, they came to our house only occasionally, but after my foot surgery they came twice a month—not only the men, but women and children, even babies. Marian enjoyed participating in the meetings, although it meant preparing a meal for as many as thirty people. For her the Bible study was a wider ministry than the "Sunday School" she had previously taught.

On weekdays I resumed translation, with Marian keyboarding and checking. Soon I finished the third draft of II Corinthians and began the third draft of Ephesians. Marian's prayer was to publish the entire New Testament by the end of December 1992, the fortieth anniversary of our arrival in Costa Rica.

"I'd be embarrassed to take longer than that!" she protested.

Yet how could the two of us possibly finish the remaining books by that time and also update the books previously published? We needed help from our sons, especially the younger ones who were already ahead of us in their grasp of the spoken language, although not in grammatical understanding and translation techniques at that point. Our sons, however, were all busy with their own ministries and studies. Timothy and Keiry were also happily busy with their baby, Rebekah Kay, born on June 8, 1989.

Interlude for Wider Ministry

In addition to translating and ministering to Cabécars, Marian and I were occasionally drawn into side ministries with Christians in Costa Rica, ministry to Americans wanting counsel concerning missions or family, or to Latins planning to be missionaries. With the tremendous church growth in the 1980s and the widespread interest in missions, it was difficult to resist invitations to be involved.

One invitation I accepted was from the pastor of the CAM church in Turrialba, the city closest to our home in Tsipirí. *Don* Carlos was a close friend, so I agreed to preach at a prayer conference late in July of 1989. However, three days before the conference I saw streaks in my right eye, like spider webs. I had had a hemorrhage in that eye the previous year, which cleared up in response to treatment. Now I phoned the ophthalmologist, a Costa Rican trained at Harvard.

"We can't take a chance on a possible detached retina," he warned, but I had no idea what that meant.

That night my eye blacked out completely, but I preached the two messages as scheduled—with one eye. Each night, after the service, the pastor and his wife questioned me in depth about the Holy Spirit. I discovered that they had invited me to preach on prayer so they could talk about the Spirit—perhaps as a result of messages I had given at other CAM churches a few years before, concerning the Holy Spirit in the life of the Lord Jesus.

After the prayer conference, I finally was able to get an appointment with the ophthalmologist in the capital. He sent me for an ultrasound. The technician assured him it was not a detached retina.

"It's probably only a hemorrhage," said the doctor—without checking the ultrasound. "However, if it doesn't clear up in six weeks, come back to see me." Then he left for vacation.

Back at the translation desk, my helpers and I finished Ephesians, Philippians, and Colossians during those six weeks. Never had we worked so efficiently!

Ignorant of the seriousness of my condition, I said to Marian, "Even if I lose my sight in that eye, what we've gotten done on the translation would almost be worth it!"

Another invitation we had accepted was to a major conference called *Avance 2000* (Advance 2000) held in the capital in late August. That conference in 1989 was the largest missions conference ever held in Costa Rica. Dr. Ralph Winters, Dr. Luis Bush, and Dr. David Bryant—each one a key leader in the worldwide missions movement—all ministered during the week-long event attended by several thousand Christians. FEDEMEC, the Costa Rican missions organization sponsoring the conference, responded to the speakers' challenge to reach the world by the year 2000 by committing Costa Rican believers to "adopt" fifty people groups for church planting. Excitement mounted as vision expanded. Young people responded to the Adopt-a-People challenge. Marian and I attended almost all sessions, participating in a seminar on the education of missionary children. Peter was deeply involved in the preparations for the conference as well as in the seminars. Our three youngest sons sat eagerly on the front row during the sessions. It was an unforgettable week for us all.

The surge of interest in world missions impacted not only our family but even some Cabécars. Peter and Timothy took Efraín to San José for the *Avance 2000* Conference and then to a missions conference in Honduras where Peter was a speaker. Seeing a tribal convert moves and inspires people deeply, yet being exhibited may engender pride and ultimately be harmful to a convert's spiritual life. Did it harm Efraín?

Peter and Debbie were near the center of this new missions vortex. By the time of *Avance 2000* they had completed three sessions of *Etno*, his cross-cultural training camp near the Cabécar territory along the Estrella River. Each session basically took several months of his time, including interviews, screening, a *"Pre-Etno"* weekend, a month or more at jungle camp, and then debriefing. When not at jungle camp, they spent most of their time near the capital in Santa Ana, which became a hub for Peter's trainees. Marian and I and our younger sons also felt strongly the heartbeat of God for the "dark half of the world." In fact, the younger ones assisted Peter at the camp as they were able.

Leading *Etno* was only part of Peter's involvement in missions. For a time he taught anthropology to potential missionaries at a seminary in Costa Rica, and he also went to the U.S. to take part in a consultation on establishing a linguistics program in Costa Rica.

Another facet of Peter's ministry was to stimulate prayer for missions. In the early days of the missions movement a Central American friend had phoned him from Guatemala, greeting him with a question, "What country did you pray for today?"—a blunt reminder that according to *Operation World* this was the day to pray for Costa Rica!

In 1986 I myself got a copy of an early edition of *Operation World*, the prayer almanac. By the time the next edition appeared, I was already "hooked." Marian joined me in prayer for the world but wanted her own copy of the book. Our burden for the unreached people groups kept intensifying as we prayed through *Operation World*.

More Months Lost

Following the *Avance 2000* Conference I returned to the ophthalmologist. Six weeks had passed since the ultrasound, but I still had no sight in my right eye. The ophthalmologist sent me to the United States, where a retinal specialist in Columbia found a badly torn retina, three-fourths detached. He sent me to Atlanta for surgery by the specialist under whom he had studied. They reattached the retina but did not promise that reading vision would return in that eye.

Recuperation at our stateside home in Columbia was pleasant. Our two youngest sons were with us, David studying by correspondence and Philip back for his second year at Columbia Bible College. He had spent the summer in Costa Rica with the Cabécars, including three weeks in remote Telire. Susanna and Prem and their little Irene were also with us, preparing to go to India as newly-appointed candidates with WEC International. Steven and Cameron lived nearby with their three boys, after spending the summer in Costa Rica on a building project as they had the previous summer. We missed seeing Priscilla and Jonathan who left in August to begin Urdu study in Pakistan. However, we were able to see most of my twelve siblings during a trip to Alabama with David as chauffeur.

A few weeks after the retina surgery, I had to return to Atlanta for a second surgery. However, little vision was restored. Weary with trying contacts and prism lenses, I eventually settled down to regular glasses, got used to some double vision, and adjusted to life with only one useful eye. When I was finally released by the eye doctor, I had lost most of a year due to my foot surgery and my eye surgeries.

Back to the Translation Desk

In February 1990 we returned to Tsipirí and focused on finishing the translation of Hebrews. Few books are as difficult to translate, but few moved me as much as Hebrews—revealing what a Savior and Priest we have in Jesus! Marian kept working on the manuscript of Revelation. One of Peter's trainees, a young woman named Marilyn who was preparing to become a translator, spent several weeks helping us. During her time in Tsipirí, she finished keyboarding the books of the New Testament which had not yet been put on the computer. By mid-1990 we had printouts available of the third draft of all the unpublished books except the last few chapters of Revelation. Translation kept moving five days a week, except for necessary trips to Turrialba or the capital.

In October 1990 I was working in my study when Marian called excitedly from the next room, "I just finished typing Revelation." Then she added, "I've now typed all of the New Testament at least once."

The next day Philip and I bowed in prayer with the translation helpers after we revised her copy of Revelation. Marian actually typed the New Testament three times—mostly on a manual typewriter. Each time she had revised what I had done, checking both the meaning of the original and the accuracy of the translation. She still ran the house, did the bookkeeping and clerical work, and edited my writing—as well as meeting the Lord alone an hour or more each morning before breakfast.

Translation is often boring, tedious work, mixed with agonizing decisions based on extensive research. Yet translating the book of Hebrews moved us to a deeper appreciation of the sacrificial offering of Jesus Christ, and translating Revelation moved us to worship. We felt like shouting "Hallelujah" with the living creatures, the twenty-four elders, the angelic hosts, and the multitude in white as they prostrated themselves in worship to the One sitting on the throne and to the Lamb.

We Lose Efraín

Meanwhile, ministry among the Cabécars had begun to sour. After five very encouraging years, a serious problem arose concerning Efraín, whose conversion had sparked the work across the Chirripó River. Up until this problem arose, Timothy and Keiry had spent much time with Efraín's family, living together in the big house Timothy had built for them. The family called Timothy *kibí*,

"elder brother;" he and Keiry called Efraín's wife *mina*, "mama."
They had sowed and harvested beans together, trekked to Telire
together, and ministered together. Believers from Efraín's group had
started two new groups further up the Chirripó River. Believers from
all over the area celebrated Holy Week together by acting out the
Easter story from the trial to the crucifixion to the resurrection—an
outdoor drama.

Efraín and Timothy had also led the believers in building a large
conference center at a place called Chimoklä which belonged to
Efraín's father. (Efraín's grandfather had lived in the area in 1895
when he received the first missionary, Mr. Jamison. A generation
later Efraín's father had welcomed Dean Lewis there.) The center at
Chimoklä came to be known as the Central Church.

Now a shadow hung over Efraín—a moral question. There had
been other hints that something was wrong. Timothy spoke with
him—only to be rejected by his disciple. In the heat of the conflict,
Timothy quoted to him the words of the Apostle Paul, "You have
many teachers, but only one father."

In the light of our concern for Efraín, Timothy called a meeting
with emerging Cabécar leaders in May 1990 to study the Scriptures
regarding church government. We met in Tsipirí at the little house
behind ours where Timothy and Keiry were now living, the house
where Peter and Debbie had lived a decade before. Young Indians
filled the room—some even perched on the rafters. Efraín, of course,
was there. I sat in the back, observing. It was beautiful to me to hear
Timothy teach the passages in the Pastoral Epistles concerning elders
and deacons and then to listen to the discussion that followed.

At the final session with the leaders, Efraín asked permission for
his stepson to read a passage from Titus: *"The laborer is worthy of his
hire."* The atmosphere became tense as Efraín challenged Timothy,
"What do you say to this?" (Unknown to us, Efraín had gone several
months previously to the pastor of the CAM church in Turrialba to
solicit a monthly offering. The money had since been taken away at
my request, for we were committed to establishing churches that
would not be dependent on outside financing.) Timothy explained

that believers should bring their tithes and offerings in order to support their pastors. Actually, there were no Cabécar pastors; the congregations were led by *de facto* elders.

This session revealed that Efraín's moral problem was compounded by his desire to be paid a salary and be named the chief leader—the "bishop." Relationships deteriorated quickly. Timothy felt the sting deeply, for a close relationship with several people was shattered in one blow. Philip and David shared Timothy's hurt, for they were also involved. All three were friends of Efraín and his family.

Soon Efraín went to town and recruited a Spanish-speaking pastor to preach at Jamáritábá, a man from a denomination that does not hold to the Trinity. Many of the believers who had been meeting with Efraín at Jamáritábá left and began meeting nearby at Ñári. Fortunately, the two newer churches further upstream were not affected, nor was the group I led. My little flock continued to trek over rugged terrain to meet at our house every two weeks.

Later Efraín abandoned his faith in Christ and accepted a position teaching the Cabécar religion and language in the new government school. His marriage—which had brought us much satisfaction just a few years before—broke up and the family divided. He had been the first of the believers to marry legally. Now he abandoned Adelina for another woman, but she continued to follow the Lord. Her brother remarked that Efraín was "like a bent nail that could not be straightened." Efraín's defection was a traumatic experience for Timothy, a trial by fire.

"Daddy, We Need to Talk"

Not long afterward Timothy and Peter came to me saying, "Daddy, we need to talk." Efraín's case had brought up serious questions: "What is the extent of our apostolic authority and when does it cease? How do we meet the need for qualified elders, and for a structure which handles discipline and yet allows freedom in the Spirit? What about the unresolved question of common-law marriages? (Most believers had mates but were not married.) Should they be legally married to be baptized, to take the Lord's Supper, to be leaders?" I had been following the standards of the CAM churches which required legal marriage before baptism and admittance to the Lord's Table. However, as my sons talked, I knew that I would cede to them; for Scripture does not mention such qualifications. The Biblical mandate for a believer is: "Repent and be baptized." The qualification for baptism is faith. The qualification for admittance to the Lord's Table is a life consistent with one's confession of faith.

The last topic discussed that day was the matter of my successor. Was it time to hand over authority to my sons? I recognized that at best I was now mostly a consultant. I realized the truth of a statement I had recently read: "Success without a successor is failure."

Even before the trouble with Efraín which produced the interchange with our sons, Timothy had initiated occasional training sessions for potential leaders. The first leadership training conference took place in 1989 with the help of Philip and David. In the meetings there was teaching on the nature of the local church and its leadership by elders. We looked for men who were stable and capable, who planned to marry legally, and who rejected all demon-oriented practices. We sought overall coordination by a group of elders while still maintaining the autonomy of each congregation.

Family Coming and Going

Soon after all the trauma with Efraín, Timothy and his family flew to the States to spend the last six months of 1990 visiting supporters and doing further study in linguistics—a needed break from the pressures of ministry. In May of that year Philip finished an associate degree at Columbia Bible College, and then studied for three months at the Summer Institute of Linguistics in Oregon. He then returned to Tsipirí to help in the ministry. Shortly after Philip came home, David finished his high school correspondence courses and left for Bible training at CBC. Marian was glad to have at least one son at home, and she appreciated Philip's help in the kitchen, as well as with the computer.

Peter and his family were in the States for a short break, but before they returned to Costa Rica, Peter flew to London for a consultation on unreached people groups—he was becoming a walking missions encyclopedia. Steven and his family had spent the summers of 1988 and 1989 in Costa Rica helping a missionary friend with construction projects, but in 1990 he did a major re-roofing project in Pennsylvania for the organization with which Susanna and Prem served. Prem helped with the project, as did Noel, Elizabeth's husband. (Elizabeth and Noel had moved to Rhode Island the year before, leaving only Steven's family in Columbia.) The three couples and their little ones had a great time together in Pennsylvania. A few months later Susanna and Prem and their little girl flew to India to begin their work in Allahabad. Meanwhile in Pakistan a new grandchild was born. Timothy Daniel, Priscilla and Jonathan Kew's first child, arrived on October 6, 1990.

A Significant Prayer Meeting

In January 1991 we Joneses in Costa Rica had a day of prayer—it had become our custom to start the New Year in prayer. When the time came for me and Marian to verbalize our prayer requests, we began, "Well, there's always the translation!" Before we realized it, Timothy was at the blackboard while Peter moderated a two-hour planning session. On the blackboard a chart appeared with a time frame for finalizing the Cabécar New Testament. We never got prayed for, but the chart clarified a plan which made the staggering task less overwhelming.

My job would be to revise the books already published. As I finished each book, Philip would check for consistency in terminology and would enter all changes on the computer. Timothy would check it for naturalness. Marian would proofread and double-check meaning. Peter promised practical help from some of his *Etno* trainees. The next two years would be among the most intense of our lives.

Getting Ready to Publish

There was much work to do. We had eight books of the New Testament to finalize for checking by SIL in Guatemala. Furthermore, we had to revise the nineteen books previously published. After I had revised Mark, Acts, and John, I passed them on to Timothy to check.

"Daddy," he commented, "Philip and I can check the other sixteen books more easily if we do it from scratch."

That ended my practical involvement in the revision. Instead I went back to work on the Old Testament, while Marian checked New Testament books for accuracy and worked out details with Timothy and Philip.

At this point, following Jonathan Kew's advice, we bought a Macintosh computer plus a better printer. Jonathan created the special character fonts we needed for the new computer. Peter and his friend Eduardo spent many hours transferring the New Testament files from our old Compaq to the Macintosh. Eduardo later helped orient Philip, who would become our key computer man. At this point we were hoping to publish by the end of 1992.

As we finalized the New Testament we asked our friends to pray for the right choice of words. In preparation for the final approval of our translation we needed to prepare a list detailing how we translated more than one hundred New Testament terms, such as "apostle," "disciple," "confess," and "believe." These terms are potential problems for people with no Christian tradition. We had to make a final decision about the term "Son of Man," which we had translated four different ways over the years. Furthermore, we had translated "anointed" a dozen ways, but ended up with three ways to express the idea.

However, we did not question our choice of the term for "God," assuming the traditional term was acceptable. This almost became a *fatal* choice. We had been taught that the native term, even though not totally satisfactory, would in time be redefined by its use in the Bible. The name *Sibö* was the accepted term among the Cabécars and Bribris, as well as related tribes in nearby Panama. We never even considered looking for an alternative. We went on happily and excitedly, determined to finish the New Testament. However, later reconsideration of this term would cause a shock wave—and much pain.

Checking in Guatemala

In April 1991 Marian and I flew to Guatemala for the first round of checking the Cabécar New Testament with Wycliffe consultants— experienced translators who had been trained to check the work of others. We arrived exhausted from getting material ready to be checked. For weeks we had worked with Timothy and Philip from breakfast until bedtime in our "translation factory," while Timothy's wife prepared our meals. Even though it was during bean harvest season we had plenty of Cabécar helpers, especially Franklin and Nasario.

During our month in Guatemala the consultants gave us a great boost when they told us they would not require us to recheck any book that had previously been published. That meant we had only eight books to check! During the checking sessions we read a portion aloud, one sentence at a time, then translated it literally back to English for the consultant to evaluate. It was a word-for-word check, not a spot check, but even so it went fast with few problems. We completed I Corinthians, Matthew, and Galatians—each book with a different consultant. We returned to Costa Rica with some suggestions to work on, but with their approval.

EARTHQUAKE

While in Guatemala, we turned on the radio one evening and heard shocking news: An earthquake registering 7.2 had caused extensive damage and even some deaths in Costa Rica—the strongest quake worldwide during 1991. The Caribbean watershed where the Cabécars live was the most affected. In fact, the epicenter was at the mountain named for the Cabécar lord of the nether world.

When we finally made phone contact with Costa Rica we learned that at our house—thirty-five miles from the epicenter—everything had fallen from shelves and cabinets. The kitchen floor was a jumble of pots and pans. The study was a sea of books and papers. Furniture shifted, even the piano. Our car was not damaged, but our garage fell onto the generator. In Chirripó, mountains moved, entire Indian farms slid to the bottom in massive landslides. Our close friends, Ray and Susie Schlabach, lost their house in the lowlands near the Bribri Indians; Susie barely escaped as it fell.

"A jumble of pots and pans"

Later we found out that one of the Cabécar believers who fled his hut during the quake went back to grab his copy of Luke. He read to his family from Luke 21, which speaks about earthquakes preceding the return of the Lord. The unbelievers among the Cabécars fear earthquakes as a sign of *sa̱ érdawá*, "the end of the world."

The devastation caused
by the earthquake in April
was compounded in August
by torrential rains which
caused massive destruction,
bringing down trees, boul-
ders, and hillsides loosened
by the quake and weeks of
aftershocks. Bridges fell and
roads were severely dam-
aged throughout the Caribbean watershed. The storm
caused even more destruc-
tion than the earthquake! It
took twelve grueling days of
pick-and-shovel work by
David and his Cabécar crew
to clear the landslides be-

"A sea of books and papers"

tween our house and Moravia. Someone jokingly called that road
"Aziel's three-mile driveway," because it fell to me to finance the
repairs even though it was a public road.

Before the storm David had not only helped our colleagues the
Schlabachs get ready to rebuild their house but had also restored our
generator shed. However, it was several months until he poured a
new foundation for our garage during a break from his studies in
South Carolina. Eventually Timothy rebuilt the garage, enlarging it to
accommodate a second vehicle. At the time we were still sharing our
ten-year-old Toyota with him, and occasionally with Peter as well.

Cabécar Elders Ordained

After returning from our month in Guatemala, Marian and I began revising the books we would work on during the next checking
session. Interruptions, visitors, and supply trips continued. On weekends our younger sons were involved in their usual ministries across
the river, while I led Sunday Bible studies at Tsipirí and the Saturday
night ministry in Spanish. In June Timothy asked that I go with him

on an overnight trek to Chimoklä to baptize some believers and ordain elders. Keiry accompanied us, with little Rebekah strapped to her back Indian-style. The five-hour trek from Tsipirí—all downhill after the first hour—was painful. Each downhill step was a jolt to my arthritic knees.

Before the evening meeting at the Central Church, I enjoyed watching Keiry—totally at ease—working with the women as they prepared supper in the conference kitchen. The next morning, Sunday, after the new believers gave a clear testimony of faith in Jesus Christ, I baptized eleven Cabécars in the rushing white waters of the Chirripó River. Timothy assisted me with the men, and the husbands helped me with their wives.

Afterwards the believers all gathered in the chapel, and Timothy served the Lords' Supper, using separate gourds for the men and the women in case some woman might be considered ritually unclean. Then Timothy called the six church leaders to the front, including Franklin and José Gilberto from my group. The setting was rather basic, even crude, with all of us in muddy rubber boots. Timothy was leading, but I joined him in praying and laying hands on the men for this first formal ordination of elders.

We already had four or five congregations of believers, most of whom were baptized. Now we were officially recognizing the natural leaders of these congregations as elders. With this, we now had structure in the Cabécar churches. Then, though I had not planned it, I took care of one final piece of business.

My Successor

I had planned to return for another baptism in August and had decided that at that time I would name my successor. However, I had not told Timothy nor had I even mentioned it to Marian. Yet, as I sat there on the crude bench I realized, "With my bad legs, I'll never make it back here in August. I must act today." So—like Samuel anointing David in an impromptu meeting in rustic circumstances—I called Timothy to the front of the chapel after the ordinations and laid my hands on him. As we stood on the muddy floor in our wet clothes, I commissioned him to oversee the emerging Cabécar churches and then prayed for him, my successor. It was the right time. It was the right place.

That afternoon I climbed slowly upward for four hours out of the Chirripó River Valley, and then headed down the last hour to Tsipirí. Supported by my walking stick, I cautiously chose each step through the muddy holes made by pack horses. I had difficulty staying on my feet, for the "shock absorbers" in my knees were totally worn out. I was now sixty-nine years old; it had been thirty-eight years since my first trek to Chirripó with Dean Lewis. As I turned into my driveway at Tsipirí, I knew I would never trek that trail again.

Timothy and Aziel baptizing at Tsipirí

After bathing in the icy creek, I lay down on the couch to be refreshed as I reveled in vibrant worship music. The trip had been worth the agony. I was glad I had commissioned Timothy. I told Marian that I was confident the Spirit had led.

Our Fortieth Anniversary

Our fortieth anniversary celebration in September 1991 was shared by fifty friends—missionary colleagues and other local friends, spiritual children, four of our own sons, their wives and children, as well as Marian's sister and family. Our oldest son, Peter, emceed the two-hour program at Santa Ana, our base near the capital, switching between English and Spanish as he spoke of his impressions of our home—the Word of God and work.

One visitor wrote later: "I'll always remember last Sunday. The sight of you two seated with your sons behind you praying for you. To know the Lord will bless each generation in your family. *'One generation shall praise thy works to another, and shall declare thy mighty acts'* (Psalm 145:4)." Another friend wrote appreciating our children's "willingness to produce children to continue the good seed." That was our vision and prayer.

With each year the family kept increasing. That summer Marian had manned the daily radio "sked", waiting for an announcement. On July 8, 1991, we heard the big news—two new grandchildren on a single day! Christiana Hope was born to Steven and Cameron, their first daughter; and Simon Carlos was born to Noel and Elizabeth, their third son. Each was the fourth child in their family. Three months later, Timothy and Keiry had a second daughter, Hannah Kristina, born on October 7. Her birth brought the grandchild count to sixteen—nine boys and seven girls.

At that time Peter and his family were gearing up for another *Etno*. He had been in Guatemala while we were there in April, doing a presentation at a missions congress and participating in a consultation on training third-world missionaries. On his return to Costa Rica he edited a manual for the Adopt-a-People movement and helped design a missions curriculum for a local seminary. Yet the growing interest in reaching the world with the gospel was not without opposition.

New Opposition

That fall, at the beginning of the yearlong celebration that would culminate with the five hundredth anniversary of the discovery of Costa Rica by Columbus, a book was published decrying the oppression of the Indians. In it our work among the Cabécars was mentioned as being dangerous and aggressive in terms of weaning the Indians away from their own religion. The book ended with an appeal for governments to remove all such workers from Indian territories. Missionary friends in other tribes in Latin America were hearing the same refrain.

Locally, a rumor surfaced that the priest threatened to gather up and burn the Scripture portions that we had published. Nothing came of it, but a few months later Efraín led a large meeting urging Cabécars not to leave the old ways. The priest—who had spoken of the need to recognize the "cultural base" of the Indians—opened the church for this meeting, the purpose of which was to announce the formation of an association of witch doctors.

Later a Korean missionary, working through Spanish, took over part of one Cabécar church across the Chirripó River. He had begun by luring the people with gifts and offering salaries for elders. When we visited him, hoping for some cooperative effort, he refused further contact with us.

"You have no membership lists, so you have no church," he claimed.

The Apostle Paul had to learn to thank God that the gospel was preached for whatever motive, but for me it was hard! I found rest in remembering that God will reward according to *His* evaluation. Timothy seemed unperturbed by the Korean, remarking that the Cabécars would have to decide for themselves what kind of church they wanted. However, Timothy did establish an association of Cabécar-speaking churches.

Other "competitors" have come and gone, but the Korean has continued disrupting the churches in various areas. We try never to forget the words of Jesus in Matthew 15:13: *"Every plant, which my heavenly Father hath not planted, shall be rooted up."*

To Guatemala Again—and Again

In the face of this opposition we pushed toward finalizing the New Testament. Other translators encouraged us.

"You may think you'll never finish the final revision and the checking, but you will," they insisted.

I had already finished revising the books we first published. Marian and Philip were working together on books not yet published in order to be sure they were faithful to the original. Timothy then read their work to new helpers to see if they understood it and if it sounded as natural as though a Cabécar had written it. Philip had also produced a new edition of the Cabécar songbook with formatting help from Paul Williams, the Bribri translator. They used the new Cabécar/Bribri fonts developed for the Macintosh by Jonathan Kew, our son-in-law. He mailed them to the "Jones Family Computer Department" from Pakistan where he assisted translators with their computer problems.

In November we flew to Guatemala for a couple of weeks to have four more epistles checked by Wycliffe. This time Philip accompanied us, not only to help with the back translation but to receive orientation regarding his part in the final computer work on the manuscript. He found the details involved in running the consistency checks somewhat overwhelming. During the checking sessions we quickly finished II Corinthians, Ephesians, Philippians, and Colossians. We even had some time to socialize with fellow translators and other missionary friends.

When we returned to Guatemala in April 1992, Timothy went with us. In Guatemala he translated the book of Hebrews from Cabécar back to English in just two-and-a-half days.

"I've never had anyone do Hebrews so quickly!" exclaimed the consultant.

For Timothy it was easy, for he was fresh from teaching Hebrews to Cabécar believers. Although Hebrews is considered the hardest book of the New Testament to translate due to the many historical allusions to the Old Testament, he had worked over the translation so thoroughly that the consultant made only a few suggestions for improvement. Finishing Hebrews in such a short time left the rest of the week for Revelation. When Timothy completed the back-translation, we all bowed in worship, praying with the Apostle John, *"Even so, come, Lord Jesus."*

While we were at the SIL Center in Guatemala, one of the members of Wycliffe made a significant comment to Marian.

"We all revise and revise," she said, "but we can't go beyond our level of incompetence. Those sons of yours have taken your translation beyond your level of incompetence."

It was true, but no credit to us. Their command of the language was far beyond ours. We have no explanation of how our sons got involved, except as friends of the Indians, and because they loved Jesus—not because we asked them to help.

The Cabécar Churches Grow and Thrive

Before Timothy arrived in Guatemala, he and Philip ministered at the Holy Week Conference for the Cabécars of the Chirripó Valley. It was the largest crowd that ever gathered at the newly rebuilt Central Church. (The building had been damaged by the earthquake and later demolished by a landslide. Furthermore, Efraín had taken the roofing that was salvaged.) Eight believers were baptized and others publicly professed Christ. The conference was a time of joy after the setbacks caused by Efraín's defection.

At the same time Peter was ministering in the Estrella Valley where after his heartbreak years before, a church was finally emerging near his cross-cultural missions training camp. There were encouraging developments as well among the Cabécars living along the Pacuare River where Franklin, one of my translation helpers, had recently spearheaded outreach.

"What motivated you to go teach the Word?" I asked him.

"When you laid hands on me last year to ordain me as an elder," he replied.

Ministry also continued in the remote Telire Valley. Marian prayed much for our sons' safety on such trips, especially after Philip's experience in 1988 when he was accosted by authorities searching for drug runners. David made a trip a few weeks later without incident, and Timothy even took Keiry there on a trek not long afterward. Philip himself spent three weeks in Telire the following year without a problem.

As the churches grew, so did the sale of Scripture portions—an average of almost one portion a day. We were encouraged that the emerging church was using the Word in the meetings, with illiterate believers learning to read as they studied the Scripture. Furthermore, some were beginning to have personal and family devotions. Only the Word applied by the Spirit could remold the animistic Cabécar culture.

In addition to the sale of Scripture, there was a steady demand for literacy materials and the Cabécar songbook, our fastest moving piece. Philip was the one most involved with music, although Steven had composed many of the earlier songs following my initial efforts and some input from Marian. In the summer of 1988 Philip had taken Bill Supplee, professor of music at Columbia Bible College, to the new group in Sinoli. Mr. Supplee had previously helped other missionaries develop ethnically appropriate Scripture songs. What a blessing it was for Philip, so creative musically, to learn from Bill, "a kindred spirit in the Lord!" Philip kept producing new editions of the songbook and even a cassette to help isolated believers learn new songs. Inspired by the Spirit, young Cabécars themselves began composing music to praise the Lord, as well as to express Scriptural truth.

It was rewarding to see believers get their lives in order. In July 1992, thanks to a new government provision facilitating the documentation of Indians, the marriages of ten Cabécar couples were legalized. Timothy and Keiry arranged a mass wedding ceremony with a Christian lawyer officiating. It was moving to hear couple after couple promise to love, respect, serve, and be faithful to each other. Although most had lived together for years, they were embarrassed even to join hands for the ceremony. (The Cabécar term for legal marriage is *julákukäk* "to join hands," but touching in public was not a normal practice.) To accommodate the crowd, Timothy had built an Indian-style chapel in the front yard of his house in Tsipirí. The night before the ceremony eighty Indians from as far as a day's trek away met to praise the Lord and to study a computer printout of a passage dealing with marriage. Twenty-seven took part in reading the forty verses of I Corinthians 7—proof that the believers were literate and were building their lives on the Word.

Joining hands in marriage

The Grano de Oro Church Survives

There were many months I could not continue to minister to the Spanish church we had planted in Grano de Oro—months in the capital recovering from the infection in my foot, months in the United States for surgery on my detached retina, and weeks in Guatemala checking translation. Yet the church survived. It was their church; they took responsibility for it. For weeks at a time the little group would meet on their own at the chapel with Ramón leading, or at least facilitating, as they sang, prayed, and read the Word. During the week they met in homes for a cottage prayer meeting. Once a month they opened the chapel for a day of prayer—signing up individually to come and pray for an hour.

At times the young people we had sent to Bible School helped out with the services. When we inaugurated the chapel, Moisés, our first graduate, led the meetings for a time. I had hoped he would continue indefinitely, but he moved to the city with his parents and siblings and began helping our friend Bob Wilmarth with construction and with preaching. Eventually he married an American associated with Bob's ministry and moved to the United States. One of Javier's sons, a young man named Cristian, studied at Elim Bible Institute, partly financed by the church. On vacations and for a time afterward he preached at the chapel before moving to the capital.

The girls who studied for the Lord's service helped in various ways, with Lourdes and Alcira teaching the children; both later married. Pércides worked full-time in a country church until her fellow student from the Guatemala Bible Institute moved to Costa Rica to court her. It was my pleasure to marry them in the Grano de Oro chapel; she and Noé went on to serve in the pastorate of a CAM church. As for Noribette, whose conversion and baptism had been so significant, she studied in San José at a seminary called ESEPA, the School of Pastoral Studies, where she met Michael Day from Wheaton, Illinois. I had the special privilege of performing their wedding in 1990 in a large ceremony at the CAM church in Turrialba. After her graduation she and Mike ministered in Grano de Oro one weekend each month while he continued his studies.

Noribette and Mike

To us it was very gratifying to have six of the young people complete their preparation for the Lord's service, especially considering the small size of the church. I had baptized twenty-two believers before the chapel was built, and then on Good Friday, 1990, I baptized four more, including three siblings of Cristian. The other person baptized that day was Elena, the one who had been instrumental in opening the door for Bible studies in Grano de Oro. All this time Luis, her husband, had denied permission for her to be baptized, but he finally relented.

Although there were never any strong leaders in the church, the ones who did accept responsibility were faithful. Ramón continued as elder after Johnny, the other elder, moved out of the area, Elena became deaconess, and Jeanette was treasurer. I had the privilege of marrying Ramón and Jeanette.

Many in the church were the children, grandchildren, or sons- or daughters-in-laws of *don* Moisés, who first hosted our Bible studies in Grano de Oro. During his last week of life, he professed faith in Christ—the answer to many years of prayer. His son-in-law Noé baptized him in the hospital. When he died, two of the sons-in-law bought the casket and were offered either candle holders for a Catholic wake or flower stands for an evangelical viewing. One reportedly responded, "Don't give us candle holders, give us flower stands; he was an evangelical!" It was my privilege to conduct the funeral at the church Noé was then pastoring. I felt great liberty in my message, and Marian played the piano for the service. *Don* Moisés' widow, faithful *doña* Chala, and all thirteen children and their extended families were there, as well as some of our own family. On the way to the cemetery, the procession stopped for rites at the Catholic Church—apparently to satisfy those who were not evangelical. We felt close to all the family in their sorrow, yet it was also a day of victory in Jesus.

The Grano de Oro chapel continued to be a blessing. The believers took good care of the property and financed improvements on the building, as well as helping pay the expenses of the students at Bible School. Now that I was no longer able to spend all day Sunday trekking to Chirripó, I changed the meetings at Grano de Oro to

Sunday afternoon, following the meeting with Cabécar believers in the morning at our house in Tsipirí. It took a while for everyone to adjust, especially since the soccer games were always played on Sunday afternoons. The girls continued to hold Sunday School on Sunday mornings for the children. It was a joy to see the chapel fully utilized on the Lord's Day.

After the church was well established, others wanted a "piece" of it. More than one individual or group came to Grano de Oro with the idea of taking over the church, whether overtly or subtly. In my early days in Costa Rica, the Lord spoke to me from the Apostle Paul's words about those who in his absence preached Christ from dubious motives, saying, *"I therein do rejoice, yea, and will rejoice"* (Philippians 1:18). Even so, I found it a bitter pill to swallow in regard to Grano de Oro. Surprisingly, the believers quietly resisted all outside efforts to take over. The credit for the survival of the Grano de Oro church goes to the Lord, who said, *"I will build my church and the gates of hell shall not prevail against it."*

Down to the Wire

Even though we had completed the necessary consultant checking in Guatemala, there was still an enormous amount of work to do after we returned to Tsipirí at the end of April, 1992. One translator was asked, "How many times do you check?" There seemed to be no end of details to check as we prepared for our son-in-law Jonathan, a specialist in typesetting Scripture, to arrive from Pakistan. During the final weeks of checking Timothy and Philip worked ten hours a day, six days a week. On some days the picture was like this: Timothy checking with his two men in his house behind ours; Philip in my study doing final polishing with his two men; me in a corner of the living room with my two men, translating Exodus; and Marian on the computer entering changes. Missionary friend Helen Richardson spent a few weeks helping with housework and keyboarding.

Meanwhile Peter and Debbie were rejoicing in the birth of Samuel Peter on May 28—their fifth child. In late July their older daughter, Joanna, then twelve, flew to Spain with a missions team from Costa Rica to evangelize at the 1992 Olympics. Young Joanna raised her own financial support for the trip; it was already becoming obvious that the Lord's hand was on her.

Nasario and Timothy checking the Synoptic Gospels at Santa Ana

For the month of August our whole team converged on our base in Santa Ana where Peter and Deb were then living. Jonathan, Priscilla, and their little son joined us. While still in Pakistan, Jonathan had created the special character fonts, as well as a hyphenation program with data sent by Philip. Jonathan had also written programs for our Macintosh to check punctuation and chapter and verse numbers, since the existing programs were written for IBM machines. Now he helped with entering changes, and then began the actual typesetting process. Timothy and Philip toiled long hours making final changes with their Indian helpers. Marian put in many hours proofreading, and I did quite a lot of it myself. Jonathan and Philip kept the work coordinated, while Peter helped in various ways. Debbie, Keiry, and Priscilla helped with meals, and the cousins had fun playing with each other.

Lencho and Philip checking the translation at Santa Ana

Twenty-two of us lived together for a month, working long hours without accident or incident. Sundays were a relief from the intense concentration. We were all pushing to the limit, for the work had to be completed before Jonathan and Priscilla left. Philip and Lencho worked outside on a bench in the yard, while Timothy and Nasario worked in an old stable as they checked the parallel passages with a makeshift harmony of the Gospels. Interestingly, Timothy at thirteen had taught Nasario, then twelve, to read. These two were the ones who made the very last changes on the translation. We had finished!

On the last night we celebrated with a pizza party. Paul and Linda Williams, our colleagues translating for the Bribris, joined us, just as they had joined us on the first day in a good time of prayer for the upcoming typesetting. Most of the talk that evening was about translation—what else! After the party, it was back to work until long after midnight, as Philip, Jonathan, and Timothy finished selecting the seventy illustrations to be included in the New Testament. Then Timothy prayed again, thanking the Lord for bringing all the loose ends together on the last day. It had been touch-and-go all along, wondering if we would finish by the deadline. What a satisfaction we all felt as we gathered up the printouts and prepared for the next step of the process.

Approved for Publication!

The next morning—after the month-long final push in Santa Ana—we were off to the airport early to face the longest line we had ever seen, while the Indian who was with us stood gazing at this scene from another world. Marian and Philip accompanied Jonathan and Priscilla to Guatemala, where Jonathan was to consult with colleagues, as well as continue typesetting. During the two weeks there Marian and Philip checked the changes that had been entered into the final copy and checked consistency of spelling in the word list that Jonathan had prepared—fourteen thousand different words, counting all variant forms as separate words. While there Marian finished the first complete proofreading of the New Testament and began the second. Her verse for that work was I Corinthians 15:58, *"...your labour is not in vain in the Lord."*

Philip and Marian proofreading the New Testament in Guatemala

The SIL office in Guatemala gave the final approval needed by IBS before publishing the Cabécar New Testament. Philip, then twenty-four, happened to be the one who took the approval form to the office for the necessary signature.

"You must be the youngest person ever for whom I've signed a final approval form," said the one in charge.

It had been almost forty years since my first attempt to write a Cabécar word. A lump formed in my throat as I wrote this and reflected.

Time to Take a Break

Philip accompanied Jonathan and his family from Guatemala to South Carolina, where Philip resumed his studies at Columbia Bible College. Marian and I soon followed to spend several months in the States. She kept proofreading for any typo, glitch, misspelling, or error in punctuation, while Philip entered corrections in his free time.

In Marian's diary for October 31, 1992, she wrote: "Spent the day finalizing the proofreading. Finished Revelation 22 at 11:10 pm. PTL!!! The end of a long, long job; a blessed job. Thank You, Lord, for the privilege of helping give Your Word to still another tribe. May they treasure Your Word like I do." Philip finished entering changes a few minutes later. Then we three celebrated, committing the New Testament to the Lord. At this point we were *really* finished. (Once published, we found *no typographical errors*. PTL!)

Now it was time to relax, for Marian was exhausted from the sustained concentration of the last months. The two-day drive to New Jersey was restful, and the weekend at Bethany Church was delightful, as we renewed sweet friendships. From there we traveled to various places in Pennsylvania, visiting friends and supporters. The weather was chilly but the visits were refreshing. We even got to see Marian's only brother. Snow flurries fell one Sunday as we traveled to report to supporting churches in Pittsburgh where we were warmly welcomed. More visits followed in Ohio, including time with the Kibbeys who had been our "neighbors" during their years in

Costa Rica. By Thanksgiving we were back in sunny South Carolina, counting our blessings in terms of rich times with the Lord's people on our trip.

In December we enjoyed a four-day family reunion at a lodge in the mountains of North Carolina. All the children and grandchildren were there except for Susanna and her family, who were detained in India. The weather was very mild, allowing the children outside playtime. We adults took turns updating each other on events since our last reunion in 1987 and sharing our hopes for the future. We worshipped together and prayed for each other. Marian and I were the last to share; what a privilege it was to have the family's input and encouragement and then to have five sons and two sons-in-law gather around, lay hands on us, and pray. We ended with the Lord's Supper and the Doxology. Marian and I felt blessed beyond measure.

After our reunion the family scattered once more. Elizabeth and Noel returned to New England. Philip went back to Costa Rica but with plans to return to CBC for the spring quarter. David finished his diesel mechanics course and returned to Costa Rica to help Peter and Debbie with *Etno* and to keep our four-wheel-drive vehicles in repair. Timothy and Keiry went to Dallas for a semester of further linguistic studies. Priscilla and Jonathan also went to Dallas while he finished typesetting the Cabécar New Testament. Only Steven and Cameron were in South Carolina near us.

As the year ended, we marked the completion of forty years since we first arrived in Costa Rica—one year studying Spanish, thirteen years of exploring and learning about Cabécar culture and language, and twenty-six years of work on the translation of the New Testament. We had grown old and weary in the effort. I was now seventy years old, but we rejoiced that no major setbacks or sicknesses had impeded the finalizing of the New Testament since we scheduled the work plan during our prayer day in January 1991. God had indeed heard Marian's prayer that our part in the Cabécar translation would be finished by the end of 1992.

Financial Hurdle

An unexpected call from Guatemala disturbed our joy over finishing the translation. We were told that cost-cutting at the International Bible Society would eliminate funding for the Cabécar Testament. This was shocking news, for we had been assured in writing that the IBS would finance the printing of our New Testament. To think that we might have to raise almost twenty thousand dollars before the Testament could go to press was daunting, to say the least.

A translator friend encouraged us: "I can't believe your friends wouldn't like the privilege of helping finance the New Testament." So, although we never solicited gifts for personal support, we invited people to give toward publication expenses. Gifts began to flow in—the largest from Marian's aunt. However, the manuscript would not be placed in the lineup of Testaments waiting to be sent to Korea for printing until its cost was fully underwritten.

In January 1993, when Jonathan finished the typesetting, he left the camera-ready copy in Dallas until all funds were in. At that point Jonathan and Priscilla returned to Pakistan to continue assisting translators there. During their six-month furlough Jonathan had given us a real boost. Were it not for his expertise we would have needed to convert our computer files to PC files. Instead, our New Testament was the first to be typeset on a Macintosh—a pilot project.

Our supporting church in Columbia got excited about the need for funds to publish the Testament. Many prayed. We reported weekly as the money came in. Eventually, there was even some left over, for the cost turned out to be far less than originally quoted. Jonathan's typesetting skill had kept costs down—the manuscript did not exceed five hundred pages, considerably less than most Testaments in previously unwritten languages. Timothy, studying in Dallas, was called in by the Production Department to answer a question about locating a map in the Cabécar manuscript. He was excited to learn that they were about to finish the negatives—two weeks earlier than expected. In April they were sent to Korea for printing.

Meanwhile, Marian and I were on the road again, this time for a couple of weeks in Alabama where we spoke at three churches and saw many members of my family. We took with us a computer printout of the beautifully formatted Cabécar New Testament, complete with maps and illustrations. (Marian's comment: "It reads *so* nicely.") We, of course, enjoyed showing the printout to our excited supporters and prayer partners. One pastor even had the whole church gather around the printout to pray that the Lord would use this Scripture. Our own prayer was that the Cabécar church would be a Word-oriented church.

Late in March we traveled to the WEC headquarters near Philadelphia to welcome Susanna and Prem and little Irene who finally arrived from India for furlough after months of bureaucratic delays. They drove back with us to Columbia for the final two weeks of our own furlough. The time we spent with them gave us a good picture of their life among the Hindu people of North India.

Back to Costa Rica

We flew to Costa Rica in time for Peter's fortieth birthday celebration in April 1993. He had just finished another session of his cross-cultural training program. The final event of this session of *Etno* was a two-week trek through Telire, the most remote Cabécar area. The Lord kept them safe from traffickers and other dangers, and gave opportunities to hold meetings with the Indians.

The day after we returned from the States, Paul Williams asked me to do a back-to-Spanish translation of Cabécar Acts. This work would help Paul, translator for the Bribri tribe, to suggest possible ways for his helpers to translate to Bribri, since the two languages were closely related. When we got back home to Tsipirí, I not only began this project, but took up work again on the rough draft of the Cabécar Old Testament where I had left off after Exodus 20. Other Scriptures, like Jonah and several Psalms, had been drafted and were ready to polish.

It was good to have pressing work facing me. In spite of my arthritis and double vision, I could still handle the job, although at a slower pace. As I continued to translate Exodus with the help of Isaac, Franklin, or Nasario, I was overwhelmed with the awesome God of Sinai. The funds for publishing Genesis and Exodus would come from what was left over after the printing of the New Testament.

In addition to translating, I continued meeting with my "little flock," rejoicing that they were becoming rooted in the Word. At one of our meetings we studied Paul's appeal in Philippians 2 to think of others as better than ourselves, to think not only of our own interests, but to think like Jesus. Although equal with God, He stepped down to become a man, a servant, and not only died, but died the death of a criminal: *"Bas jérikö Cristo Jesús jérika käi."* (Think like Jesus Christ thought.) To this Franklin responded, "That makes me feel ashamed." Israel said, "There's no one that doesn't seek his own self-interest."

Others in the group of twenty responded in like fashion as they felt the force of the Word in their own tongue. We ended in prayer—men and women alike—praising Jesus who is now exalted far above all, seated at the right hand of God. To see former animists respond positively to this Scripture the first time they heard it was worth the forty years of preliminary work!

In July when the group met to study Paul's testimony in Philippians 3 of leaving all behind in order to follow Christ, I asked Franklin, "Do you feel called to serve the Lord?" He answered firmly, "Yes, I do feel called. If I didn't, I wouldn't be here today. I'd be somewhere else, doing my own thing." Franklin made numerous trips to Pacuare to teach the Word to Cabécars in that area.

As we waited for the printed copies of the New Testament to arrive from Korea, there was a new emphasis on teaching reading. Two of the Cabécar churches had started their own schools. Other groups wanted to begin schools to teach the Word, as well as reading, writing, and arithmetic. But the focus was on teaching their children the Word at home. Isaac had already taught his own boys to read and was interested in helping others teach. Marian had just finished the fourth in a series of primers she had begun long before the final push on the New Testament. A computerized version of the alphabet book I had hand-produced early in the 1960s was now ready for another reprinting with new artwork. Our alphabet had been in use far and wide, but officials were trying to institute a new one. The recently developed alphabet was untested, used by no one. "It's not our alphabet," said the Cabécars. We kept praying that the use of our alphabet, the one we developed for the New Testament, would not be prohibited.

Excitement ran high in July when we heard that the shipment of the published New Testaments would arrive shortly, but that news proved to be a false alarm. Although not affiliated with the International Bible Society which published the Testament, the Bible Society of Costa Rica graciously agreed to guide the shipment through customs when it did arrive. The former director of the Spanish language school promised to pay the customs charges; he wanted the privilege of having a part in this event! Suspense continued to mount as we laid plans for the dedication of the Cabécar New Testament. In faith, we set the date for October 17, 1993, not knowing whether the books would arrive in time for the grand celebration at Tsipirí.

— 25 —

Enjoying the Fruit
1993 to 1997

"For thou shalt eat the labour of thine hands:
happy shalt thou be, and it shall be well with thee."(Psalm 128:2)

On October 12, 1492, ships from Spain arrived in the New World, irrevocably impacting every Indian tribe in the Americas. Now, just over five hundred years later, another ship arrived in Costa Rica bringing the Cabécar New Testament to a tribe already irrevocably impacted by the Word of God. With only five days to spare before the dedication service, the Bible Society of Costa Rica received the shipment after shepherding it through the customs process.

Almost miraculously, in one of the wettest months of the year, the weather cleared. Ten four-wheel-drive vehicles—including the one transporting the precious books—negotiated the muddy hill down to the Tsipirí Valley for the overnight celebration. Nearly one hundred fifty Cabécars assembled in Tsipirí for the opening service on Saturday evening. A few had walked as many as four days to get there. Well over a hundred non-Indians also crowded into the chapel that night.

"May God be praised," echoed through the hills around our clearing in the jungle. Over and over as the various groups of Cabécars were introduced, they spoke of being "one in Christ"—one with believers they had not met before. The highlight of that first meeting, apart from the joyous singing, was hearing a group from across the Chirripó River who quoted extensive portions of Scripture. One girl recited most of Luke 21. The Cabécars were ready for the complete New Testament!

Joyous singing at the dedication

The Dedication of the Cabécar New Testament

The actual dedication service on Sunday morning, October 17, 1993, was all we had hoped for. Our middle son, Timothy, led the meeting in the Cabécar language, with summaries in Spanish and English. After a spirited time of worship, I gave a historical review of our work and Marian spoke of her involvement in the translation. Then followed the proper string of appropriate speakers: among them were Peter, as eldest son; next, representatives of the Evangelical Alliance of Costa Rica, of CAM International, of Wycliffe Bible Translators; and lastly, my nephew, who at the time was pastor of our first supporting church. All speeches were brief, but worthy of the occasion, and honoring to the Lord.

Finally the long-awaited moment arrived. Alberto Reyes, head of the Bible Society of Costa Rica, spoke: "The Bible is to be read, the Bible is to be lived, the Bible is to be distributed." Then as he opened the first box of Cabécar Testaments, *don* Alberto presented a copy to me and one to Marian. The congregation crowded around to get a better look at the Book; many even climbed on the benches in order to see! We, too, were seeing the Book for the first time. I cried—I knew I would!

Timothy dedicating the New Testament in prayer

The Spirit was moving. Timothy gave the dedicatory prayer in Cabécar. Jack Hoey, a friend from a supporting church in Pittsburgh, prayed in English. Rodolfo Saenz, president of the Evangelical Alliance, prayed in Spanish. Then Timothy suggested that Israel, one of the young translation helpers, should pray. And did he pray—pleading for families to use the Book, for parents to teach it to their children. He prayed as a sinner broken before a holy God—an appropriate final prayer.

Climax of the Celebration

As the celebration climaxed, our second son Steven sang a song of his own, picturing old Spanish ships carrying gold away and another ship now bringing true treasure to stay. Then I presented a copy of the New Testament to each Cabécar who had helped me with the translation over the years—three of them for more than twenty years. Philip, our fourth son, gave copies to the younger men, all believers, who had helped him and Timothy at least a month with the final revision. Some clutched their Testaments, some were near tears. Others asked for a chance to pray, still others embraced me. This from Indians who rarely show emotion or affection. And finally I gave a Testament to Peter, Steven, Timothy, Philip, and David, my five sons. They had grown up on the trails with me and had been such a part of it all.

Nasario, Franklin, Isaac, and Philip reading their copies

And then the celebration was over. But the teen-age daughter of missionary friends was so moved she just stood there, even after the three-hour service of which she understood little. Her father said it had been an anointed meeting. The Lord had given us the blessing we asked for. Marian had prayed that He would smile on us, and He did!

Aziel and Marian with their copies of the New Testament

"As I watched the Indians praising God," remarked a believer from our Spanish church who was present at the dedication, "I remembered how as an unbeliever I used to serve liquor at my father's bar, thinking *don* Aziel would never change these drunken Indians." But her former customers were different now, and so was she. Her sister, realizing that if we had not come to minister to the

Cabécars, she might never have heard the Gospel, commented, "We're like grafts into your Cabécar ministry."

Unfortunately, our three daughters were unable to attend the dedication. Priscilla and her husband, Jonathan, who had typeset the Testament for us, were serving the Lord in Pakistan. She phoned later, wanting to hear all the details. Susanna and her husband Prem had recently returned to India. As for Elizabeth and her husband Noel, they remained in the United States where she was caring for newborn Matthew Conrad, their fifth child, who was born September 23, the day the ship carrying the Testaments had docked in Costa Rica.

The After-Meeting

Most visitors—fellow missionaries, trainees from Peter's program, and friends from the capital—left after the Sunday morning dedication service. By the time they got to their vehicles, the rain was already pelting down. The four-wheel-drive vehicles proved their worth, plowing up the hill out of our "hole" and through the three miles of mud on the road, where over the years we had worn out a Jeep, a Land Rover, and two Toyotas.

There were over a hundred Indians who lived too far away to walk home before nightfall. That evening Marian and I and our sons met with them for a moving time of worship and praise. Then Timothy asked for volunteer readers. (Most had been motivated to learn to read by their desire to read the Word.) About twenty of them jumped up and got in line for the reading of the entire book of Revelation. Most of them read a whole chapter, while those in the audience followed the text and corrected their mistakes. Our sons David and Timothy each read a chapter. And finally at 1 a.m. Marian had the "fun," she said, of reading the last chapter. What a way to end the dedication day!

As the believers met in the rustic tin-roofed building with its dirt floor and walls of split logs, our stateside visitors met in the den of our house to praise the Lord in English. There were two ladies from a supporting church in New Jersey and two men from a church in

Pittsburgh, a supporter from Alabama who came with my nephew and his family, plus our son Steven who had come from South Carolina with his wife and their four children. Our son Philip had flown down from Columbia Bible College to share in the dedication weekend.

Logistics of the Occasion

An enormous amount of work filled the days before the celebration. Timothy and a crew of Cabécar volunteers bore the brunt of it, enlarging the Indian-style outdoor kitchen and quadrupling the size of the chapel. David, with his chain saw, provided boards for the backless benches and made a noise shield for the generator. He also built sleeping quarters for guys. I was responsible for new outhouses and for extra accommodations for visitors. Keiry, Timothy's wife, was in charge of cooking for the crowd. We bought three pigs, plus rice, beans, and sugar by the sack. David hauled a trailer loaded with green bananas from a plantation hours away. Debbie, Peter's wife, took care of meals for the stateside visitors.

Cost of the New Testament

Originally, the cost of printing the Testament was estimated at ten dollars per copy, but we sold them for less than a third of that amount. Indians lined up after the dedication service to buy copies. Many friends helped underwrite printing costs. Actual cost turned out to be less than the estimate, with the surplus saved for future publications.

The real cost? Four decades of missionary support, including the cost of vehicles and a base in the jungle. Years of paying language helpers, reams of paper, plus typewriters and computers. Years of analyzing the language, years of sticking to it, years of checking for comprehension and accuracy. Years of praying. The cost? It cost Tyndale his life to give us the English Bible. Whatever the cost, the Lamb is worthy.

The Cabécar New Testament represented the fulfillment of our vision: a church where there had been none, with a New Testament in the hands of the believers, and a family of our own, following the Lord. Forty years of trekking steep trails, crossing swift rivers, eating boiled green bananas. Forty years of learning the language, deciding on an alphabet, and analyzing the grammar. Twenty years of teaching home Bible classes with a new Scripture portion coming out every three years, while waiting for significant response to the Word. More than twenty years of training our children, teaching them the Word, sadly sending them off to school and gladly welcoming them back, years of seeing each child commit himself to the Lord and His service. Twenty years of watching them find spouses to bring to their jungle home. In the Cabécar New Testament were capsuled forty years of prayer, tears, and joy.

Overwhelming Response

An avalanche of cards and letters—eighty of them—poured in from prayer warriors and supporters, as well as from friends and family. So many had invested so much during those forty years. Now as they received our report on the dedication, they were thrilled, challenged, and inspired. Two verses quoted in one card summed up our feelings: *"Weeping may endure for a night, but joy cometh in the morning"* (Psalm 30:5), and *"He shall see of the travail of his soul, and shall be satisfied"* (Isaiah 53:11). Although some spoke of our sacrifice, we felt *privileged* to have given the Word to an unreached group. Furthermore, we realized that we did not do the job alone. Scores of people helped: Indians, consultants from the Bible Society and from Wycliffe Bible Translators, family members—particularly Timothy and Philip, as well as our wider network of prayer and financial supporters. Ultimately, we knew that only through God could we have done it. To God be the glory!

The wife of my college roommate wrote: "In your recent letter to us you thanked us for a monetary gift with the remark, 'You have done so much for us and we have never done anything for you.' Bob and I had tears in our eyes when we read that. You have done MORE for us than you will ever know—represented us in Costa Rica, translated a New Testament (something I always dreamed of doing during Wheaton days), *prayed* for us and our children, given us wisdom and help in example and words, made us feel that living in and trekking through the jungle is 'normal!' And then we have been privileged to get to know your extended family."

I was never sure how clearly my twelve siblings understood our work, but one sister, Mary, certainly did. She wrote, "The pamphlet describing the celebration was one of the most moving things I've read in a while. My heart swelled with joy at the accomplishments and the magnitude of potential in that area now. It has been a magnificent experience for me just to have read all the news. And of course spiritually it had to have been deeply satisfying to see the culmination of the many years' work—but at the same time there must be a sense of urgency at the needs still existing."

Julian, a CAM colleague and close friend, had identified with us more than we realized. He wrote: "Since 1957 we have rejoiced, prayed, agonized with you, prayed some more, and watched the progress of the translation. Your singleness of purpose and 'pressing on' attitude has been a true example of one who follows his calling."

I wrote Paul, Julian's brother, lamenting his absence and he responded with the following poem, dated November 4, 1993:

I was not there, Aziel, but I imagined it,
Imagined people, friends, and laborers.
Imagined songs in Spanish, songs in English,
songs in that strange tongue I cannot understand.
These are the incense of the ones who do the work,
Our offering, blessing for our God,
And blessing for the other thousand thousand tribes.

I was not there, Aziel, but I imagined other things,
Imagined days of jungle trails and children's birth.
Imagined days of anguish, days of "joy right through the roof,"
These are the heritage of those who do the work,
Our treasure, riches to sustain us in our lives,
And bless our children, and their children's children's lives.

A Church for the Book

The fact that there was now a literate Cabécar church, ready to receive the New Testament, was almost as significant as completing the Book. One may translate by dint of hard work, but only the supernatural action of the Holy Spirit can bring about saving faith in the work of Christ and allegiance to Him as Lord, as well as transform the worldview of a tribe. As we kept talking to everybody about Jesus, and leading simple Bible studies, and as the printed Word was widely read, a small but significant "critical mass" of interested people emerged.

More and more were ready for the New Testament. Some who had attended our meetings merely to learn to read were "hooked" on the message. (We never had a literacy program, but we had a very popular alphabet book and a few primers.) Furthermore, we *used* each portion of Scripture as soon as it was published, starting with the Gospel of Mark, reading it to visitors, as well as studying it in meetings. When we met for Bible study, a thought from the passage would suggest a song. A need that someone voiced would lead us to pray together. First, however, I had to figure out how to pray in Cabécar. There were no native prayer forms, for no one ever called on God. Rather, the Cabécars used rituals to, hopefully, influence the supernatural world.

By 1993, however, the church was well established. There were believers scattered throughout Cabécar territory, with scores already baptized. Congregations were meeting regularly in several areas, led by ordained elders. Believers carried a stack of Scripture portions to the meetings, as they anxiously waited for their New Testament.

The Impact of the Word

We, of course, watched for reactions of the Cabécars to having the full New Testament in one volume. Most of the believers quickly colored the edges of the new Book with red pens, explaining that they wanted it to look like the Spanish Bible. The cover of the Testament was black, as they had requested, but we had failed to pick up their desire for red edges! Beyond their superficial reaction to the appearance of the Book, we were particularly listening for response to its message.

"How is the Word of God affecting you?" I often asked.

"The book of James reveals my pride," Juan responded.

"Sinai makes God more fearful," said Isaac, who had helped translate Exodus, "but Calvary makes Him more loving."

"God takes care of the birds though they don't plant or harvest," commented Franklin, referring to a verse in Luke 12, "so He will take care of my family when I lose work time to serve the Lord."

Another who was affected was Rodrigo, a new believer who brought me a song he had written, based on a praise passage in Revelation. Soon he came with one from Philippians 2, about how Jesus humbled himself.

One day a girl named Heidi came asking for a copy of Romans.

"Do you read?" inquired Marian.

"No," she replied, "but my brother is teaching me. Now read me a passage!"

When Marian finished Romans 1, Heidi demanded more. After Romans 3, she asked for Colossians 3. Then I read her Mark 7 with its list of sins which proceed from our hearts. This touched her. She admitted her immorality and prayed to receive Christ.

One of my former translation helpers, however, was not impressed.

"Now we know that the Word has no power," he declared sarcastically when he learned that a married believer was having an affair with a girl in my "little flock."

We had a published New Testament, but this was only a beginning. Truth had to be internalized; believers had to be tested. Syncretism, the combining of pagan and Christian beliefs, would plague the believers and eventually require radical surgery—a painful action that would threaten unity.

Back to Work after the Dedication

We had no desire just to walk away once the dedication was over. After sending down roots for more than four decades, we wanted to see the Cabécar church using the completed New Testament—to savor the fruit of our labors! How good it was to go to meetings with the Testament in a single book instead of several! Twice a month I continued leading the group that met at Tsipirí.

My most important job at this time was a new task: translating the Cabécar Testament back into Spanish at the request of Paul Williams who was working on a translation for the Bribri Indians. Because of the close relationship between the two languages, my work would help Paul cast his translation in a more natural form. Not only was I involved in this "back-translation" but I also continued Old Testament translation, working on Joshua, while Marian was checking exegesis and keyboarding Exodus.

Recording the New Testament

Timothy also shifted focus toward the Bribris for a few months. He and Keiry lived with a Bribri family in order to gain a better understanding of the similarities and differences between the Bribri language and Cabécar. However, his major ministry project after the dedication was the audio recording of the Cabécar New Testament. This lengthy task delayed his polishing Genesis and Exodus for publication, although he did, of course, keep up his day-by-day ministry to the Indians. His first step toward the recording was to build a studio on our property in Tsipirí. Next he needed to find and train Cabécars to read the various parts of the dramatized production.

The actual recording was done in 1995 with the aid of two technicians, themselves Indians from Guatemala, who spent six weeks in Tsipirí financed by a ministry called "Hosanna!" Although few Cabécars could read when we first arrived in Tsipirí, as people came to know the Lord they taught themselves to read in order to study the Scriptures. However, commas and periods, intonation and phrasing were a mystery to most, slowing the recording process as

Timothy coached the Cabécar readers. Lencho, a bright young man who had worked on finalizing the translation, helped Timothy do the coaching. When crickets, chain saws, and downpours added their noise to the recordings, Timothy had to take time out to make the studio more soundproof—using anything available in Tsipirí, from old quilts to egg cartons!

The project required a different reader for each speaker in the New Testament—more than twenty in all. Marian felt honored to be asked to read Elizabeth's words in the first chapter of Luke. After the initial recording was completed, Timothy and his family flew to the States for a break before the final step of his involvement in the project. While there, he took an intensive course in Hebrew to aid him in continuing work on the Cabécar Old Testament.

Other Projects

Philip's big project after the dedication was a new series of literacy primers, an outgrowth of the project begun years earlier by Marian. For the illustrated series, a graphic artist from the States spent a week in Tsipirí producing culturally sensitive drawings of Cabécars and their world, adding to the set already made by artistically-inclined Philip. Our overloaded computer system strained to handle all the graphics. And Philip's time was limited, for he was constantly ministering to Indians and helping Timothy with the recording project, as well as helping in other aspects of our work. Eventually five primers emerged, totaling one hundred fifty pages, all tested by Philip in actual teaching.

David also had a burden for teaching reading, particularly to those in remote Telire. Some young men from Telire whom David had invited to the dedication spent time in Tsipirí following the celebration, while he taught them to read and urged them to teach others. Their time with David gave them a chance to rest after their four-day trek, struggling with live pigs which later appeared in the bowls of beans and pork served to visitors at the celebration. Benancio, one of the fellows from Telire, returned to Tsipirí six months after the dedication to spend several weeks doing manual labor by day and studying reading with David in his free time.

Another part of David's ministry was to maintain our vehicles. He not only spent a lot of time working on Peter's twenty-year-old Toyota, but he also converted my old "work horse" into a pickup for his needs. After the dedication I had bought a used Isuzu Trooper, a small vehicle suitable for us now that our family was grown. It was not intended to be a work horse, for at the age of seventy-one I was weary of the effort that thirty years of life in Tsipirí had required. I was not too weary to continue ministering, but I was glad that our sons were now bearing the responsibility for hauling passengers and supplies, as well as hauling rocks to fill the ruts that still marked our muddy road.

Time to Reconnect and Report

On May 12, 1994, David took us to the airport in Costa Rica, and that night Steven and his family, as well as Philip, met our plane when we arrived in South Carolina for a six-month furlough. The first main event on our schedule was Philip's graduation that month from Columbia Bible College. He had received an associate degree there before taking two years out to help finalize the New Testament. Now he got his bachelor's degree and returned shortly to Costa Rica to continue his literacy project.

That summer was gladdened by the birth of four more grandchildren. Mark Kaleb, Timothy and Keiry's third child, was born on May 5. Marian was delighted to see him before we left for the States. However, she did not get to see Susanna and Prem's second child, Judson Vikram, for he was born in India on June 19. Nor did she see Priscilla and Jonathan's second son, Christopher James, who was born on July 10 in England. We both enjoyed being in Columbia for the birth of Steven and Cameron's fifth child, Mary Grace, on September 11. Then we were blessed to be present the following month, along with her other grandparents, when she was dedicated to the Lord.

In Columbia, over the porch of our home I put up a sign, "Movnomo" [move-no-more] which I acquired when my mother died. Her father, a Methodist preacher—after a life of moving from parsonage to parsonage—had put it up over the porch of his retirement home. Inside the house, we converted one small room into an office and began to get some of our books and papers in place. Steven built a wall of shelves and cabinets for the books we had shipped from Costa Rica—books damaged by years of humidity, termites, and roaches in Tsipirí. I spent hours in the office working on the back-to-Spanish translation of the Cabécar Testament for our colleague working on the Bribri Testament. For exercise I tamed the overgrown back yard.

While in the States, Marian and I visited relatives and attended family reunions. On July 4 we traveled with Steven and his family to the annual Jones Reunion, where one hundred twenty-eight of my parents' descendants and their spouses gathered—including twelve of my parents' thirteen children, and many of their fifty-six grandchildren, plus many great-grandchildren, and the first great-great-grandchild.

Although we had missed many reunions of my extended family over the years, I never felt "cheated" by being obedient to God's call to missions. Neither did I feel that I had made a sacrifice. Marian and I had fulfilled an incredibly rich calling of God. What a privilege! Now in our later years we enjoyed more frequent contact with my brothers and sisters.

"Show and Tell"

With great anticipation Marian and I visited our supporters and prayer partners, showing them the beautiful Cabécar New Testament. The first to see it were friends at Bethany Free Church in New Jersey, our home church as newlyweds, and one of the first churches to support us. From there we traveled to New England to visit supporters and to see for the first time Elizabeth and Noel's fifth child, Matthew.

On another trip we contacted supporting churches in Alabama and Chicago, with a side trip to Dallas to see Priscilla and Jonathan. They had come to the States for a few months while he worked on a special project for translators. That gave us a chance to see their new baby, Christopher.

Our final long trip took us to Ohio and Pennsylvania. We showed the New Testament, shared things the Lord had taught us, and made new friends. On each trip we contacted a wide network of individuals along the way. As always, the Lord opened one-on-one ministry opportunities as friends opened their hearts and homes to us.

Not until after a lifetime of relating to personal supporters did I realize the bond that often develops—one of those enriching "fringe benefits" of obedience to God's call. Most churches and individuals had given and prayed during our whole missionary career. Eight of our supporters were also our spiritual children! When one of our supporters discontinues giving, we feel nostalgia over the loss of a fellow-warrior, rather than pain over the loss of financial help.

Shortly before leaving Columbia, we met with the board of Christian Missions, Inc. to discuss our future, now that the New Testament was published. The consensus was that Marian and I should continue as active missionaries but with a reduced level of involvement, dividing our time between Columbia and Costa Rica.

Our board was also in transition. The original board members resigned, saying they were no longer needed since the translation was done. We very much appreciated their having put their names "on the line" for us and backing us for fifteen years. The other members, including Dr. Charlie Davis, and Dale and Joan Kibbey, who once lived near us in Costa Rica, continued faithfully serving Marian and me as well as our sons. Furthermore, our original bookkeeper, Sandra Barber, kept on serving under the new board. These faithful friends were characteristic of the many who believed in us and backed us, even before there was visible fruit among the Cabécars.

Costa Rica Again

Leaving our home in Columbia, where we had enjoyed being near our son Steven and his family, we flew back to Costa Rica on November 25, 1994, for a joyful meeting with our other four sons, two daughters-in-law, and eight grandchildren. With our three daughters and their families so far away, it was good to have family nearby. After a few days in the capital to rest and buy supplies, we loaded our bags in our little Trooper and traveled five hours through the mountains to Tsipirí, our home so full of memories.

When we first built our jungle house in Tsipirí, life was hard but simple. Little by little we finished the house, developed an adequate water system and improved the jeep road. Slowly we analyzed the Cabécar language, decided on an alphabet, started translating, and then began holding Bible studies. Ours was a simple one-orbit operation: we did everything. As our family grew, the children learned to work alongside us.

Now the house was more comfortable and we had some basic conveniences, but life was more complex, and we were no longer solely in charge. Several other buildings dotted the landscape behind our house—a garage, Timothy's house, his office and studio, the chapel/school and cooking-eating area, houses for Indians, outhouses, and even a playhouse! Multiple orbits swirled around us; we were caught in the vortex of ministries and projects, of comings and goings.

The three youngest sons were involved in leaders' meetings and outreach trips, in literacy projects, Scripture promotion, and literature production. A daily radio schedule linked us with colleagues. When we went to the capital, where our oldest son was based, there were phone calls and faxes to keep us in contact with the rest of the children, with the Mission, and with other ministries.

The highlight of our first weeks back in Tsipirí was Timothy's conference for Cabécar church leaders. Seeing the believers once more made up for the two weeks of steady rain and sticky mud which preceded the conference. What a joy to see jungle Indians working through Romans 6. And what a blessing to baptize Franklin and Zoila. Franklin, my translation helper, was an elder in the church but had waited years for his wife to be willing to express her faith publicly. Actually, it was through her that he first came in contact with the gospel a few years after Marian had taught her—then a giggling teenager—to read.

Editing the New Testament Recordings

Before cassettes could be produced from the recordings done in Tsipirí, the tapes needed to be edited. To oversee this process Timothy drove to Guatemala in 1996 with Keiry and the kids, arriving broke after paying border-crossing fees in five countries during the three-day trip. The transmission on his Toyota suffered on the war-scarred roads, but was repaired with used parts and borrowed money.

At the studio in Guatemala, Timothy learned to edit sound waves on the computer and make necessary adjustments to improve the quality. The editing itself was a struggle until a technician arrived from the States to repair the computer and teach the local staff new techniques.

"I'll be slower to tell the Cabécars to rejoice in all things after my struggle to praise the Lord in the circumstances here," Timothy later commented.

Two full years after the initial recording sessions the cassettes of the dramatized New Testament finally arrived in Costa Rica—fifty sets of seventeen cassettes each. The recordings proved a blessing to believers in outlying areas, many of whom could not yet read with ease. The technical knowledge that Timothy gained during the process later enabled him to produce other recordings.

Ongoing Translation Work

Timothy's ministry was varied, but translation was his favorite job. Eventually he and Franklin, who had helped me for many years, worked together polishing Genesis, which had been through several drafts since my initial one. At home, Franklin finished a preliminary draft through II Samuel. After learning about Solomon while doing the draft, Franklin wanted to work on his writings, so he began trying to translate Proverbs. Lencho, the Cabécar whom Philip taught to keyboard, put preliminary drafts onto the computer for Timothy, making some corrections as he went along. Philip himself was involved in the process, evaluating style and naturalness. I, of course, continued my back-to-Spanish translation of the Cabécar Testament as an aid to the Bribri translation team—my fourth handwritten copy of the New Testament.

Peter Goes International

Peter continued to develop *Etno*, his cross-cultural training center near the Caribbean coast. Deb and the children enjoyed life there during the yearly training sessions. After the weeks at jungle camp, one group of trainees went to Chirripó to stay with believers there, while the more hardy ones trekked with Peter and David up the Estrella Valley and over into the Telire Valley. After they contacted Cabécars throughout the unresponsive, sparsely populated area, they crossed the 7,000-foot ridge into the Chirripó Valley. There they made their way downstream to join Timothy who was leading an Easter conference. What an impact it made on the trainees to see more than a hundred Cabécars gathered to worship the risen Christ!

By the mid-nineties Peter and Deb spent most of the year at our base near the capital where the children could attend school and Peter could give time to developing his ministry. FEDEMEC, the Costa Rican mission agency, was functioning well. Several Costa Ricans supported by their local churches were now on the field. Peter was already speaking annually for FEDEMEC on the challenge of the tribes. He also was involved in preaching missions to Hispanics in the United States, and involved in COMIBAM—the Hispanic counterpart to Urbana. His international ministry kept expanding.

In 1995 FEDEMEC asked Peter to fly to Africa to encourage their missionaries serving in Mali, all of whom had been trained at *Etno*. On his return trip he contacted mission leaders in Spain and in London regarding future placement of missionaries from Central

America. When he got back to Costa Rica from Africa, he commented to us that for the first time in his life he had experienced being in a country where he understood no language—a culture shock for him.

"Telire for Jesus"

A Costa Rican helicopter pilot wanted to work out a trip with our sons and veterinarian Bob Wilmarth for a Cabécar outreach. "Telire for Jesus" finally came together in May of 1995, but traveling by helicopter was a deviation from our usual "keep-it-simple" approach. In our methodology we tried to stick to what the average Cabécar Indian could do in communicating the message and relating to his world. To reach the Indians, we walked and talked—it was that simple! Psychologically, slogging though the mud, fording white-water rivers, sleeping on crude beds of river cane, and eating unpalatable food enabled us to "think Indian" when trying to make the gospel meaningful.

A fifteen-minute helicopter ride took Peter and Timothy, the vet, and two goats to Telire. Steven, who was in Costa Rica framing a building for Peter, accompanied them. The banner they took with them read: *"Jesucristorä Säqueclä Täliresca"* (Jesus Christ is Lord of Telire).

Philip and David had gone ahead by foot—a three-day trek—to make plans for meetings, promotion of the New Testament, and the goat project. While Bob doctored the Indians' animals, our sons translated for him. During the meetings Steven played his guitar and sang, and his brothers did the teaching.

As they prepared to leave, the weather turned ominous. Flying through a driving rainstorm, bucking a strong headwind, the pilot maneuvered the helicopter through rugged ravines over white-water rivers. Since then I have shuddered many times, thinking of what could have happened to the priceless cargo in that overloaded wind-tossed helicopter.

Peter, Steven, Timothy, Philip, and David in Telire

Our sons followed up the outreach as they continued to trek the trails with the message of Jesus: talking, praying, and reading Scripture until the news about Jesus began to crack the resistance in Telire. Within a year they had baptized the first believer. There are now churches near the most sacred mountain of the Cabécars.

And the "Competition?"

Never, in the early years as I trekked, talked, and translated, did others make a serious attempt to win the Indians. An initial, short-lived effort had ended over fifty years before we arrived. However, once we had planted churches, others came—some trying to take over churches, and some starting their own. This may be a bitter test for the pioneer until he commits it to the Lord of the harvest, who rewards *"every man...according to his own labour"* (I Corinthians 3:8).

Now in the mid-1990s the Korean missionary, who had begun working among the Cabécars a few years before, continued to follow our trail of churches, starting his own by attracting people with gifts and by paying Cabécars to oversee in his absence. Pastors also came from Spanish churches in the city with giveaways and with promises of tin roofing for chapels.

In the Estrella Valley our sons met a self-styled "pastor to the Cabécars of Estrella and Telire." Though he claimed to be an Indian, he did not know the language. A few Sundays later when we attended church in the capital we were shocked to hear this man speak, claiming sixteen hundred converts—more than the total population of the area. Using Peter's name in his appeal for support, he received an offering of several hundred dollars. The following week he appeared on Christian TV, saying he must now target Chirripó "where there are no churches." The host church had failed to check him out—a "con man" with a record of already having deceived other churches in the capital!

What did we do about the competition? We tried to teach the believers to be discerning, like the Apostle Paul who warned the Ephesians elders of "grievous wolves." One of the men in my "little flock" remarked with discernment, "Those who are enticed by giveaways will last only as long as the gifts last."

Gradual Withdrawal

Even before the New Testament was published, we began to think about relinquishing our hold on our life's work. Actually, our sons had already taken hold of the load and leadership of the work among the Cabécar Indians. That left us free to spend part of each year in the States, rather than slamming the door suddenly on more than forty years of ministry in Costa Rica.

Years before in a personal day of prayer, I had asked the Lord that one of my sons would carry on my work. Now it was obvious that replacements were on hand—a rather delicious fruit of the labor of our hands! Having given David my old Toyota, we then took our Costa Rica properties out of our names and divided them between our sons who lived there. On each trip to South Carolina we took a few of our keepsakes with us.

"Retirement" was the word I continued to avoid. My mindset was as much set for ministry as ever. We were only changing locations. For practical and emotional reasons, we planned to wind down gradually, as we pulled up roots in Costa Rica and put down deeper roots again in the States. Financially, we found that whether beginning or ending our missionary career, we were still living by faith.

As part of our gradual withdrawal we spent five months in the United States in the summer and fall of 1995—a refreshing time. We really enjoyed our house in South Carolina, and I personally enjoyed working in the yard, often with the help of Steven and Cameron's three boys. Marian was happy with Steven's expertise in remodeling the kitchen. Having a son nearby helped compensate for the other children being so far away.

One highlight of our months in the States was our own family reunion—four days of sharing our concerns and joys, interceding for each other, and enjoying the grandchildren. All the children were present but Priscilla and her family, who were in Pakistan. Another highlight was the opportunity to repeat at church the parenting class I had taught there in 1974.

Soon we were back in Costa Rica, back to heavy rains and the flip side of living in the "land of eternal spring"—mud, mold, and mildew, as well as roaches, spiders, ants, and other creatures. On Sundays I led services for my "little flock" and on weekdays I worked on the back-translation of the Cabécar Testament. Saturdays were given to maintenance, like repairing one of the local bridges which fell in shortly after I drove across it. Another job that kept us busy at odd moments was sorting through papers, pictures, books, and keepsakes. We were looking ahead to the day when we would be based at our small apartment in the capital, rather than in Tsipirí.

The "Bombshell"

By this time, six of our children had married: Peter and Deb in 1975, and then Steven and Cameron, as well as Susanna and Prem in 1982, followed by Elizabeth and Noel in 1985, and finally Priscilla and Jonathan, and also Timothy and Keiry in 1988. Our two youngest, although now adults, continued with us—when they were not in the States studying, or in Chirripó with the Indians. Marian particularly enjoyed having Philip and David around, giving a helping hand and keeping us company.

Over the Christmas holidays in 1995 Marian and I were at our base in the capital with Peter and Timothy and their families—a happy, festive, noisy season—when our two remaining singles each dropped a bombshell!

Late one evening Philip came by our apartment and, to our total surprise, asked our blessing on his interest in Saukeen, one of Peter's trainees who had recently returned to Costa Rica on medical leave after four years in China.

The next night, Christmas Eve, David hung around the apartment, admitting he, too, wanted to talk.

"What's her name?" I asked, still reeling from the night before.

"Lucy," he stated, mentioning another of Peter' trainees slated to leave for Pakistan in a few months. We were stunned, but approved and gave our blessing.

"Philip and David's news stopped the whole Jones family for four days!" remarked a visitor who was helping Timothy with a remodeling job at our base.

On Christmas morning Marian was alone in our apartment, trying to absorb her emotional overload at this sudden turn of events. She was not unhappy. In fact, she was very satisfied with the boys' choices, for she already knew and respected both the girls. However, it was just *too much, too fast!* Opening the book I had given her for Christmas—Elisabeth Elliot's *Keep a Quiet Heart*—she read until this sentence grabbed her: "A quiet heart is one that is content with whatever the Lord gives." That was the Lord's word to Marian. It put her heart at rest.

To reinforce the initial shock, both girls were wearing engagement rings within a week, and the two couples were planning a double wedding on April 20, 1996. (Philip had even prayed that he and David would both find wives at the same time!) Now there were phone calls, faxes, and e-mails inviting Priscilla in Pakistan, Susanna in India, Steven in South Carolina, and Elizabeth in Rhode Island.

After recovering from our surprise, Marian and I rejoiced at the Lord's answer to our prayer for godly wives that fit our sons and our family. Brought up in an evangelical home, Saukeen had become interested in missions while studying at the University of Costa Rica, where she majored in English. Her parents, Alvaro and Bienvenida Cob, had given their daughter a Chinese name in recognition of *don* Alvaro's father who had emigrated from China and married a Costa Rican girl. After finishing her *Etno* training, Saukeen had gone to China to serve among an unreached people group until the Lord redirected her to serve with Philip among the Cabécars.

In contrast to Saukeen, Lucy was raised in a strongly Catholic city, where her widowed mother, Elsi Solano, lived near the church. Lucy came to know the Lord as an adult through a charismatic group in that church. When pressured to make a choice of church affiliation, she and her older brother left the group and helped start a Bible church. Eventually, she felt the Lord's call to service and quit her job in order to train at *Etno* and then study nursing. As she continued preparing at nursing school, she had asked Marian to pray with her about the people group that was on her heart. Neither she nor Marian had any inkling that her future would be with the Cabécars.

We knew that cross-cultural marriages involve extra adjustments for everyone, but Philip and David's plans gave us a certain sense of relief regarding their future, as well as our own move toward closure in Costa Rica.

Double Wedding, Double Blessing

From the platform I watched — with a lump in my throat as first Lucy and then Saukeen marched in while Marian's brother-in-law played "Jesu, Joy of Man's Desiring." Lucy came in with her brother and her widowed mother, and Saukeen with both parents, according to local custom. Philip and David had already come down the aisle with Marian to wait for their brides.

Our oldest granddaughter, Joanna, was one of the bridesmaids, as was daughter-in-law Keiry. Six young granddaughters were flower girls, each wearing a wreath of fresh rosebuds in her hair to match the wreaths the brides wore. Little grandson Timothy was one of the ring bearers. Our son Timothy was Philip's best man; David's best man was our son Steven.

The procession was a long one, with the traditional Costa Rican honor attendants—older married couples—then bridesmaids and groomsmen, flower girls and ring bearers for each bride. A master of ceremonies introduced each one who came in, a Costa Rican custom. And then, in keeping with local practice, the two couples took seats on the platform, as a contemporary worship group set the tone of the two-hour celebration.

I felt unusual liberty in focusing my meditation on communicating the knowledge of God through the family from generation to generation. Missionary colleague Dennis Smith had his own words for David and Lucy before he led them in their commitment. Then our oldest son, Peter, spoke to Philip and Saukeen before leading them in their vows. Following prayer and the laying on of hands, Steven sang a song he had written for the occasion, and then Marian's brother-in-law at the piano accompanied Lucy's brother on the trumpet for the triumphant recessional.

The whole occasion was characterized by joy in the Lord and Christian love. The crowd present for the wedding and the meal which followed numbered almost four hundred. We were glad that all of our children came, not only from the States but from Pakistan and India. With the new brides we were now a family of forty.

Final Family Celebration at Tsipirí

A week after the wedding, thirty-four of us, including the new daughters-in-law, gathered in Tsipirí, our family home for thirty-three years. Our grandkids played in the icy swimming hole and entertained themselves with the toys and books that our children had grown up with. The little ones enjoyed the playhouse and the swings.

On Saturday night, with almost one hundred fifty Cabécars at the chapel in Tsipirí, we introduced our children—the ones unknown to the new believers. Our daughters had a chance to see the growing Cabécar church, which did not yet exist when they left home. To climax the meeting, Timothy gave a message on purity, a very sensitive issue in Cabécar culture. Then, to introduce Philip and David's brides and to teach the concept of marriage, he led the two couples in an exchange of vows. The Indians left at dawn after spending the rest of the night watching the "Jesus" film and "Pilgrim's Progress."

After dinner on Sunday, the family gathered in the den for "Sunday night," our final hymn sing all together in Tsipirí. Wonderful, hearty singing was followed by Peter's reading from Revelation 21 and 22 about our eternal home. We ended with an emotional time of reminiscing, sharing troubles, encouraging and praying for each other. It was a very special Sunday evening, more than just the replaying of a tradition. Once again, we experienced God together as a family—*a key factor in children's embracing the faith.*

Leaving the "Job Site"

The next day the "exodus" from Tsipirí began, each one taking away some favorite books and mementos. Priscilla and Susanna and their children stayed on longer and the newlyweds too. With their help we took down pictures, cleaned out closets and cupboards, pulled out boxes and footlockers, and opened steel barrels. Among the treasures we found were Marian's graduation picture as valedictorian of her high school class, and my army discharge papers. I spent many days going through old files. Much paper went into our trash burner, some went to our apartment in the capital, and some eventually went to our house in South Carolina, along with books, pictures, and sentimental items.

"Do you feel bad about leaving?" asked Benjamín, my old helper, when he came to say goodbye.

I responded by telling him that Marian felt more emotion than I did because she designed the house and we raised our children there. Personally, I felt that we had finished a job and were now cleaning up the job site—to go on to the next thing the Lord had for us. It was time to regroup after fulfilling our God-given vision. Our roots were deep in Costa Rica but the cloud was moving, and so were we.

The group of Cabécar believers that I called my "little flock" met with us for one last time in Tsipirí. After the regular Bible study, I read Paul's farewell from Acts 20. Marian served a meal, and then we all gathered outside for a photo before the believers walked home—some a couple of hours—in the rain. This group had met with me for almost fifteen years, the first permanent group in the Chirripó area. In my absence, Philip would lead them. He and Saukeen were now living in the little house behind ours.

Finally, we loaded our trunks and boxes into my old army trailer and then climbed into Timothy's big Toyota, also heavily loaded. He drove with chains on as we "crawled" up the hill from Tsipirí, swaying and sliding over the ruts and bumps. As usual, he began with the lowest gear of the four-wheel drive and gradually shifted up as the mud got less, and the roads got better. Then, when out of the worst of the mountains, he shifted into normal gear, as we had done on every trip for three decades with no accidents and few incidents.

We soon found a place for everything in our little apartment in Santa Ana, then decorated the walls with some of our pictures, and set up housekeeping with utensils from Tsipirí. In Santa Ana we packed over two dozen boxes of books and personal effects to ship to the States as air freight—the first of several shipments. In the last shipment, we even sent my favorite Costa Rican easy chair!

Goodbye, Grano de Oro

We had hardly gotten settled in Santa Ana, when we returned to Tsipirí in our little Trooper to take care of a few final details, the most important being to bring closure to our ministry in Grano de Oro. The Spanish church had asked for one more service before we left them to meet on their own. The "icing on the cake" was that Hector and Adilia had asked to be baptized that day!

We all gathered at the river in Grano de Oro on a sunny Sunday in June, as I baptized Hector and Adilia and one other. This brought to twenty-eight the number of those from this tiny village that I had baptized Later in the chapel we worshipped, celebrating the Lord's Supper. My final word to the group was from Acts 20: *"I know this, that after my departing shall grievous wolves enter in among you... And now, brethren, I commend you to God, and to the word of his grace..."* There had already been several efforts by others to take over the group. Nevertheless, like Paul, we eventually had to commend our work to the Lord.

Then came the surprise! The brethren had planned a goodbye for us: a time of sharing a special Costa Rican meal of chicken and

With Pércides, Noé, and family at the chapel in Grano de Oro

rice, followed by two cakes. Afterwards they took our picture as we opened their gift, a tray engraved with Scripture references in appreciation of our twenty-one years leading them.

Although we were leaving, the church was not without occasional oversight. By this time Mike Day had graduated from seminary and had helped with the ministry for extended periods. His wife, Noribette, who was raised in Grano de Oro, had previously graduated from the same seminary. Men from Mike's home church in the States had even come to Grano de Oro to build a parsonage beside the chapel. Eventually Mike and Noribette moved on to a much wider ministry, overseeing the Awana program for all of Costa Rica. Noribette's sister Pércides and Noé her husband, both Bible School grads, later ministered in Grano de Oro.

Goodbye, Tsipirí

After the farewell in Grano de Oro we returned to Tsipirí to spend a day packing up the last of our personal belongings. The next day dawned dark and gray. Light rain was falling, but I thought we could make it without chains. Marian and I climbed into the Trooper and prayed—we never took for granted that we would get out successfully. No one was there to say goodbye. As we drove away, Marian looked back and said, "Goodbye, house!" Then she added, "Thank you, Lord, for thirty-three years here." This was our real *Adios* to Tsipirí and to our life's work.

As we crossed the Tsipirí creek, I revved up, already in four-wheel drive and double-low, hoping to make it up the long, slick hill. We did—without chains! How often we had put on and taken off chains—a muddy, gooey mess. (At times I had needed the help of the winch when all four wheels were spinning—even with chains—and mud was flying everywhere.) As I looked at the ditches I had dug, and the road I had maintained, I was glad that no more would I have to shovel landslides, cut fallen trees, or repair the road and the shaky bridges!

Our house in Tsipirí would now become Timothy's until he developed the property he had acquired for a Cabécar center in Grano de Oro. Marian and I would stay in Santa Ana for several days until we left for Columbia where we would spend six months, another step in our gradual withdrawal.

Before we left for the States, however, we attended one more wedding, as Moisés, originally from our Spanish church, married Cathy, who was in Costa Rica studying Spanish. Most of Moisés' family members were there—several that I had baptized and taught when they lived in Grano de Oro. Again we were enjoying "the labor of our hands."

"Coming Home"

At dawn on June 19, David and his bride Lucy took Marian and me to the airport near our base in the capital. At dusk that evening, as we circled to land in Columbia, Marian remarked, "I feel like I'm coming home after forty-three years." The labor of our many years in Costa Rica was finished except to tie up loose ends. Although we were not yet pulling out of Costa Rica, we were beginning to focus more on stateside ministry.

We felt so blessed, with family at both ends of the journey! Our oldest daughter Priscilla and her family were at the airport to meet us. Priscilla and Jonathan, on a working furlough from Pakistan, had rented a house just up the street from ours. They would be in and out, and the grandchildren would come down to play. In spite of our children's families being scattered worldwide, the Lord gave grace for the separations and granted us times of reconnecting!

A week after our arrival in Columbia we went back to the airport to pick up Philip and his bride Saukeen on the first leg of their trip to China and India. After visiting their friends and supporters in the States and Canada, they spent six weeks in China seeing the places where Saukeen had lived during her four years there, and then three weeks in India visiting Susanna and Prem who, according to Philip's report, were happy and well-adjusted after several hard years.

We ourselves were happy in our house on Winyah Drive. More and more it began to feel like home, reducing the pull of our house in Tsipirí. Settling in was a long process, however, as we gradually found places for the contents of the boxes we had shipped from Costa Rica. We were used to shipping things to Costa Rica and going through customs there, but going through customs in South Carolina was a first for us—part of our reverse culture shock.

During our months in the States we did some traveling, especially to the R K Jones Reunion. Philip and Saukeen were with us at the time, so she met over a hundred of Philip's relatives. Another trip that Marian and I took was to upstate South Carolina for a reception for Moisés and Cathy, whose wedding we had so recently attended in Costa Rica. Our network of relationships from Costa Rica was now linked to South Carolina!

Unfortunately, we did not get as far as Rhode Island, so we missed getting to meet another new grandchild, Abigail Joy Sánchez—Noel and Elizabeth's sixth child—born September 6, 1996. We would have to wait until we returned to Costa Rica to meet another granddaughter, Ruth Kimberly Jones, the fourth child of Timothy and Keiry, who was born on October 24 of that year.

Winter in Costa Rica

Early in December we returned to "the land of eternal spring." Although it was winter in the States, it was dry season in Costa Rica. Even so, when we drove to Tsipirí, we encountered the usual mud, rain, and chill. We were happy to be "home" with Timothy and Keiry and the grandkids. Our yellow house was now painted a bright Costa Rican blue, my study had become the guest room, and the recording studio was the new office and translation room.

Our real joy while at Tsipirí was to worship with more than a hundred Cabécars who braved the weather to attend a six-hour service. Several congregations took part, as did Peter, David, and the *Etno* trainees who were then finishing their weeks among the Indians. The meeting included a report from Philip and Saukeen who had just returned from their travels in China and India.

Not only did we visit Tsipirí, but we spent a few days in Estrella, near the Caribbean coast, where Peter and his family lived, as well as David and Lucy. We also spent time at our apartment in Santa Ana near the capital; while there we started working on this book.

My seventy-fifth birthday on February 22—Washington's Birthday and mine—was a real jubilee. All five of our sons were there, for Steven and his family had arrived early in the month to begin a seven-month construction project for a missionary friend. Even my cousin Bill Tate came from the States for the occasion. The sons' wives fixed fried chicken for dinner and put seventy-five candles on the cake; I blew them out on the first try! The sons and grandchildren did an impromptu enactment of scenes from my life, including spanking the children with my belt, and driving the jeep as we bumped, slid, and spun on the road to Tsipirí. Dale Kibbey, CMI board member, was there and captured the hilarious production on video. To climax the evening my cousin showed an old family video which included our grandfather Tate celebrating *his* seventy-fifth birthday!

The next day Costa Rican friends and missionary colleagues joined us for a reception. Peter led the program, Steven led the singing, and the three younger sons and their wives ended the time by praying over me—the afterglow of a great weekend.

In March 1997, on the eve of our departure for the States, one of Peter's trainees came across the city, an hour by bus, bringing gifts and an encouraging word about our ministry and about the Lord's blessing on our children.

Spring in South Carolina

The dogwoods and azaleas on our property in Columbia all bloomed early, seemingly just for our enjoyment during this, our first springtime in the States since 1985. A month later when we left for five weeks on the road, even the oaks had leaves.

Beginning with a missions conference in Alabama where I was the speaker, we watched spring regress as we traveled north to Chicago. There the trees were bare and the weather cold, but the fellowship was warm. We spoke in three churches and in an inner-city school, as well as being interviewed in a missions class at Moody Bible Institute and also at a radio station. In between times there was always one-on-one ministry.

Continuing through Ohio where we saw board member Dale Kibbey again, we headed for chilly Pennsylvania where we visited supporters in Pittsburgh and spent a weekend in Philadelphia with our daughter Susanna and her family, just arrived from India for a few months' leave. New England was not warm either, but it was great to visit our youngest daughter and her family in Providence before heading home, with other visits along the way.

We even did a bit of sight-seeing at Gettysburg, where I was moved to learn that Alabama troops bore the brunt of one battle, leaving fallen comrades strewn everywhere. The impact of that visit somehow closed a chapter in the life of this Southerner.

The friends we contacted as we traveled were people who had prayed for us and supported us throughout our missionary career. What a bond we felt with them. They had believed in us even when we were young, untried, and unknown. This long, intense, and satisfying journey was like a valedictory trip!

Returning to warm South Carolina, we reflected on memories of our travels: stimulating conversations, counseling with parents seeking to raise children for the Lord, networking with people concerned for the lost and for a meaningful walk with God. This was the season for us to be "missionaries-at-large."

Peter Drops His Bombshell

Peter's cross-cultural training program, *Etno*, was becoming widely known, resulting in more and more invitations to preach at missions conferences in Latin America, as well as at Hispanic congregations in the United States. In 1997 he spoke at conferences in Mexico, Guatemala, and Panama, and preached in Los Angeles, Phoenix, Reno, and in Florida. His wider ministry that year included a consultation with mission leaders in London about some *Etno* grads serving in Africa and then a trip to Spain for more missions conferences.

As Peter flew back to Costa Rica from Spain, the Lord spoke to him, giving him new vision. His eight-page letter outlining his plans to relocate in Spain was a totally unexpected bombshell. Although it took us hours and days to absorb the news, we were convinced that the Lord was in this vision. In Spain he would be much closer to *Etno* grads and other Spanish-speaking missionaries who by then were serving in Africa and Asia. The proximity would enable him to travel to encourage and counsel these new workers.

During the transition from Costa Rica to Spain, Peter and Deb came to the States with their five children for a long-delayed sabbatical. Their two oldest, Jonathan and Joanna, had just graduated from high school in Costa Rica. In Columbia, Jonathan began working for a landscaping company and Joanna enrolled in the Bible College. Peter himself soon began work on a master's degree at the seminary connected to the college.

Their move had implications for our family in Costa Rica. We would have to adjust some of our property decisions, for Peter would no longer be based in Santa Ana. Although he hoped to return for annual *Etno* sessions, his nineteen years of increasingly effective ministry in Central America had shifted to a much wider focus.

A Special Anniversary

People often asked me how Marian and I had stayed together so long. For our forty-sixth anniversary on September 8, 1997, I listed ten items I felt were significant:

+ *We made and kept our vows to be faithful, for better or for worse.*
+ *We did our duty whether we felt like it or not.*
+ *We believed that children were a blessing from the Lord.*
+ *We saturated our lives and home with the Word of God.*
+ *We went forward on our knees together, with prayer and fasting.*
+ *We depended unashamedly on the power of the Holy Spirit.*
+ *We sought the Lord and His kingdom above our personal pleasure.*
+ *We invested in the kingdom for our future financial security.*
+ *We opted for a simple lifestyle and Biblical values.*
+ *We lived like pilgrims looking for the city of God.*

Our anniversary was very special and very personal. We gave each other a book, we went out for breakfast and supper, and we attended a missionary prayer meeting. I gave Marian a bouquet of

two roses, and she gave me a card on which the printed verse said it
all:

> *I think of you and how*
> *our lives have intertwined;*
> *two cords, separately insignificant,*
> *wrapping around each other,*
> *weaving something new*
> *and stronger altogether.*
> *And the third Cord braided through makes us stronger yet;*
> *making one from three...*
> *strength in unity...*
> *strong enough to withstand time.*
> *A cord of three strands...*
> *You, me, and the Lord working together*
> *to strengthen forever the bonds of marriage.*
> — *Alvalyn Lundgren*

These words captured the key to this book, *"Two are better than
one... A threefold cord is not quickly broken"* (Ecclesiastes 4:9,12). We are
a team of two, yoked together for life, with a common double vision.
Finally, before she signed her name and noted *our* verse, Psalm
9:10—which is engraved in our rings—she wrote these words:

> *My heart is so content to be with you*
> *just to know we share*
> *a deepening relationship built on love,*
> *on trust, and on growing in the Lord.*
> *I thank God for you and for the life*
> *He is allowing us to build together.*

It was a privilege to celebrate another year together, walking with
the Lord. It all fit the final song at our wedding, "Together with
Jesus."

That fall, following our anniversary in September, we welcomed
Steven and Cameron back from eight months in Costa Rica where he
had worked on a house for a missionary friend while Cameron
studied Spanish. Then we said good-bye to Susanna and Prem who
had spent the summer with us in Columbia. Traveling with them was

a young woman from Ecuador who had completed her cross-cultural training at *Etno* in Costa Rica and was on her way to serve in India. Priscilla and Jonathan also returned to Asia after a working vacation in England. Their family had increased to three, two sons and a daughter, with the birth of Elizabeth Grace on April 23, 1997. Little Elizabeth was our twenty-fifth grandchild. Our own Elizabeth drove down to Columbia that fall with Noel and their six children to spend a week with us.

Besides enjoying our own family, Marian and I traveled to the annual reunion of my brothers and sisters and their families. All thirteen siblings were together for the first time in many years; we did not know then that it would be the last before the circle was broken by death. At home in Columbia, Marian and I were busy with ministry locally and with phone calls and faxes from Costa Rica. We also immersed ourselves in old diaries and prayer letters as we worked on the early drafts of this book.

Forty-five Missionary Years

We had arrived in Costa Rica on December 31, 1952. As we neared the end of 1997—forty-five years after our first flight to our adopted country—we decided to choose "forty-five" to define the years of our service there. And how should we celebrate forty-five years of service in our beloved Costa Rica? Return, of course! On December 31, 1997, Peter, our firstborn, drove us to the airport to catch a plane to Miami where we boarded LACSA Flight 621—the same airline and the same flight number as our first flight. Yet this flight took just two-and-a-half hours on a 737 rather than six hours on a DC-3. At the time of our original flight, Marian had been expecting Peter. Now, as we landed in San José, we were greeted by our two youngest sons, Philip and David, and their wives. They grabbed our baggage, loaded it into our Trooper, and drove us to our city base in nearby Santa Ana. There our son Timothy and his family were waiting for us. Together we welcomed the New Year in prayer—so different from that first New Year's Eve in Costa Rica when I was whisked away to a meeting and Marian cried herself to sleep in our dingy quarters.

Marian and I rejoiced in the fulfillment of our double vision. We had reached a tribe for God and we had raised a family for God. Providentially, the children had become a key part in fulfilling our vision of reaching a tribe. The lives of the children were proof that our vision of raising a family for God had been fulfilled as well. We knew that it was only the Lord's grace that had brought us to this point. In spite of our weaknesses and limitations, He had worked through us—and in spite of us—to fulfill the vision He had given so many years before.

What if we had never gone to Costa Rica to reach the Cabécar Indians? What if we had not waited all those years until the harvest? And what if our friends had not kept on praying and giving for long years before there was any return on their investment? Would there ever have been any Cabécar believers or a Cabécar New Testament? Perhaps, but we would have missed having a part in what the Holy Spirit was doing in our day among every tribe and tongue.

To God be all the glory. One more tribe has been reached. There is now a growing church among the Cabécar Indians. We were privileged to have a part in reaching them for Jesus. He alone is worthy!

~ *Epilogue* ~
The Story Continues
1998 to 2010

A dozen years have passed since Marian and I completed our gradual withdrawal from ministry in Costa Rica. We end our story with an update on our children and on the work in Costa Rica, as well as on ourselves.

A Family Raised for God — August 2005
Aziel and Marian with their eight children and their spouses,
thirty-two grandchildren (two with spouses),
and the first great-grandchild

The Family Today

Peter: After Peter finished his Master's of Divinity at Columbia Biblical Seminary, he and Debbie moved to Spain in the fall of 2002. Serving now under an Hispanic mission, they continue to work with

Spanish-speaking missionaries, several of whom are former *Etno* trainees. Peter teaches locally and travels extensively in Africa and elsewhere, while Debbie manages hospitality for their group. They return annually to the United States for Peter to minister in missions conferences and seminars for Hispanics, as well as traveling back to Costa Rica for seminars and even another session of *Etno*—his cross-cultural training program.

Peter and Debbie's oldest son, Jonathan, is working in South Carolina. Their older daughter, Joanna, is married to Joshua Fleming. After graduating from Bible College, Joanna and Josh did further study and are now headed for missionary service with their little daughter Charis. The middle son, Luke, is married to Soraya Benson; they live in Costa Rica with their new baby, Leyla. Luke holds a job and both he and Soraya are studying. Sara, the younger daughter, is married to Rayner Rojas, who is in ministry with his father, the pastor of a church in Costa Rica. They have two children, Adriel and Sara Faith. Samuel, the youngest son, recently finished high school.

Priscilla: Priscilla and Jonathan Kew served ten years in Pakistan, relocating to England in 1999 to facilitate Jonathan's ministry—designing fonts and typesetting Scripture in languages using Arabic-based script. He resigned from Wycliffe two years ago and is now separated from Priscilla, who continues as a member of Wycliffe, working part-time in the linguistic library. Most of her time is spent looking after their children: Timothy, now twenty and studying at Cambridge, Christopher, sixteen, and Elizabeth, thirteen.

Susanna: Susanna and Prem Shastri continue serving in India. Prem teaches Hindi at the Language Institute which he started, but is involved in various other ministries. Susanna helps with administration and teaches English; she also oversees sixteen-year-old Judson's studies. Their daughter Irene recently graduated from Villanova and currently helps her parents in India.

Steven: Steven and Cameron live near Columbia, South Carolina. He is a contractor whose business serves as a platform for ministry, not only locally but in Costa Rica and elsewhere. Having them close by has been a great blessing to us.

Their oldest son, David, graduated from the University of South Carolina and recently started Law School. He is married to Claire Fuziol; they have a baby girl named Moravia. The middle son, Joseph, graduated from Clemson University and is married to Jennifer Fisher; they too have a baby daughter, Callie. They live in Baltimore, where he works as a supervisor for a bridge-building company. The youngest son, Daniel, is in college, as is their older daughter, Christiana, while Mary Grace, the youngest child, is in tenth grade.

Elizabeth: Elizabeth and Noel Sánchez live in Providence, Rhode Island. Noel is a contractor who specializes in restoration of old houses. He and Elizabeth serve in their local church. Their oldest daughter, Ruthanne, graduated from the University of Rhode Island and is married to Jared Holloway; they have a daughter, Katherine and a newborn son, John. The oldest son, Andrew, lives nearby and works with his dad. The next son, Santiago, is in college; he is married to Kristen Tanza. They live on Long Island with their son Aiden, born this year. The three youngest children: Simon, who graduated from high school this year, Matthew, a junior, and Abigail, in ninth grade, continue to live at home.

Timothy: Timothy and Keiry no longer live in our original house at Tsipirí, but have developed a large property a few miles away on the hill called Jakúbata, which overlooks the village of Grano de Oro. This has become the "nerve center" of the Cabécar ministry with an office for his ongoing translation work and a large chapel with adjacent kitchen for hosting conferences. Timothy has been confirmed many times over as my successor.

Timothy and Keiry have also run a hostel for Cabécar youth attending the local high school; this affords further opportunities for discipling and for teaching a work ethic. They also provide housing for those who help with translation and for transient Indians who work the acreage. The coffee, milk, cheese, and other farm products are a source of income, as well as helping to feed the families of the workers.

Their own home is on this property, a rambling house for their six children and their many visitors. Their oldest child, Rebekah, studies dentistry at the University of Costa Rica, where her sister, Hannah, studies business. Their son Mark is in high school, while Ruth, John, and Abigail study at home as well as in the local school. These last two were born after we left Costa Rica: John Kristopher on September 25, 2001, and Abigail Keila on July 7, 2003.

Philip: Philip and Saukeen live on our old property in Tsipirí. Since we left Costa Rica, four children have been born to them: Emily Joy on July 19, 2000, Christine Faith on March 23, 2002, Jacob Emmanuel on October 14, 2004, and our youngest grandchild, Anna Hope, on December 17, 2006, her Daddy's birthday. Saukeen is homeschooling the older three, while Philip ministers to the Cabécars. He has spearheaded programs for preparing young adults to take equivalency exams, while he also discipled them and taught a work ethic. Furthermore, he has had occasional opportunities to orient teachers for the regional office supervising Indian education. Currently, he is helping Timothy with translation.

David: David and Lucy continue working with Cabécars in Estrella and Telire, but David has felt a call to work with the Bribri Indians as well. In 2000 they relocated from Estrella to the Bribri area near the Panama border, where they bought property and built a home. They have two sons: Andrew Noel, born April 8, 1999, and Levi John, born October 6, 2000. Lucy homeschools the boys. David is active in evangelism and discipling believers, as well as training Indians in practical skills. Currently, however, he helps with translation. His newest vision is to reach across the border to the Guaymí Indians of Panama, a group much larger than the Cabécar and Bribri tribes combined.

The Cabécar World of 2010

The Cabécar world of today is not the isolated world that we encountered in the 1950s, nor even the 1970s when the government established a reservation system to protect Indian lands from the encroaching Latins. The 1990s saw a massive influx of financial aid, even from foreign governments, following the devastating earthquake of 1991. Then in the mid-1990s the government began to establish health posts and also primary schools. Now there are dozens of one-room schools scattered throughout the mountains, with sixty schools serving almost two thousand children in the Chirripó area alone. The growing Cabécar population, numbering perhaps five times what it was when we arrived in the area, now receives much aid from the government in the form of monthly stipends, resulting in a decreasing motivation to work.

In the light of demographic changes and changes in communication and transportation patterns among the Indians, Jakúbata, the hill above Grano de Oro where Timothy lives, proved to be a wise choice for the Cabécar Ministry Center. Electricity reached the area several years ago. Timothy has provided land for the installation of a cell phone tower and also for collecting seismographic data. Grano de Oro itself is still a small village at the end of the Latino world, but it is the main access point to the Chirripó area where the majority of Cabécars live. The village buzzes with commercial activity, as well as a medical clinic, a large primary school and a secondary school. Numerous vehicles enter and leave the village daily—a few even owned by Indians.

Modernity is even beginning to reach Tsipirí, six miles into Cabécar territory southeast of Grano de Oro. Houses—financed by foreign organizations and built of sawed lumber—now dot the road toward Tsipirí and even deeper into Indian lands. Philip supervised the improvement of the last bad stretch of the road to Tsipirí, cutting driving time to Grano de Oro in half. As yet there is no electricity in the Tsipirí area nor beyond, but the government has financed solar-powered battery systems for the Indians. Philip himself now has a hydroelectric plant that provides 24-hour power.

There is now a provisional road to the Chirripó River, which trucks and motorcycles can navigate in dry weather rather than having to park near Tsipirí before heading toward Chirripó. Yet packhorses are many and foot traffic is heavy, not only with Cabécars hauling out produce and bringing in supplies, but with government teachers and health workers hiking to their posts.

The Cabécar area that stretches for several miles along both sides of the Chirripó and Pacuare Rivers and their tributaries has changed less than the area around Grano de Oro and Tsipirí. The same is true of the area along the Estrella and Telire Rivers. Even so, the modern world is slowly encroaching. David has been active in teaching Cabécars and other local people certain practical skills such as using a chain saw and milling lumber. This has enabled them to build sturdier houses and has also provided a way for them to meet their own needs rather than hire outsiders.

One of the greatest needs in the Telire area is for sturdy bridges to provide access to the outside world. Logs that are laid across the narrowest points of the river to serve as bridges tend to wash away with each new flood. This isolates the Indians from medical help and supply sources. David has teamed with another American interested in helping meet this need. With cables supplied by the government and transported in the government helicopter, David and his friend, along with their helpers, have built two suspension bridges across the Telire River for foot traffic.

The Cabécar Churches Today

The total area occupied by the Cabécars is too large for any single person to oversee. The believers are spread throughout the mountains, where as yet no roads have been built. Timothy, Philip, and David have divided the area, with Timothy overseeing the churches in upper Chirripó and upper Pacuare, Philip looking after the work in lower Chirripó, and David responsible for Estrella and Telire, as well as probing into remote San José Cabécar, the ancestral home of the Cabécars. Though each supervises a different area, they maintain their unity and are in frequent contact. Furthermore, each relates to the leading believers in their area. These relationships are informal rather than structured, for the Cabécars have never had any formal structure in their culture. Outreach trips provide opportunities for our sons to disciple the leaders who accompany them. Believers also make outreach trips on their own.

A Tribe Reached for God — September 2010
The church at Tsipirí, one of many Cabécar churches

As fruit of a half-century of ministry, there are now at least a dozen churches meeting in different areas of the four river valleys which comprise Cabécar territory. Most of these churches have their own buildings, though newer, smaller groups meet in homes. Some of these buildings are sturdy structures with cement floors, which have replaced the original buildings with dirt floors. This has been done on the believers' initiative and has been financed by them, with occasional help and advice from our sons as to construction. Even in the remote Telire area David has helped erect church buildings. In Tsipirí an attractive chapel designed by Philip has replaced the temporary structure built in 1993 for the dedication of the New Testament.

However, a church is a body of believers, not the building in which they meet. Years ago when the Cabécar reservation was established by the government in 1976, I stood with six hundred fifty

Cabécars awaiting the arrival of the president to celebrate the occasion. The president, however, failed to show up. This led Marian to begin praying for seven hundred Cabécars to be ready to receive the Lord Jesus when He returns. At the time this number was beyond the limit of my faith, for there were no baptized believers yet. Several years ago I asked Philip how many Cabécars were now believers.

"I think we now have *more* than seven hundred," Philip said. Then he thought a bit and added, "We probably have more than seven hundred believers already *baptized*." That could mean that perhaps ten percent of the Cabécars are now believers. What an awesome thought!

With Isaac, an elder at the Tsipirí church,
and his wife Oliva and family

The church among the Cabécar Indians is growing. Timothy reported recently that people are still coming to the Lord. Furthermore, there is now a large number of second-generation believers. The loosely-organized churches are led by local elders, usually two elders in each group. The meetings are informal, with a time of singing and group prayer, after which various ones will share what the Lord has been showing them from the Scripture. No one is in a hurry. Dogs and children wander in and out of the services. Marian and I have been privileged to attend Cabécar services while visiting our sons during recent years. We have been encouraged by hearing the believers pray for us. Furthermore, Indians who never showed affection nor voiced appreciation have gladdened our hearts with their love and thanks for bringing them the good news of the Lord Jesus. One of the elders still writes me occasional letters.

The churches are loosely linked to each other through occasional meetings at the large chapel on Timothy's property in Grano de Oro. These are happy occasions for isolated believers who seldom have contact with others who know the Lord. Since most believers must walk several hours to reach the chapel, these meetings are overnight affairs, beginning at dusk and lasting several hours before a late supper, prepared in the church kitchen by the women and served in the adjacent dining area. After the meal, families sleep on the chapel floor, while youth enjoy each other's company until weariness overcomes them. In the morning after a prayer service and breakfast, they make their way through the mountains to their home areas.

Occasionally believers from as far away as Telire will trek to these meetings. At times David brings a group from Estrella in his vehicle. The meetings were originally designed for the leaders to report to each other, but Cabécar culture ignores such restrictions. Others always tag along, and all are welcome. Each group brings a greeting from the congregation they represent; some share a song or a Scripture; everyone enjoys the fellowship.

Issues in the Cabécar Church

A crucial issue which surfaced after we left Costa Rica was the matter of syncretism, that is, the continuing of pagan practices along with Christianity. This was not a new issue, but one that began to come to a head in the late 1990s. Some believers defended such matters as curses, divination, witchcraft, and appeasement of demons, by insisting that Sibö had told the Cabécars to do these things. Sibö is the name used for God among the Cabécars, the neighboring Bribri tribe, and even tribes across the border in Panama. From the beginning of our ministry we had used the name "Sibö," believing, as had been suggested to us, that over the years as the believers studied the New Testament, their previous concept of God would be corrected.

We had assumed that "Sibö" was a generic term, yet we eventually came to realize that it was the name of a specific being, a sort of glorified shaman, as reflected in stylized drawings used in certain Cabécar ceremonies. The name "Sibö" permeated the whole Cabécar New Testament, unwittingly fostering syncretism.

In confronting syncretism, Timothy, Philip, and David spent three years seeking the Lord fervently and focusing on the true nature of God in their teaching. After much teaching, prayer, fasting, and crying out to God, they began to question the continued use of the Cabécar name for God. They had been reading much in the prophets and noticed how drastically the prophets dealt with false gods. In 2001, our sons, each apart from the other, rejected the name, struck it out of their New Testaments and burned the extra copies. It was an agonizing decision, but they were at peace. They were free.

Some of the Cabécar believers also questioned the name "Sibö." They, too, had been earnestly seeking the Lord. A few had visions of Sibö rebuking them for rejecting his name. However, rejecting the name was too much for other believers; they remained in bondage to the old ways. Yet Isaac, a leading elder, testified that when he was filled with the Spirit and repudiated that name, he no longer felt strongly pulled to go back to the old ceremonies—he was free! He, too, struck the old name out of his New Testament, as did the other faithful believers. The churches stabilized. New believers must reject the old name and give up pagan practices before being baptized.

Although Marian and I did not know, until after the fact, that the extra copies of the New Testament had been burned, we fully backed our sons. We had left them in charge. They would have to live with their decision—and would face the task of revising the translation. They had been deeply involved with us in finalizing the original New Testament, so they felt responsible—at least in part—for using the native term for God. Furthermore, they fully understood what an arduous task awaited them.

Personally, I was sorry we had used the name "Sibö" when translating, yet I did not feel the weight of that choice until three years later when the Lord spoke to me in the wee hours of the morning, saying that I had offended Him. I ended up burning our extra copies of the New Testament. Marian had her own encounter with the Lord and made a public confession, even as I did in a letter to our family and friends.

The translator's choice of a term for God is not merely an academic issue. God is jealous, He allows no rivals. He said to Isaiah: *"I am the LORD: that is my name: and my glory will I not give to another"* (Isaiah 42:8). "LORD" in capital letters in our Bibles actually stands for "Yahweh" or "Jehovah," the specific personal name of God. No one shares His glory. If pagans must repent of false gods, so must we as translators.

With the change in the term for God, it has been easier for the believers to desist from divination, which had been a major issue, and other pagan practices. Issues such as death ceremonies have been handled as they came up, with some major victories. The matter of marriage customs, particularly as to who can marry whom, is under consideration and prayer.

The issues which surfaced in the Cabécar churches once the matter of syncretism was dealt with were not theological, such as the term for God, but moral and ethical. These were not new issues among the believers, but needed to be dealt with once the basic issue of syncretism was past. They are still issues in the lives of some of the believers—issues of morality such as fornication and adultery, as well as ethical issues such as stealing, lying, envy, jealousy, resentment, gossip, filthy talk, laziness, irresponsibility, pride, and lack of compassion—all the sins common to fallen humanity.

How can believers be discipled and inspired to live worthy of their calling? Prayer is needed. Workers are needed. Our sons and the Cabécar leaders are stretched. Two new couples have begun ministering in recent years. Both couples, like our sons, are Americans married to Costa Ricans. They are learning the Cabécar language and have access to areas of the tribe that our sons are not effectively reaching. Others are seeking to minister to the Cabécars through Spanish. Their lack of understanding of the language and culture seriously limits their effectiveness. Furthermore, some do not value a spirit of unity with the Cabécar-speaking congregations.

The Revised Cabécar Testament

When the extra copies of the original Cabécar Testament were burned in 2001, Timothy's first priority was to decide on a new term for God. He and his helpers, with input from Philip, David, and others, spent many months considering options before finally settling on *Säkeklä*, the Cabécar word for "Lord." This is a generic term, of which there are enough variant forms to handle all occurrences, such as in the phrase, "the God and Father of our Lord Jesus Christ."

Another decision we had to make involved changes in the alphabet. Philip had petitioned the government in 2001 for the use of our alphabet in the schools being established for the Cabécars, but this was denied. This meant that in revising the translation they would need to adapt to the government alphabet created years later than ours.

Nine years had already passed since we sent the original New Testament off to the printer. More than half the copies of that Testament had been distributed before the rest were destroyed. It was time for a revision. However, computer systems and programs had also changed during that time. The original computer files were no longer readable. One of Timothy's helpers spent many months scanning the original Testament so that Timothy could make global changes to incorporate the new term for God and the new alphabet.

Within a year after making the changes, the gospel of Matthew was revised and printed, as well as a new Cabécar songbook and cassettes of all the songs. Work on the Old Testament went on concurrently, as well as audio recordings. The next year Mark was printed and John the following year. These were actually retranslations and not merely revisions. Drafts of other Scriptures were available for teaching.

What a thrill it was for us to see the entire New Testament in print again in December, 2006, when we visited our sons in Costa Rica. We had arrived just in time for the annual Christmas conference at the Cabécar Ministry Center near Grano de Oro. After we were greeted by many of the believers, Timothy announced, "I have a surprise for you." He handed us one of the first copies of the partially revised Cabécar New Testament—with the corrected name for God and the authorized alphabet—photocopied earlier that day.

With schools now located all over the reservation and hundreds of young readers, there is much demand for the Testament. However, only a minimum are printed as needed, for revision is ongoing. Newer editions also contain Genesis 1 to Exodus 20, plus several Psalms. Hopefully, the retranslation will be completed by the end of 2010.

The Bribri New Testament

In the late 1950s, as I explored the four river valleys where the Cabécar Indians lived, I kept hearing of the Bribri Indians living over the next ridge toward Panama. After exploring the Bribri area, I sent out a call for someone to reach this closely related tribe. Eventually, Ray and Susie Schlabach began the Bribri translation. Later, Paul and Linda Williams joined them and finished the task. My contribution, which I completed after we returned to the States, was a literal translation into Spanish of the Cabécar New Testament for the benefit of the team working with Paul. The Bribris have much in common with the Cabécars, including a belief in Sibö. However, that name was not used in the final draft of the translation, but rather a term related to the term used in the revised Cabécar Testament.

The dedication of the Bribri New Testament in August, 2007, fulfilled my original vision for this tribe. Marian and I flew to Costa Rica and joined the four hundred Indians and visitors present at the happy event. Our sons, Timothy, Philip, and David (and their families) attended, along with a number of Cabécar believers. Peter and his family came from Spain. David had helped with the logistics of producing the audio version of the Bribri Testament and also had a part in the program at the dedication.

Spanish Churches in Grano de Oro and Turrialba

Every visitor entering the village of Grano de Oro passes the small chapel with its sign announcing: "Iglesia Evangélica." There has been no significant growth in the congregation, but the brethren continue to meet regularly for worship, prayer, and Bible study and have improved the building by adding a multipurpose room. When we visited in December, 2006, we joined them there for the traditional chicken and rice dish and then went outside to watch the children break open the *piñata*.

The church currently has no pastor, although Noé and Pércides still minister there from time to time. Pércides' sister Noribette and her husband Michael Day are still in charge of the Awana program throughout Costa Rica, but their mother, *doña* Chala, the widow of the patriarch in whose home the church began, is now with the Lord. Their cousin Moisés, whom we also sent to Bible School, now lives in South Carolina; we enjoy seeing him and Cathy occasionally.

From Grano de Oro to Turrialba, the road passes through the town of La Suiza where we once lived. The flourishing CAM church in that town grew from the tiny seed we planted during our time there in the early 1960s. The city of Turrialba is the regional hub serving the Cabécars who live along the Chirripó and Pacuare Rivers. A thriving commercial center, it is also the location of the only hospital for miles around. All the government offices for the county are located there. We still maintain connections to believers at the large CAM church we attended when we lived in Turrialba in the 1950s. In 2003 the church presented us and our sons a lovely plaque in honor of our work among the Cabécar Indians, inscribed with 2 Corinthians 4:5: *"For we preach not ourselves, but Christ Jesus the Lord; and ourselves your servants for Jesus' sake."*

It was at the church in Turrialba that we met *don* Emilio and his wife, *doña* Flora, who became close friends in 1963 when Emilio built our house in Tsipirí. Over the years their home became our private rest stop whenever we went to town on errands; their son even became my orthopedist. Although Emilio later left Flora, she continued to provide us a wonderful haven, serving us coffee before our rough ride back home, often on a stormy night.

When Marian and I left Costa Rica, *doña* Flora continued to welcome our sons; she became a confidante for their wives and a grandmother to their children. In 2005 Timothy's wife, Keiry, brought Flora to the United States—the trip of a lifetime. Marian and I took her to Alabama; when she returned to Costa Rica, she excitedly told everyone that she had met my sisters. In 2007 we got the sad news of her sudden death. Timothy, Philip, David, and their families were among the mourners who packed the CAM church for her funeral. Our sons even helped carry the casket up the long hill to the cemetery.

The Overflow

The years since Marian and I left Costa Rica have been marked by annual trips to touch base there, as well as travels within the United States to reconnect with family, friends, and supporters. When not traveling, we minister here in South Carolina, especially at St. Andrews Evangelical Church which we joined after our return from Costa Rica. Our ministry stems from the overflow of our life in Tsipirí where I felt God "doubled in size" as I prayed daily for the Lord's protection, provision, and power. We had proved Him adequate and wanted to share with anyone, anytime, anywhere.

With our life's work behind us, we still minister out of the overflow, whether teaching, preaching, leading home groups and prayer meetings, or discipling one-on-one. Ministry grows out of meeting the Lord. The best time of each day for me and for Marian, established long before our marriage, is meeting the Lord each morning—she in the bedroom, I in the den. We still pray together the last thing before going to bed. Every Monday morning we take an hour or two for special prayer for each other and for the children and their families. Our common love for the Lord and daily prayer together is still the cement of our love for each other.

These years have been a time of ongoing renewal. After a lifetime of limited corporate fellowship in the jungle, the fellowship at St. Andrews Evangelical Church truly is a rich reward; it helps make up for our children being so far away. For me personally, Scripture memory has been a major source of renewal. Since my days at Moody Bible Institute when I was discipled by the Navigators, I continued memorizing verses until I bogged down in Costa Rica when I tried to learn them in Spanish. Then one day in 1997 as I recalled the blessings of Scripture memory, I pulled out the stained and battered boxes of verses and decided to try to relearn them. Beginning slowly with one pack of twenty-one verses, I continued reviewing until by 2007 I had recovered them all—more than 850 verses. With so much of the Word always "in my mouth," as in previous years, and walking with the Lord in renewal, I am almost overwhelmed! Overwhelmed not only by His Word, but by the Lord Himself! As the Psalmist says, *"...there is none upon earth that I desire beside thee"* (Psalm 73:25).

Our interest in missions is as strong as ever. We follow closely the news of what God is doing around the world. Each day we pray for a different country, using *Operation World* as a guide. In recent years we have led a lively weekly prayer meeting at church, focusing on missions. At conferences we continue to motivate others to intercede.

Here in Columbia at our "honeymoon house," Marian and I enjoy living together: working, reading, writing, and talking. We need each other—we stimulate each other. We are grateful to the Lord for the measure of health we still have, despite the concerns that come with age. We deeply appreciate those who continue to pray for us and support us.

Although we have passed through painful moments during the last dozen years, including a difficult time stemming partly from our lack of foresight when disposing of our properties in Costa Rica and now the troubled marriage of one of the children, we have also celebrated some significant milestones in these later years: our 50th anniversary and our 55th, my 80th birthday and my 85th, Marian's 70th and her 75th and 80th, as well as our trip to Israel in 1999, and a complete family reunion in 2005 with all the children and their entire families. The Lord has blessed us in an amazing way.

Looking back over my life and ministry, I have few regrets. I am one of the most fulfilled men I know. By God's grace, Marian and I have been able to fulfill our double vision of raising a family for God and reaching a tribe for Him. What a long way the Lord has brought this barefoot preacher's kid from Alabama! If I were young, I would love to go for another unreached tribe.

Whatever the Lord has in our future, we embrace it. We will always echo the shout of the Moravians: "Let us win for the Lamb the reward of His sacrifice!"

It is a privilege to serve Him!

He is worth it all!

He is worthy!

Amen!